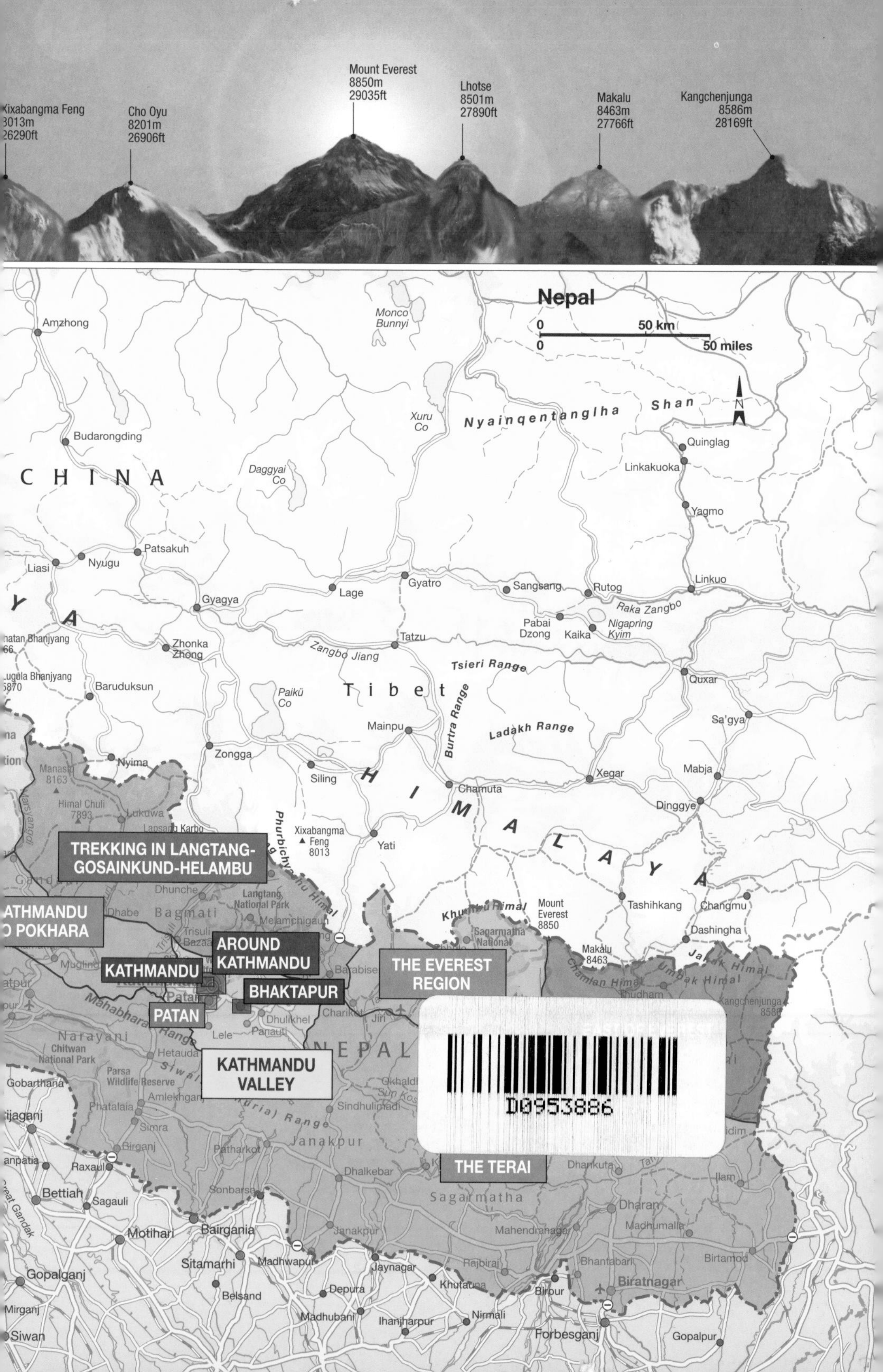
Mount Everest
8850m
29035ft
Cho Oyu
8201m
26906ft
Lhotse
8501m
27890ft
Makalu
8463m
27766ft
Kangchenjunga
8586m
28169ft
Nepal
0 50 km
0 50 miles
CHINA
Tibet
HIMALAYA
Nyainqentanglha Shan
Amzhong
Monco Bunnyi
Xuru Co
Budarongding
Daggyai Co
Quinglag
Linkakuoka
Yagmo
Patsakuh
Liasi
Nyugu
Gyagya
Lage
Gyatro
Sangsang
Rutog
Linkuo
Raka Zangbo
Pabai Dzong
Kaika
Nigapring Kyim
Tatzu
Zangbo Jiang
Zhonka Zhong
Tsieri Range
Quxar
Baruduksun
Paikü Co
Burtra Range
Mainpu
Ladakh Range
Sa'gya
Zongga
Nyima
Siling
Chamuta
Xegar
Mabja
Dinggye
Xixabangma Feng 8013
Yati
Tashihkang
Changmu
Dashingha
Mount Everest 8850
Makalu 8463
Kangchenjunga 8586
TREKKING IN LANGTANG-GOSAINKUND-HELAMBU
AROUND KATHMANDU
KATHMANDU
BHAKTAPUR
PATAN
THE EVEREST REGION
KATHMANDU VALLEY
THE TERAI
NEPAL
Langtang National Park
Bagmati
Narayani
Chitwan National Park
Parsa Wildlife Reserve
Janakpur
Sagarmatha
Mahabharat Range
Khumbu Himal
Sagarmatha National Park
Dhulikhel
Panauti
Lele
Hetauda
Amlekhganj
Simra
Birganj
Raxaul
Bettiah
Sagauli
Motihari
Bairgania
Sitamarhi
Madhwapur
Gopalganj
Belsand
Mirganj
Siwan
Jaynagar
Depura
Khutauna
Madhubani
Jhanjharpur
Nirmali
Forbesganj
Gopalpur
Biratnagar
Birtamod
Bhantabari
Dharan
Dhankuta
Ilam
Dhalkebar
Mahendranagar
Rajbiraj
Sindhulimadi
Jiri
Charikot
Barabise
Dhunche
Sonbarsa
Patharkot
Gobarthana

INSIGHT GUIDES

NEPAL

Contents

Introduction

History

Features

Insights

MINI FEATURES

PHOTO FEATURES

Places

Travel Tips

TRANSPORT

ACCOMMODATION

EATING OUT

ACTIVITIES

A – Z

LANGUAGE

Maps

THE BEST OF NEPAL: TOP ATTRACTIONS

From the high peaks of the Himalayas to the crowded spaces of the Kathmandu Valley and the steamy jungles of the Terai, Nepal is rich in unforgettable experiences.

◁ **Durbar Square, Kathmandu**. At the very core of the Kathmandu Valley, this crowded Malla-era cityscape is part open-air museum, part living, breathing place of worship and commerce. See page 161.

△ **Boudhanath**. Set amidst the crowded spaces on the eastern edge of Kathmandu, this magnificent Buddhist monument is the hub of a thriving Tibetan community, with monks, monasteries and momos aplenty. See page 172.

▽ **Swayambhunath**. Standing atop a monkey-infested hill, this great white stupa has been watching out over Kathmandu for millennia; its courtyard, bedecked with prayer flags and crowded with statuary, still offers the ultimate view of the city. See page 171.

▽ **Bhaktapur**. Of all the medieval temple towns of the Kathmandu Valley, Bhaktapur feels furthest removed from the modern world. The beetling alleys are free from traffic, and around every other corner lies another temple-filled square. See page 183.

△ **The Kathmandu Valley**. Ringed with high hills and studded with spectacular temples, the Kathmandu Valley offers endless opportunities for exploration, from the alleys of Sankhu to the forests of Shivapuri and the epic mountain views from Nagarkot and Dhulikhel. See page 195.

◁ **Pokhara**. Pokhara's lakeside is the perfect place to relax after the rigours of a trek, or simply to take in the vision of the Annapurnas, reflected in the smooth waters of Phewa Tal. See page 218.

△ **Bandipur**. On a high ridge in the Middle Hills, the streets of this tranquil little town are lined with beautiful 18th-century buildings and a growing number of boutique guesthouses. See page 214.

△ **The Annapurna region**. A sacred massif at the heart of Nepal, the long white ridge of the Annapurnas is a powerful presence, and its flanks are traversed by some of the best trekking routes in the country. See page 227.

△ **Lumbini**. Out in the hot flatlands of the Terai, the birthplace of the Buddha is suffused with an air of slow-paced tranquillity amongst the pilgrims, mendicants and epic sunsets over dusty plains. See page 299.

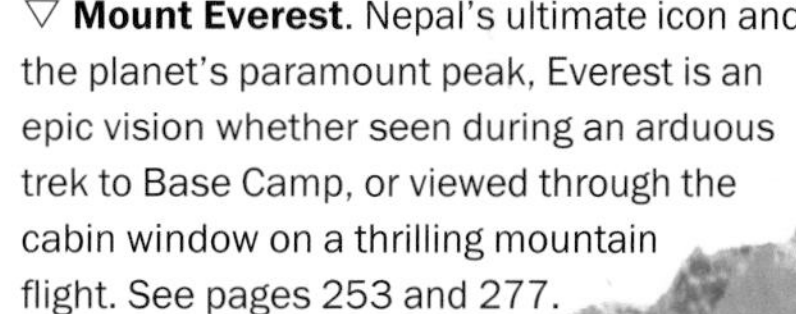

▽ **Mount Everest**. Nepal's ultimate icon and the planet's paramount peak, Everest is an epic vision whether seen during an arduous trek to Base Camp, or viewed through the cabin window on a thrilling mountain flight. See pages 253 and 277.

THE BEST OF NEPAL: EDITOR'S CHOICE

Nepal's temples, treks, adventures and experiences... here, at a glance, are some recommendations to help you plan your journey.

Lions outside Kumari Bahal in Durbar Square.

VIEWING WILDLIFE

Chitwan National Park. Deep in the forests of southern Nepal, Chitwan is one of Asia's great national parks, home to tigers, rhinos, bears and crocodiles. See page 288.

Bardia National Park. In the remote western Terai, this park is home to tigers and wild elephants and all manner of exotic birdlife. See page 295.

Koshi Tappu Wildlife Reserve. In the eastern Terai, this beautiful riverine reserve is remarkably rich in birdlife, and forms a major staging post for migrant species. See page 283.

Langtang National Park. Red pandas thrive in the dense bamboo groves of this beautiful mountain region, which is also home to elusive upland ungulates and a handful of snow leopards. See page 243.

Shey-Phoksundo National Park. This vast and fabled mountain park is home to blue sheep, wolves and the majestic and ghostly snow leopard. See page 304.

BEST TEMPLES AND RELIGIOUS SITES

Pashupatinath. On the banks of the Bagmati River, the smoking funeral pyres and meditating sadhus instil this sacred spot with a profound atmosphere. See page 173.

Kala Bhairav. The ceaseless stream of devotees lighting candles and offering prayers before this terrifying deity underscores the role of Kathmandu's Durbar Square as a living place of worship. See page 161.

Changu Narayan. On a narrow ridge, this temple is lavishly endowed with Licchavi-era carvings and is still a major place of pilgrimage. See page 199.

Dakshinkali. Set in the cool forests in the furthest southern reaches of the Kathmandu Valley, this tiny temple is the scene of spectacular blood sacrifices, demonstrating the depth of religious faith in Nepal. See page 205.

Janaki Mandir. Far from the beaten tourist track in the Terai town of Janakpur, this magnificent Mughal-style temple is dedicated to Sita, wife of the god Rama. See page 285.

Travelling by elephant-back.

Pashupatinath is the place to see sadhus.

TOP TREKS

Porters assisting on a trek in the Langtang Valley.

Annapurna Circuit. Nepal's original teahouse trek, the route around the mighty Annapurna Massif still sets the standard for Himalayan journeys. See page 229.

Everest Base Camp. Everest Base Camp is the ultimate goal for many trekkers, but the real highlight of the trek is the journey through the Sherpa homeland. See page 257.

Langtang Valley. Away from the crowds of the other teahouse trails, this trek leads through lush forests to grand glacial vistas. See page 243.

Annapurna Sanctuary. From the subtropical foothills, this fabled trek leads through dense rhododendron forests to the icy amphitheatre at the heart of the Annapurnas. See page 237.

BEST ADVENTURES

Whitewater rafting. Running the wild white water of Nepal's rivers is a thrilling experience. See page 330.

Mountaineering. The peaks of the Himalayas are the ultimate testing ground for top-flight mountaineers, the less experienced can venture up more modest peaks. See page 129.

Mountain biking. The tracks and trails of the Kathmandu Valley and the Middle Hills offer endless opportunities for lung-busting ascents and thrilling descents. See page 329.

Aerial adventures. Take to Nepal's skies by hang-glider, paraglider, microlight or hot-air balloon for unforgettable thrills and views. See pages 143 and 329.

The road to Tibet. The Friendship Highway from Kathmandu across the Tibetan frontier is one of the world's greatest roads, and Lhasa is still a destination steeped in legend. See page 248.

Whitewater rafting.

Revellers celebrate Holi in Kathmandu.

CULTURAL EXPERIENCES

Bisket Jatra. The biggest and most boisterous of the Kathmandu Valley's many festivals, this New Year's celebration is marked by the progress of a huge chariot through the streets of Bhaktapur. See page 87.

Holi. This Hindu festival marks the coming of spring, and sees tourists and locals alike cheerfully doused with colour. See page 91.

Prayers in a Tibetan gompa. The rumble of drums, the sounding of horns and the clashing of cymbals opens the daily recitations of Buddhist texts in monasteries around Boudhanath and Pharping. See pages 172 and 204.

A meal in a bhojanalaya. Be it a plate of steaming momos or a platter of dal bhat with unlimited refills, a meal amongst the locals in a humble eatery offers an authentic taste of Nepal. See page 320.

A Kathmandu rickshaw ride. A journey through the teeming alleyways of Kathmandu's old quarters on the seat of a rattling cycle-rickshaw is an essential experience – but don't expect to get anywhere very quickly. See page 311.

Carpets and crafts. From Tibetan carpet-weavers to Newari metalworkers, Nepal is home to myriad artisans plying ancient trades and crafting the exquisite artefacts on offer in the boutiques and craft-shops of the Kathmandu Valley. See pages 165 and 167.

Elephant-back safari. Of all the ways to view Nepal's wildlife, edging through the *phanta* grass of Chitwan or Bardia atop a swaying pachyderm – with a tantalising glimpse of a rhino or tiger always a possibility – is the ultimate experience. See pages 290 and 296.

A porter in Nepal's Everest region.

Tri-shaws for hire in Kathmandu's Durbar Square.

NEELAM

Prayer flags at the Maya Devi Temple.

A window onto some of the world's highest peaks in the Manang Valley.

A COUNTRY IN BETWEEN

Slotted in between giant neighbours, Nepal's small space contains a staggering diversity of landscapes and cultures and forms a travel destination of legendary stature.

A bronze lion souvenir for sale in Patan.

Nepal is a nation in between. Strung along the glittering length of the central Himalayas, its narrow breadth spans one of the most dramatic geographical and cultural transitions on earth. From the heat and dust of the Terai to the wind-scoured wastes of the trans-Himalaya, Nepal is both the buffer zone and the point of contact between the disparate worlds of the Indian subcontinent and Sino-Tibet. Its own character has been forged at the crackling junction between mountain and jungle landscapes, Hindu and Buddhist religions, Tibeto-Burman and Indo-Aryan ethnicities, and northern and southern architectural, artistic and culinary traditions. This is also a country straddling the space between medievalism and modernity, democracy and despotism, war and peace.

Buddhist Manapanahom prayer stones.

Long locked away from the outside world, Nepal maintains a formidable allure for travellers, and the name "Kathmandu" alone is enough to set feet itching. The country is home to eight of the world's ten highest mountains, and since the mid-20th century the Himalayas have been drawing intrepid adventurers to test their mettle on sky-scraping summits. Today thousands of trekkers arrive each year to traverse the high-altitude homelands of Sherpas, Gurungs and Tamangs, and the lower hills have become an adventure playground for climbers, kayakers, rafters and mountain bikers. There is more to Nepal than mountains, however. A turbulent dynastic past and a rich religious syncretism have left the country speckled with palaces and temples, showcases for rarefied traditions in woodcarving, sculpture and metalwork. In the steamy lowlands of the south, meanwhile, the mighty sal forests and vast expanses of riverine grassland are the setting for some of Asia's finest national parks.

That a country this diverse has faced Himalaya-sized obstacles on its journey is inevitable. Since it was first forged from a clutch of competing fiefdoms in the 18th century, Nepal has been marked by conflict, manifest in palace coups, royal massacres and Maoist uprisings. But the civil war that racked the country at the turn of the 21st century is now over and Nepal is slowly settling into its current role as a uniquely diverse nation in the narrow slot between the superpowers of modern Asia.

The mountainous landscape around Kyanjin.

THE COLLISION ZONE

Nepal's mountainous landscape is a legacy of a cataclysmic collision between the Indian subcontinent and the Eurasian landmass.

The story of the Himalayas begins with an almighty impact. The sheer scale of that collision – between two huge slabs of the earth's crust – is illustrated in one simple fact: the summit of Mount Everest, the world's highest mountain, is made up of limestone originally laid down in the depths of a turbid sea. Nepal's landscape, then, is the wreckage of a continental crash, an episode of inconceivable geological violence, played out across millennia and still unfolding today.

The Tethys Sea

Some 250 million years ago, in the Late Palaeozoic era, the portion of the globe now occupied by Nepal and India lay deep beneath the surface of an ocean known to modern geologists as the Tethys Sea. The waters of this ocean teemed with primitive marine life forms, amongst them the spiralled black ammonites, the fossils of which would be revered by Hindus as an embodiment of Vishnu many millions of years later.

Deep layers of sediment were deposited at the bottom of the Tethys Sea – the muddy run-off carried out by rivers from continents where dinosaurs were taking form, and the calcium-rich particles of smashed seashells and crumbled corals. Over the ocean's 200 million-year lifespan those layers reached a depth of some 4,500 metres (15,000ft). By around 70 million years ago, however, the days of the Tethys Sea were numbered, for far away to the south, the continents were on the march.

The shifting plates

The theories of plate tectonics and continental drift were only conceived in the early 20th century. Earlier geographers had supposed

Gosainkund Lake.

that mountain ranges had formed as a cooling earth shrank, its skin wrinkling like a raisin. But today we know that the surface of the planet is divided into great slabs of varying thickness, all born along on the slow convection currents of the earth's semi-molten mantle beneath.

What is now the Indian subcontinent started out in the southern hemisphere as part of a vast continent consisting of the jumbled jigsaw of modern Africa, Australia, Antarctica and Southeast Asia. This mega-continent, usually known as Gondwana, began to break apart during the Jurassic era. The Indo-Australian Plate split away and began to drift northwards at the formidable rate of 20–25cm (8–10ins) per year. The Indian section of the plate travelled some

4,400km (2,700 miles), crossing the equator and squeezing the Tethys Sea into an ever narrower channel until finally, some 50 million years ago, just as the first mammals were taking form, it crunched into the vast northern bulk of the Eurasian Plate. When continents collide carnage ensues, and the Himalayas were the result.

Formation of the Himalayas

Mount Everest was not made in a day. The upheavals caused by the impact of the Indo-Australian and Eurasian plates may have begun 50 million years ago, but they continue apace today: the Indian subcontinent is still driving under the Eurasian landmass, triggering earthquakes and thrusting the Himalayas ever upwards. However, the pace of change is not constant and the ongoing birth of the Himalayas has been punctuated by a series of stupendous periods of uplift followed by intervals of comparative quiescence.

An early episode of upheaval occurred during the Upper Eocene era (38 to 45 million years ago), flinging the one-time bed of the Tethys Sea up into vast mountain ranges, buckling, bending and cooking the sediments into all manner of improbable angles. It was, however, the intense mountain-building epoch of the mid-Miocene (7 to 26 million years ago) that created the major structure of the present-day Himalayas. Another significant bout of uplift occurred about 2 million years ago, and the final major upheaval ensued during the Pleistocene period, between 1 and 2 million years ago – at a time when the progenitors of mankind were beginning to stir.

The power of erosion

The moment that the Himalayas began to rise, the converse process of erosion got under way too. As continental drift forced the bands of buckled rock upwards, wind and water were

Dramatic vistas on the Annapurna Trail.

THE EARLIEST SETTLERS

Very little is known of the earliest human activities in the Himalayas, and the facts tend to be shrouded in myths and legends. Some of the more far-fetched explanations for the supposed existence of the yeti (see page 107), for example, make it an early humanoid, abandoned by the evolutionary process. There is also the legend of Manjushri, the Tibetan saint who came across the mountains and saw a large lake, then cleft a mountain in half to let the water out, creating the Kathmandu Valley. While the yeti remains in the realm of crypto-zoology, modern geologists confirm that the valley was indeed once a lake.

working to wear them back down. Modern geographers believe that the great rivers of South Asia – the Indus, the Ganges and the Brahmaputra – were in existence before the mountains began to rise. Their headwaters do not coincide with the natural watershed of the Himalayas; instead they lie beyond it on the heights of the Tibetan Plateau. As the landmass rose beneath them they did their best to maintain a southward course, carving deep clefts through the mountains and bearing the resultant sediments away towards new oceans. In some places the rising ridges trapped the rivers for a time, forming great lakes within the ranges until the water finally cut its way out. The Kathmandu Valley was once such a lake.

Water in another form – ice – has had its own impact. During the last ice age a great meandering network of glaciers spanned the Himalayas, stretching down through the foothills towards the plains of India, with the lower limit of glaciation reaching some 1,500 metres (4,900ft) below its current level. Although the glaciers have retreated, they continue to grind away at the mountains today. Each year fresh snow accumulates and is compressed into ice to depths of several hundred metres. The weight pushes the glacier's lowest edge down the mountain, scraping away debris and carving out the valleys. Meanwhile, the monsoon rains pound at the southern flanks of the mountains, and the constant freezing and thawing cracks the rocks, causing them to shed their outer layers. But for all this, the process of plate tectonics is still winning the battle: the Himalayas continue to rise by some 5mm every year.

Mountain geography

Today the Himalayas stretch some 2,400km (1,500 miles) across Asia, from northern Pakistan to southeast China. They set the tone for the climate of the continent: the mountains

The Dudhkoshi River.

TENSIONS AND EARTHQUAKES

Ever since the first collision of continents the Himalayan region has been subjected to compression, contortion and elevation, and the area is still adjusting to the impact today. The Indian subcontinent continues to push into Eurasia, as evidenced by the frequency of slips along the major fault lines beneath the Himalayas. Minor tremors are common all along the length of the Himalayas, and major earthquakes are not unknown. The last catastrophic quake to rock Nepal was in 1934. Measuring 8.4 on the Richter Scale, it caused widespread devastation. An earlier quake of similar magnitude took place eight centuries earlier in 1255.

stop cold northern airstreams from getting to India, keeping its upper reaches far warmer than places of similar latitude elsewhere on earth. Conversely, they also stop the wet monsoonal weather systems of the Indian Ocean from heading north, turning the Tibetan Plateau into a high-altitude desert and leaving great sweeps of aridity stretching beyond into Central Asia.

Mountain relief is asymmetrical, with rock strata inclined to the north, leaving steep southern faces. The south-tending spurs of the main Himalayan range are covered with temperate forests, their steep valleys marked with occasional waterfalls. North of the main range, the prospect is much more desolate with bare mountain slopes and undulating valleys filled with rock debris and sparse vegetation. Summers are short; winters are severe with high snowfall, low temperatures and strong winds.

Jharkot, near Jomsom.

In the northwest of the country a fourth, trans-Himalayan range defines the boundary between Nepal and Tibet. Peaks of between 6,000 and 7,000 metres (19,700–23,000ft) lie about 35km (22 miles) north of the main range. This region lies beneath the rainshadow, and wind-eroded landforms predominate. This is part of an essentially Tibetan landscape and climate, a world away from the wet, fertile zone south of the mountains.

The Middle Hills

South of the Himalayas, is the Mahabharat Range, rising to heights of between 1,500 and 2,700 metres (4,900–8,900ft). Arrayed between the outer rampart of the Mahabharat Range and the mighty rise of the Himalayas is a mass of tangled valleys and steep slopes generally known as the Middle Hills, or the *Pahar*. This region is the cradle of Nepal's cultural collision zone between China and India – the Kathmandu Valley lies deep within the Middle Hills. The climate in this region is moderate. Summer maximum temperatures are about 30°C (86°F) and mean winter temperatures about 10°C (50°F). Winters can be frosty, but they are dry and snowless, while summer monsoons bring substantial rain.

> *Himalaya means "Abode of Snow", and the mountains are sometimes seen as an embodiment of Himavat, the Hindu god of snow and the father of the goddesses Ganga, who takes the form of the River Ganges, and Parvati, the wife of Shiva.*

The characteristic landforms in the Middle Hills are sinuous ridges, dissected by numerous river valleys. While the smaller valleys make narrow, steep defiles, the larger ones have an easy gradient and a wide open character. Landslides and landslips are very common in these areas and the tributary streams, laden with detritus, unload sprawling alluvial fans as they emerge into Nepal's southernmost geographical region, the Terai.

People are often surprised to learn that Kathmandu's latitude – about 27°41 North – is the same as that of southern Florida and Kuwait, and slightly south of New Delhi.

Phewa Tal at dawn.

The lowlands

South of the Mahabharat Range one final Himalayan outrider shadows the east–west line of the higher ranges. This is the Siwalik Range, sometimes known as the Churia. These modest hills generally rise to heights of 750–1,500 metres (2,450–4,900ft), and at their base lies the low, level region, 25–40km (15–25 miles) in width, commonly known as the Terai.

Geographically speaking the Terai is simply the northernmost part of the great alluvial plains of north India. It is predominantly flat and overlain with silt and sand. Taking full advantage of the monsoonal deluges as well as the nutrient-laden rivers, the Terai is formidably fertile. Between the Siwalik and Mahabharat hills lie the *dun*, or Inner Terai valleys. These longitudinal valleys are slightly higher than the Terai itself, but have a similar climate with wet summers and rampant tropical vegetation. Summers are very hot in the Terai and the *dun*, with temperatures often rising well beyond 38°C (100°F). Winters are much cooler, with temperatures falling to 10°C (50°F). Most

MONSOON RAINS

The monsoon begins in June and lasts for almost four months, but its distribution of rain varies. Eastern Nepal is affected first by the wet winds from the Bay of Bengal and has a longer monsoon and more rain. The west of Nepal lies in the hinterland of the monsoon's progress and is under the influence of the *lhu*, the dry wind that blows across western India. The high Himalayas block the northward passage of the rains and much of the northwest lies in the rain shadow; Jomsom gets less than 30cm (12ins) of rain, while Pokhara, 65km (40 miles) further south and exposed by a dip in the middle ranges, receives over 300cm (120ins).

The name Siwalik means "tresses of Shiva", and these interlocking hills are said to be the long, matted hair of the Hindu god. They stretch right across the top of the Indian subcontinent as far as Pakistan.

rain falls during the June–September monsoon, which is heaviest in the east.

Living with the landscape

In the epic timeframe of plate tectonics, the impact of human culture on the landscapes of Nepal has lasted mere moments. And when compared to the monumental marks left on the mountains by rivers and glaciers, the occasional road cutting or dam seems like little more than a pinprick. But when it comes to surface geography and ecology, mankind has changed much of the scenery beyond all recognition. Forests have vanished; seemingly impossible slopes have been terraced, cities have sprawled, and vast expanses of agricultural land have spread across what was once jungle.

However, the landscape influenced culture long before the culture shaped the landscape; the livelihoods of the various peoples of Nepal have always been dictated by the altitude at which they live. And it was only in the 20th century that population pressures and modern technology saw traditional harmony give way to environmental destruction.

Life has always been hardest in the far north of Nepal, at sky-scraping altitudes and deep beneath the trans-Himalayan rainshadow. The Thakalis of the Kali Gandaki Valley and the people of Manang, Mustang and Dolpo live amidst harsh terrain which has always made farming difficult. These trans-Himalayan people turned instead to trading for a source of income, traversing the mountains on foot, plying short routes from village to village or crossing the great divide between Tibet and India at the head of mule trains and yak caravans.

Further south, where the monsoon rains reach high up the southern slopes of the Himalayas, agriculture has always proved more successful, and mountain pastoralists have succeeded in growing potatoes at 4,000 metres (13,000ft) and barley still higher up. In the Middle Hills, meanwhile, the mild subtropical climate and adequate rainfall create a favourable zone for agricultural settlement. The Tamangs of central Nepal, originally from Tibet, assimilated into the local culture through farming, carving remarkable terrace systems out of the slopes. The clearing of forest for agriculture, however, has hastened the process of soil erosion and denuded the very fertility that first drew the attention of farmers to the hillsides. The patches of level ground within the Middle Hills have proved more resilient. In the Kathmandu Valley the moderate climate permits three harvests a year.

At a glance the Terai seems as though it should have always been the cradle of settlement and culture in Nepal, with its warm climate, easy terrain and fabulously fertile soils. However, those same conditions also made it a breeding ground for malarial mosquitoes – not to mention much larger dangerous animals – and for much of its history it was the preserve of only a few hardy settlers. But in the more recent past malaria has largely been eradicated, and the Terai has been transformed into an extensive belt of farmland, with settlers from the crowded and overworked Middle Hills clearing forests and draining marshes to make new space alongside the indigenous Tharus with their own elaborate system of irrigation, homestead construction and rotational grazing.

Terraced fields at Manakamana.

Tilling maize in the Terai.

Jung Bahadur Rana and family.

DECISIVE DATES

Early history: 800 BC–AD 1200

800–600 BC
The Kiratis, Nepal's first known residents, arrive from the east and settle in the Kathmandu Valley.

c.543 BC
The Buddha is born at Lumbini.

350–100 BC
The Mauryan emperor Ashoka visits Lumbini; Buddhism spreads through the region before a subsequent Hindu resurgence.

AD 300–600
The Licchavis take control of the Kathmandu Valley.

637
Chinese pilgrim Hsuan Tsang visits Nepal.

c.640
The Licchavi princess Bhrikuti marries King Songtsen Gampo of Tibet and is subsequently credited with converting Tibet to Buddhism.

c.650–1200
Nepal slips into the "Dark Ages" under the Thakuris; Tibet and Kashmir invade.

Malla and Shah Dynasties: 1200–1846

1200
Ari Malla becomes the first Malla king.

1350–1482
Malla rule extended beyond the Kathmandu Valley.

1482
The death of King Yaksha Malla sees the Kathmandu Valley divided into rival city-states.

1768–9
Prithvi Narayan Shah of Gorkha conquers the Kathmandu Valley and founds a unified Nepal.

1790–2
Nepal tussles with China over Tibet and ends up obliged to pay tribute to China's Celestial Emperor.

1814–6
Nepalese expansion into India leads to two years of war with the British, ending with the "Treaty of Friendship"; a British representative is installed in Kathmandu and the first Gurkha troops serve the British.

The Rana Dynasty: 1846–1951

1846
The "Kot Massacre" sees Jung Bahadur Rana establish the Rana regime of hereditary prime ministers. The Shah kings are reduced to puppet status.

1852
Mount Everest is discovered to be the highest point on earth.

1857
Nepal supports Britain during the Sepoy Rebellion in India and regains former territory in the Terai in return.

1901
Chandra Shamsher Rana builds the Singha Durbar and establishes the first colleges in Nepal.

1911
Britain's King George V visits Nepal as a guest of the Ranas.

1923
Britain recognises Nepalese sovereignty.

Monarchy Restored: 1951–1990

1951
King Tribhuvan regains power with the support of India and

Gurkhas in 1815.

The Nepalese monarch, Chandra Shamsher Rana, in 1926.

the Nepali Congress Party; foreigners are allowed to travel in Nepal.

1953
Edmund Hillary and Tenzing Norgay climb Everest.

1959
Nepal holds its first election; China closes the Tibetan border.

1962
King Mahendra takes direct power and introduces the *panchayat* system of government.

1972
King Birendra inherits the throne.

1980
After unrest Birendra calls a referendum which narrowly reaffirms the continuance of the *panchayat* system.

1989
India enforces a trade embargo on Nepal in an attempt to encourage reform.

Democracy and Revolt: 1990–Present

1990
Following pro-democracy riots, King Birendra lifts the ban on political parties and introduces a parliamentary system.

1991
The Nepali Congress Party wins the general election; G.P. Koirala becomes prime minister.

1994
A coalition takes power with Manmohan Adhikari of the Communist Party of Nepal (CPN) as prime minister, but the election result is subsequently overturned by the Supreme Court, heralding a long period of political chaos.

1996
The Maoists launch the decade-long "People's War".

2001
Crown Prince Dipendra kills 10 members of the royal family, including the king, before turning the gun on himself. The unpopular Gyanendra is crowned king and becomes Nepal's constitutional monarch.

2005
King Gyanendra assumes direct rule, accusing the government of failing to end the Maoist uprising.

2006
After mass demonstrations the king restores power to parliament; the Maoists declare a ceasefire and join negotiations.

2008
The Maoists win the general election; all political parties agree to abolish the monarchy at the first parliamentary session and Nepal becomes a republic.

2011–3
Wrangles over a proposed new constitution see a series of short-lived governments and a general parliamentary stalemate; attempts to set up a Truth and Reconciliation Commission to investigate events during the civil war stall in the courts.

Celebrating the lifting of the ban on political parties, 1990.

Mandala of Vishnu, a Newar artwork, dated to 1681.

ROYAL DYNASTIES

Nepal's history emerges from myth over 2,000 years ago with the start of a long relay of royal regimes centred on the Kathmandu Valley.

Nepal's past is spectacularly blood-soaked. From the 18th century to the 21st century the country's history is riddled with assassinations, uprisings, massacres and coups. In fact, two points in the Nepalese narrative stand out as near miraculous: that one man managed to forge a single nation from a plethora of feuding fiefdoms; and that the subsequent state survived at all.

The territory that now comprises Nepal has always been part of the Himalayan buffer zone, a strip of mountainous country running from Bhutan in the east to Kashmir in the west. This was, and is, the point of transition between the Indian subcontinent and the Sino-Tibetan world, a stage set for cultural and religious syncretism and with every opportunity for clear-eyed middlemen. Deep into prehistory small states have flourished along the length of the Himalayas. Most were tiny and transient, but where trans-Himalayan trade routes intersected with a pocket of unusually fertile ground a more sophisticated – if still geographically limited – kingdom could sometimes develop. Prior to the 18th century most of what we now think of as "Nepalese" history is in fact that of one such pocket – the Kathmandu Valley.

Early kingdoms

Legend tells that the Kathmandu Valley was created when the god Manjushri, a manifestation of the Buddha, drove his celestial sword through the hills at Chobar, draining a vast lake to create a slab of level, mountain-encircled land. The valley was indeed once a lake, and its fertile floor was an obvious place for a small state to develop.

The earliest recorded history of the Kathmandu Valley teeters on the brink of myth. The Indian epic the *Mahabharata*, which dates in parts from the first millennium BC, mentions that the region was ruled by the Kiratis, and indeed it was these people – who endure today as the Rais and Limbus of eastern Nepal – who held sway in the valley for several centuries around the first century AD. Buddhism, which had emerged from the plains of north India in the 6th century BC, had reached this proto-Nepal, and the Mauryan emperor Ashoka – or at least his emissaries – may have visited the valley in the 3rd century BC following his pilgrimage to the Buddha's birthplace at Lumbini.

Combat between King Padmottara and Duhprahasa from Svayambhu Purana, sacred legend of Nepal.

History takes firmer form around AD 300 when the Kiratis were shunted aside by the Licchhavi dynasty. Serious temple-building got under way and the Kathmandu Valley developed as a successful trading centre on the routes between India and China. In AD 637 the Chinese pilgrim Hsuan Tsang visited and left a description that is still recognisable today: "The houses are of wood, painted and sculpted. The people are fond of bathing, of dramatic performances, of astrology and of blood sacrifices. Irrigation, carefully and skilfully applied, makes the soil rich. Both Buddhism and Brahmanism (Hinduism) flourish in the main temples, which are wealthy and well supported. Commerce prospers and trade is well organised." The people that Hsuan Tsang met in the streets were the Newars, still the dominant ethnic group of the valley today, and the area was known by a variant of their name – "Nepa", which in turn would become Nepal.

Despite the prosperity and order which Hsuan Tsang described, in the early 7th century the Licchhavi period gave way to a lengthy episode of obscurity under the Thakuris – Nepal's own "Dark Ages" about which little is known. Trade across the mountains continued, however, despite periodic incursions by armies from Kashmir and Tibet, and in the 10th century the Thakuri king Gunakama Deva founded the city of Kantipur, known today as Kathmandu.

The Malla golden age

The true golden age of the Kathmandu Valley began with the arrival of the Mallas in 1200. The first Malla king, Ari Malla, founded a dynasty which would last for more than 500 years, and which would preside over a spectacular flourishing of arts and architecture.

Greatest of the Malla kings was Jayasthiti Malla. In the late 14th century he unified the valley, established the social order underpinned by the Hindu caste system and built a legal framework for the state. This legacy of stability lasted for two generations and Jayasthiti Malla's grandson, Yaksha Malla, even managed tentatively to extend his rule beyond the Kathmandu Valley as far as Gorkha and the central Terai. However, on Yaksha Malla's death in 1482 the kingdom was divided between his children. Each became ruler of one of the four valley towns – Kathmandu, Bhaktapur, Banepa and Lalitpur (now known as Patan) – and each established an independent ruling dynasty. The brief moment during which the Mallas had the potential to found a greater Himalayan nation had passed, and from now on they turned inwards, still gathering their incomes from trade, but focusing their political energy on a glorious, if ultimately unproductive, artistic rivalry.

The word malla means wrestler, and legend has it that Ari Malla, founder of the Malla dynasty, was given the name after his mother unexpectedly gave birth at a wrestling tournament.

Each of the valley's city-states vied to achieve pre-eminence in architectural splendour. Newari artistry reached its apogee, and magnificent multi-roofed temples mushroomed in the Durbar squares of the rival capitals. The legacy of this period is still writ large in the cityscapes of modern Nepal, but it enervated the Mallas as a political power, and left them ultimately doomed, for beyond the Kathmandu Valley history had been continuing apace.

A 17th-century wooden sculpture of Vishnu.

The rise of Gorkha

While the Mallas had been stacking their tapered temple roofs ever higher into the Himalayan sky, away to the south there had been great political changes in the Indian subcontinent. The Delhi Sultanate and the subsequent Mughal Empire had replaced Hindu political dominance in north India with Muslim rule. As a consequence a number of Rajput chieftains of the Kshatriya caste had moved into the hills and carved out their own small kingdoms amongst the indigenous peoples. In 1559 one of these chieftains, Druvya Shah, had seized the little hill town of Gorkha, three days' march west of Kathmandu. Gorkha was a formidable stronghold, but it was just one of some 60 similar fiefdoms that speckled the Middle Hills. Nothing suggested that it would one day be the wellspring of a modern state, until the birth, in 1722, of a man named Prithvi Narayan Shah, nemesis of the Malla kings and founder of the Nepalese nation.

An image of assembled Gurkhas in 1820.

According to legend, shortly after ascending to the modest Gorkha throne, Privthi Narayan Shah looked out from a ridge on the edge of the Kathmandu Valley at the distant trio of Malla temple towns. "The thought came to my heart," he later recounted, "that if I might be king of these three cities, why, let it be so." It was a project that would take quarter of a century and the careful assembly of an impressive, if motley, fighting force of disparate hill tribes who came collectively to be known as "Gorkhas", and later as Gurkhas.

Over the years the Gorkha army slowly coiled itself around the Kathmandu Valley like a python. A number of tentative forays were beaten back, but the Malla realm was essentially enchained by Prithvi Narayan Shah's forces. In 1768 the increasingly desperate Malla kings issued a cry for help to a new power that had recently emerged in the south, and that looked as though it would soon entirely usurp the crumbling Mughal Empire. The British East India Company responded favourably and an expeditionary force of 2,400 men set out from Calcutta at the height of summer with the aim of rescuing the Mallas. They only got as far as the Terai, however, before running into Nepal's formidable natural defence system – the virulent strain of malaria known locally as *ayul* (and called "owl" by the hapless British). The disease so decimated the British troops that it only took a small Gorkha unit to deflect them. By the time the sickly survivors had beat their ignominious retreat to Company territories it was all already over in the hills: Privthi Narayan Shah had swooped on Kathmandu, choosing the day of the Indra Jatra festival, when most of the inhabitants would be drunk or at prayer, for his final assault. The Malla reign was over, and the years of Shah dominance had begun.

The Shahs

Prithvi Narayan Shah did not stop at the Kathmandu Valley. His forces had an irresistible momentum that carried them westwards through the Kirati country all the way to the borders of Sikkim. By the time he died of fever at Nuwakot in 1775 all of what is now central and eastern Nepal – and a little more besides – was ruled from Kathmandu. On his deathbed the founding father of this new nation forbade his descendants to divide the country amongst themselves: he was well aware that this was what had fatally hobbled the Mallas.

Prithvi Narayan Shah had forged a formidable military machine in the Gorkha army. After his death it continued to grow, creating its own impetus for fresh conquests. The third Shah king, Bahadur, conquered the long stretch of hill country west of Kathmandu, successfully toppling each of the petty principalities of the so-called *Chaubisi Raj*, the "21 Kingdoms" of the western Middle Hills. The marches of the Nepalese state had already reached their modern limit, but the military momentum was unstoppable, and at times it caused the Shahs to overstretch themselves.

In the latter years of the 18th century the Gorkha armies made a number of forays into Tibet, including a raid on Shigatse during which they looted the fabled Tashilunpo monastery. These incursions led to the first setbacks: in 1792 a formidable Chinese-Tibetan army launched a counter invasion, which resulted in a chastened Nepal being obliged to send tribute to the Chinese capital. The Shahs did not learn their lesson, however, for they now swung southwards, and in doing so ran headlong into the rising power of the British in India.

By the dawn of the 19th century the Mughals were presiding over a lame-duck empire, and the British East India Company – still a quasi-commercial organisation but by now operating as the de facto colonial wing of the British Crown – was unmistakably the main player in north India. With Gorkha troops pushing ever further across the Terai and into the Gangetic plains, conflict was inevitable, and between 1814 and 1816 Britain and Nepal were at war.

Lalitavistara manuscript images, as commissioned by Captain Robert Knox of the East India Company.

Despite their staggering superiority in terms of manpower and weaponry, the victory that the British eventually won was not entirely decisive, and they baulked at the prospect of actually invading Nepal and tackling the Gorkha soldiers on their home ground. However, they were able to draw up a rather prejudicial "Treaty of Friendship" during peace negotiations at Segauli. Nepalese acquisitions in the western Himalayas and in the north Indian plains were hived off and made British territory, and the borders of Sikkim were re-established under British guarantee. Nepal's frontiers had been fixed, though within them the Shah dynasty would be free to do as they pleased, and as far as the British were concerned the country would serve as a comforting buffer zone, protecting their own realms from the machinations of the Chinese and Russians.

The Segauli treaty made one further demand: a British residency would be established in Kathmandu as the first official representation of a foreign power that the country had ever hosted. Nepal had long been suspicious of Europeans. Two wandering Jesuits had passed safely through Kathmandu in 1661 while travelling from China to India, but a party of Capuchin missionaries who followed met with disaster when it was discovered that they had come to win converts. The Nepalese accepted the British representative with great reluctance; the only land they would provide for the residency building was a grubby and ill-omened plot two miles north of Kathmandu, known locally as "The Abode of Demons", and the incumbent residents were granted no power and little freedom. They did, however, have a ringside seat for all the courtly carnage that would ensue in the coming decades.

Intrigue and infighting

With the capacity for territorial expansion curtailed, the Shah dynasty turned in on itself. For decades the Kathmandu palace was a hothouse of intrigue and assassination and the entire dynasty was chronically unstable. Indeed it is probably only because Nepal had a framework of frontiers defined by outsiders, and because large chunks of the countryside had been granted as personal fiefdoms to senior military figures who then ran them with little recourse to Kathmandu, that the country survived at all.

A series of weak kings took to the throne, frequently ascending at a young age and necessitating a lengthy period when effective power was in the hands of a regent – often an uncle or a dowager queen. While a claim to the throne itself depended on direct descent from Prithvi Narayan Shah, the role of regent could be seized by anyone within the royal household capable of sufficient Machiavellianism, and this fact was largely responsible for the endless round of plotting, politicking and literal backstabbing that marked Shah rule in the first half of the 19th century. In 1845 the British Resident, Henry Lawrence, wrote of the palace that "so much blood has been shed during the last half-century and there is so much to avenge that sooner or later each individual must look to judicial murder or assassination as his fate."

This culture of assassination reached its climax on the night of 14 September 1846. At around 10pm the minister for civil affairs Gagan Singh, who was also the lover of Queen Rajya Laxmi Devi, junior wife of the ineffectual King Rajendra, was murdered on the rooftop terrace of his home. When the queen – who had long been plotting to ensure her own son's ascent to the throne – heard the news she ordered all senior military and civil officers to gather in the courtyard of the Kot, an arsenal across the northern Durbar Square from the Hanuman Dhoka Durbar. Ensconced on an

Kathmandu in 1921.

EVEREST DISCOVERED

The first European to grasp the extraordinary nature of Nepal's mountains was the map-maker James Rennell, who in 1788 observed that the summits could be seen at a distance of 240km (149 miles), suggesting heights of 8,000 metres (26,250ft)-plus. Nepal was out of bounds for British surveyors, but bearings were taken from afar on several mountains, including one identified as Peak XV, which proved to be the highest point on earth. Strenuous efforts were made to discover the mountain's local name. This proved fruitless, and so in 1865, Peak XV was named Mount Everest, for the former Surveyor-General of India, Sir George Everest.

upper balcony the furious queen demanded of the massed ranks of the aristocracy, crowded in the darkness below, that the identity of the murderer be revealed. Tensions mounted; shots were fired, and a bloodbath ensued. More than 30 members of the cream of Kathmandu's courtiers died, as well as untold others. Before the massacre was even over Queen Rajya Laxmi Devi had handed the roles of chief minister and commander-in-chief to the young officer whose men were doing the shooting, Jung Bahadur.

Whether Jung Bahadur had deliberately engineered events leading to the Kot Massacre is still a point of debate, but he took advantage of the opportunity it presented to effect a coup and found a dynasty that would hold the power in Nepal for the next century.

A 19th-century oil painting of Mount Everest.

Rana rule

In the aftermath of the Kot Massacre – with most of his potential rivals dead – Jung Bahadur moved swiftly to sideline both the king, and the queen who had granted him his new positions. He adopted the regal moniker "Rana" and made himself prime minister. He later also awarded himself the pseudo-royal title of "maharaja". The Shahs were not actually deposed, but they were reduced to the status of figurehead, essentially imprisoned within the palace while Jung Bahadur Rana and his descendants ran the country.

The Ranas are often presented as the villains of the Nepalese piece, but their rule brought to an end a lengthy period of courtly carnage and engendered a degree of political stability. While a certain amount of intrigue inevitably continued, the hereditary system that Jung Bahadur Rana established did away with default regencies, and ensured, in theory, that the ruler of the day would have served an apprenticeship. He gave the major Nepalese military commands to his brothers in descending order of seniority on the understanding that as the holder of each position – including that of prime minister – died or resigned, the incumbent of the post below would move up to take his place. And as the brothers moved upwards, the next generation – starting with Jung Bahadur's sons and followed by his nephews – would take their place on the ladder.

Britain's King George V was one of the few foreigners invited into Nepal by the Ranas. A total of 39 tigers and 18 rhinos were killed during his 1911 hunting trip to the Terai.

The Ranas also proved adept at dealing with their British neighbours who, by the middle of the 19th century, were the undisputed masters

A number of foreigners transgressed the Nepalese travel ban, including the boastful Henry Savage Landor, and the Japanese Zen Buddhist monk Ekai Kawaguchi who stayed for 15 months en route for Tibet.

of the Indian subcontinent. In 1850 Jung Bahadur Rana made a ground-breaking visit to Britain. He was the first South Asian Hindu ruler ever to do so; he and his entourage of fabulously attired courtiers were fêted by British society, and he carried away a clear impression of the power of an industrialised nation.

The British had been recruiting Gurkha troops since the signing of the 1816 Treaty of Friendship. In 1857, when local sepoy soldiers across British India turned against their officers, the Gurkha units were amongst the few that remained loyal. Though many in India – including the enfeebled final Mughal emperor – believed that British power was about to be annihilated, Jung Bahadur, with his first-hand experience of Europe, judged otherwise. He made an immediate offer of assistance and led a column of 9,000 men to the aid of the stricken colonialists. Once the rebellion was crushed a grateful Britain returned the Terai tracts seized in 1816 to Nepal. Though the Ranas maintained a policy of official isolationism, restricting access to the country to all but the British Resident and a handful of carefully vetted guests, and responding with hostility to any unofficial incursions, they had done enough to ensure the benevolence of the rulers of the Raj.

As the 19th century drew to a close, neo-classical Rana mansions sprouted across the Kathmandu Valley. Village lifestyles remained essentially medieval, but the Ranas did abolish *sati* (the Hindu tradition of widows immolating themselves on their husbands' funeral pyres) and emancipate many of Nepal's bonded slaves. Trade across the Himalayas continued, but Nepal's most significant connection to world events was through its military tradition: some 114,000 Gurkhas saw active service in World War I. In 1923, in a further show of gratitude, Britain acknowledged Nepal's outright sovereignty. The country's independent future was assured.

Pashpati temples in 1905.

THE PUNDITS

In 1802 the British embarked on a mission to map the entire Indian subcontinent. By the middle of the century the survey had reached the fringes of Nepal. Knowledge of potential invasion routes through the mountains was deemed essential, but the country was out of bounds to foreigners. But in 1863, the surveyors hit upon the idea of using Himalayan traders to work on their behalf. Nain Singh and Mani Singh from the Kumaon region were the first of these explorer-spies, later known as the Pundits. They were trained in covert surveying techniques and sent out in the direction of Nepal and Tibet.

In March 1865 the Pundits headed for the hills. Nain Singh made a successful 2,000km (1,200-mile) return journey to Lhasa, and Mani Singh completed a clandestine circuit of western Nepal. These were the first of many such journeys through forbidden territory. The British were anxious to preserve good relations with the Ranas, however, so the efforts of the Pundits were kept strictly secret.

As a result, the name of Hari Ram, another Kumaoni Pundit, is largely forgotten. Between 1871 and 1886 he made a series of epic circuits of the Himalayas, exploring the Everest region, traversing the mountains as far as the Kali Gandaki gorge and scouting out the country between Kathmandu and Pokhara. He did more to put Nepal on the map – literally – than any other individual.

Chandra Shamsher Rana, maharajah from 1901 to 1929.

FROM MONARCHY TO REPUBLIC

In the last 100 years Nepal has opened up to the outside world, wrestled with democracy and civil war, and made the shift from monarchy to republic.

As the 20th century rolled on Nepal struggled to come to terms with its place in the new Asia. The Shah kings remained essentially imprisoned in the royal palace while the Rana aristocracy ran the country. Chandra Shamsher Rana, who ruled from 1901 to 1929, had wrought a number of changes: there was now limited electricity in the Kathmandu Valley. But when the first motorcar arrived in the 1930s it had to be carried across the Mahabharat Hills by porters. The country had also remained formidably isolated from the outside world with the ban on foreign travellers still strictly enforced. The journalist Percival Landon, who visited in 1928, estimated that no more than 120 Englishmen had entered the Kathmandu Valley before him, and none had been permitted to set foot in the surrounding hills.

Nepal's founding father, Prithvi Narayan Shah, had had a profound understanding of the country's eternal quandary as a small state between the vast Indian and Chinese spheres. It was, he once said, "like a yam between two boulders". By the middle of the 20th century huge changes were taking place in both those boulders. Nepal's isolationist oligarchy could not hope to remain unaffected, but when the country eventually opened up it struggled to deal with the modern concept of democracy – a struggle which continues today.

The return of the king

During World War II Nepal reprised its long-established role as a source of formidable fighting men for the British Army: 45 Gurkha battalions served with the Allies. But favour with the colonial power would carry little weight in post-war Asia; the age of European empire – and with it the age of client maharajas – was coming to an end. By the time India gained independence in 1947 and Mao's communists took control of China in 1949, Nepal had its own nascent political movements and the days of the Ranas were numbered – though, as if to prove that Nepal was still a land apart, the coming change would be centred on the resurgence of the 200-year-old Shah dynasty.

British Gurkha army pipers on the northwest frontier of India in 1930.

King Tribhuvan Shah was just five years old when he ascended to the throne in 1911. He spent most of the next four decades strictly contained within the sprawling quarters of the Narayanhiti Palace, a gilded cage built four years after his ascension. However, he managed to pick up on the changes wracking the world beyond the walls and found sympathy with the newly formed Nepali Congress Party which, inspired by recent changes in India, was urging reform. In India itself, meanwhile, Jawaharlal Nehru's new socialist republican government had scant sympathy for the Ranas. Surreptitious contacts were established; the Indian embassy in Kathmandu was given secret instructions to aid the Shahs, and the scene was set for a long-delayed royal counter-coup.

In late 1950 King Tribhuvan made a request to be allowed to leave his palace for a picnic in the forests of Nagarjun. The prime minister, Mohan Shamsher Rana, was already suspicious of the king's intentions, but the request was granted. On 6 November the royal motorcade rolled out of the palace with the king at the wheel of his own car. As they were passing the Indian embassy at Sital Niwas, Tribhuvan swerved suddenly to the left: the embassy gates were standing open for him, but they closed with a crash as soon as the car was inside. The king claimed political asylum, and was flown to Delhi on an Indian Air Force jet.

The new King Mahendra in 1956.

The first tourists to Nepal – a total of 600 – were admitted in 1951. The number has since grown to an annual total of around half a million and tourism has become a cornerstone of the Nepalese economy.

Though the Ranas had held the reins of power for a century, the captive king had always remained the symbolic head of the country, and once he had slipped from their grasp they no longer had the advantage. Faced with irresistible political pressure, Mohan Shamsher Rana agreed to step down. On 16 February 1951 Tribhuvan returned to a hero's welcome in Kathmandu; two days later, with the support of the Nepali Congress and the approval of India, he proclaimed a multiparty democracy.

Democracy is a tricky business, however, and for a decade a succession of appointed cabinets and prime ministers came and went without providing an effective government. However, the fall of the Ranas did allow Nepal to engage with the outside world. Roads, schools and hospitals were built and the first foreign travellers were welcomed into the country.

The Ranas had already tentatively let a few mountaineering parties into the Himalayas; now the door was thrown open – just as the Chinese invasion of Tibet severed alternative access from the north. In 1953 Edmund Hillary and Tenzing Norgay successfully climbed Mount Everest.

Democracy delayed

King Tribhuvan died in March 1955 and was succeeded by his son, Mahendra. The political merry-go-round continued: between 1951 and 1960 Nepal had no fewer than 10 different governments. The first general election was eventually held in 1959, with the Nepali Congress returned to power and B.P. Koirala appointed prime minister. By this point, however, the new king had decided that he was unsatisfied with his ceremonial role: in 1960, backed by the fiercely loyal Royal Nepalese Army, he declared a state of emergency, dissolved parliament, arrested the cabinet, and assumed direct rule. Two years later he issued a new constitution, banning political parties and investing all real powers in the king.

The new political scheme was based on the Mahendra's conviction that Western-style parliamentary democracy would not work in Nepal. In its place he instituted the *panchayat* system, based on the traditional five-man village council. It offered locally elected, non-party representation and government at ward, village and district levels. At the national level a Panchayat Assembly was established to ratify decisions taken by a Council of Ministers appointed by the king. Nepal had in effect become an absolute monarchy once again.

King Mahendra died in 1972, and his son Birendra inherited the throne. Throughout the 1970s discontent with perceived corruption and stalled development mounted, and eventually erupted into riots in Kathmandu at the close of the decade. Mahendra ordered a referendum offering a choice of democracy or a continuation of the *panchayat* system; the existing system was endorsed by a narrow majority, and though the constitution was modified to grant more powers to the assembly the king maintained ultimate control. Freedom of speech remained curtailed and the powers of the police and army remained unchecked.

Reform and civil war

On 18 February 1990, the 40th anniversary of the original declaration of democracy, Nepal's outlawed political parties announced a campaign to restore the multiparty system. Demonstrations swept the country and tensions grew

Hippies in Nepal, 1970.

THE HIPPIE TRAIL

Today's travellers to Nepal are following in the footsteps of the long-haired pioneers of the 1960s and 70s. In the years following World War II offbeat adventurers began to travel by road from Europe to Asia. They were few in number, and usually well funded, but in the 1960s, as Western counterculture developed a fascination with Indian spirituality – not to mention cheap South Asian marijuana – a thickening stream of young "freaks" thumbed their way eastwards. Fabled way-stations developed along the trail – Istanbul, Kabul and Kashmir. But for most people Kathmandu was the ultimate destination, an exotic, spiritual city where the dope was cheap and the living was easy.

The hippies congregated in the cheap lodges of Jochne south of Kathmandu's Durbar Square, an area still known as "Freak Street" today. No one really knows how many people traversed the "trail". Compared to modern tourist figures the numbers were negligible, and the hippie heyday was brief: most were evicted from Nepal ahead of King Birendra's coronation in 1975, and the Islamic Revolution in Iran and the Russian invasion of Afghanistan in 1979 effectively severed the overland route. But the hippies created the concept of big trips on small budgets, and in doing so paved the way for today's backpackers and the huge industry that supports them, everywhere from Nepal to Goa to Bali.

as police shootings of protesters spurred further dissent. On 6 April a crowd rallied at Kathmandu's Tundikhel and began a march down Durbar Marg to the Royal Palace. Police tried to turn the crowd back with tear gas; when that failed, they opened fire. The violence shocked the country and prompted major reforms. King Birendra lifted the ban on political parties, and the *panchayat* system was dissolved.

The new 1991 constitution defined the country as "a multi-ethnic, multi-lingual, democratic, independent, indivisible, sovereign, Hindu and constitutional monarchical kingdom". The king's power was now limited but he retained political influence. Multiparty democracy had finally arrived, but it did not bring stability. The Nepali Congress Party (NCP) traded power back and forth with the Communist Party of Nepal (CPN), and a succession of short-lived coalition governments exacerbated the endemic corruption and inefficiency.

At the royal family's funeral, 2001.

At the beginning of 1996 a Maoist splinter group of the CPN declared what they called "People's War" against the government. It began with attacks on foreign factories and raids on state-run banks, but it swiftly developed into a full-blown civil war. The Maoists took control of large swathes of the countryside; their own bloody raids met with violent reprisals from the Nepalese Army, and development shuddered to a halt. The war lasted for a decade; atrocities were committed on both sides, and an estimated 13,000 people were killed.

By the dawn of the 21st century many outside observers were quick to declare Nepal a mess. The civil war had reached a state of violent stalemate which made development projects effectively impossible, and the democratic system was chronically ineffective. In fact, the only genuinely stable institution in the country appeared to be the Shah monarchy – but all that was about to change.

The royal massacre

At around 9pm on the night of 1 June 2001 people on the streets of northern Kathmandu heard the sound of gunfire from the Narayanhiti Palace. No one was particularly concerned: Crown Prince Dipendra was a well-known firearms enthusiast and he often liked to shoot his weapons in the palace gardens. In fact, the 29-year-old, Eton-educated crown prince had just gunned down 10 senior members of the royal family, including his parents and his brother and sister, before turning the gun on himself. He had effectively annihilated the Shah dynasty.

As news of the bloodbath – as dramatic and decisive as the Kot Massacre 155 years earlier – seeped out, Nepal went into shock. Dipendra had actually survived his self-inflicted injuries, and for two days he reigned as king – from an intensive care unit in a military hospital – before ultimately succumbing. The late king's brother Gyanendra – who had previously been crowned as a three-year-old puppet by the Ranas when Tribhuvan fled to India in 1950, and who had been in Pokhara at the time of the massacre – ascended to the throne. As national grief subsided the conspiracy theorists went into action. Gyanendra was already unpopular before he became king, and rumours soon spread that the whole affair had been his doing, or that of his son Paras, who had a reputation as a hell-raising playboy and who had somehow survived the shooting on 1 June. Such theories – as well as others of plotting by the Indian secret services or the CIA – are still common in Nepal. The general belief, however, is that Crown Prince Dipendra, who drank heavily and was known to use drugs, was acting out of frustration because of his parents' disapproval of his intended bride.

The destruction of the direct Shah line meant that Nepal's people would no longer be inclined to acquiesce to the country's monarchic default mode – though at first King Gyanendra failed to realise this.

The birth of the republic

After the royal massacre Nepal's parliament continued to lurch from crisis to crisis. Cabinets collapsed and prime ministers were unseated on a regular basis, and the Maoists took advantage of the chaos to make fresh gains, edging their control closer to Kathmandu. As the violence worsened the tourist industry – which had continued to grow throughout the instability of the 1990s – began to suffer.

The 2001 royal massacre fulfilled an ancient prophecy that the Shah dynasty would survive for just 10 generations. King Birendra was the tenth legitimate Shah king.

In February 2005, responding to government ineptitude and the growing Maoist threat, King Gyanendra seized power and assumed direct rule. He lacked popular support, however, and the following spring mass protests erupted across Kathmandu. International condemnation followed the deaths of 16 demonstrators at the hands of security forces, and Gyanendra bowed to the inevitable. Parliament was restored and one of its earliest moves was to strip the king of all but ceremonial status. The change was enough to bring the Maoists to the negotiating table, and then to join an interim government.

In April 2008 the Maoists won a dramatic electoral victory. Pushpa Kamal Dahal, formerly a guerrilla leader known as Prachanda, became prime minister, and a month later parliament voted by a huge majority to abolish the monarchy. Gyanendra was evicted from the Narayanhiti Palace and Nepal became a Federal Democratic Republic.

Prachanda, head of Nepal's Maoist party.

Though both tourism and development have dramatically rebounded since the end of the civil war and the resumption of democracy, Nepal still faces huge challenges. Parliament has largely maintained its form for short-lived and ineffectual coalitions; efforts to draft a new constitution and to establish a Truth and Reconciliation Commission to investigate the years of violence have foundered, and the Maoists continue to encourage occasional public demonstrations to bolster their parliamentary demands. Peace, however, has returned to the countryside, and Nepal is open for business once more.

Vegetables for sale at Asan Tol market in Kathmandu.

Tyeuda

Nepal has a surprisingly diverse ethnic make-up.

THE NEPALESE

For such a small country, Nepal is astonishingly diverse in its ethnic make-up, from ancient tribal societies to refugees from neighbouring lands.

Nepal's ethnic make-up is as complex and convoluted as its geography. The country is home to a grand tangle of languages, cultures and origins, wrapped around the high ridges and deep valleys. There are around 100 different ethnic groups, and a similar number of languages and dialects.

As with so many of its characteristics, Nepal's wide variety of ethnicity reflects its position as a point of contact between the Indian and Sino-Tibetan worlds. The country's population – approaching 30 million – is fairly evenly split between Tibeto-Burman peoples with their East Asian features and mountain origins, and the Khas groups, whose roots run south into the subcontinent. In the Middle Hills, meanwhile, ancestry from both angles has coloured the culture.

In a wider region so often wracked by communal violence, Nepal has shown a remarkable resistance to ethnic tension. Ever since the rise of Prithvi Narayan Shah and the foundation of the Nepalese state, a loose sense of "Nepaleseness" has grown, fuelled in large part by the increasing dominance of the Nepali language, and linking, if not entirely unifying, the disparate groups. In the 21st century, however, all the peoples of Nepal – from the Sherpas living in the shadow of Mount Everest to the Tharus tilling their fields in the heat of the Terai – are facing the new challenges of increasing urbanisation, an erosion of old social orders, a bitter legacy of civil war, and all the other complications of a desperately poor country advancing unsteadily into the modern age.

Mountain people

In the northernmost mountain areas most of the peoples share a loosely Tibetan heritage and linguistic culture; this region borders onto Tibet itself, after all. These peoples are often known collectively as Bhotiyas, a name derived from the archaic term for Tibet, *Bhot*, but they encompass numerous individual ethnicities, including the most famous of all Nepal's ethnic groups, the Sherpas (see page 53).

A mountain dweller.

Life across the mountain region is tough, with communities perched precariously on narrow ledges and precipitous slopes. Settlements are few and far between; interaction with other villages requires long journeys and much of the year is spent in temporary shelters, moving with the seasons to provide grazing for domestic yaks, sheep and goats. Underpinning mountain society is a deeply rooted religious tradition typified by variations of Tibetan

Buddhism, at times combined with local shamanism and traces of the indigenous Bön faith.

Amongst the harshest of all mountain regions is Mustang, home to around 15,000 people. These Lopas ("People of Lo") – the local name for the area – live in oasis villages on a reddish-brown rock desert, battling against freezing winds to cultivate grains and potatoes in sheltered plots.

The Tamang

The most numerous of all Nepal's mountain peoples are the Tamangs. Their settlements – with sturdy, stone-built houses – appear on the northernmost rim of the Kathmandu Valley and stretch northwards to Langtang and beyond. Tamangs account for around six percent of the total Nepalese population.

The Tamangs are certainly of Tibetan origin, but how exactly they established themselves in Nepal is unclear. Some of their own legends tell of a flight from Tibet during a period of religious persecution, but the best-known story translates the name Tamang as "horse soldiers" and claims that they were cavalrymen who stayed behind and settled after the various historical Tibetan incursions into Nepal. Today, most Tamangs are small farmers, although some work as porters and craftsmen and they can often be spotted in Kathmandu, either toting *rhadis* (flat-weave carpets) for sale or carrying large *doko* baskets with headstraps supported on their foreheads. The men and boys traditionally dress in loincloths and long black tunics; in winter, they wear short-sleeved sheep-wool jackets, frequently with a *khukri* knife thrust in the waistband. Women wear above-the-ankle saris of home-made cotton, and blouses adorned with ornaments and jewellery.

Most Tamangs belong to the Nyingma sect of Tibetan Buddhism; their regions are dotted with gompas, and many young Tamang men and boys join the ranks of the lamas. However, there is also a lively tradition of folk religion, and the *Bompo*, or shaman, has an important role in many village rituals. Tamangs traditionally marry outside their *thar*, or immediate clan. They also had a long tradition of both polygamy and polyandry, though both are now very rare.

Young and old in Bandipur.

The Thakalis

Bridging the gap between Tibet and the Indian subcontinent, many of Nepal's mountain peoples have a long history as traders and middlemen. While trans-Himalayan trade has long since dried up, some have successfully redeployed their skills in modern Nepal, most notably the Thakalis of the upper Kali Gandaki, east of the Annapurna Massif.

Over the centuries, the Thakalis have emerged as the most successful entrepreneurs in Nepal. Their careers began with the salt trade between Tibet and India, but today they have spread into all spheres of contemporary life – including construction, politics, business, academia and the arts. The secret of this expansion is the *dighur* system. A group of friends or relatives pool a given amount of money, sometimes thousands of rupees each, and give the whole sum every year to one among them. The recipient uses the sum as he sees fit; whether he loses or gains money is his own affair, and his only obligation is to feed the *dighur* (group). A self-financing device based on mutual trust, the system does away with interest rates. Most Thakalis still living in their mountain homeland are small farmers, growing barley and potatoes, but they have developed a successful sideline playing host to passing trekkers in their lodges and cafés.

People of the Middle Hills

The Middle Hills form the heartland of Nepal, and it is here that the currents of culture and ethnicity from both north and south have intertwined most thoroughly. While there are groups of both essentially Khas and Tibeto-Burman origin here, most show at least some signs of intermingling.

Early European travellers often described all the people of this long strip of hill country as Gurkhas, but there is no such single ethnic group. Prithvi Narayan Shah, the founder of the Nepalese state, recruited his army from amongst the Gurung, Magar, Rai, Limbu and others, and Gurkha troops today show a similar diversity of origin (see page 215).

A unifying feature of the ethnic groups inhabiting the Middle Hills, is that agriculture is the principal occupation. While the landscape is at times challenging in its steepness, it has all the moisture and fertile soil that the higher zones lack, and a highly developed farming culture has grown up on the steep hillsides, with intricate terraces and long-established villages. The Middle Hills, as the crucible of Nepalese history, are also home to its traditional urban and courtly culture, and it is here that Nepal's syncretic blend of Hinduism and Buddhism is most highly developed.

The Kiratis

The earliest known inhabitants of the Kathmandu Valley were Kirati people who settled there in the 7th century BC after a westward migration from Assam and Burma. Though eventually usurped in the Kathmandu Valley by

An example of Thakali life can be seen in Marpha in the Annapurnas. Clean and organised, the village has running water and a drainage system, a relative rarity in Nepal.

A wizened face in Jharkot.

the Licchavis, people of Kirati origin still live in the eastern reaches of the Middle Hills.

The Rais and Limbus both claim Kirati descent. Both groups traditionally practise subsistence agriculture. They have generally proved more resistant to Hinduism and Buddhism than other groups, and many still practise the indigenous belief system, Kirat Mundhum, with its blend of shamanism and ancestor worship. Notions of caste have had little influence on the Kirati peoples. The Limbus practise a form of matrilineal descent: although women traditionally follow their new husband to his home or community, they bring with them the household deities that will define the spiritual identity of the new family, and inherit the belongings of their own mother.

Both Rais and Limbus have a reputation as warlike peoples – Limbu means "bearers of bows and arrows" – and both groups have provided troops to the Gurkha regiments since the days of Prithvi Narayan Shah.

The Gurungs

The Gurungs are one of the most widespread of the hill peoples, occupying the valleys and ridges from Gorkha to the slopes of the Annapurnas. Of Tibeto-Burman descent, they contribute a large proportion of the modern Gurkha regiments.

The Gurungs are traditionally farmers and herders; they cultivate maize, millet, potatoes and mustard seed for its oil. Cattle are kept and buffaloes provide meat, but sheep – which thrive in the hills – are of paramount importance. Most families own perhaps a dozen sheep, grouped in village flocks of 200 to 300. Four or five shepherds take them to the upper pastures from April to September, when the shearing is done. The flocks return to the village in October, for the Dasain festival when

A potato farmer in the Langtang Valley.

REFUGEES IN NEPAL

Following the Chinese invasion of Tibet in 1950, long periods of oppression ensued as an atheist Communist regime took control of what had long been a feudal theocracy. It is estimated that more than 100,000 Tibetans fled, including the Dalai Lama and many other members of the religious hierarchy. Some 15,000 exiles crossed the Himalayas into Nepal.

The Tibetans have been remarkably successful in forging new lives. They have built up a thriving wool industry (see page 84) and created a centre of Tibetan Buddhism at Boudhanath (see page 172). However, the Nepalese government's frequent reliance on Chinese aid means the "Free Tibet" movement in Nepal is largely conducted underground.

Nepal is also home to more than 50,000 Bhutanese refugees. Originally of Nepalese origin, the Lhotshampas migrated during the 1880s in search of farmland, and settled in southern Bhutan. They retained their Hindu culture and religion but for a century enjoyed a largely peaceful co-existence with the dominant Buddhist Drukpas of Bhutan. However, in 1985 the Bhutanese government, threatened by the Lhotshampas' infiltration into politics, issued legislation that all citizens adopt the Drukpa culture. Many Lhotshampas took to the streets in protest and violence erupted. More than 100,000 fled to Nepal, where they continue to live in refugee camps.

Mountain celebrations occur on the full-moon days of May, June, July, August and November, including the Yartung festival of Muktinath, and the Dyokyabsi fest of Mustang.

all the family gathers; then they head south for the winter, sometimes as far as the inner Terai hills. Wool is soaked and washed, then woven in traditional patterns by Gurung women.

Gurungs, for the most part, have adopted Tibetan Buddhism, but in the lower valleys they have added a significant Hindu influence to their culture. Pork meat is taboo for traditional Gurungs.

The Newars

While they constitute just five percent of the total population, the Newars of the Kathmandu Valley have had a vital role in the history of Nepal. Their own name is thought to share an origin with "Nepa", from which the word Nepal itself developed. The Newars show clear traces of descent from both Tibeto-Burman peoples – possibly the original Kirati inhabitants of the Kathmandu Valley – and Indo-European peoples from the Indian subcontinent. Their religious tradition – a melange of Hinduism and Buddhism with all manner of local idiosyncrasies – is also typical of the synthesis of Middle Hills culture.

The Newars have a more developed urban culture than any other group in Nepal. The original Newari settlements of the valley and beyond reflect concern for the prudent use of valuable agricultural land. Often located along ridge spines, Newar houses clustered around sites of religious significance, expanding on the basis of each family's structure. Villages extended laterally along these plateaux, leaving the fertile low-lying areas for farming. In this way, organic wastes found their way to the farms, adding nutrients to the soil.

A Newar house can only be built with sacred permission, which must come prior to the foundation-laying ceremony and then again after the roofing of the house. The extended family is the cornerstone of Newari society and acts as both a support and a refuge. From an

The topi is a traditional Nepalese hat.

NEWAR RITES OF PASSAGE

From birth to death, special rites and celebrations mark the important events of a Newar's existence.

One of the more colourful initiations is when the young girls are "married" to the god Narayan before they reach puberty, with all the symbolic rituals of a typical wedding. Although the human marriage will come later, it will technically be her second, thus ensuring that the girl will never become a widow and also making any future divorce a mere formality.

In a country where death often comes early, age is also respected and celebrated. The old are venerated, and when a relative reaches the auspicious age of 77 years, seven months and seven days there is a re-enactment of the *pasni*, or rice-feeding ceremony, which all children go through when they are seven months old.

When death finally comes, the deceased must be taken, often in the pre-dawn hours, to the cremation ghats by the riverside. The sons must walk three times around their parent's corpse, carrying the butter lamp that will be placed on the face of the deceased. As the priest sets the pyre ablaze, the dead person's relatives have their heads shaved and ritually purify themselves with a bath in the sacred river. The ashes are scattered in the river which flows into the sacred Ganges.

early age, a Newar learns how to fit within the social nucleus and how to relate to clan and caste, through respect for relatives and patron deities. Joint families can include three generations with 30 or more members.

Beyond the immediate family structure, Newars are bound by their *guthi* or brotherhood. *Guthis* maintain local temples and communal services, organise feasts, festivals and processions, arrange burials, maintain family sanctuaries, care for the ailing and elderly, and even assist in the collective preparation of fields. The *guthi* provides substantial advantages to its members and is indicative of the social rank and economic potential of each family. This institution, present since Malla times, has been a key prop of social stability and continuity.

Hitching a ride on the train to the Indian border.

Brahmans and Chhetris

The Hindu caste groups are the most obviously "Indian" of all the peoples of the Middle Hills. They are also by far the most numerous people in the country: Brahmans and Chhetris make up around 30 percent of the total Nepalese population, and it was their language, Khas Kura, which became the national lingua franca in the form of Nepali.

Though they have clear Indo-Aryan cultural roots, the so-called Khas people have been settled in the western hill regions of Nepal for many centuries, and probably represent an intermingling of ancient immigrants from the south with indigenous Tibeto-Burman peoples. However, they have a clear notion of Hindu caste. The Brahmans – often known as Bahuns in Nepal – belong to the high Hindu priest caste, while the Chhetris are of the Kshatriya or warrior caste.

Brahmans and Chhetris are predominantly subsistence farmers. However, the literary and priestly tradition of the Brahmans has given them important roles in modern Nepalese government, education and business. Similarly, most of the ruling families, including the famous Ranas, have been Chhetris. Some Chhetris, particularly the Thakuris and those with a background as rulers, claim descent from princely Rajputs of the Suryavanshi or "solar lineage" who fled into the hills in the face of Muslim dominance of north India. Such origin

The Tharu were able to thrive in the lowland Terai because of their mysterious immunity to the virulent strain of malaria known locally as ayul – and to fearful early British travellers as "owl".

myths are common to ruling clans the length of the Western Himalayas as far as Kashmir and may often reflect a desire for royal legitimacy rather than historical fact. Nonetheless, the Brahmans and Chhetris remain distinctly more orthodox in their Hinduism than most other Nepalese.

Peoples of the Terai

The Terai Hindus tend be close in both culture and ethnicity to those across the border in the Indian states of Bihar and Uttar Pradesh. Indeed, until the establishment of the Nepalese state, and then again until the return of the Terai territories to Nepal by Britain after 1857, the people of the plains were bifurcated by no national boundary. As a consequence society here is organised on typically Indian-style caste lines. Although the caste system has lost its legal support, the higher castes still control most of the region's wealth and carry political clout. Villages are typically clusters of 30 to 100 dwellings, with bamboo walls plastered with cow dung and mud. Concrete walls and cement roofs are signs of wealth.

Lowland groups such as the Tharu, Danuwar, Majhi and Darai live in the southern, northeastern and western Terai. Rajbansi, Satar, Dhimal and Bodo peoples live in the far eastern districts of Jhapa and Morang. Muslims are found in significant numbers along the central and western Terai.

Numbering about half a million, the Tharu are the most ancient people inhabiting the Terai, though they encompass a considerable diversity of tribal cultures. In most areas, the Tharu grow rice, maize, wheat, barley, lentils and mustard and keep livestock. While many Tharu have adopted fairly orthodox Hindu beliefs, some maintain their own belief systems of animism and ancestor-worship.

The Dangaura Tharu of the Deokhuri Valley have managed to preserve their traditions to the greatest extent. They live in villages of mud longhouses, with as many as 150 family members clustered together under one roof. The small entrances to the houses lead into a large central room, which is often decorated with wall-paintings, nets and hanging baskets. Animals live on the right; on the left the family rooms are divided by tall grain jars providing both privacy and storage. Dangaura usually wear white, and the women are tattooed with peacock designs. They often marry by sister exchange: two families exchange their sons and daughters. During the wedding ceremony, the newlyweds knock their heads together as a sign of union.

Modern society

The steady advance of roads into remote rural areas; the coming of electricity, mobile phone coverage and internet access; a rapidly growing population, increasing urbanisation, and a mobility unknown a generation ago; not to

A Terai village woman.

NEPALESE IN INDIA

Some 4 million Nepalese citizens live and work in India, but there are many more Indians claiming Nepalese descent. The greatest such concentration is around Darjeeling, the result of the campaigns against Sikkim by the armies of Prithvi Narayan Shah, and of later migration during the days of the British Raj. While the Indian Nepalese have a wide range of ethnic origins they often refer to themselves collectively as Gorkhas. Indeed, while the term Gorkha carries no ethnic implication in Nepal itself, it does in India; there have even been calls for the Darjeeling area to be separated from West Bengal as a state called Gorkhaland.

mention the lingering impacts of decades of political turmoil and civil war – all have served to shake the traditional foundations of communities and societies across Nepal.

Nepal's population has been growing rapidly for decades, with a current rate of increase of around two percent annually. Together with improved transport links the growth has led to significant internal migration. The eradication of malaria in the Terai in the mid-20th century suddenly opened up large swathes of fertile territory to settlers from the overcrowded Middle Hills, and the indigenous Tharus suddenly

Working in a Terai rice field.

found themselves farming alongside Gurungs, Newars and Magars. Population growth has also fuelled immigration beyond national borders. While the British and Indian Gurkha regiments ensured that the concept of going abroad to seek a fortune had long currency in Nepal, it was an exclusive pathway. Today, however, many thousands of Nepalese – mostly, but not always, young men – travel abroad to work. The more coveted positions are in construction and service in the Middle East and Southeast Asia; those unable to find such opportunities head south to India to work in sectors ranging from agriculture to tourism.

Nepal's generally patchy modernisation, and the stagnation exacerbated by the long years of political conflict, has left the country with some unenviable development indicators. Average annual income is little more than US$1,000, and around a quarter of the population lives below the poverty line. National literacy rates stand at around 60 percent, and while school attendance has led to dramatic improvements in younger generations, the decade of civil war disrupted education across much of the country.

While Nepal has made concerted efforts to improve the lot of women – and while one of the key characteristics of the Maoists was their strident insistence on the liberation of women from traditional cultural and religious ties – there is still an obvious disparity between the lot of the sexes. Female literacy lags its male equivalent by around 40 percent, and while women have been given increasing legal parity with men in terms of social and financial rights, in remote rural areas government dictates often carry less weight that deep-rooted social mores. Child marriages still take place, and trafficking of young girls for the sex trade and domestic servitude both within Nepal and to India remains an issue.

However, mostly in the towns – and to a lesser extent also in the countryside – there have been some improvements in the lives of both men and women in recent years, and especially since the end of political violence in 2006 allowed stalled development to resume in outlying areas. Infant mortality rates have dropped by more than half in the last 20 years; school attendance has improved and incomes have crept upwards. And while some of the more positive social frameworks of traditional society may have fractured with increasing mobility, there is also now more room for marriage across communities, and for women to pursue education and careers.

Tourism too, in the areas where it dominates, has brought its own dramatic benefits in terms of incomes and access to the wider world. However, during the worst violence of the last decade, which coincided with a general global travel downturn, many Nepalese discovered that becoming dependent on tourism means being beholden to political and economic factors far beyond your own control in a world where events in Kathmandu, London or New York can ultimately bankrupt a village trekking lodge on the slopes of the Annapurnas.

The Sherpas

Of all Nepal's myriad ethnic groups, only one has found international fame, its name a byword for mountaineering prowess and resistance to the rigours of altitude.

Many foreigners are unaware that "Sherpa" is even an ethnicity, mistakenly believing that the word is simply the professional tag for high-altitude guides and porters. "How long have you been a Sherpa?" is a question well-travelled Sherpas are used to hearing.

People of the east

Sherpa, in fact, means "people of the east". They are of Tibetan origin and headed west to settle the valleys in the lee of Mount Everest sometime around the 16th century, possibly to escape persecution during the ascendancy of a rival Tibetan Buddhist sect. Today they number around 150,000, living in the Solo-Khumbu region, with smaller communities in Langtang and Helambu, as well as significant numbers settled in Kathmandu.

In Solu Khumbu the Sherpas were able to take advantage of a relatively fertile environment to raise crops and livestock, particularly yaks. The introduction of the potato – which thrived in the Solu Khumbu – brought a degree of prosperity. Their greatest boon, however, was from trade with their former homeland: Sherpas controlled the passage of goods across the Nangpa La between Nepal and Tibet. Though the Chinese invasion of Tibet in the 1950s ended this long-standing way of life, Sherpas had the good luck to be able to cash in on the nascent mountaineering and trekking businesses. They played an important part in the first ascent of Mount Everest in 1953, and Tenzing Norgay, originally from Thame, a village in Khumbu, was one of the first two climbers to set foot on the summit.

Sherpas today

The influx of trekkers and climbers has had its benefits and its disadvantages. It has undoubtedly brought a new prosperity, and almost every Sherpa family has come to depend in one way or another on the trekking industry. However, tourism incomes have also disrupted traditional social patterns. Kathmandu, where most trekking companies have their headquarters and hire their crews, has become a dominant focus for Sherpa life, with many moving there for part or all of the year. The wealth that some Sherpa families have earned through tourism has allowed them to fund expensive educations for their children, carrying them far from traditional village outlooks and lifestyles. Many young Sherpas are now being drawn by the attractions of a larger world beyond even

A hardy Sherpa mountaineer.

Kathmandu: the United States, Japan, India or the Middle East.

Yet as a people who left their homeland to settle in a bleak, upland region, the Sherpas have long form in adaptability, and they have come to terms with tourism and rapid modernisation better than many other once isolated peoples. Sir Edmund Hillary, who worked with the Sherpas for half a century and devoted much of his life to helping them, found them "cheerful, hard-working, agreeable and lacking in any sense of inferiority... They introduce you so readily into their culture and religion; they ask so little from you except politeness and friendship; they laugh so easily at your jokes and their own."

In Gorkha's Upallo Durbar.

The distinctive figure of a sadhu.

RELIGION

Nepal is coloured by a complex pattern of interwoven religious traditions, from the dominant Hinduism and Buddhism to tantric cults and tribal shamanism.

Religion is practised out in the open in Nepal. From the gaggle of supplicants forever crowding around the Ashok Binayak in Kathmandu's Durbar Square to the ever-smouldering funeral pyres of Pashupatinath, and from the rumble of drums and calling of conch-shell horns in the Tibetan monasteries of Boudhanath to the blood-spattered courtyard of Dakshinkali, faith and worship is as much a part of public life as commerce and consumption.

Nepal is dominated by the two major indigenous religions of the Indian subcontinent: Hinduism and Buddhism. According to the most recent census data around 80 percent of the population is Hindu, and indeed, until the abolition of the monarchy Nepal was the world's only constitutionally Hindu nation. This is not the whole story, however, for while only around nine percent of Nepalese people are declared Buddhists, the dividing line between Hinduism and Buddhism here is not always obvious.

As with so much else in Nepal, geography demarcates religion. In the low levels of the Terai a Hinduism bearing a close resemblance to that across the border in north India dominates, while high and dry in the trans-Himalaya, the clatter of prayer wheels and the fluttering of candy-coloured prayer flags show that Tibetan Buddhism sets the tone. But in the convoluted ranges of the Middle Hills the threads of faith form an almighty knot of practice and belief. It is said that if you ask a Newar from the Kathmandu Valley whether he is Hindu or Buddhist, he will probably answer "Yes"!

The religious complexion of the country is further complicated by all manner of indigenous and localised traditions. In the high mountains, Tibetan Buddhism has absorbed, but not always completely consumed, the older Bön faith; communities the length of the country have their own lively shamanic traditions, often coinciding with a notional adherence to Hinduism or Buddhism; and ancient spirit cults tied to specific locales have successfully insinuated themselves into wider orthodoxies. Meanwhile, the esoteric currents of Tantrism flow through both mainstream faiths.

Buddhist prayer wheels.

Hinduism

"Hinduism" simply takes its name from "India", which was in turn named for the Indus River. Today over a billion people regard themselves as Hindu, most in India and Nepal, with smaller numbers in Bangladesh, Sri Lanka, Indonesia and elsewhere. However, the term was only

The sacrifice of a male chicken, goat or buffalo is not only a way to pay obeisance to the gods; it is also a means of releasing an "unfortunate brother" from his imprisonment as an animal in readiness for his next reincarnation.

popularised as a catch-all word for the massed adherents of myriad interconnected South Asian religious traditions by European adventurers and colonialists in the 18th century. Today Hinduism still encompasses a vast variety of –

A mural depicting Shiva at Kathmandu's Pashputi temple.

sometimes contradictory – belief and practice.

The roots of the religion can be traced to the Aryan immigrants from Central Asia who settled in the northwest of India around 1700 BC. They recorded the Vedas, a collection of more than 1,000 hymns defining a polytheistic religion. Out of this grew the caste-conscious Brahmanism, linking all men to the god-creator Brahma. The Brahmans, or priest class, were said to have come from Brahma's mouth; the Kshatriya or warrior caste (known as Chhetris in Nepal) came from his arms; the Vaisyas, artisans and traders, appeared from his thighs; and the Sudras, or serfs, sprang from his feet.

Hinduism has no formal creed or universal governing organisation. Brahman priests serve as spiritual advisers to upper-caste families, but the only real authority is the ancient Vedas, bolstered by a series of later epics in which many of the familiar Hindu gods are defined. Different sects have developed a particular affinity with one or another deity; especially with Brahma "the creator", Vishnu "the preserver" and Shiva "the destroyer".

Most Nepalese Hindus regard Brahma's role as being essentially completed. Having created the world, he can now sit back astride his swan and keep out of everyday affairs. Both Vishnu and Shiva, however, remain very important.

Vishnu, whose duty it is to assure the preservation of life and of the world, appears in many different avatars, among them Narayan, the embodiment of universal love and knowledge, the princely Rama, and the blue-skinned Krishna. Both Buddha and the kings of Nepal were also regarded as incarnations of Vishnu.

Despite all the devotion paid to Vishnu, it is Shiva who gets the most attention in Nepal. Like Vishnu, Shiva takes different forms. He is Pashupati, the lord of the beasts and the tutelary god of Nepal. He is also Mahadev, lord of knowledge and procreation, symbolised by the phallic *lingam*. And he is the terrifying Tantric Bhairav, depicted with huge teeth and a necklace of skulls, intent on destroying everything he sees, including ignorance.

One of Shiva's sons, by his consort Parvati (also known as Annapurna Devi, goddess of abundance), is the elephant-headed Ganesh. It is Ganesh's responsibility to decide between success and failure, to remove obstacles or create them as necessary.

RELIGION AND LITERATURE

While the Vedas provide the scriptural foundation of Hinduism, later religious texts come in the form of mighty epics that have a hold on faith and imagination in India, Nepal, and across Asia. The *Ramayana* is the story of the brave and virtuous Rama and his beautiful wife Sita, who is captured by the demon Ravana and carried away to the island of Lanka. In the epic, Rama enlists the aid of Hanuman's monkey legions and the eagle Garuda to rescue Sita.

Krishna is the central figure of the other great Indian epic, the *Mahabharata*, particularly in the part of the tale known as the Bhagavad-Gita.

The idea of "new beginnings", manifest in the doctrine of reincarnation, underpins the Hindu caste system. Hindus believe that they must accept and act according to their station in life, no matter what it may be. Their birthright is a reward or punishment for actions – *karma* – accrued in a previous life. Their behaviour in this life will help determine the course of their next one.

> *Lord Buddha preached that one must follow the Middle Way, thereby rejecting all extremes of pleasure and pain.*

Women singing at Janakpur's Janaki Mandir.

Teachings of the Buddha

Brahmanism was the dominant faith in the Indian subcontinent at the time of the emergence of Buddhism in the 6th century BC. The new religion's founder, a Sakya prince named Siddhartha Gautama, was born around 543 BC near present-day Lumbini (see page 293). At the age of 29, he convinced his charioteer to take him outside the palace grounds where he lived a life of protected luxury. The sight of an old man, a cripple and a corpse persuaded him to abandon his family and his lavish lifestyle for that of an ascetic. For the next five years, Gautama wandered, attempting to find a solution to the suffering he saw. Finally, while meditating under a pipal tree near Varanasi in India, he achieved enlightenment.

From then on, as Buddha, the "Enlightened One", he preached a doctrine based on the "Four Noble Truths" and the "Eightfold Path". We suffer, he said, because of our attachment to people and material objects in a world where nothing is permanent. We can rid ourselves of desire, and do away with suffering, by living our lives with attention to right views, right intent, right speech, right conduct, right livelihood, right effort, right mindfulness and right meditation. The "self", according to Buddha, is an illusion trapped in the endless cycle of *samsara*, or rebirth, and created by *karma*, the chain of cause and effect. By following the Buddhist doctrine, the *dharma*, he preached, one can put an end to the effects of *karma* and achieve *nirvana*, which is essentially extinction of "self".

Buddha preached his doctrine for 45 years before dying at the age of 80. In the following centuries many doctrinal disputes arose, leading to various schisms in the Buddhist philosophy. Most significant was the break between the Theravada or Hinayana school, which adhered more closely to the original teachings and which today predominates in Southeast Asia and Sri Lanka, and the Mahayana school, which spread north and east from India.

It was Mahayana Buddhism that took hold in Nepal. One of the central beliefs of all Mahayanists is that one can achieve *nirvana* by following the example of bodhisattvas, or "Buddhas-to-be". These enlightened beings have, in the course of many lifetimes, acquired the knowledge and virtues necessary to attain *nirvana*, but have indefinitely delayed their transcendence to help other mortals reach a similar state of perfection.

> *The 14th Dalai Lama, Tenzin Gyatso, was chosen at the age of two in 1937. Exiled from Tibet since 1959, he currently resides in Dharamsala in northern India.*

Sadhu paraphenalia.

The Buddhist emperor Ashoka, of India's Mauryan dynasty, is believed to have made a pilgrimage to the Buddha's birthplace near Lumbini in the 3rd century BC. He or his missionaries may have introduced some basic teachings while building stupas in the Kathmandu Valley. Nearly 1,000 years later, in the 7th century AD, a Tibetan king, Songtsen Gampo, invaded the valley and according to legend carried back a Nepalese princess, Bhrikuti, as his wife. Both the Nepalese lady (later incarnated and revered as the Green Tara) and the king's Chinese consort, Princess Wencheng (who became the White Tara), were Buddhists, and they persuaded Songtsen Gampo to convert to Buddhism.

Tibetan Buddhism and Bön

Although Buddhism reached Tibet from Nepal, in time a religious influence flowed back across the Himalayas in the opposite direction. Tibetan Buddhism has taken on unique aspects, drawing in part on the indigenous Bön religion of the trans-Himalaya. This shamanistic faith, elements of which still exist in Tibet and some remote corners of Nepal, has certain affinities with Buddhism including a belief in karma, which indicates at least an influence from, if not an origin in, the proto-Hindu Aryans. The followers of Bön, known as Bönpos, believe that their religion was brought to the Tibetan regions from somewhere in the west, possibly Kashmir, by a decidedly Buddha-like figure called Shenrab. The obvious parallels allowed for a fusion of Buddhism and Bön, and the older faith contributed its fearsome panoply of demons and nature spirits to the Tibetan Buddhist belief system.

There are four main sects of Tibetan Buddhism. The most important of these is the Gelugpa (Yellow Hats), the central figure of which is the Dalai Lama. The others are the Kagyupa (Red Hats),

Nyingmapa (Ancients) and Sakyapa (People of the Earth). Each group has made important contributions to the Tibetan Buddhist doctrine.

According to Tibetan Buddhism universal cosmic forces and the energies of individual humans are one and the same, and through meditation it is possible to harness these energies. This concept sometimes slips into the realm of the occult: skilled Tibetan monks are said to be able to levitate or to travel across land at the speed of the wind.

Learning proper meditation, under the guidance of a personal teacher, is the first step toward understanding the doctrine of interdependence. The most important tools of meditation are mantra (sacred sound) and mandala (sacred diagram). In mantra meditation, chanting of certain syllables is believed to intensify the spiritual power of those indoctrinated to the meaning. Mandala meditation requires one to visualise certain circular images to assist in orienting the self to the universe.

The mantra Om mani padme hum ("Hail to the jewel in the lotus") is written on prayer wheels to aid meditation. Prayer flags offer thoughts to the wind.

Another important aspect of Tibetan Buddhism is the perception of death. Accounts of pre-death and post-death experiences are an integral part of Tibet's religious scriptures.

Syncretism and practice

While both Hinduism and Buddhism have themselves absorbed many individual traditions, in Nepal, and especially in the Middle Hills and the Kathmandu Valley the two faiths have combined in a remarkable syncretism.

Many of the Kathmandu Valley's Newars are notionally Buddhist, in the sense that their family priests are Tantric Buddhist gurus rather than Hindu Brahmans. Such classification, however, has never prevented a villager from worshipping the Hindu gods who are the village's patron deities. Many Buddhists regard the Hindu trinity of Brahma, Shiva and Vishnu as avatars of the Buddha; Hindus likewise revere the Buddha as an incarnation of Vishnu.

While the political leaders of the Kathmandu Valley have long been Hindus, it was only from the time of King Jayasthiti Malla in the 14th century that a degree of Hindu orthodoxy began to develop with influence from India. Even the Malla family deity, the goddess Taleju, was an import from South India. This trend was strengthened when the present Shah dynasty

Buddhist wall-paintings at Mangen Choling Monastery.

acceded to the throne, adopting as its patron deity a deified Shaivite yogi, Gorakhnath. The later Ranas, meanwhile, bolstered the caste system by enhancing the wealth of the ruling class.

Amongst the general population of the Kathmandu Valley, however, a degree of open-handed heterodoxy endured, and continues to inform religious practice in the 21st century. Every day before dawn, when sacred cows and stray dogs roam aimlessly in empty streets and farmers hurry to market with their loads of vegetables or chickens, men, women and children set out for Hindu and Buddhist temples, carrying ritual offerings *(puja)* for the multiple gods of their pantheons. They carry small copper plates piled high with grains of rice, red powder and tiny yellow flower petals to scatter on the deities' images. Afterwards, they mix the offerings into a paste and apply a small amount of the mixture to their own foreheads, between the eyes: this is *tika*, a symbol of the presence of the divine.

Puja such as this are made at any and all times in Nepal, for any occasion or celebration. Offerings renew communion with the deities most important to each individual's particular community or inclination – or to their concerns on a given day. Ritual sacrifice is another foundation of Nepalese Hinduism. At the time of Nepal's biggest feast, the Dasain festival of early autumn, some 10,000 animals, mainly goats, are sacrificed in the space of a few days, while at a number of specific temples, most notably the Dakshinkali Temple in the southwest of the Kathmandu Valley, there are routine weekly sacrifices.

Tantrism

Nepal's religions, whether Hindu, Buddhist or otherwise, are strongly influenced by the practices of Tantrism, a heterodox and mystical thread running parallel to more orthodox faith in a similar fashion to the Sufi tradition within Islam. Tantric practices run the gamut from deployment of magical symbols to active engagement with the temporal world as a form of worship, through music, dance and even sex. Tantrism originated in India, but while the centuries of Muslim dominance, British colonialism and modern secularism have largely eliminated its more esoteric elements there, it has lived on in Nepal.

Tantra is a Sanskrit word, referring to the basic warp of threads in weaving. Literally, Tantrism reiterates the Buddhist philosophy of the interwovenness of all things and actions. But Tantrism, with its roots in the Vedas and the Upanishads (pre-Buddhist Brahmanistic verses) is more than that. In its medieval growth, it expanded the realm of Hindu gods and rites, and added a new element to the speculative

Buddhist prayer flags flutter.

philosophy and yogic practices of the time. Within Buddhism, it created a major trend called Vajrayana, the "Path of the Thunderbolt", which reached its apogee in Nepal.

The *vajra*, known as the *dorje* in Tibetan Buddhism, is the ritual object for Tantric Buddhist monks, a double-headed sceptre, at each end of which are five pinched digits, said to represent the infinite in three dimensions. It is the symbol of the Absolute, a male instrument. Its female counterpart is a bell *(ghanta)*.

The prolific Tantric gods are represented in numerous human and animal forms, often with multiple arms, legs and heads as symbols of the omnipresence and omnipotence of the divine. Many of these deities have a terrifying appearance, such as forbidding Bhairav, bloodthirsty Kali, or Shiva, who in Tantrism is both the creator and destroyer. Tantrism substituted action and experience for contemplative meditation. This eventually evolved into all manner of esoteric practices, sometimes of a sexual nature, designed to generate a state of divine bliss. Shaktism is one such cult, praising the *shakti*, the female counterpart of a god. Some ritual Tantric texts proclaim: "Wine, flesh, fish,

A mountain lama.

SHAMAN PERFORMANCES

Dressed in a long robe and a headdress of peacock feathers, protected by straps or bells, ironmongery and cowries, and armed with his flat, double-sided frame drum, the shaman often accompanies his spiritual performance with the recitation of a myth that may continue for many hours, revealing both his prodigious memory and his gift for storytelling.

The story, which is usually sung to the accompaniment of the drum, begins with the origin of the world, and continues with the appearance and ultimate resolution of crises between the forces of good and evil. The therapeutic power of these stories should not be underestimated; the bards of ancient Tibet, for example, were regarded as the protectors of the kingdom.

Part of the shaman's technique involves forging an identity between the myth he recites and the circumstances of the pathology with which he is faced. Through ritual performance and sheer thespian virtuosity the shaman relates the myth to the everyday world; the mundane and the supernatural merge, and healing is achieved in sympathy with the narrative's resolution.

Today, the theatricality of shamanism has entered the commercial world: many shaman performances are now given in hotels for the entertainment of tourists.

women and sexual congress: these are the five-fold boons that remove all sin."

At a higher level, Tantrism is an attempt to synthesise spiritualism and materialism. Practitioners seek to expand their mental faculties by mastering the forces of nature and achieving peace of mind. The image depicting sexual union is called *yab-yum*, not unlike the Chinese *yin-yang*, a symbol of oneness in polarity. Around Kathmandu Valley *yab-yum* and other erotica are carved in wooden relief on the struts of temples. Their significance depends less on what they show than on who looks at them.

A sadhu in Durbar Square, Kathmandu.

Shamanism and folk religion

Given the broadly syncretic nature of so much religious practice in Nepal, aspects of ancient traditions, long predating the arrival of either Hinduism or Buddhism, are often hidden in plain sight. Small village shrines or pilgrimage sites may well have been sacred spots for millennia; local deities given space in the inclusive Hindu pantheon may be indigenous spirits in disguise. But besides these scattered traces, a number of more distinct local religious traditions endure.

Amongst the Rais, Limbus and other broadly Kirati peoples of the Himalayas, a belief system known as Kirat Mundhum survives. As with indigenous religions throughout the mountain regions of South Asia, Kirat Mundhum shows hints of early Aryan beliefs, combined with localised animism and ancestor worship, and threads from later Shaivite Hinduism and Tibetan Buddhism. The different ethnic groups have their own specific beliefs and traditions, but a unifying element is the practice of shamanism.

Though the term shaman is of Siberian origin, the concept of the faith healer and spirit medium is universal. In Nepal these specialists are generally known as *jhankri* and *dhami*, though each ethnic group has its own variation on the form. A shaman is a man (or occasionally a woman) who mediates between this world and the supernatural realm of ghosts, demons, deities and ancestral spirits. His task is generally to maintain the proper relationship between the temporal and unseen worlds, and to reset the balance when it has been upset. Since the commonest manifestation of imbalance is illness, the shaman is often first and foremost a healer.

The methods which the healers use to tackle spirits and diseases are legion. Shamans may make use of spirit possession. Once possessed, the shaman falls into a trance which may involve violent shaking and wild dancing. Possession may be accompanied by dramatic demonstrations of the power temporarily bestowed by the gods: licking red-hot iron, for example, or tying swords in knots. Speaking through the possessed shaman, spirits can answer questions, make oracular statements and banish evil influences.

Another common shamanic approach involves the healer achieving ecstasy – literally "standing outside". The patient has fallen ill because his soul or life force has been stolen by a malign entity, perhaps a witch, a demon or the ghost of a restless dead person. The shaman must leave his body and fly through the other world in search of the lost soul and bribe, cajole or force the captor into relinquishing it.

Animal sacrifice is a common prerequisite of shamanism, even amongst nominally Buddhist communities. The sacrifice is an important component of the commerce between the two worlds in which the shaman is the broker. The client wants something from the spirits and in exchange for this concession he must send across something from the domestic sphere, such as a chicken, a goat or a pig.

The Himalayan region is a rich store of medicinal plants and the shaman's repertoire includes a mastery of herbal lore. The plants are not cultivated but must be gathered from the wilderness. Pharmaceutical knowledge is only one branch of an overall familiarity with the undomesticated. Images of the hunt also characterise many of the rituals that are performed over the course of the long shamanic nights: malign ghosts must be tracked down, and lost souls recaptured like wild animals.

Among the skills a shaman must learn is divination, which is essentially a magical diagnosis to establish the cause of a problem. Methods include the scrutiny of egg yolks or the entrails of animals; the way grain moves on a lightly tapped drumskin; the number of beads in a section of a rosary (used primarily by Buddhist shamans); or, among the Rai people of east Nepal, the way in which pieces of sliced ginger fall on a sample of the patient's clothing.

Besides its central role in tribal religions and the spiritual life of remote communities, shamanism also forms a religious underground in many Hindu and Buddhist communities of Nepal, running parallel to the activities of the orthodox priests of these religions. Hindu and Buddhist functionaries do offer many of the traditional services of the shaman. But spirit-mediums of Nepal still endure.

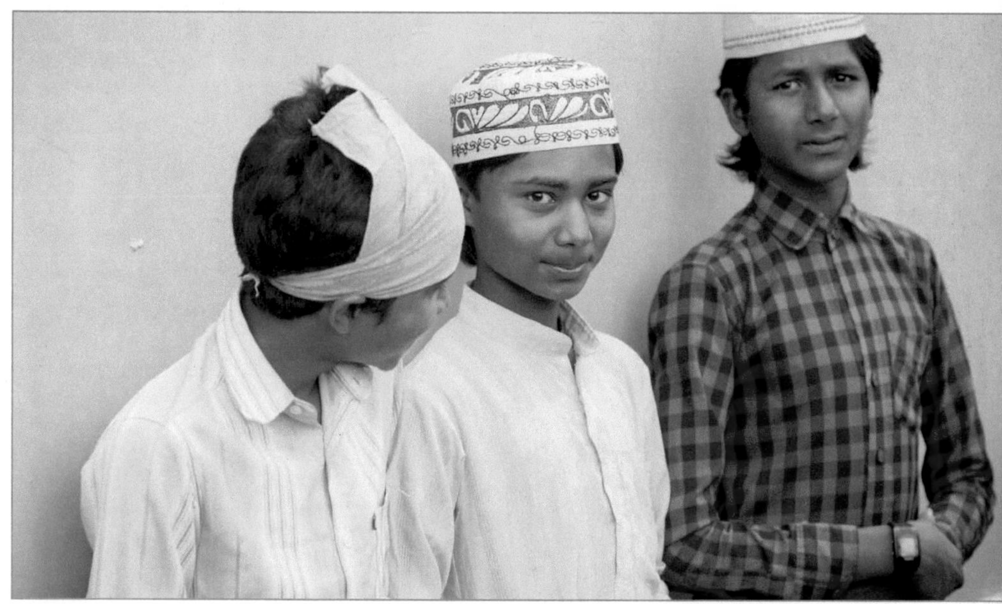

Boys after Friday prayers at Kathmandu's Jama Masjid.

NEPAL'S MUSLIMS

Visitors walking along Kathmandu's Durbar Marg at Friday lunch time may be surprised to see dozens of bearded, shalwar-kameez-clad men heading for a large green building nearby. This is the Jama Masjid, Kathmandu's main mosque. Muslims make up around 4.5 percent of Nepal's population. Most live in the Terai; their communities often predate the establishment of Nepal and they are closely related to their Urdu-speaking co-religionists across the Indian border.

Many of Kathmandu's Muslims claim Kashmiri descent. Some are the distant descendants of settlers who arrived during the Malla era; others are more recent arrivals who turned up with their handicrafts following the tourism boom. There are also Muslims of Tibetan origin, members of a little-known community overshadowed by their more numerous Buddhist brethren. Churaute Muslims live in the Middle Hills, mainly working as farmers alongside their Hindu neighbours. Almost all Nepalese Muslims are Sunni.

Locals often proclaim Nepal a beacon of religious tolerance, pointing to the absence of the Hindu–Muslim violence common in neighbouring India. However, in September 2004 the killing of 12 Nepalese workers by militants in Iraq prompted a sudden storm of anti-Muslim violence. Demonstrators set fire to Kathmandu's Jama Masjid and looted Muslim-owned shops.

Buy every spice under the sun at the Asan Tol market.

FOOD AND DRINK

Nepal's cuisine draws on influences from north and south and encompasses a diversity of dishes, from hearty mountain broths to delicate Indian-style desserts.

As with everything from architecture to religion in Nepal, the local cuisine draws on influences from either side of the Himalayas, and then creates something distinctly Nepalese from these contrary currents. In wayside tea stalls and elaborate palace restaurants the length of the country you'll catch a hint of Indian spice, an echo of Chinese technique and an underpinning of Tibetan heartiness. Cuisine is often defined by altitude: the staples change as the continent rises towards Himalayan heights, from tangy Indian pickles and traces of Mughal influence in the Terai, to pounded barley and butter tea in the trans-Himalaya.

Staple foods

Rice is grown throughout the Terai and the Middle Hills, and Nepal's most famous dish is the ubiquitous *dal bhat*, a stolid staple that has earned the country an unwarranted reputation for culinary blandness amongst travellers. *Dal bhat* simply means "lentils and rice", and this combination is indeed the foundation for daily meals in many parts of Nepal. *Dal bhat* is generally served on a large metal platter, along with a dollop of *tarkari* – vegetable curry – and a number of *achaar* pickles. In homes and upmarket restaurants it simply serves as a foundation for all manner of tasty side-dishes, though in truck-stops and trekking lodges it can indeed be decidedly dull.

Rice does not grow at high altitude, and on the southern slopes of the mountains the staple is formed by another grain – maize, pounded with water into a sticky paste called *dhindo* and served with meat or vegetables. Higher still, across the Himalayan watershed and beneath the rainshadow, the stodgy Tibetan staple, *tsampa*, made from pounded barley, appears.

Momos, probably the best-known Nepalese foodstuff.

Newari cuisine

The Kathmandu Valley, originally the country's hub of the country, was where the most elaborate cuisine developed, both around the humble hearths of the villagers, and in the grand courtly kitchens of the ruling class. Flavourings – cumin, turmeric and coriander – show a clear Indian connection, but the dishes are generally milder and less oily than in India itself; chilli is used sparingly.

The Newars – and most other Nepalese people – are generally far less inclined to vegetarianism than Hindus and Buddhists in India, and though they baulk at beef, buffalo meat is widely eaten. The daily staple, and the cornerstone of any Newari meal, is *chiura*, the hard, beaten rice sometimes also known as *baji*. Unhusked short-grain rice is first boiled, then dried in the sun before being pounded into wafer-thin flakes. The technique originally developed as a means of storage and fuel preservation: *chiura* keeps for months, and is ready to serve without additional cooking. It can be eaten as part of any meal, and a Newari breakfast is often *chiura* mixed with tea or curd into a kind of crunchy porridge. The main meal is usually eaten in the afternoon, and typically features *chiura*, soya beans or other pulses, and potatoes boiled with garlic and ginger. Newars typically eat with their right hand, sitting cross-legged at floor level, and during a family gathering or celebration a great circle is arranged, with those deputed to serve keeping the plates topped up with *chiura* and a wide variety of meat and vegetable dishes.

Enjoying a morning cup of chiya.

Newari meat dishes include *chhowela* – buffalo or chicken marinated with spices and cooked in a tandoor oven. There are a number of different breads, including *bara*, a thick, spongy pancake made from lentil flour, and *chatamari*, the Newari version of the pizza with minced buffalo meat and tomatoes on a thin rice flour base. *Sel roti* is also made of rice flour, sweetened, kneaded into rings and deep-fried. The Kathmandu Valley's endless round of festivals are often accompanied by elaborate family meals. Wild boar is the meat of choice for special occasions such as the Shivaratri festival, and a traditional wedding party includes an epic 84-course dinner.

The grand, multi-course Newari feasts are best sampled in a family home, or in one of Kathmandu's upscale Newari restaurants. At a humbler level food stalls on the streets serve simple snacks, with the commonest of all being the momo, meat- or vegetable-filled dumplings cooked in a large steamer and served with chilli or coriander sauces. Momos first arrived in Kathmandu with Tibetan traders, and the Newars adopted them as their own.

Tibetan food

In the high, dry world beyond the Himalayas delicate Indian-style spicing was unknown, and rice was a wildly exotic grain from a far-off and fertile land. The development of the local cooking style was driven by the need to keep warm and find nourishment in a place where agriculture was limited and winter temperatures plunged far below freezing, and Tibetan food shares an impetus with the cuisines of cold countries the world over.

Tibetan-style dishes make up the indigenous cuisine in mountainous regions of Nepal such as Mustang, Solu Khumbu and Dolpo. Trans-Himalayan traders, meanwhile, gave broths and noodles to the Newars, and in more recent years Tibetan refugees have brought hearty mountain dishes to the milder climes of the Middle Hills and the Terai.

The original basis of the Tibetan diet is pounded barley. This *tsampa* is sometimes mixed with pungent yak butter tea (to which salt, not sugar, is customarily added). The Tibetans also picked up on the art of noodle-making from China, and gave it a more robust spin. The best-known Tibetan dish in Nepal – besides the ubiquitous momo – is *thukpa*. A variation on noodle soup, this broth generally contains a

Potatoes and chillies are essential ingredients, not only in Nepal, but across Asia. And yet they – and the papaya – originate in South America and only reached Asia when Portuguese traders arrived in the 16th century.

Caste impacts on cuisine in Nepal, and the concept of ritual pollution meant that high-caste Hindus were often unable to accept food from those of lower rank. Culinary caste rules were enshrined in civil law in Nepal until 1962.

mass of chopped vegetables and flat noodles, as well as chicken or buffalo meat. A particularly hearty variation is *thenthuk*, which is thicker than standard *thukpa*, and comes with large squares of pasta.

served as *dhudhbari*, with the milk balls soaked in cream scented with rosewater, saffron, cardamom and pistachio.

Another milk product, found all over Nepal is curd, used as an ingredient and eaten as a dish in its own right. Curd is usually made from cow's milk, but the most celebrated version is the *juju dhau* of Bhaktapur, the "king curd" made from buffalo milk, which has a higher fat content. The curd is set into earthenware dishes which absorb the excess liquid leaving a rich, creamy yoghurt with the consistency of a crème brûlée.

The Nepalese staple, dal bhat.

Nepalese desserts

Nepalese desserts closely follow the Indian tradition of rich, milk-based sweets. In towns and cities across the country sweet shops offer a colourful array of fudge-like treats, usually stacked in neat piles behind a glass-fronted counter, and then served up on tiny metal plates, or packed in boxes to be eaten at home.

Burfi is the classic Indian and Nepali sweet – a dense, creamy milk fudge, flavoured with cardamom and cut into diamonds. *Burfi* is sometimes decorated with thin layers of edible silver leaf. Milk is also the basis of *rasbari*. The milk is heated and split with a dash of vinegar then strained and the remaining solids are formed into balls. These are most lavishly

A CUP OF CHIYA

Everywhere from the alleys of Kathmandu to villages in the lee of the Annapurnas, the tea stall is a Nepalese institution. Tea originated in southern China, but trade routes have carried it to every corner of the globe. The word for tea in virtually every language comes from one of two sources – the Fujianese term *te*, or the Cantonese word *cha*. Nepal takes the latter route, and calls its national drink *chiya*. Equal measures of milk and water are brought to boil; black tea leaves are added, along with a spice blend of cardamom, nutmeg, cloves, cinnamon, ginger, pepper and star anise; the mixture is strained into a small glass.

Boudhnath Stupa in all its glory.

Basanta Pur in Durbar Square.

ARCHITECTURE

Nepal's distinctive architecture naturally draws on numerous influences from outside its borders, while at the same time maintaining an original style all of its own.

Over a distance of little more than 100km (60 miles), Nepal's vernacular architecture runs the gamut from the wattle-and-daub of the steamy Terai to the rammed earth walls and poplar-wood roofs of the bleak Tibetan Plateau. It was in the temperate valleys of the Middle Hills, however, that an identifiably "Nepalese" tradition developed, drawing influence and inspiration from both India and China, but at the same time creating new conventions and exporting them across the mountains to Tibet and beyond. This rich stylistic tradition reached its apogee in the crucible of the Kathmandu Valley from the 13th century as the rival Malla kingdoms of Kathmandu, Patan and Bhaktapur turned architecture into a form of bloodless warfare, striving to outdo one another with epic expressions of artistry that drove the pagoda roofs ever higher into the clear blue sky.

A detailed column at Kathmandu's Royal Palace.

Early styles

The earliest traces of Nepal's formal architecture are hard to discern. The period is mostly represented by stupas or *chorten* – memorials to holy men consisting of solid domes. This is a form that appears to have been indigenous to Nepal, and that later spread across Asia as the pagoda. The mighty Swayambhunath (see page 171) on the edge of Kathmandu is often claimed to be the oldest structure in Nepal, but it has been rebuilt and overlaid so many times over the centuries that it has little to tell us about the antecedents of pagoda architecture. The earliest stupas were probably rudimentary structures.

The yellow colouration smeared across the bone-white domes of the great stupas at Boudhanath and Swayambhunath is a wash of thin yellow clay which is splashed on to the monuments during festivals to make the dome resemble a lotus flower.

Quite when the classic wood-and-brick combination that is still the watchword of Nepalese architecture came into common usage is unclear: the earliest surviving temples in this form date from the 12th century. What remains from the earlier Licchavi period (4th to 9th centuries) are exquisite pieces of statuary, such as those at Changu Narayan (see page 199) and Budhanilkantha (see page 199). The intricate Newari woodworking style was almost certainly in use by this time, however: while the monsoon damp has ensured that Licchavi-era timber has long since rotted away in the Kathmandu Valley itself, to the north, in the drier climate of Tibet, there are pre-9th century buildings showing the tell-tale traces of Newari craftsmanship.

The later Malla period, around the 17th century, was the heyday of Nepalese architecture, marked by a veritable orgy of temple-building. The arrival of Prithvi Narayan Shah and the end of Malla rule in 1769 brought an abrupt close to this glorious architectural excess, and besides

In the Royal Palace.

the occasional extension, little of note was built for the best part of a century. Once the Ranas had wrestled de facto rule from the Shahs, however, a new kind of regal architecture came to the fore, with ostentatious stuccowork mansions, inspired not by the pagodas of old Nepal but by the palaces of 19th century Europe. This bout of Europhile building was the last major architectural epoch in Nepal before steel, glass and concrete arrived in force.

Newar temples and shrines

The classic manifestation of Newari architecture is the brick-built temple with a tapering stack of tiered roofs. The style probably originated in India more than 1,000 years ago, but

The 13th-century Nepalese artist Arniko is sometimes credited with introducing the pagoda to China. In 1262 he travelled to the court of Kublai Khan at Xanadu, where he was celebrated for his artistic skill.

once it reached Nepal it was given multiple local twists.

All Newar-style temples are based on this concept, but they differ wildly in shape and size. The main structures are built of brick, often faced with special glazed bricks *(dachi appa)*. The heavy multi-tiered roofs are supported by carved timber struts *(tunasi)* and are usually covered with small clay tiles *(jingathi)*; the grandest temples have gilded copper or brass roof coverings.

Temples can be square, rectangular or even octagonal in plan (though only those dedicated to Krishna can be constructed in the latter form). They range in size from tiny neighbourhood shrines a few square metres across to epic structures on the scale of the Taleju Mandir in Kathmandu's Durbar Square (see page 164), which is more than 30 metres (100ft) high. Most principal temples have three roof tiers; the smaller attendant shrines generally have two. There are only two free-standing temples with five roofs in the Kathmandu Valley: the Nyatapola Temple in Bhaktapur and the Kumbeshwar Temple in Patan.

A very different style of temple is the *shikhara* – a tower-like structure built of brick, stone or terracotta. These temples display a more obvious Indian influence, and are similar to the Hindu temples found across north India. The name *shikhara* is drawn from the Sanskrit term for mountain, and the temple form is thought deliberately to echo the outline of the mythological Mount Meru. While the style may have already reached Nepal from the south by end of the Licchavi era, most surviving *shikhara* temples date from the 17th century onwards. Mahabuddha in Patan (see page 180) is a particularly striking example. Like most other religious buildings the *shikhara* is set on a stepped plinth and encloses a small sanctuary containing the principal divinity. The main structure is generally symmetrical in form around a central spire or tower, which is capped with a *gajur*.

Newari houses

While the great Durbar squares – the ceremonial gathering places at the heart of Kathmandu, Patan and Bhaktapur – feature neat ranks of temples, and make a planned virtue of the open spaces between, the cities that have swollen around them grew organically in a tangle of alleys and overhangs. Newari urban dwellings are usually clustered around interlocking courtyards *(chowks)* or arrayed in terraces. In places the streets turn into tunnels, completely roofed in by the upper storey of the house above. Typically the houses comprise two or three storeys, and where the ground floor is not used as a shop or a workshop it remains unadorned with a low door flanked by two small windows. The walls are built of the small rectangular red bricks that set the colour scheme of old Nepalese towns, while the windows are framed by intricately carved wood and shuttered with delicate latticework. The living area of a house is marked by a special window consisting of either three or five bays known as *tikejayal*.

In the standard three-storey house, the second floor is the main living area. The spine wall is replaced by a row of twin columns forming a large, ventilated, hall-like room suitable for family gatherings. The kitchen and the family shrine are usually located in the attic.

Vihara: the Buddhist monastery

As well as the towering pagoda-style Hindu temples, the Kathmandu Valley has its own array of Buddhist architecture. These are not the Tibetan-style gompas (see page 268) that stud the bleak trans-Himalayan regions (and that have sprouted more recently in the Tibetan refugee communities), but the indigenous Newari monastic buildings known collectively as *viharas*.

Viharas come in two styles, the *bahil* and the *bahal*. The *bahil*, set on a raised platform above street level, is a two-storeyed structure surrounding a courtyard. Except for the main entrance, consisting of a small, central doorway flanked by two blind windows in the main elevation, the ground floor is sealed off

Small stupas at Swayambhunath.

EROTIC ARCHITECTURE

Nepal may be a socially conservative nation, but some of its sacred architecture is decidedly more expressive. The friezes and roof struts of a number of Malla-era temples in the Kathmandu Valley display some remarkably graphic erotic images. There are scenes of well-endowed male figures enjoying the ministrations of skilful courtesans, any number of distinctly unorthodox sexual positions, and even representations of elephants *in flagrante delicto*.

The purpose of these images is unclear. A well-worn myth has it that they are intended to ward off the bashful and virginal goddess of lightning, but this seems most likely to be a glib tale invented for tourists long after the fact. Hinduism is certainly replete with more abstract sexual imagery – particularly in the phallic *lingam*, a manifestation of Shiva, and its female counterpart, the *yoni* – and Tantrism incorporates the notion of the sexual image, the *yab-yum*, as a symbol of oneness in polarity. However, the figures on Nepal's temples appear to be mortals rather than deities. It is possible that they were simply a humorous indulgence, added by the woodworkers in the same way that medieval masons carved comic gargoyles on European churches.

Amongst the temples most notable for their erotic decorations are the Pashupati Mandir in Bhaktapur and the Jagannath Mandir in Kathmandu's Durbar Square.

Because of their religious significance, the kitchens or shrines of high-caste dwellings are out of bounds for strangers and members of lower castes.

from the outside. Arcaded porticoes on all four elevations overlook the internal yard. Directly opposite the main entrance is the free-standing shrine with a passageway around it. The shrine itself is a small rectangular room containing the principal icon.

The *bahal* is also a two-storeyed building enclosing a courtyard, but, unlike the *bahil*, both its ground and upper floors are subdivided into several rooms. The building is generally of a more robust construction, set on a low plinth and overlooking a sunken courtyard. The main entrance, flanked on either side by windows, leads into an anteroom with benches. As in the smaller *bahil*, the main shrine is situated opposite this entrance and consists of a large, enclosed room containing the statue of the main deity. In the four corners of the building are stairways to the upper floor, each leading to

A traditional round house at Ramkot.

PALATIAL ARCHITECTURE

All the palaces in the Kathmandu Valley built by the Malla kings are recognisable for their extravagant style and, in the major cities, for their scale and complexity. These buildings are much larger than typical domestic homes. As prestige buildings they were often constructed in competition with the rival kingdoms elsewhere in the valley. The palaces exhibit the best examples of their period of architecture, since the local craftsmen were encouraged to produce the finest quality of workmanship. They are solidly built, not as fortresses but rather as examples of artistic beauty, and they incorporate aspects of religious, monastic and domestic architecture.

A dramatic change in style can be seen in the vast white stucco palaces introduced by the Rana regime from the mid-19th century. Most of these palaces boast several hundred rooms and scores of courtyards. Vast workforces were pressed into service to build them – the mighty Singha Durbar which now houses Nepal's parliament was completed in less than a year. The external decorative stucco was made from local clays, copying the intricate designs at that time popular in Europe. The interiors were furnished with reproduction period furniture and decorated with crystal chandeliers and mirrors, all echoing the neoclassical revival that had swept Europe the previous century.

a separate group of three-room units with no intercommunicating doors or passages.

Perfect symmetry is achieved in *bahals* by projecting the central and corner sections of the brickwork on all facades and by the placement of windows and doors on a central axis. Although unglazed, the quality of the brickwork is excellent and is usually left exposed on the external facades. The interior facades are rendered with a mud plaster and whitewashed. A carved tympanum or *torana* indicates the entrance to the *bahal* and to the main shrine.

Garu is a typical high mountain village.

Dharmasala: public resthouse

A building common to all traditional Newari settlements is the *dharmasala* or public resthouse, a place designed to accommodate passing travellers or pilgrims. These resthouses can range from the simple *pathi*, a small shelter usually standing at the intersection of important routes, to the *mandapa*, which formerly served as the town assembly hall. These resthouses were usually constructed by wealthy individuals or religious groups, who were also responsible for their upkeep.

Sattal is a general term for the larger public building enclosing a courtyard. The *sattal* was intended for longer sojourns by members of religious communities. *Sattals* are commonly found in the durbar squares of royal Newari towns, and might originally have quartered the palace guard. The two-storeyed unit consists of a simple rectangular platform with a small door at the rear leading into the shrine. The upper floor is reached by an external stairway at the back.

The *mandapa*, meanwhile, is a square, single or multi-storeyed building mainly designed as a community hall. It is generally a free-standing open pavilion, with a high roof supported by pillars. Sometimes a second storey rises above in classic pagoda-roofed temple form. The Kasthamandap in Kathmandu is the grandest of all *mandapas* (see page 161).

High-altitude architecture

Far from the fertile fields and teeming spaces of the Kathmandu Valley, the vernacular architecture of the high mountains has developed to cope with the harsh conditions prevalent at extreme altitude. Walls are built of thick rammed earth or large mud bricks. Windows – if there are any at all – face south and west to avoid the worst of the chill. Roofs are flat and built of clay laid on brushwood or stones. More sophisticated roofs are laid with a mix of clay and oil which is rammed in great ceremony by singing workers. The Buddhist gompas of the high mountain regions are built in the same way, although the rough, plain outer walls may hide beautiful painted murals within.

A craftsman relaxing in Bhaktapur's Potter's Square.

ARTS AND CRAFTS

Nepal has a long history of arts and crafts, from religiously inspired painting and metalwork to traditional dance rituals and folk music.

Art, religion and daily life are inextricably intertwined in the Kathmandu Valley, where images of deities preside over local water taps and laundry is laid out to dry on the tiered steps of magnificent multi-roofed temples. The valley's tremendous artistic wealth was created by its original inhabitants, the Newars (see page 49), who drew on the rich cross-cultural influences brought in by successive waves of traders, pilgrims, religious scholars and refugees. Motifs were adopted from Hinduism and Buddhism, while stylistic influences came from India, China and Tibet.

Most works of art were commissioned by wealthy patrons for donation to a temple or monastery. Portraits of people are rare, but the gods are all-pervasive, rendered in a highly formalised context according to iconographic canons that dictate a deity's pose and appearance, down to the smallest details. Creativity was expressed in the general composition and the skilful rendering of fine details.

Sculpting a metal deity statue.

Statuary

Some of the most glorious art to emerge from valley ateliers are cast images of gilt, copper and bronze deities, produced by the ancient "lost wax" technique (see page 180).

This technique – which was probably pioneered by the Indus Valley Civilisation of modern-day Pakistan some 5,000 years ago – has been practised in Patan since at least the Licchavi era. The initial image is rendered in wax, which is then used to create a reverse-image mould of clay. Small images are created with a single mould, but even very large metal statues are sometimes created using the lost wax technique, with multiple parts cast and then fixed together. Finished statues may be coated with gold and inlaid with semi-precious stones such as coral, turquoise or agate. These statues generally follow the Tibetan Buddhist tradition, with numerous images of the Buddha in his traditional poses. The Patan Museum has excellent examples of the process.

Stone sculpture also abounds throughout the valley. Stone was the first medium Nepalese artists fully mastered, and Licchavi-era pieces from as early as the 5th century are still breathtakingly powerful. Sculptures generally depict Hindu deities, Vishnu being a particular favourite. A slightly less solemn form are *makara*, stone water spouts carved in the form of serpents with water gushing from their open mouths. These are set in *dhunge dhara* (sunken stone baths), which serve as a multi-purpose public bath, laundry place, water source and social centre.

Paintings

The classical paintings of the Kathmandu Valley blend cultural influences from India and China with an exquisite sense of form and colour. Gracefully posed figures are depicted in highly stylised and symbolic settings.

The favoured traditional medium was the scroll painting, which was easy to transport for use in teaching, worship or decoration. Called *thangka* in Tibetan and *paubha* in Newari, they constitute two very distinct schools of painting. *Thangkas* depict deities, either peaceful or wrathful. The painstaking level of detail in these traditional paintings can be astonishing, and the artists have followed a complex set of rules for each individual image. Modern renditions of *thangkas* crowd Thamel's tourist shops today, though in terms of detail these are distinctly inferior to any of the traditional works.

Paubhas are uniquely Newari paintings involving more vibrant and flowing renditions of deities. Traditional *paubhas* may appear as horizontal scrolls up to 12 metres/yards long, which were intended to be slowly unrolled. In this way they functioned as storytelling devices, somewhat akin to comic strips. Modern *paubha*-derived paintings produced for the tourist trade use Naïve folk-art style to depict animals, and an assortment of minor deities and valley landmarks.

In the souvenir shops of Patan and Kathmandu there is also now a trend for quaint images of Nepalese village life, painted in oil or acrylic on canvas. Formal, European-style portraiture and landscape painting first appeared in Nepal during the Rana era, but these Orientalist scenes are a product of the tourist trade and have only come to the fore in the last few decades.

Outside the valley, a vigorous folk-art tradition continues in paintings rendered in vivid colours on handmade paper by the Maithili women of Janakpur in the Terai (see page 286). These striking paintings utilise folk designs originally painted on the walls of houses. Centuries of tradition and legend are condensed into a highly stylised symbolic art, in which every motif carries a wealth of meaning. Pictures may depict a range of subjects, the most common being deities or fertility symbols such as bamboo, fish or

Crafting a pot.

Clay pots drying in the sun.

Paints made out of mineral and vegetable dyes are still used on traditional thangkas, as well as an abundance of gold-based paint on the more valuable works.

whimsical pregnant elephants. The main images are surrounded by intricate borders and detailed designs fill all empty spaces.

Metalwork and pottery

Simple, useful crafts are an equally vibrant tradition in Nepal. Metalware includes brass water pots or *ghada*. Despite the rise of imported plastics, many families still prefer to use a traditional *ghada* – as overflowing hardware shops in Kathmandu's Asan Tol area, and busy workshops in the backstreets of Bhaktapur attest. Other metal vessels include the graceful *anti*, used to pour *rakshi* at festival feasts. Finely wrought ritual items are more formal in use, such as oil lamps, incense burners and the classic metal baskets favoured by Newar women to carry temple offerings. The patina of age makes it easy to distinguish old pieces from shiny new products.

Another ancient art still practised in Patan is *repoussé*, which involves hammering metal sheets into intricate embossed designs, generally used to create the lavish temple ornamentation so abundant in the Kathmandu Valley. Metalworkers also excel in creating finely detailed accessories such as temple bells and implements, and fine jewellery in gold and silver.

Unglazed red clay pottery formed from the rich soil of the Kathmandu Valley is a common and highly practical product produced by the local *kumals* (potters). Pottery is used for a variety of purposes, including storing traditional yoghurt – the unfired clay soaks up the excess liquid creating a particularly thick and creamy curd. Flowerpots, small and large, in the form of rhinos, elephants and griffins are among the more amusing variations.

Potter's Square in Bhaktapur is the best place to observe the pottery-making process from start to finish. Heavy clay is shaped on spinning wheels into vessels, formed into a final shape, then baked in temporary kilns of straw.

Weaving is still an important skill.

A WEALTH OF JEWELLERY

Nepal is famous for its silver jewellery, often set with semi-precious stones. Silver and gold are sold by the *tola*, a measurement equalling 11 grams (0.3oz); the fine craftsmanship is included in the price. Traditional jewellery designs tend towards the dramatic, ranging from necklaces of old silver coins favoured by hill women to Tibetan ornaments composed of enormous chunks of antique turquoise, coral and amber. The most popular semi-precious stones include tourmaline, citrine, aquamarine, ruby and garnet which are found in the Ganesh Himal region, and amethyst and sapphire, imported from Tibet.

Textiles and clothing

Nepal's major export is handwoven Tibetan carpets, which make unique and functional souvenirs, as do pashmina shawls and scarves – a fashion accessory in the West, but a centuries-old standard in the Himalayas (see page 85). However, handwoven cloth – from the red-bordered black *patasi* cotton sari worn by Newar peasant women to the intricately patterned *dhaka*, usually distinguished by its colourful geometric patterning and used for all manner of garments, most famously the classic *topi* hat, worn by Newari men – embodies the country in its very weave.

Playing a flute.

Kathmandu is also an outlet for other Asian fabrics, from brilliant Chinese brocades and delicate silks to sturdy Bhutanese cloth. Old Bhutanese textiles of cotton and wool, intricately woven with silken thread, are particularly interesting. The modern Nepalese clothing industry centres around rayon dresses produced for export. More distinctive garments include the striking designs of local boutiques, utilising local hand-weaves of linen, *allo* (nettle), hemp and silk.

Handicrafts

Nepal offers a cornucopia of miscellaneous handicrafts. Handwoven baskets range from the ubiquitous *doko*, Nepal's own "backpack", to the elegant coiled baskets of the Terai, decorated with cowrie shells and coloured grasses.

Another distinctive symbol is the wickedly curved *khukri* knife, the preferred weapon of Gurkha soldiers (see page 215) and a handy tool for hill men across the country: a *khukri* can be used to sharpen a stick or lop off a goat's head with equal ease.

Soft, textured handmade *lokta* paper, produced from the soaked and pounded bark of the daphne shrub, is produced in a range of colours. Colourful wooden toys, block-printed fabrics, cushion covers and hand-knitted sweaters are also abundant in local handicraft shops.

Indian handicrafts – many of them from Kashmir, the great souvenir centre of South Asia – can be easily found on the streets of Kathmandu as well. These include silk carpets, chain-stitch tapestries and brightly painted papier mâché wares – though hawkers may attempt to pass off mass-produced Kashmiri trinkets as local wares.

Performance arts

Like the visual arts, Nepal's traditional music and dance are deeply influenced by religion. They range from exuberant expressions of folk songs to the highly sophisticated dance-dramas of the Kathmandu Valley. This traditional wealth has come under pressure from

Hindi-language film and pop music imports in recent years, and the local efforts at mainstream pop culture have generally tried to emulate Bollywood rather than local traditions. However, the recent rise of small-scale radio stations and the internet has brought a new vibrancy to the local folk scene.

Nasa Dyo, the god of music and dance, presides over Newari music and dance, and a special invocation or worship to him precedes all performances. In the old sections of Newari towns, Newar men still gather to sing *bhajan*, devotional hymns accompanied by harmonium and tabla. Evening walks in the old bazaar may uncover songs wafting out from a resthouse or upstairs window, and during major festivals such as Indra Jatra, the singing goes on all night. *Dhimay* bands are still popular with farming castes in the valley towns. These two-headed cylinder drums are played while marching during festivals and *pujas*, and competitions of skill are held. A group of *dhimay* drummers with accompanying pipers is also an essential accompaniment for a traditional wedding procession.

Wandering minstrels or *gaine* were the major carriers of Nepalese folk music. These itinerant musicians were generally regarded as untouchables or outcastes by settled Hindu communities; the name *gaine* simply means "singer". The *gaine* refer to themselves as *Gandharva*, and claim descent from the celestial musicians of Hindu mythology. They traditionally roam from village to village, accompanying themselves with a small four-stringed wooden fiddle or *sarangi*. In pre-radio days, the *gaine*'s long, topical ballads served as an important means of spreading news. While most people of *gaine* descent are now settled in towns and villages, a few can still be spotted plying their traditional trade in the back streets of Kathmandu during the Dasain season, and the Pokhara Valley is one of their remaining strongholds.

Dance

While folk dance shows are held year-round at tourist hotels, festivals and weddings are the setting for authentic performances. Often these performances are marked by humorous or satirical dance, as in the wild masquerade of Gai Jatra. For the most part Newar women do not dance in public, except at the wonderful festival of Teej (see page 90). Female roles are therefore traditionally performed by men dressed as women – although some younger women are now beginning to participate in the larger towns. Spontaneous village dances range from the shuffling line dances of Tibetan-influenced peoples to circles of hand-clapping viewers clustered around a solo performer, and the dancing of the Tharus of the Terai, in which women do often take part.

Costumed, masked Newar dancers perform during festivals such as Dasain, enacting trance-like dance-drama pageants depicting various religious themes such as the 10 avatars of Vishnu or the Ashta Matrika ("Eight Mother Goddesses").

Carved masks for sale.

The Newari Buddhist ritual dance tradition of *charya nritya* dates back to 7th-century India. A combination of worship, meditation and performance, it was originally only performed inside temple precincts to audiences of initiated male members. The Tibetan Buddhist equivalent is *cham* dancing, in which richly costumed monks impersonate deities in performances that can last for days. These ceremonies combine religious symbolism with equally important social get-togethers – an occasion for locals to mingle, chat and celebrate. Best-known are the dance-dramas of Mani Rimdu, performed yearly at Buddhist monasteries in Solu Khumbu.

NEPAL'S WOOL INDUSTRY

The rise of Nepal's Tibetan carpet trade, from a cottage industry to the country's single largest manufacturing business, is a remarkable success story.

Over the past half-century the carpet trade has transformed from a self-help scheme for newly arrived Tibetan refugees to become an enormous industry. By the 1980s carpet exports were generating a third of Nepal's foreign currency earnings. The industry has been badly hit by competition from cheaper Chinese rugs and scandals about child labour in recent years, but while it is no longer the booming business it once was, carpets remain an important aspect of the Nepalese economy.

Producing old from new

Most modern Tibetan carpets are now woven from a blend of New Zealand and Tibetan wool; the latter is preferred for its greater durability and lustre. The standard carpets feature a ratio of 40–60 knots per square inch, while the best have up to 100 knots per square inch.

The carpets are woven in private homes or in cavernous factories where the weavers sit shoulder-to-shoulder as they deftly knot the yarn according to patterns drawn on graph paper. Weavers work long hours, from dawn to dusk, to meet the demands of the tourist market.

The finished product is trimmed to accent the contours of the design, then immersed in a chemical bath to soften the wool and make it more lustrous. A more recent trend is to add a "tea wash" to the finished rug to produce an antiqued golden sheen.

Weavers at Baje Carpet Industries in Jawalakhel. Tibetan carpet factories are not only a place of work but of social activity, with weavers chatting and singing throughout the day.

Tibetan carpets use the senna loop, an ancient technique in which the yarn is knotted around a gauge rod and slipped out with each row.

The finished article: rolled-up Tibetan carpets.

Pashmina shawls for sale.

PASHMINA SHAWLS

As well as carpets, Himalayan wool is also transformed into pashmina shawls, a modern fashion item which is steeped in the history of trans-Himalayan trade.

The secret of the pashmina is its combination of feathery weight and great warmth. It is woven of the fine wool of the *changthangi* goat of the high Himalayas. The wool was traditionally carried down from the high valleys by traders and woven into rich cloth in way-station settlements. Its alternative name – cashmere – is drawn from the original centre of the industry, Kashmir, and early agents of the British Empire often scoured the mountains in search of the tricks of the trade.

Workers spin the thread and weave the fabric on special wooden looms, often combining it with silk to add sheen, lustre and durability. Dyed in brilliant jewel tones or subtle pastels, this luxury fabric is now transformed into all manner of clothing.

Pashminas can be bought all over Nepal, particularly in the many shops around the Thamel district of Kathmandu, though the cheaper offerings may not be made entirely from authentic *pashm* wool.

Knitting in the Langtang Valley.

Raw wool drying in the sun.

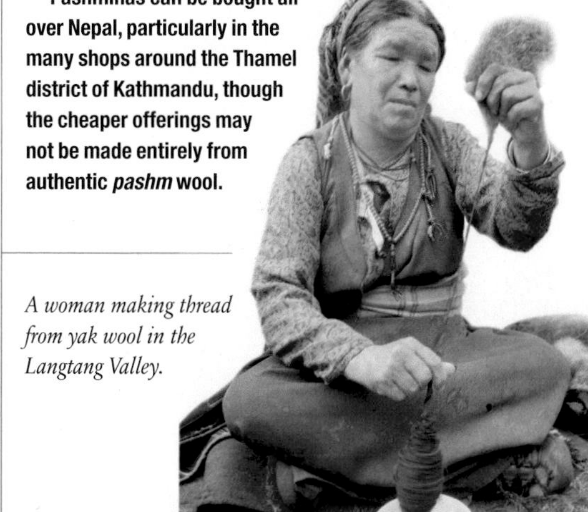

A woman making thread from yak wool in the Langtang Valley.

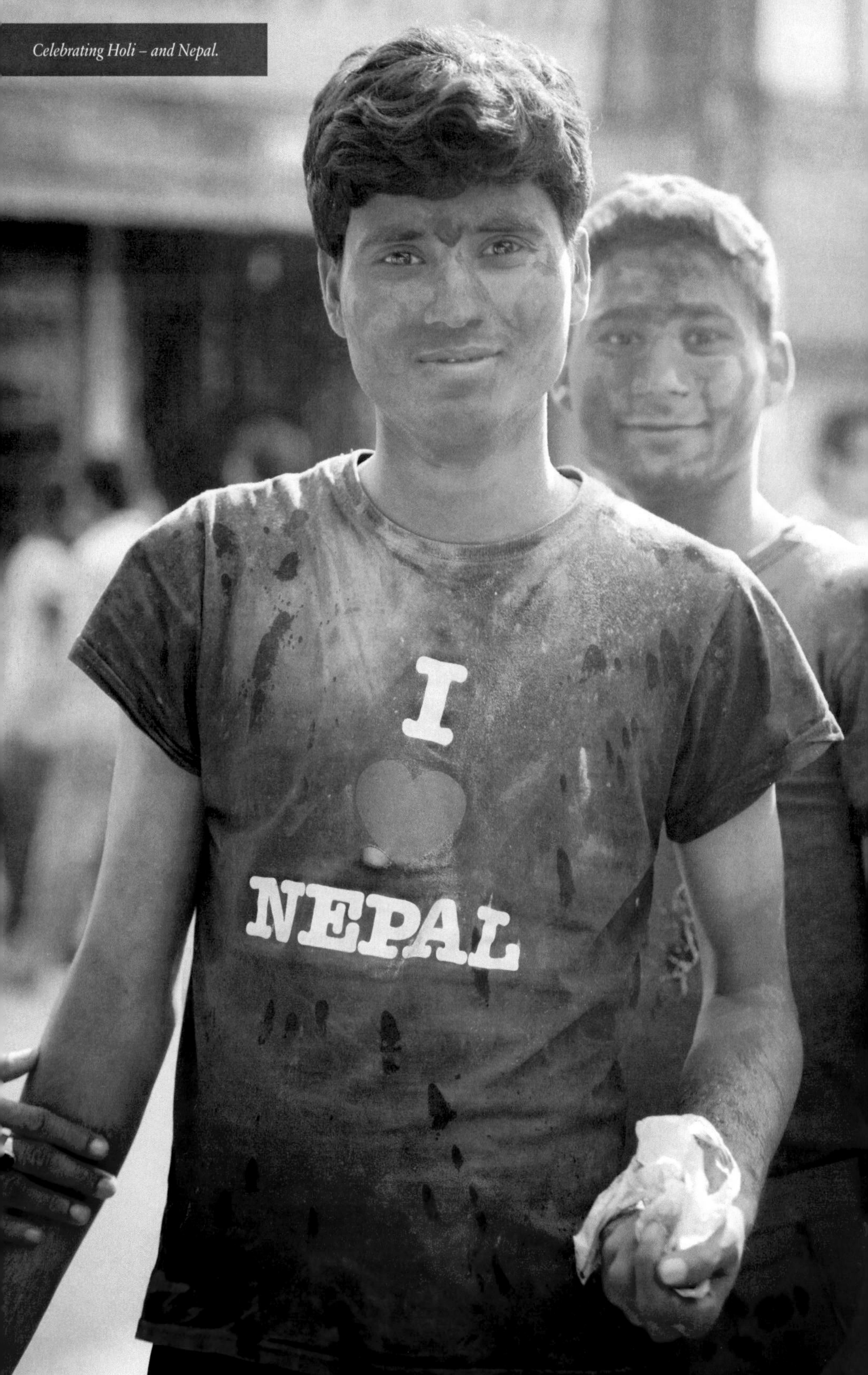

Celebrating Holi – and Nepal.

FESTIVALS

With an annual calendar packed with festivals, visitors are likely to witness at least one colourful event regardless of when they arrive.

In Nepal, it is often said, every other building is a temple and every other day is a festival. There are more than 50 festivals, many lasting several days or even weeks, each year. Some, such as Bhaktapur's boisterous Bisket Jatra, are epic undertakings with crowds of thousands and attendant tourist hordes and camera crews; others are little-known local affairs in the compound of some forgotten village shrine.

The majority of Nepal's festivals have a religious underpinning, tied to one or both of the two great religions of the land, Hinduism and Buddhism. Hindu festivals generally combine mass pilgrimages and *puja* offerings at temples followed by large *melas* (fairs), feasts and animal sacrifices. Buddhist festivals tend to be quieter, but equally colourful. Adherents of both faiths, however, often participate in one another's festivals.

Some of the great religious events celebrated in Nepal are universal to the wider Hindu or Buddhist world – the chaotically colourful spring festival of Holi, for example – and some are based on a comparatively recent regal decree. But others have their roots in local traditions and folk beliefs that predate the arrival of any world religion in the Himalayas. There are thousands of gods and goddesses, demons and ogres to be appeased; the various seasons must be honoured, and there are essential rites for the blessing of seeds to be planted and crops harvested.

The major festivals are listed here according to the months in which they are normally held. Always check locally with tourist offices, however, as dates can vary due to the lunar calendar and complicated astrological calculations.

Making offerings of food at a temple.

Baisakh (April and May)

Baisakh (usually starting on 13 or 14 April) is the first month of the Nepalese New Year, which is marked by the week-long **Bisket Jatra** celebration in Bhaktapur. Three days before New Year's Day itself, a spectacular tug-of-war takes place to determine the direction the great chariot of Bhairav will take through the city streets. On New Year's Eve, a huge pole, or *yasin*, is raised in memory of the legend of Bisket. Over the following days each neighbourhood parades its own god. West of Bhaktapur in Thimi, **Bal Kumari Jatra** is celebrated all night long with torchlight processions and devotees covered with orange powder dancing and playing *dhimay* drums. **Matatirtha Snan**, the Nepalese version of

Mothers' Day, takes place near Thankot and is for persons whose mothers have died during the year. Living mothers are also honoured.

The birthday and enlightenment of the Lord Buddha, **Buddha Jayanti**, is celebrated with pilgrimages and celebrations at Buddhist shrines during the full moon. Swayambhunat, Boudhanath and Lumbini temples are particularly colourful at this time.

The lunar cycle is divided into two halves, "bright" and "dark", and within each half are 14 specific lunar "days" on which festivals are held.

Thame monastery, high in the Khumbu region of east Nepal, holds its **Mani Rimdu** dance-drama festival in May during which Sherpa monks enact age-old legends and evoke protector deities. A similar festival is held at Thyangboche during November and December.

Jesth (May and June)

Sithinakha is the birthday of Kumar, the handsome warrior son of Shiva, and is celebrated at Jaisedewal, south of the Kathmandu Durbar Square. This is also traditionally a day for people throughout the Kathmandu Valley to clean their wells, so as to prepare them for the monsoon rains.

The **Ganga Deshara** festival attracts thousands of Hindu devotees to the holy river confluence at Khaptad National Park in west Nepal (see page 304).

Asadh (June and July)

Tulsi Bijropan is one of the most important *Ekadasis*, the eleventh day of each lunar fortnight, when no animal can be slaughtered and a day of fasting is mandatory. Primarily a woman's ritual, the *tulsi* (basil) plant is planted in a specially chosen place within the home and then reverently worshipped.

Celebrating Mothers' Day with a festival at Mata Tirtha Hindu temple near Kathmandu.

In Khumbu and Helambu the **Dumje** festival features much noisy revelry, for the purpose of driving out the evil forces that have gathered around the villages over the previous year.

Srawan (July and August)

Patan sees one of its biggest and most spectacular annual festivals in the summer. During **Bhoto Dekhaune** a sacred jewelled waistcoat *(bhoto)* is ritually displayed in front of the crowds. This is the culmination of the festival of **Rato Machhendranath**, the protector deity of the valley, who is paraded through Patan for one month in his huge 2-metre (6ft) -high chariot, and given offerings of rice to ensure good monsoon rainfall.

Traditionally the last day for rice planting, **Ghanta Karna** is the night of a terrifying local demon. According to legend the demon was outwitted by Krishna, who tempted him into a deep well by disguising himself as a frog and trapped him there. Small boys make leafy arches and collect money in the street in order to pay for the demon's funeral.

The birth of Krishna is celebrated at **Krishna Jayanti** all over the country; on the Krishna Mandir in Patan, women carrying oil lights keep vigil all night long.

Raksha Bandhan or **Janai Purnima** is the full-moon day *(Saaun)* on which every Brahman male must renew the sacred thread worn over his shoulder and all Brahmans and Chhetris receive a new thread around their wrists. At the sacred Gosainkund Lakes, high in the Helambu region, thousands of devotees throng to bathe and make offerings.

Snake gods *(nagas)* are widely worshipped as controllers of rainfall, earthquakes and guardians of treasure in Kathmandu Valley. During **Naga Panchami** prayers are said at Pashupatinath and pictures of the *nagas* are displayed on every house. Milk, the snake's favoured drink, is offered to the images.

Late summer is the time for the important **Yartung** festival celebrated annually by mountain people with wild horse racing and much drinking of millet beer. Muktinath, high in the Kali Gandaki valley, is an important centre of this festival.

Bhadra (August and September)

During the festival of **Gai Jatra**, musical processions of little boys dressed as holy men and stylised cows wend their way through Kathmandu, Patan and other Newar settlements in the valley. Originally devised as a comic-relief parade to cheer an inconsolable queen who had lost a son to smallpox, these rituals also ease the spiritual transition of those who have died during the previous year.

Holi revellers.

The most spectacular of all the Kathmandu Valley festivals is the eight-day **Indra Jatra**, which is best seen around Kathmandu's Durbar Square. The Hindu god Indra is fêted with dancing and processions, and homage is paid to the *Kumari* (Living Goddess, see page 162). Bhairav is also honoured during this festival, the only time the great mask of Seto Bhairav is exposed to the public, with *chhang* (millet beer) pouring from his mouth to refresh revellers.

Gokarna Aunshi or Fathers' Day is celebrated with ritual bathing at the Mahadev temple by the river at Gokarna for those whose fathers have died during the previous year.

Teej, three days after full moon, is the most colourful women's festival in Nepal, celebrated over three days. After fasting and ritual bathing, a period of dancing and singing takes place. Pashupatinath is the best place to watch these caste women in their finest red saris and jewels. Offerings are made to their husbands, and their sins are washed away.

Ashwin (September and October)

The 10-day festival of **Dasain** is the most important Hindu festival and life throughout the country comes to a standstill for up to a fortnight. Families gather to worship the mother goddess Durga who is assuaged with offerings and animal sacrifices. An enormous communal sacrifice takes place in Kathmandu's Hanuman Dhoka. Priests swirl through the streets of Patan for eight nights prior to the main day, Vijaya Dasain, when families feast together on the sacrificial meat.

Kartik (October and November)

Diwali or **Tihar**, the "Festival of Lights", is a more joyous five-day holiday of family gatherings, feasts, gifts and offerings. Cows, dogs and crows are blessed with treats, and brothers travel for days to receive a *tika* from their sisters on Bhai Tika. On the fifth day lamps are lit in all homes to attract the attention of Lakshmi, the goddess of prosperity. This is also an auspicious day for gambling.

It is hard to miss the sounds, let alone the sights, of the Tihar (Diwali) festival. Nepalese children rejoice in setting off firecrackers throughout the event in streets all over the country.

Chhath takes place during the Diwali festival and is an important event for the Maithili people of Janakpur in the Terai. Women pray and bathe in sacred rivers and make offerings to the sun god, Surya. They also paint their distinctive murals on exterior walls, which remain in place until the spring.

The Newars also celebrate **Mha Puja** at this time to honour the self and to mark their calendar New Year.

The **Mani Rimdu** dance-drama festival is held at Thyangboche Monastery in the Khumbu, high on the trekking route to Everest. Monks enact Sherpa legends and evoke the protector gods with colourful masked dances, celebrating their victory over the older Bön religion.

Reminiscent of Mani Rimdu are the dance festivals of **Dyokyabsi**, which are celebrated at various monasteries in the Thak Khola (upper

Crowds attend the procession of the goddess Kumari's chariot on the last day of Indra Jatra at Durbar Square in Kathmandu.

Kali Gandaki river valley) and Mustang during the months of October and November.

Haribodhini Ekadasi welcomes Vishnu back from his annual four-month sleep in the underworld. The festival is marked by a pilgrimage around the Kathmandu Valley to the temples of Changu Narayan, Bishankhu Narayan, Sekh Narayan and Ichangu Narayan, culminating at Budhanilkantha.

Marga (November and December)

Yomari Purnima is celebrated by Newars with a *mela* at Panauti in December. A special dumpling *(yomari)* is made out of rice flour and molasses, and ritually offered to the family rice store for protection.

Indrayani Jatra takes place in Kirtipur at new moon, when deities are paraded in the streets.

Bala Chaturdashi is a night-time vigil held at Pashupatinath during new moon, when Hindu families pray and make offerings to their dead relatives.

Pousch (December and January)

In Janakpur in December the festival of **Biha Panchami** re-enacts Ram and Sita's marriage from the great Hindu epic entitled the *Ramayana*, complete with an extraordinarily colourful five-day procession of elephants, horses and chariots.

Maha (January and February)

A rare "fixed" event in the Nepalese festival calendar is **Maha Sankranti**, which is held on 14 or 15 January. While most festivals are based on the lunar cycle and so migrate back and forth through the Gregorian calendar, this is a solar event held to coincide with the entry of the sun into the constellation of Capricorn. It is traditionally seen as heralding the start of spring, and is an important day for ritual bathing in sacred rivers. This is a particularly important day at Devghat, which is located north of Narayangharh.

Basant Panchami is the festival of spring on the fifth day after the full moon, and also of Saraswati, goddess of learning. Students, artists, weavers and schoolchildren gather at the temple of Swayambhunath to celebrate, and schools across the country are brightly decorated.

Nepalese people marry according to the lunar calendar, choosing auspicious days on which to wed. The wedding party is preceded by a brass band, followed by the bride, dressed in red.

The Hindu shrine of Pashupatinath or the nearby village of Sankhu are the places to be for the ceremony of **Maha Snan**, which centres on the ritual in which Lord Shiva is washed with milk, yoghurt, honey and *ghee*, then dressed anew.

Falgun (February and March)

One of the most beautiful celebrations of the year is **Losar** or Tibetan New Year when Tibetans and Sherpas parade around the freshly decorated stupa of Boudhanath.

Women sing and dance at Pashupatinath Temple during the Teej festival.

Shivaratri, the birthday of Shiva, the Hindu god of destruction and rebirth, is one of the great festivals of the year. Thousands of pilgrims flock to the *mela* at Pashupatinath for the happy celebration and all-night vigil. Sadhus, or *yogis*, some dressed in nothing but a loin cloth and carrying a metal trident, gather from all over India and Nepal in order to perform rites.

The rowdy week-long festival of colour, **Holi**, is a rather chaotic springtime carnival during which children roam the streets pelting each other (and anyone else who gets in the way, including unsuspecting tourists) with water balloons and coloured powder. Wear your oldest clothes and have fun.

The gaai (cow), the sacred Hindu animal, is thought to assist the path of the deceased to heaven, leading them by its tail.

Chaitra (March and April)

The horse festival of **Ghodejatra** takes place on the Tundhikhel in Kathmandu with a display of horsemanship and gymnastics. The same evening, the festival of **Pasa Chare** assures protection against an underground demon in a midnight procession.

Another two separate festivals occur simultaneously towards the end of March. Ritual offerings are made to the goddess Durga at midday on **Chaitra Dasain**, exactly six months to the day before the spectacular Dasain festival of October. **Seto Machhendranath** is a four-day procession through the streets of Kathmandu, eight days after full moon, in which the deity of compassion is paraded from his temple in Asan Tol in a towering chariot and visited by the *Kumari*.

During the full moon is **Chaitra Purnima**, when Buddha's mother Mayadevi is worshipped by thousands of pilgrims in Lumbini.

Nepalese devotees carry traditional torches during festivities on the last day of the Rato Machhendranath festival.

NEPAL'S CALENDARS

As well as the Gregorian calendar, four other calendars are used simultaneously in Nepal. The official calendar is the Vikram Sambat; day one of Vikram Sambat was 23 February 57 BC, and the 12 months are determined by the lunar cycle. The year begins in mid-April with the month of Baisakh, followed by Jesth, Asadh, Srawan, Bhadra, Ashwin, Kartik, Marga, Pousch, Maha, Falgun and Chaitra. As the lunar year consists only of 354 days it requires seven additional months every 19 years. While government, newspapers and other official institutions use the Vikram Sambat, there have been recent moves to reinstitute an alternative system, the Nepal Sambat, which began in AD 879.

In addition, the Nepalese year is also divided according to the Shaka Sambat which counts AD 78 as Year Zero, and which is used by Buddhist astrologers and some orthodox Hindus. There is also a Tibetan calendar, known as the Bhot Byalo, which was first introduced in 127 BC.

The seven days of the Nepalese week are named after the planets. They are: Aityabar (Sunday – the day of the sun), Somabar (Monday – the day of the moon), Mangalbar (Tuesday – the day of Mars), Budhabar (Wednesday – the day of Mercury), Bihibar (Thursday – the day of Jupiter), Sukrabar (Friday – the day of Venus) and Shanibar (Saturday – the day of Saturn).

A dancer performs to mark the beginning of the Indra Jatra festival in Kathmandu.

A blackbuck herd on grassland in the mist at sunrise.

An elephant ride is a great way to see wildlife.

FLORA AND FAUNA

Nepal's narrow strip of territory contains a staggering range of natural habitats, home to a wide array of wildlife, much of it living within national parks and reserves.

Nowhere else in the world does the landscape change so dramatically over so short a distance as in Nepal. From the mountain deserts of the trans-Himalaya down through lush valleys and into the steamy swamps of the south, the country is home to an incredible diversity of flora and fauna. Deforestation, poaching and human–animal conflict have all had an impact here, but Nepal has an impressive number of national parks, with large swathes of protected territory ranging from the bleak wilderness of Shey Phoksumdo to the dense tropical forests of Chitwan.

Vegetation zones

Nepal's enormous variation in altitude, aspect and climate produces dramatic changes in vegetation over remarkably small distances. The tropical Terai and lower Siwalik (Churia) hills extend up to about 1,000 metres (3,300ft) and are followed by the subtropical zone from 1,000 to 2,000 metres (3,300–6,500ft). The warm temperate belt runs from 2,000 to 3,000 metres (6,500–10,000ft) and is succeeded by the cool temperate or subalpine zone, which ends with the treeline at about 4,000 metres (13,000ft). Most of the remaining vegetation falls within the alpine belt between 4,000 and 5,000 metres (13,000–16,500ft). Still higher up lies the *nival* or aeolian zone, a windswept desolation of snow and ice. Across this south–north transition there are further localised differences generated by variations in rainfall. Eastern Nepal experiences a longer wet season than the west, while those areas to the north of the Himalayas are arid due to a strong rainshadow effect. This is more pronounced in northwestern parts of the country.

Mountain blooms.

The tropical belt

The vegetation of the tropical Terai plains remains remarkably uniform throughout the length of Nepal. The cornerstone of the Terai forest is the mighty sal tree, valued for its timber. Amongst the other key trees of the lowland jungle are crape myrtle, dillenia, and the so-called "marking-nut tree", *Semecarpus anacardium*, which produces an indelible ink-like dye traditionally used by laundry workers to mark clothes for identification.

There are many other plants here that have been utilised by mankind over the centuries. The broad-canopied beleric tree produces the small, hard *bedda* nut, which has mild narcotic properties. *Holarrhena antidysenterica*, sometimes known as bitter oleander, is called *dudh kare* locally. *Dudh* means "milk" and the tree produces a milky sap used in ayurvedic medicine. Some ethnic groups bury their dead infants near the roots of this tree so they will have milk to drink in the afterlife.

The eastern and central regions of the Terai are dominated by various species of the large evergreen chinquapin, which produces small chestnut-like seeds which are roasted in their shells and eaten by villagers. The lower forests include bombax, the "silk cotton tree", and red kamala, which produces the striking vermillion powder traditionally used in Hindu rituals. Further west, where the weather is drier, forests of chir pine stretch down into the lowlands. This evergreen is an important source of resin and turpentine.

Rhododendron flowers are often pickled by villagers but honey made from the nectar contains a natural hallucinogen, producing bizarre visual distortions.

Rhododendrons bloom on a hillside near the Gosainkund mountain range.

The temperate zone

The temperate zone in eastern and central Nepal is characterised by mixed broad-leaved forest, usually on north- and west-facing slopes. Laurel is the touchstone species here, along with magnolias, tree-ferns and screw pines. Evergreen oaks begin to appear at 1,200 metres (4,000ft) and share the upper temperate forests with various species of maple.

The vegetation of the temperate hill zone in western Nepal is generally quite different. Oaks and rhododendrons dominate here, giving way to mixed deciduous forests higher up, featuring chestnuts, maples and walnut trees. Conifers are also much more in evidence in western Nepal, including the majestic deodar, also known as Himalayan cedar, which forms magnificent forests along the Karnali River. As the altitude creeps upwards the West Himalayan spruces appear, along with the silver fir and the blue pine.

Another important temperate and tropical plant is the bamboo. Twenty species occur in Nepal and they are fundamental to the lifestyles of many ethnic groups. The Rai creation myth gives pride of place to bamboo as one of the first living things to have emerged from the womb of the goddess-creator. One survey counted 57 bamboo artefacts used in a single Rai house. Common items include baskets, mats, cradles and water vessels, but there are also more exotic objects such as bows and arrows, rat-traps and a brush used in shamanic seances.

Much of the tree line in Nepal is defined by birch. Its papery bark is used by highland villagers for a number of purposes including as a ceiling material in flat-roofed Muktinath and as a natural greaseproof paper for wrapping yak butter.

Rhododendrons

The lavishly coloured *Rhododendron arboreum* is the official national flower of Nepal. Known locally as *laliguran*, they are found from around 1,100 metres (3,600ft). The scarlet colour of the flower fades with altitude, progressing through paler shades of pink until it turns white at about 2,500 metres (8,200ft). Colours of other rhododendron species range from white, cream and yellow to lilac and purple. Generally they grow as modest shrubs, but in some regions they can tower up to 15 metres (50ft) high.

Rhododendrons generally decrease in stature with altitude and dwarf species form a low carpet in certain alpine areas. People of the alpine zone value dwarf rhododendrons for incense and as a substitute for snuff. The diminutive *Rhododendron nivale*, which attains a height of just 5cm (2 inches), holds the altitude record for woody plants at 5,500 metres (18,000ft).

Alpine plants

Vegetation above the treeline is divisible into moist and dry alpine scrub. In addition to dwarf rhododendrons, there are several species of juniper. Primulas grow in abundance (there are some 70 species in the Himalayas); larkspurs, fumitories, edelweiss, anemones and gentians flower into October, and the ice-blue Himalayan poppy is found on lower hillsides. The alpine regions are also home to a staggering array of orchids – a grand total of 319 different species. All orchids are protected by law and their export is banned. The arid western regions of Mustang, Dolpo and Manang are dominated by the thorny caragana bush, which thrives in the harsh environment.

Butterflies and moths

Eleven of the world's 15 families of butterflies are represented in Nepal and 614 species have been identified. The moth tally, meanwhile,

Orchids abound in the jungles of the Terai.

MEDICINAL PLANTS

In a country where modern medical facilities are few, it is natural that a vast lore of medicinal herbs should still be in use. Nepal has 600 indigenous plants with recognised therapeutic properties, more than half of which occur in the subtropical zone. Some are in high demand on the international market and large quantities are exported in bulk to India, Europe and the Far East.

A number of lichens are valued as medicinal plants. Some 352 species, grouped in 67 genera, have been identified in Nepal. Two species of *Parmelia* are especially in demand in India for use in spice and incense. Lichen extracts are used in perfume and some are valued for their antibiotic properties. Lichens cover a vast altitudinal range and the wealth of species found above the treeline remains practically unstudied.

Ferns, too, include a number of species (30 are listed by the Nepal Pharmaceutical Association) with medicinal properties, valued for use in respiratory ailments, for intestinal worms and for the treatment of cuts and bruises. In total there are 375 species of ferns, grouped into 84 genera, although the diversity decreases as one moves westwards to the drier regions. Young shoots of several varieties are eaten as a green vegetable and may even be found on sale in the markets of Kathmandu.

runs to over 5,000 species including the giant atlas moth, the world's largest moth with a wingspan of nearly 30cm (1ft). Once again, it is the country's dramatic variation in habitat that allows for such diversity, with both Palaearctic and Oriental species found in abundance.

Relatively traditional farming practices have kept Nepal a haven for many species that have all but vanished in countries where industrial agriculture dominates. The rare Queen of Spain fritillary – which is severely threatened in Europe – is frequently encountered, and there are some half-dozen species of clouded yellows, a Palaearctic genus that has extended its range down to the Terai. It is also not unusual to spot the death's head hawk moth, which is critically endangered in Britain.

The butterfly season varies with altitude. Lowland species proliferate between March and November, and a few may be seen throughout the winter months. During the wet season, greater size and brighter colours are the rule. The highland season is considerably shorter than the lowland, lasting only from May to August.

The most spectacular butterflies of the Terai and the Middle Hills are undoubtedly the swallowtails. Other highly visible species include tawny tigers, close relatives of the American milkweed or monarch. They can afford to fly unhurriedly as their orange-and-black wings warn predatory birds that their bodies contain poisons. This colour scheme has proved so successful that it is mimicked by perfectly edible species. The swallowtail family is also represented in the opposite altitudinal extreme. The rare banded apollo has been found only at 5,000–5,500 metres (16,500–18,000ft), protected from brisk temperatures by its hairy body.

Ancient forest near Gosainkund.

Birdlife

Nepal is a paradise for bird-lovers, with more than 850 species recorded, representing 10 percent of the world's avian population in just 0.1 percent of its surface area. Species range from the mighty hornbills of the Terai forests to the slow-circling eagles and vultures of the high mountains. Spring is the best time for birdwatching, while the Terai in the winter months plays host to myriad migratory species taking time out from the long commute between Siberia and the Indian Ocean.

Changing altitude defines the range of many species, but there is also a clear east–west division, marked by the Kali Gandaki Valley: three species of titmouse and two nuthatches do not occur east of the river, which also represents the western limit of such birds as the blood pheasant, the brown parrotbill, the golden-breasted tit babbler and the rufous-bellied shrike babbler.

Cranes are a key species of the Terai, and some eight species of stork ply the rivers of the lowland national parks. At a higher altitude an impressive selection of birds of prey make use of mountain thermals. Lammergeyers, golden eagles and Himalayan griffon vultures can all be spotted circling above upland valleys, while around the Kathmandu Valley kites are a common sight. The mountains are also home to a large number of high-altitude passerines, including a number of mountain finches, rose finches, accentors and redstarts.

Pheasants are common in the forests of the Middle Hills and at higher altitude. Nepal's national bird, the *danphe* or Himalayan monal, lives throughout the alpine regions. The females have dull brown plumage, but the males have vivid, metallic-blue upper bodies, similar in colour to the feathers of a peacock, a black underbelly and a crest.

At lower altitudes the Indian roller, with its vivid turquoise wing feathers, can often be spotted, as can the hoopoe, a common bird throughout the northern Indian subcontinent.

Lowland animal life

Most of Nepal's large animal species live in the lush forests of the Terai, part of a tropical, monsoonal habitat that stretches along the southern flanks of the Himalayas.

Amongst the most striking of all these animals is the greater one-horned rhinoceros (also known as the Indian rhinoceros). These huge beasts once roamed the length of the Terai, but hunting and habitat destruction reduced them to a tiny pocket of fewer than 100 individuals in the Chitwan area by the middle of the 20th century. Since then, however, concerted conservation efforts have seen numbers bounce back to over 500, and several individuals have been reintroduced to the Bardia national park to help bolster the national population. The preferred habitat of these primeval beasts, with their great folds of skin, is the marshy grassland where they like to wallow in the muddy pools.

Nepal's national bird, the danphe or Himalayan monal, is also known as the Impeyan pheasant after Lady Mary Impey, who founded a zoo in late-18th-century Calcutta and commissioned hundreds of detailed paintings of South Asian birdlife.

A few hundred gaur survive in Chitwan and on the densely forested lower slopes of the Siwaliks. These huge wild cattle, with their distinctive black hides and white lower legs, can weigh up to 1,500kg (3,300lb). They are most easily glimpsed in the spring when they descend to open areas to feed on the fresh new grasses. The rare nilgai or blue bull frequents the riverine forest of Bardia, as does the smaller and more graceful blackbuck.

Tawny tiger butterfly.

Various deer species can be seen in the national parks. Most numerous and gregarious is the elegant chital or spotted deer which gather in large herds in the spring. There are also the stately sambar, the stocky hog deer and the tiny, tusked muntjac or barking deer, named for its dog-like alarm call. The endangered swamp deer or *barasingha* is mainly confined to the Bardia National Park.

Wild pigs are found throughout the Terai, as are two common species of monkey – the langur with its silver-grey coat and black face, and the olive-coloured rhesus macaque. Both species also range well up into the mountains. Another large inhabitant of Terai forests is the sloth bear. Although they mainly feed on termites, these creatures have a reputation for aggression, and are feared by villagers.

A few wild dogs, known as *dhole*, course through the Chitwan area and other parks in search of prey. More common throughout the Terai is their scavenging relative, the golden jackal.

The Terai also hosts a great variety of smaller mammals including mongooses, civets, martens, and honey badgers. There are a number of small cat species including the jungle cat, the fishing cat and the leopard cat, as well as larger leopards, and, of course, tigers.

Few animals attract so much attention as the

A pair of large griffon vultures perched on a tree branch above the jungle valleys.

Royal Bengal tiger: revered and feared in equal measure, eternalised in the pages of Blake and Kipling, subjected to concerted slaughter by generations of maharajas and colonialists, and pushed to the brink of extinction by poaching and habitat loss. As with the rhino, there have been valiant efforts to protect the tigers in recent years, and numbers have stabilised. Most of Nepal's tigers live in Chitwan, with smaller pockets in Bardia and Sukla Phanta. Chitwan's tigers also range into the neighbouring Valmiki Tiger Reserve in India.

Tigers tend to hunt in the long grasses and floodplains around the Terai rivers. They are highly secretive and largely nocturnal and it is only a few lucky visitors who catch a glimpse of these splendid creatures.

A tiny population of Gangetic dolphins survive in the lower reaches of the Karnali River, but pollution and environmental disturbance have pushed them to the brink of extinction. The dolphins are almost blind, and they use sonar to pick their way through the murky waters of the rivers. More common in the rivers are two species of crocodile. The gharial is a specialised fish-eater with an elongated snout. It is harmless to man. The marsh mugger eats anything it can catch and lives mainly in the oxbow lakes. Pythons frequent the edges of ponds and streams, while the world's largest venomous snake, the king cobra, can also be found in the Terai, along with a number of smaller, though no less poisonous, kraits and vipers.

Mountain mammals

While most of Nepal's large animals – elephant, rhinoceros, gaur and tiger – are restricted to the lowland Terai, the high-altitude national parks play host to their own population of mammals.

Sagarmatha National Park, centred on the Everest region, is home to the largest concentration of Himalayan tahr anywhere in the animal's wide range from Pakistan to Sikkim. The preferred altitude of this wild goat coincides with the upper haunts of the ghoral or Himalayan chamois. This goat-antelope may be found at altitudes of more than 4,000 metres (13,000ft) to as low as 900 metres (3,000ft) where it descends to raid village crops. The ghoral and its near relative, the strange-looking serow which prefers forest habitats, were popular targets of colonial-era hunters, and are still widely targeted for their meat outside protected areas.

Another crop-raider is the bear. There are two species in the mountains of Nepal. The Himalayan black bear, like the sloth bear of the Terai, has a white V-shaped bib, and ranges through the Middle Hills up to the limit of the forest. The Himalayan brown bear, a Palaearctic species, is more confined to higher altitudes.

Hindus regard monkeys as holy, thanks to their association with Hanuman, the monkey god of the Ramayana, who led his simian army to the aid of Rama in his battle against the demon Rawana.

The shaggy black sloth bears of the Terai's forests are known in both Nepali and Hindi as bhalu, a term familiar to fans of Rudyard Kipling through the name of Baloo, the affable bear in The Jungle Book.

Both are hunted for their gall bladders, which are in demand as ingredients for Chinese medicine. Bears probably rank as the most dangerous of the high-altitude species, and though they generally shy away from human contact, their habit of raiding farmers' fields does lead to occasional clashes with villagers. Leopards range to a far higher altitude than their cousin, the tiger, and though they are very hard to spot they can be encountered right up to the tree line throughout the Himalayas. They also occasionally clash with villagers by taking livestock.

Packs of Himalayan wolves – lighter, rangier creatures than their European and North American cousins – roam at high altitude and prey on the various mountain ungulates. Smaller predators include the ubiquitous red fox and

A greater one-horned rhinoceros.

Himalayan brown bear.

TIGER CONSERVATION: NEPAL'S SUCCESS STORY

One of the most dramatic conservation success stories in Nepal is the comeback of the Bengal tiger. After the unrestrained royal hunts of the past, the tiger population of Chitwan's jungles dwindled to a few dozen. But when Chitwan was declared Nepal's first national park in 1973, tigers began to rebound. By the turn of the 21st century the total tiger population of Nepal had reached around 350, with most of them living in Chitwan. The Maoist insurgency provided a window of opportunity for poachers, and by 2008 tiger numbers had plummeted once more by over 50 percent. But they have bounced back yet again and there are now around 130 tigers in Chitwan, and a national total of about 200 individuals.

Unfortunately, the number of tigers outside national parks is now negligible because of habitat loss. The disappearance of jungle corridors between parks also means that overcrowding is becoming a problem. Adult males require a territory of as much as 60 sq km (23 sq miles). Where territories overlap there are frequent fights. Wounded tigers cannot hunt their natural wild prey and may turn into man-eaters, picking on cattle and humans on the park's fringes.

The tiger is at the top of the food chain: the act of protecting tigers protects the habitat on which it depends, and it has become symbolic of Nepal's entire conservation effort.

Yaks

The mighty, lumbering yak is one of the iconic beasts of the Himalayas, and a vital source of food, clothing and transport for the people of the Tibetan regions.

Yaks occupy a significant place in Tibetan life, and the Tibetan term for the animals is itself revealing: the collective expression is *nor*, meaning "material wealth", recalling the old English synonymy between cattle and chattel.

Yaks can carry twice as much as a person and are used during treks and expeditions.

However, the Tibetans' appreciation of their indigenous bovine has never extended to outright veneration – these are no sacred cows, and yaks are eaten without qualms throughout the Tibetan world. The Buddhist reluctance to take life poses some small stumbling blocks, but some indigent is usually willing to take on the slaughter in exchange for a portion of *digsha*, literally "sin-meat". Nothing is wasted. The head is often dried and eaten as a festive dish during New Year celebrations, while the horns may be used to adorn doorways and rooftops as a deterrent against demons.

Adapted for altitude

Yaks are perfectly adapted to high altitudes, and function best between 3,000 and 6,000 metres (10,000–18,000ft). They were originally domesticated from the wild *drong*, now rare due to unchecked hunting. *Drongs* are huge – a bull may stand up to 2 metres (6ft) and weigh almost a ton. They also have a nervous temperament and very large horns. Bred down to more manageable proportions, yaks rarely exceed half a ton in weight and most are considerably smaller.

Pastoral patterns accord with the yak's natural inclination to follow the receding snow up to the high grasslands in warmer weather and to retreat to lower settlements at the onset of winter. Yaks can obtain water by eating frozen snow and can dig down to eat the grass beneath. They have also been a major form of transport in trans-Himalayan trade, especially in the long-distance commerce in salt.

Yak bounties

Dairy products head the list of the yak's bounties. Yak milk contains about twice as much fat as that of lowland cattle and has a rich, golden appearance. Fresh milk is rarely drunk but is subjected to processing: yogurt is a favourite. Butter is also extracted by churning the milk. It is consumed mainly in tea or as a lubricant for *tsampa* (barley flour), but is also smeared on faces and heads as protection against the high-altitude climate. Butter is given as an offering at monasteries, where it is used to fuel votive lamps and to make religious sculptures. The residual buttermilk is boiled and the solids skimmed off and made into cheese *(churpi)* by the Sherpas. *Churpi* is delicious if eaten within a few days, but beyond that consuming the hard, dried cheese is daunting. *Churpi* should not be confused with the eminently edible yak cheese, made by Tibetan refugees to a Swiss recipe.

The most obvious adaptation of yaks to their environment is their fur. The longer, coarser hair is used for making ropes, slings, sacks and blankets. It also provides the raw material for the black tents of the Tibetan nomads. The weave allows smoke to escape and light to enter, while the oil on the hair keeps the structure waterproof. Yak-hair tents are also warmer and more durable than canvas, which can be shredded by winter winds. The soft wool beneath the hair is spun into yarn for clothing or felted to make boots. Usually the fur is pulled out by hand.

The yak's tail is valued in central Nepal for royal flywhisks and healing aids for shamans. The shaman may brandish it while dancing or plunge it into boiling water before whipping the illness out of the patient.

the yellow-throated martin, which lives in the alpine forest areas.

No animal has been the object of hunters' attention as much as the musk deer, which ranges from around 2,000 to 4,500 metres (6,500–14,800ft). The musk, secreted by the male in a pod under its tail, is valued in Chinese medicine, Tibetan incense and the Western perfume industry. Although strictly protected, musk is worth several times its weight in gold and a single pod may yield over 50 grams (2oz), providing the incentive for poachers to risk the penalties.

Above the tree line, between 4,000 and 5,000 metres (13,000–16,500ft), it is often possible to see the blue sheep, locally known as a *bharal*. With exceptional luck one also might glimpse the blue sheep's chief predator, the elusive snow leopard (see 106). This elegant cat has long been persecuted for its beautiful coat, paler and thicker than that of the common leopard, and because of its penchant for domestic sheep, goats and occasionally even yaks. It is found throughout the Himalayas, but it is notoriously difficult to spot.

National parks

Nepal has a staggering number of nationally protected landscapes for such a small country. In total there are 10 national parks, three wildlife reserves and one hunting reserve, all administered by the National Parks and Wildlife Conservation Department, as well as several scheduled conservation areas. These 17 protected regions account for around 12 percent of Nepal's total area. Nepal's best-known national parks lie in the low, level reaches of the Terai, and are major tourist attractions in their own right.

Chitwan National Park

Chitwan National Park, located in the central inner Terai region, was the country's first national park and is today the best known and the place most often visited by tourists bent on wildlife-watching. This former royal hunting reserve is home to more than 50 species of mammals including the vast majority of Nepal's rhinos, as well as tigers and elephants. Chitwan also hosts around 450 species of birds. Two of the most spectacular birds found in the park are the Bengal florican and the giant hornbill. Adjacent to Chitwan is the Parsa Wildlife Reserve, which is home to Nepal's largest resident herd of wild elephants.

Nearly a quarter of Chitwan National Park consists of alluvial floodplain at only 150 metres (500ft) above sea level. The remainder is low hills rising to 760 metres (2,565ft), covered with tropical deciduous forest, dominated by the towering sal tree. The grasslands are interspersed with riverine forests, featuring shisham, simal bombax and bilar trees. The grasslands periodically flood during the monsoon between June and September, when 90 percent of Chitwan's annual 2,150mm (85ins)

Rhesus monkey at Pashupatinath Temple outside Kathmandu.

of rain falls. This introduces a dynamic element into the ecology, changing river courses so as to create ox-bow lakes or *tals* where wildlife congregates.

Another factor of great importance is fire. The dying grasses have been burnt annually for centuries so that fresh shoots can appear. Now controlled by the park authorities, thousands of local villagers are first permitted to collect grass for thatching in January before the copped stubble is subjected to managed burning. The black, burnt areas become a mosaic of grasses in different stages of regeneration, providing grazing for ungulates during the dry months. Fire tends to preserve the grassland at the expense of the forest saplings, although the brief "cool burn" in the sal forest does not affect the fire-resistant mature trees.

Other Terai national parks

After Chitwan, the most frequently visited protected area is the Bardia National Park, situated in the far western Terai. It is comparable to Chitwan for its richness of wildlife, including tigers and wild elephant herds. The park lies along the alluvial floodplain of the Geruwa River. Its many islands are covered with tall grasses and a rich assemblage of riverine forest. A key characteristic of Bardia are

Gharial crocodile.

the *phantas*, the short grassland meadows on the forest edge which make for fine wildlife-viewing zones.

Rhinos were reintroduced into Bardia from Chitwan in the 1980s, but after initial success, attempts at re-establishment have been hampered by poaching, which continued largely unchecked during the instability of the Maoist uprising. With the return of peace preservation efforts have been stepped up once more.

There are a number of other national parks and reserves strung along the length of the Terai. The Koshi Tappu Wildlife Reserve is located on the Koshi River in the east Terai and contains the only population of wild buffaloes in Nepal. It is also a sanctuary for a wide range of migratory waterfowl. Sukla Phanta Wildlife Reserve in the far western Terai, not far from Bardia National Park, contains a large population of swamp deer, as well as a few tigers and elephants and a range of other wildlife, including more than 450 species of birds. As its name suggests, it is also known for its tall, savannah-like *phanta* grass.

High-altitude parks

High in the trans-Himalaya, the Shey-Phoksundo National Park is Nepal's largest national park covering an area of 3,555 sq km (1,373 sq miles). This is a stronghold of the snow leopard, as well as the blue sheep.

Far less remote is the Shivapuri National Park, which occupies the northern rim of the Kathmandu Valley. It was gazetted in 2002, and though it lies within easy reach of the capital, it contains a remarkable amount of pristine forest and is renowned for its abundant birdlife – a total of 177 species have been recorded, as well as leopards, brown bears and over 100 species of butterfly.

Other parks include the Sagarmatha National Park encompassing not only the peaks and valleys of the southern half of Mount Everest (Sagarmatha is the Nepali name for Everest) but also many Sherpa villages. Sagarmatha is probably the best place in Nepal to catch a glimpse of the endangered monal pheasant. Further west Langtang National Park, in the mountain region of central Nepal just south of the Tibetan border, was gazetted in 1976. The red panda lives mainly on bamboo in the forest canopies of this park.

THE SNOW LEOPARD

Hard to spot, snow leopards are formidably well adapted to life at altitude, with thick fur and an exceptionally long tail, used for both extra insulation while at rest, and for balance while hunting on precarious mountainsides. They live above the tree line, and prey on the various breeds of mountains goats, as well as smaller mammals.

Snow leopards range throughout the great mountain ranges of Asia, from the Bhutan Himalaya to the Hindu Kush, but they are so thoroughly elusive that estimates of their numbers are notoriously unreliable. Naturalists believe that between 300 and 500 individuals live in Nepal.

The yeti

Nepal's most famous wild animal dwells in the shady realms of cryptozoology, a mythological creature that has left just enough tangible traces to keep people guessing.

Early European travellers in the Himalayas tended to dismiss as colourful legend the local stories of giant ape-men, but in 1899 the explorer Laurence Waddell

The footprint of the "abominable snowman", taken near Mount Everest in 1951.

described finding a trail of huge footprints. In 1921, during a reconnaissance of Everest, Colonel C.K. Howard-Bury saw dark figures moving across the snow and, as shadowy accounts continued to drift in, the yeti took shape in Western consciousness. Its usual name comes from the Tibetan *yeh-teh*, meaning "man of the snowy places", but it gained an additional glamour in 1921 when a journalist mistranslated an alternative appellation, *metoh-kangmi*, as "abominable snowman".

As the race for the summit of Everest quickened, the yeti kept pace. Sherpas told climbers stories of the creature, and the critical moment came on a November afternoon in 1951 when Eric Shipton took clear photographs of a trail of huge footprints high on the Menlungtse Glacier. Suddenly it seemed that there really was something out there.

Hunting the yeti

According to the Sherpas there are three distinct species of yeti. There is the huge, cattle-eating *dzu-teh*, which is almost certainly based on accounts of bears. There is also the *thelma*, a small ape-like creature which may be inspired by garbled reports of the Assam gibbon. Then there is the *miche*, a man-sized ape for which there is no obvious explanation. Fossils of giant orang-utans have been found in the Himalayas, and some claim that such a creature could have endured in the remotest valleys.

Several expeditions have set out in search of the yeti, though none have returned with more than images of melting footprints. In 1960 Sir Edmund Hillary led a foray bound by a Nepalese government order that no yetis were to be killed. Hillary's team borrowed the famous "yeti scalp" from the monastery at Khumjung; it turned out to be made from the hide of a wild goat.

Yet despite a singular lack of concrete evidence, and despite the general scorn of the scientific community, the yeti myth has proved remarkably resilient. A Sherpa girl was reportedly attacked by a yeti in 1974; mysterious whistling cries are still heard, and strange footprints still appear on high mountainsides. The author Bruce Chatwin – never shy of spinning a yarn – claimed to have seen yeti tracks in the Gokyo Valley in 1983.

Myth and reality

Perhaps the most convincing interpretation of the yeti comes from the great Tyrolean mountaineer Reinhold Messner. In 1986, at nightfall in a remote valley in eastern Tibet, he had a terrifying encounter with a huge beast that moved upright through the forest. The experience sparked an enduring fascination with the yeti, and he soon discovered that throughout the region tales of the yeti were often indistinguishable from stories of the *chemo*, or Tibetan brown bear, which often walks on its hind legs.

Messner became convinced that all tangible evidence for the yeti was based on traces of the brown bear. But he argued that those who would dismiss the yeti as nothing more than a bear, and those who would cling fervently to the idea of a real undiscovered ape-man, were all missing the point. The yeti, ultimately, is a synthesis of a real creature, probably a bear, a mass of indigenous folklore, and the universal human inclination to populate the wild places with fabulous beasts.

Rice paddy fields.

ENVIRONMENTAL ISSUES

Threatened by the pressures of population growth and tourism, Nepal's fragile environment needs to be carefully managed.

The Himalayas might seem like a mighty, immutable presence, but Nepal's natural environment is remarkably fragile. Precipitous hillsides struggle to hold their thin cladding of topsoil; fast-flowing mountain streams are sensitive to the slightest changes in the landscape around them, and high-altitude ecosystems maintain only the most tenuous of balances in their extreme surroundings. Add to that the fact that Nepal is one of the poorest countries in Asia, almost completely without historical infrastructure, riven by violent political instability and corruption over recent decades, and with a booming urban and rural population, and it's easy to understand that the environment here has been placed under severe pressure.

While all the neighbouring countries of South Asia face significant environmental and developmental challenges, Nepal has its own peculiar set of circumstances. The people of Nepal make much of the fact that theirs was the one corner of the Indian subcontinent never properly brought under the aegis of the British Empire. But while nationalists may take an understandable pride in that point, a record of unbroken indigenous sovereignty has bequeathed certain disadvantages. When India gained independence from Britain it inherited an established infrastructure of roads and railways, as well as the rudiments of urban planning in the larger cities and a quasi-modern government bureaucracy to boot. Nepal had no such legacy to lean on. In the mid-20th century the place had scarcely a single stretch of navigable road; the tiny strips of railway that inched into the Terai were themselves merely British-built offshoots of the Indian network, and there were no power plants or municipal services. Nepal has been struggling to catch up ever since.

Nepal's mountains attract many tourists.

Social impact and road-building

The people of Pokhara saw their first mechanised wheel attached not to a whistling steam train, a car, or even a bicycle, but to the undercarriage of a DC-3 which winged its way down over the mountains and landed on a grassy field in the middle of the town in one afternoon in 1952. This, then, is a country that was shunted from the medieval era to modernity without time to catch its breath.

Roads were deemed essential to the existence of a functioning 20th-century nation-state, and willing foreign governments were ready to build Nepal all the roads it wanted. From the 1950s onwards, twisted coils of asphalt began to creep up the steep mountainsides, down the foothill slopes, along river gorges and across the plains. In 1956 the Indian-funded Tribhuvan Highway opened, connecting Kathmandu to the border at Raxaul. A few years later the first long-haul buses and trucks came belching into the capital, bringing with them the dust and fumes that have clogged the air there ever since.

Other roads soon followed, with Nepal's giant neighbours often vying for funding control. The people of Pokhara would quickly get used to the wheel: in the early 1970s the Prithvi Highway opened, built with Chinese funding this time, connecting the town to Kathmandu. From these and other highways, tributary roads burrowed off into the hills, linking once-isolated townships to the outside world. Two generations ago the journey from Chitwan to Gorkha took some three weeks; the trail traversed perilous malarial jungle and traced swift-flowing rivers and beetling ridges. Today that same journey takes less than three hours. The road may be pitifully thin – a fragile thread of asphalt stretched across a precipitous mountainside – but it is plied by a torrent of sleek Japanese cars and smoke-belching buses.

Speedier access and communications have introduced new concepts and a growing materialism from the outside world, and have also facilitated major political changes and greater interaction within. Today Gorkha is full of the trappings of the modern age. Corrugated roofs reflect sunlight off new buildings, and the bazaar is festooned with brightly coloured plastic goods. In addition to the obvious material advancement, the roads have brought profound demographic changes. Once-isolated villages are now populated by people from all over Nepal and beyond.

Nepal's landscape is a delicate ecosystem.

Until very recently, there were six directions in Nepal's remote hills: north, south, east, west, up and down. The terrain kept the inhabitants of these lands isolated, but also self-sufficient. The construction of roads has eased the vertical and introduced unaffordable "luxury" goods into a formerly cashless society. The roads, the rapid mechanisation and the dramatic population growth, meanwhile, have also brought enormous new pressures on the environment, far beyond the problem of exhaust fumes.

Deforestation

Many of the developmental and environmental problems that Nepal faces are the product of a

In the rainy season, landslides can wipe entire sections of Nepal's highway network off the map and lead to dozens of deaths in mountain villages.

rapidly growing population. The most recent census recorded a national population of 26.5 million, with an annual growth rate approaching two percent and rising. Some projections predict that the total population will have reached 44 million by 2035.

The country's road network has been steadily expanding since the 1950s.

Nepal's Middle Hills, including the Kathmandu Valley and the area around Pokhara, have long suffered from the pressures of population. This was always the most fertile and hospitable tranche of the country – above the malarial swamps of the Terai, but well below the snowline.

Steep hillsides are notoriously unstable, prone to landslides and severe erosion during the monsoon rains, but the intrepid inhabitants of the hill country have long known how to live with nature. Mountainsides were sculptured with meticulously engineered terraces to save the soil from washing away and to help grow food on dry slopes with only a thin skin of topsoil. Long before development specialists were talking about ecological sustainability, mountain dwellers practised rotational grazing on the summer pastures and learned how to tap the forests' resources for food, fodder and fuel without doing permanent damage. Across Nepal, many communities had laws governing the use of their forests, some with forest guards and public deliberations over what penalties transgressors should pay.

By the early 20th century, however, a rapidly increasing population was already placing unsustainable pressure on traditional land management, and forcing emigrants out of the overcrowded Middle Hills to seek new plots in the steamy Terai, or to seek fortunes in towns or abroad. The trend has only continued, with yet more pressures added to environment and rural society over the last half-century.

In hindsight, the most disastrous single blow to Nepal's forests was the nationalisation of all forest lands in 1957, a centralist decision which did away with the traditional interest of local communities in nurturing resources and land, and which instigated uncontrolled overuse to the detriment of all. Meanwhile, hill farmers have been driven to cultivate ever-steeper slopes, slashing forests and shrubs to make way for the plough. Booming birth rates and burgeoning families mean that sons inherit ever-smaller plots of land, making agriculture as a sole occupation less and less viable. In some communities, a traditional land distribution system long prevented the division of land among successive generations. The Sherpas, for example, passed all land to the eldest son, leaving younger brothers the choice of sharing his household (and his wife), striking out alone elsewhere, or joining a monastery. This practice also served to keep the population stable. The system has largely broken down as the Sherpa regions have come into increasing contact with the outside world, and in some areas found an unexpected prosperity from mountain tourism – and tourism, of course, has brought its own environmental challenges.

The impact of tourism

Many of Nepal's environmental and social concerns preceded the arrival of tourists, but the demands of an alien influx have undoubtedly left a major mark on a country that was for so long isolated from the outside world. Some of the effects of tourism are positive; others are not.

Agricultural land by Phewa Tal.

SACRED MOUNTAINS

The pre-Vedic tribes of the Indo-Gangetic plains were probably the originators of the enduring Hindu reverence for mountains, which later blended with localised mountain-veneration in the remote communities of the foothills. The idea of the looming mountains as the home of gods and ancestral spirits was an obvious one: they were clearly an essential life-giving force. During the rains they act as monsoon traps, bringing moisture to farms and water to rivers; in the dry season, the snow and glaciers are huge storage systems for ice that melts in spring, supplying water to downstream areas. The snows themselves, meanwhile, rest on the border between the temporal and spiritual, between earth and heaven.

Many peaks – Annapurna for example – were regarded as the manifestations of individual deities. Shiva in particular – customarily represented as the phallic *lingam* on a smaller scale – was often seen in the vast form of the Himalayas. The Siwalik Hills are sometimes said to represent the matted tangles of his long, uncut hair. Mount Kailas, meanwhile, rising above the Tibetan Plateau in a perfect cone, is another symbol of Shiva.

The ultimate sacred mountain is Mount Meru, the mythological centre of the universe in both Buddhist and Hindu theology. It is said to be a million kilometres high – surely a challenge for even the hardiest mountaineer.

Tourism pumps millions of dollars of hard currency into Nepal every year. Trekkers and mountaineers contribute a particularly significant share, staying for longer periods than most other tourists and carrying their cash into far-flung corners of the country. The labour-intensive mountain tourism industry provides a wider and more equitable distribution of cash in the hills, where it is most needed. Crucially, that income is more likely to stay within the country than to be spent outside on costly imports to furnish Western-style hotels and restaurants.

There is great potential to develop tourism-related cottage industries and food production to further stimulate the rural economies – for example setting up small-scale handicraft centres in the hills and organising vegetable and meat production units to supply trekkers with fresh produce. Elsewhere, tourism has revived the dying arts and crafts of Bhaktapur, and has fuelled a successful carpet industry.

However, while the positive impacts of tourism in terms of standard of living are obvious, there are also manifold downsides. The influx of foreign exchange contributes to inflation and disrupts local markets. Newfound income is making its way into mountain communities accustomed to centuries of subsistence living, driving prices for basic commodities way beyond what farming families can afford. Foreigners' intended generosity, or ignorance over a fair price, has the same effect: at Khumbu's Namche Saturday market, the only people who buy eggs, which until recently were carried on porters' backs out of respect for the mountain god who dislikes chickens, are lodge-owners who can pass the hefty price on to trekkers. Tourism is also a notoriously volatile trade in countries with a record of instability. During the worst years of the Maoist uprising many outlying areas

Farm oxen.

HEALTH HAZARDS

Nepal's child mortality rate stands at around 43 deaths for each 1,000 live births – close to the global average, but 10 times that of the United Kingdom. However, in remote rural areas the statistics are far grimmer. In parts of Humla, infant mortality stands at a shocking 30 percent. Most die of respiratory infections exacerbated by breathing the smoke of cooking fires, and from diarrhoea caused by insanitary conditions. Across the country, contaminated water kills thousands of children. Some experts say a tap with clean drinking water would do more for the general health of most of Nepal than a fully equipped hospital.

were wiped off the tourist map, and a slew of news stories featuring street demonstrations and heavy-handed crackdowns in Kathmandu saw bookings cancelled and top-end hotels standing empty.

Perhaps most serious of all are the concerns about the lack of sustainable tourism development, and the strains placed by mountaineering and trekking on the fragile environment of the Himalayas. The Barun Valley in eastern Nepal and the trekkers' "highways" through Solu Khumbu and the Annapurnas are stark examples of the damage done by uncontrolled visitor traffic. In the Barun, the moraines are crumbling because mountaineering expeditions on Mount Makalu have uprooted the dwarf junipers to burn at the base-camp kitchen. The Annapurna Sanctuary's frail ecosystem is also slow to recover from the tramping boots of the thousands of trekkers who visit it every year.

The denuded forests all along the Annapurna and Solu Khumbu trails are tragic reminders of the effects of indiscriminate tourism. While admirable initiatives such as the Annapurna Conservation Area Project (see page 115) require trekkers to be self-sufficient in cooking fuel, in many areas lodge-owners still rely on wood supplemented by yak dung to cook for hungry guests. Even when trekking agencies supply kerosene for their clients' cooking needs their large groups of attendant porters may be left to gather their own fuel.

At lower altitudes, rapid and unplanned tourism development has an impact in a country where basic utilities are rarely adequate. On the once sleepy shores of Pokhara's lake, a rash of ugly concrete hotels has sprouted across what was tranquil farmland a decade ago, placing additional strain on water supplies and sewerage systems and leading to increasing challenges in waste disposal.

According to some estimates, one job is created for every 7.5 tourists who visit Nepal, a ratio that rises to one job to every three visitors in the trekking industry.

Deforestation is all too evident on this mountain slope.

KEEPING NEPAL TIDY

Like the proverbial goose that lays the golden egg, the tourism goose also fouls its nest. Conservation-minded planners in Nepal, conscientious trekking agencies and trekkers are worried that more hikers will mean more litter along the mountain trails. Toilet paper, biscuit wrappers and non-biodegradable rubbish mark the over-trodden trails and campsites, although growing ecological awareness has prompted clean-ups in many areas. Toilet facilities, if they exist at all, are often poorly maintained or dangerously close to water sources.

Slowly, awareness is growing. Initiatives such as the Annapurna Conservation Area Project are teaching the lodge-owners how to build decomposing toilets and to keep rubbish pits. Some trekking agencies have vowed to take away their trash, but the problem then remains of how to dispose of it at roadheads or airfields.

Even the high mountains have not escaped the problems. At almost 8,000 metres (26,250ft), the South Col of Mount Everest was long dubbed the "world's highest rubbish dump". The area is still strewn with discarded oxygen cylinders, stoves and climbing gear, but in recent years clean-up sessions and a "garbage bond" that all expeditions must deposit in Kathmandu have improved matters.

Mitigation efforts

There is, however, some cause for optimism. Some ecologists argue that deforestation in the hills has largely been halted, and recent satellite data reveals that forest cover has actually increased by as much as 15 percent in parts of the Middle Hills in the last 30 years, even as deforestation continues apace elsewhere. This is largely due to the success of Nepal's community forestry programme, which has attempted to undo the damage rent by the earlier nationalisation of forests through handing back the task of managing forests to local communities.

The Annapurna Conservation Area Project (ACAP) has worked effectively to mitigate the negative impacts of tourism (see page 115) on both environment and society, and management initiatives in other mountain areas are attempting to emulate its success. Debate, meanwhile, continues over the opening up of more new trekking areas. Prior to 2002 large areas of Nepal's mountains were entirely off-limits to foreign tourists; today most of the country is officially open, although permits are required for visits to many remote areas. In some cases – most notably Mustang – these permits are prohibitively expensive, keeping tourist arrivals to an elite few. Residents and champions of some newly opened regions point to the unimagined wealth that uncontrolled tourism has brought to the Annapurnas and the Everest region, while others point to the bare hillsides and plastic waste in the same places and urge caution. It has even been suggested that heavily burdened regions such as Khumbu be closed for several years to allow them to rejuvenate. Regardless of the various arguments offered, most agree that the government and tourism industry must plan for the future so as not to spoil the object which attracts tourists here in the first place.

Hydroelectric potential

The great rivers of the Indian subcontinent all rise in and around the high mountains of the Himalayas, and the various tributaries that descend through Nepal's Middle Hills

Accessing clean drinking water remains a problem.

ANNAPURNA CONSERVATION AREA

In the remote valleys around the Annapurna Range, an innovative organisation has been working for the past 30 years to mitigate the negative impacts of tourism and to ensure sustainable development – with remarkable success. The Annapurna Conservation Area Project (ACAP) was set up in 1986 by the King Mahendra Trust for Nature Conservation and granted management control of the 7,600-sq km (2,934-sq mile) Annapurna Conservation Area. Around 90,000 tourists visit annually and obviously have a significant impact on the local environment and society. However, under the careful aegis of the ACAP, earlier deforestation has been reversed; lodge owners have been trained in environmentally friendly fuel use and waste management, and the funds raised by the Rs2,000 fee that all tourists entering the Conservation Area must pay have been ploughed back into a large number of social welfare projects. One of the organisation's key current activities is establishing alternative trails where new roads have eaten into traditional trekking routes.

A core principle of the ACAP is to ensure that local people – and there are some 120,000 within the Annapurna region – are active stakeholders in the management process. The success of the ACAP has prompted attempts to organise similar systems in areas such as Makalu-Barun near Everest.

eventually feed into mighty watercourses such as the Ganges. The sheer volume of water heading south from the mountains, along with the hilly terrain, has made Nepal an obvious location for the development of hydroelectric power.

The country's total feasible hydropower potential is estimated at 83,000 megawatts, one of the highest potentials per capita in the world. So far, however, a mere 700 megawatts have been harnessed, largely with the help of foreign investors. The main obstacle to more dams is the initial capital needed for construction, and the Nepalese government's traditional reluctance to accept large-scale assistance from the rival superpowers that hem it in – India and China. Both countries have made concerted overtures to both Nepal and other small countries along the line of the greater Asian mountain system: Bhutan and Burma have more readily accepted Chinese and Indian investment in hydroelectricity.

Amongst the generation plants that have already been built in Nepal is the Upper Bhote Koshi Project, opened in 2001 at a cost of US$98 million. The plant produces up to 44 megawatts. Still larger is the Kali Gandaki plant, built with Asian Development Bank aid and generating up to 144 megawatts.

In Nepal's national parks, the dos and don'ts for travellers can be summarised very simply by the old saying: "Take nothing but pictures, leave nothing but footprints."

Hydroelectricity is not without its opponents, however. There is a risk that large numbers of people may be displaced by the rising waters upstream of the huge dams that are constructed to power the turbines, and environmentalists point out that the projects can severely disrupt the natural flow of sediments and nutrients downstream. Endangered species, such as the Gangetic river dolphin, may also be badly affected by changes such as this.

A huge new project is currently planned on the West Seti River in the far west of Nepal. The plant is expected to produce up to 750 megawatts of power, although campaigners claim it will have a devastating impact on the surrounding area. In 2012 the Nepalese government agreed a contract that would allow the project to be part-funded by the same Chinese power company that built the controversial Three Gorges hydroelectricity plant in China.

Ethical, sustainable tourism is the key to Nepal's future.

Responsible travel

Individual travellers can make a difference with minimum effort by making simple but informed decisions about where to stay and eat, and what to buy.

The idea of "sustainable tourism" is well established, and for over a decade the government of Nepal has been touting the term in its travel slogans. However, in a country with myriad political challenges, and a tourist industry dominated by fragmented private enterprise, much of the onus must fall on the tourists themselves. "Responsible travel" is the watchword. Even the most ethically minded travellers can be forgiven for wanting simply to enjoy their holiday and for protesting that individual efforts are meaningless. However, small choices can, collectively, make a big impact.

Ethical trekking

Is the hot water in your lodge heated by solar power? Is the inn constructed from local materials? Is it necessary to order food from a lodge menu that requires exotic ingredients shipped in from the far-off cities if there are local dishes available?

Trekkers can help save the forests simply by bringing adequate clothing and thus not relying for warmth on the lodge fireplace. Group trekkers can choose a trekking company which is environmentally conscientious, one which uses kerosene on all treks, and which provides warm clothing for porters on high-elevation treks.

With so many agencies and operators offering very similar packages – from cultural tours to treks and safaris – it is always worth looking at the final destination of the cost of your holiday. There are plenty of long-established and highly professional local operators in Nepal, offering everything from cultural tours to treks and safaris. Choosing their services over those of a large foreign operator is not only better for Nepal; it will likely save you money. Many specialist tour operators also have programmes to channel a portion of their profits into community or environmental projects in the areas where they work.

Cultural considerations

Across Nepal – in both rural and urban areas – it has become common to see schoolchildren asking for sweets or money. Most local NGOs strongly discourage handouts. If you want to give, donate to a local charity, and if you want to provide books or learning materials, give them directly to a school.

Locals observe tourists wherever they go, looking at what they wear, carry and eat. Tourism often raises expectations of local people, which by itself may not be bad, but these expectations may be unrealistic and can enforce a sense of inferiority. Guidebooks customarily advise you to avoid ostentatious displays of wealth, but whatever you wear or carry is already ostentatious, such is the enormous income disparity between visitors and most locals. Still, it pays to make an effort, and above all

Local travel agencies advertising.

to be respectful of local customs and friendly and engaging with local people.

Ethical shopping

Simple choices can also make a difference when it comes to shopping. Avoid any animal products that may have been made from an endangered species. The famed *shahtoosh* pashmina, made from the wool of a rare Tibetan antelope, is officially banned in Nepal, but it may be offered under the counter by traders in Kathmandu – it is, of course, to be avoided, as are antiques of questionable provenance.

A number of NGOs have helped to set up fair-trade handicraft outlets, such as Sana Hastakala (see page 328), and in Tibetan refugee areas there are carpet-weaving cooperatives.

Climbing to Thorung La Pass on the Annapurna Trail.

Trekking on Ama Dablam in the Everest region.

TREKKING

For those who seek breathtaking mountain scenery, nothing can beat the exhilarating treks of the Himalayas.

Mention Nepal and many people will immediately think of trekking. In the 50 years since the first commercial trekking party headed into the Himalayas the country has become one of the foremost destinations for those bent on plotting a path along mountain trails. A huge service industry has developed around trekking, from travel agencies and equipment suppliers to German bakeries, and whole generations of mountain villagers have grown up working in the tourist trade. As a consequence Nepal offers some of the best facilities in the world for those wishing to walk independently but with the minimum of planning and equipment. There are few other countries where you can set out on a month-long trek, far from surfaced roads, and yet be confident of a comfortable bed and a slice of hot apple pie every evening.

Conversely – to quieten the complaints of those who would condemn the well-trodden "teahouse trails" of Annapurna and Everest as overly commercialised – almost the entire length of Nepal is now open for exploration.

Once closed areas have been gradually derestricted, and the end of the Maoist insurgency has opened any number of formerly restive regions to walkers. There are always new passes to be pioneered, and as often as not there are empty trails plied only by local villagers just across the valley from the busiest of routes. And above all – quite literally – the mountains remain the same indescribable epic of rock and ice that drew the first trekkers to Nepal, and that will be drawing them forever more.

Trekking history

The first people to ply the mountain trails were local traders and pilgrims, but the antecedents of organised trekking in the Himalayas can be traced to the colonial era. Early European explorers often headed for the hills in a fashion that would leave most modern trekking parties looking positively primitive. A group of just half a dozen travellers might require hundreds of porters to carry their equipment. Full-size dining furniture might be lugged on yak-back across mountain passes, and supplies ranged from vintage port to tinned salmon. Such expeditions, cumbersome though they may have been, were often bound for the blank spaces on the map; more closely analogous to today's hikers were the Victorian "sportsmen". Hunting was a passion for many a red-blooded British officer in 19th-century India, and heading for the high mountains of Kashmir and Ladakh in

On the trail to Manang.

pursuit of mountain goats was a favourite way to fill the lengthy periods of leave.

Nepal, however, lay outside the British Empire. It was strictly closed to foreign visitors, and besides a few hardy trespassers neither explorers nor hunters had the pleasure of testing its trails. It was only in the mid-20th century that the Nepalese government began to ease the restrictions. The high peaks of the Himalayas were already the object of fevered attention from mountaineers, and they leapt at the chance to approach them from the south without the need for a lengthy loop through Tibet. In 1949 a small British expedition led by Bill Tilman was allowed to visit Langtang, north of Kathmandu. Late in the season, with the monsoon approaching, Tilman, Peter Lloyd and an aspiring but as yet unknown Sherpa by the name of Tenzing Norgay (see page 137), crossed the Bhote Kosi and explored the extreme southeast corner of the Ganesh Himal.

Jimmy Roberts, the founding father of trekking in Nepal, retired to Pokhara in 1975, where he kept an extensive collection of rare Himalayan birdlife. He died at the age of 81 in 1997, and his ashes were scattered in the Seti Khola River.

The Marsande River.

TREKKING CHARGES

In 2008 the Nepalese government introduced the Trekking Information Management System (TIMS), a registration card that all trekkers must obtain from the Tourist Reception Centre in Kathmandu, or through a travel agency. The card costs US$20 for individuals, or US$10 for group members. Trekkers also have to pay a national park or conservation area entry fee – usually Rs1,000 – where applicable. These can also be paid at the Tourist Reception Centre, or on the ground at park checkpoints. Permits for trekking in restricted areas, including parts of Mustang and Dolpo, are still required, and are obtained through trekking agencies.

These first foreign explorers all shared a willingness to endure the rigours of a rugged landscape cut off from all communication and modern amenities. There were no roads, and for months only local food and basic camping accommodation were available. However, within a few years the successful first ascent of Everest had created an enduring public fascination with Nepal in the West. At the same time a nascent tourism industry was beginning to blossom in Kathmandu.

It was only a matter of time before someone thought to organise a commercial trek – not for the purpose of exploration, mountaineering or hunting, but simply for the pleasure of moving through the mountains on foot. That man was Lieutenant-Colonel Jimmy Roberts. After an illustrious military career in a British Gurkha regiment, Roberts had gone on to forge a stellar reputation as a mountaineer. He was already familiar with the logistics of organising trips deep into the Himalayas, and so in 1964 he placed an advert for a trek to the base of Everest in *Holiday* magazine. Three sporting middle-aged American women responded and an industry was born.

Tourism continued to grow rapidly in Nepal.

Trekking through cornfields at the base of Thulo Shyafru.

Between 1966 and 1970 the number of annual visitors quadrupled to 46,000, and by 1976 it had topped 100,000. And as Roberts' "Mountain Travel Nepal" – still operating today – and other new agencies led increasing numbers of well-heeled travellers into the hills, cash-strapped hippies were branching out on their own from Pokhara, paying a few paisa for overnight accommodation in village homes, and laying the foundations of the low-budget teahouse trails.

Today well over half a million tourists visit Nepal each year. Many of them come to trek; their journeys contribute a huge share to the country's foreign exchange earnings and the business which was pioneered in the 1960s now provides a living for thousands of Nepalese people.

The impact of trekking

Mountain tourism has been a boon to many of Nepal's hill economies, providing seasonal jobs to hundreds of skilled guides and to the thousands of subsistence farmers who work as porters. Those with the acumen to set up a business – be it a Kathmandu-based travel agency or a simple guesthouse on a mountain trail – have seen their fortunes transformed.

During the 1950s mountaineering rescued the economy of the Khumbu region just at the time that trans-Himalayan trade with Tibet was obliterated. With the Chinese invasion and the

GREAT HIMALAYA TRAIL

If the Annapurna Circuit is not enough, there is always the option of tackling the Great Himalaya Trail. A number of explorers have made successful traverses of the Himalayas, and the idea of a connected trail running the entire length of the range has been discussed for decades. In recent years the 1,700km (1,000-mile) Nepalese section of the route has been plotted, running from Kanchenjunga to Humla. It typically takes around six months to complete the route. Eventually it is hoped that the trail will stretch all the way from Nanga Parbat in Pakistan, the Himalayas' western buttress, to Namcha Barwa, its eastern rampart in Tibet.

closing of the border Sherpa farmers who for centuries had depended on trade as a source of supplemental income suddenly faced very tough times.

However, the Sherpas, living year-round at elevations upward of 3,000 metres (10,000ft) and long familiar with transnational commerce, proved naturally adept at scaling precipitous heights and well equipped for dealing cannily with outsiders. As trekkers followed in the footsteps of mountaineers to Everest Base Camp their fortunes flourished. Many of those who so diligently served the early foreign expeditions went on to found their own successful trekking agencies.

A hike along a stone trail in the Khumbu Valley, past colourful teahouses.

The closure of the Tibetan border left the Thakali people of the upper Kali Gandaki Valley in the Annapurna region facing a similar dilemma. The choice was to continue trying to eke out a living in this high mountain desert, without the supplemental income from trade, or to move to lower, more productive farmlands far from their heritage and homeland. Tourism arrived at exactly the right moment, and many Thakalis turned their well-reputed traders' inns, known as *bhattis*, into trekkers' lodges. Today they offer the cleanest, most popular accommodation on the circuit, and serve some of the best food.

There were no roads to speak of when the first foreigners arrived in Nepal. Not even the capital was linked to the outside world. In 1950, the French mountaineer Maurice Herzog – who had just climbed Annapurna in the first successful ascent of a peak over 8,000 metres (26,250ft) – had to walk all the way from the mountain to Kathmandu to receive his royal congratulations. The members of the team with frostbitten toes were carried on the backs of porters. The earlier Everest explorations had set out from Darjeeling through Tibet, but even after Nepal was opened to foreigners, the trek from Kathmandu to Everest Base Camp still took more than a month.

Nowadays Nepal's east–west road network plus its scattering of mountain airstrips make the mountains much more accessible to visitors. In just a few weeks, trekkers can reach Everest Base Camp and see much of Khumbu, or make a circuit of the Annapurna Massif.

Trekking accommodation

The mushrooming of small lodges along popular trekking routes, many converted from homes that once served the trans-Himalayan traders, has sped tourism's inroads into certain mountain areas. The early budget travellers of the 1970s often wandered the hills unaccompanied, staying in village teahouses, coining the phrase "teahouse trekking".

Villagers quickly caught on and built more lodges. Most are simple shelters offering wooden cots and basic meals. Others, particularly in the Annapurna and Solu Khumbu areas, are more elaborate, patterned after Alpine huts with wood-panelled dining areas, private rooms and flower-filled terraces. Conveniently spaced along the trail, teahouses have enabled independent trekkers to travel light, without tent, food or cooking gear.

While lodge-to-lodge trekking gives a taste of Nepalese home life, along with the charm can come problems. Not all lodge kitchens are hygienic and sickness out on trek can delay travellers. Despite the cosmopolitan menu offerings on the busiest trails, elsewhere the monotony of *dal bhat* (rice and lentils) can be tedious, as can the lack of privacy.

At a more rarefied level, however, many modern trekking agencies provide a service echoing the elaborate provisions of the 19th-century expeditions. Indeed, Nepal has set the standards for quality adventure travel worldwide. It is not uncommon for a group of six trekkers to be accompanied by an entourage of 12 to 15, comprising porters, a cook and several kitchen staff, two or three Sherpas and a chief guide called a *sirdar*. The porters carry all food needed for the trip, camp equipment including sleeping and dining tents, stools and the members' personal belongings. Each night, camp is made by a stream or water source, often in an idyllic setting beneath the snow-crested Himalayas or overlooking a jigsaw pattern of brilliant green rice paddies. The *sirdar* (usually fluent in English) oversees the entire operation from the hiring and firing of local porters, to seeing to the clients' comfort and safety.

Many first-time trekkers, especially those used to backpacking, feel their conscience twinge upon seeing the porters, some just teenagers, bend under two or three duffel bags. But to mountain villagers, who have transported all kinds of loads on foot for centuries, such work is a chance to earn hard cash to buy household necessities. The camaraderie that grows between clients and staff, despite there often being a language barrier, is heartfelt and is one of the bonuses of trekking with an agency.

Breaking camp in Thame.

Planning a trek

Many trekkers find it easier to let the experts do all the preparatory work. The assistance of a professional agency in arranging for any relevant permits, equipment, food and transportation, hiring reliable staff and arranging porter insurance (a government requirement) can certainly help make the most out of limited time.

Treks need not be long and rigorous: they vary from two to three days' walking on relatively easy, low-level terrain to demanding expeditions of three weeks or more. Do not make the mistake of thinking a short trek is necessarily easier – there are still hills and less time to get fit and into the trek rhythm.

Trekking with an agency, self-sufficient in all aspects, often allows you the chance to penetrate deep into the Himalayan wilderness, leaving behind overcrowded trails.

Entry into the Dolpo and Mustang areas requires special permits and is limited to those with a registered agency who must be self-sufficient in food and fuel. Dolpo and other remote, food-poor regions simply do not have any surplus to support teahouse trekkers.

Most of Nepal's trails have been in use since long before the arrival of trekkers. They began life as routes of communication between villages. The only trails that didn't are those leading to mountain base camps.

In 1978, a total of 18 summits ranging in height from 5,587 metres (18,330ft) to 6,654 metres (21,830ft) were opened as "trekking peaks" to groups for a relatively modest permit fee. In 2002, a further 15 mountains were added.

Pack donkeys crossing a cable bridge.

Trekking peaks

For many adventurous travellers the thought of standing on some sky-scraping summit, looking out across the roof of the world, has an intense allure that surpasses even the appeal of crossing the highest of trekking route passes. Financial and physical constraints may leave Everest the preserve of an elite few, and the other 8,000-metre (26,250ft) peaks are off-limits to all but professional mountaineers, but there are plenty of more modest mountains.

SPECIALITY TREKS

A more structured approach and an educational forum appeals to some travellers, and companies now combine scientific, religious, photographic, art and cultural study with a trekking holiday. Tour leaders double as instructors in yoga, herbal medicine, photography, birdwatching, sketching and cultural interaction. Family treks can be planned with a less ambitious schedule, finding time for children's activities and extra staff to tend to youngsters. Pony treks are conducted out of Pokhara for those who do not wish to or cannot walk. A group of blind trekkers recently set a world record climbing 6,654-metre (21,830ft) Mera Peak.

The term "trekking peak" may suggest that an ascent requires no further skills than the ability to walk. This is most definitely *not* the case. To attempt a trekking peak it is necessary to have some previous climbing experience as well as knowledge of how to use equipment such as ropes, ice axes and crampons. It is true that some designated trekking peaks are routinely climbed without complications by large commercial groups – these include, amongst others, Island Peak, Mera, Tent Peak and Chulu Far East. However, this is mostly due to good leadership and the use of experienced Sherpas to carry loads, fix ropes and blaze the trail.

Also among the 33 trekking peaks are several coveted summits, such as Kusum Kanguru, Hiunchuli, Fluted Peak and Kwangde, which over the years have acquired a reputation of inaccessibility that has attracted some of the world's most respected climbers. They offer technical routes of the highest standard and are not suitable for even the most ambitious amateur.

The trekking peaks are concentrated in the Khumbu and Annapurna regions, which are also the most popular trekking destinations. As yet there are no trekking peaks in the more recently opened areas such as Dolpo, Dhaulagiri, Manaslu or Kanchenjunga. However, as once off-limits regions continue to open up, more mountains will likely be made accessible.

The draw of the mountains

Beyond Nepal's obvious practical advantages in terms of trekking infrastructure, many trekkers find that mountain journeys here have a unique appeal that is hard to define. This is doubtless partly down to fantasies of Shangri La and the Orientalist notions that have become inextricably tangled with authentic indigenous mysticism and mythology in Western imaginings of Nepal, Buddhism and the Himalayas. But what many trekkers find most easily and obviously attractive, aside perhaps from the mountains themselves, is the Nepalese people. This is a country that has been welcoming travellers since the earliest days of trans-Himalayan trade, and as a consequence remote and impoverished villages have often tackled the psychological challenge of dealing with an influx of affluent aliens with remarkable success. Old traditions of hospitality have not been subsumed by commercialism, even on the busiest trails, and neither has a well-attested local sense of humour. Village life often seems to continue unhindered by the clicking of trekking poles and the rustle of Gore-Tex.

The word trek comes from Afrikaans and means "to pull". It entered English after the "Great Trek" – the movement of Boer settlers through South Africa in the 1840s, but was popularised as a term for mountain hikes in the mid-20th century.

A kitted-out guide in the Thorung La Pass.

The endless mountain scenery – so radically removed from familiar cityscapes – has its own calming impact, and the process of slowing the tempo of life to walking pace is a sure way of peeling away the stresses of modernity. The low ache of limbs after a day's steady progress along the trail, a wordlessly smiling interaction with a gaggle of village children, the simple reward of a home-cooked meal in a rustic lodge, time to read a battered paperback in the afternoon sunlight, the sense of glorious isolation as a mountain valley fills with blue shadow at dusk, and the breathless release in the cold wind at the apex of a high pass with a new prospect beyond: these are the unquantifiable yet uniquely addictive rewards of trekking in Nepal. One visit is rarely enough.

Mountaineers push for the summit of Everest.

MOUNTAINEERING

Nepal has long been a mecca for mountaineers, and the slopes of its giant peaks have been the stage for some of the most dramatic stories of exploration and endurance.

Eight of the world's ten highest mountains rise from Nepal's mountain spine, and many of its lesser peaks stand higher than the tallest summits of Europe and America. The entire northern flank of the country is defined by the Himalayas, a saw-toothed ridge of rock and ice levitating over the horizon in a long white line. This, then, has always been the ultimate playground for the mountaineering elite. The stories of the first ascents of the awesome 8,000-metre (26,250ft) giants of Nepal's mountain pantheon are true epics of human endeavour. In a frenetic "Golden Decade" in the mid-20th century, hardy European climbers struck out into the unknown from bleak base camps, and with a seemingly ceaseless momentum ticked off each of the highest tops in the space of just ten years.

That, however, was not the end of the story, for once the summits had been reached there was always the challenge of a return by a more difficult route, of an attempt without supplemental oxygen and of climbing harder and faster than those who had gone before. And for those willing to lower their sights by a thousand metres or so, there is still an appealing array of virgin summits waiting to be bagged. Today, with organised fee-paying parties slogging up Everest in their dozens each year, it's easy to forget that mountaineering remains a deadly serious business. Many of the pioneers came to grief on the slopes, and though tweed and hobnailed boots have given way to synthetic fibres and plastic, avalanches, sudden storms and the sheer crippling impact of altitude remain as hazardous as they ever were. Himalayan mountaineering is still a sport engaging the outer limits of endurance.

Tents at Everest Base Camp.

The early days of mountaineering

One summer's day in 1949 the British mountaineers Bill Tilman and Peter Lloyd, and a young Nepalese Sherpa called Tenzing Norgay, made it to the top of a 5,928-metre (19,450ft) mountain by the name of Paldor in the Lantang region. Tilman's party was one of the very first foreign expeditions to be allowed into the remote upper reaches of Nepal, and Paldor was the first of the country's mountains to be scaled by outsiders. Within the next ten years, however, Tilman's successors would have tackled every 8,000-metre (26,250ft) mountain from Kanchenjunga to Dhaulagiri.

Mountaineering as a sport had begun in Europe a century earlier. Mont Blanc had been climbed for the first time in 1786, but it was only in the second half of the 19th century that the sporting gentlemen of Victorian Europe overcame their horror of rugged landscapes and began to scale mountains for pleasure. The early name for the sport – alpinism – reveals its dominant venue, and until the turn of the 20th century most mountaineering took place in the Alps of France and Switzerland.

Early attempts at Himalayan peaks took place either within British domains, or via the Tibetan back door. The true age of mountaineering in Nepal – and the brief but heady heyday of high-altitude pioneering – began in the years following Tilman's ascent of Paldor. Nepal was a far cry from Switzerland, however, and the effort required to tackle 8,000-metre (26,250ft) mountains was enormous. Vast armies of climbers, porters and Sherpas marched towards base camps to lay siege to the peaks. The expeditions often lasted for months.

Once the virgin summits had been scaled, those at the cutting edge of mountaineering looked towards more difficult routes on steeper ridges and faces. In recent years, Himalayan endeavour has taken individuals to the very limits of endurance in solo, turbo-charged, record-breaking climbs. The mountains have seen an increasing number of wild performances – flying in hot-air balloons or hang-gliding and ski descents. However, high-performance Himalayan climbing remains the preserve of the extreme few because of the high level of expertise required, and the majority of mountaineers are confined to the traditional approach using established camps, fixed ropes, bottled oxygen and the careful assistance of armies of Sherpas.

Lhotse's south wall.

Everest – highest point on earth

In 1921 the ill-fated mountaineer George Mallory described his first view of Mount Everest. It was, he wrote, "a prodigious white fang excrescent from the jaw of the world".

As the highest peak on earth it was inevitable that Everest – known as Sagarmatha in Nepal and Chomolungma in Tibet – would gain a disproportionate amount of attention from mountaineers. Standing at 8,848 metres (29,028ft), it had challenged the skills of British climbers over several decades prior to the opening up of Nepal. Mallory and others had been obliged to attempt the mountain from the north, and they had always met with failure and sometimes with tragedy. The closing of Tibet coincided fortuitously with Nepal's opening, and efforts were renewed to find a way to the top from the south side of the mountain.

The leading lights of British mountaineering were soon probing the corrugated foothills east of Kathmandu to find an approach to the Khumbu. Fresh from his assault on Paldor, Bill Tilman traced a way to the foot of the Khumbu icefall in 1950 and the following year Eric Shipton's team went through the icefall to reach the Western Cwm. The British, however, were not alone in their endeavour and all but lost the great prize in 1952 when a Swiss expedition came close to success.

The following spring another British expedition headed for the mountain. The team was led by Colonel John Hunt, a highly decorated British Army officer who had been born in Shimla in the foothills of the Indian Himalayas. Hunt had been chosen for his organisational skills as well as his mountaineering experience, and he presided over the summit attempt with a keen military eye. His team was made up of the finest mountaineers of Britain and New Zealand as well as the most experienced local Sherpas and an accompanying army of 350 porters.

Hunt had his men inch their way up and down the mountain over the course of some seven weeks, ferrying equipment and supplies to a series of staging posts on the South Face. During a crossing of the Western Cwm in late April, one of the New Zealand climbers, Edmund Hillary, was saved from tumbling into a crevasse by the same Sherpa who had stood with Tilman and Lloyd on the summit of Paldor four years earlier. A powerful bond was forged.

On 2 May Charles Evans and Tom Bourdillon made the first reconnaissance of the Lhotse Face, reaching the expedition's highest point so far. On the same day, Hillary and Tenzing – now climbing as a team – made a staggering return journey from Base Camp to Camp IV in a single day. By now these two partnerships – Evans and Bourdillon, and Hillary and Tenzing – had emerged as the most likely candidates for the final summit bid.

Throughout May the team continued to inch its way up the mountain, with more high camps and supply dumps established, followed by further retreats to lower altitude. On 21 May Wilfred Noyce and Sherpa Annullu made it to the windswept saddle of the South Col at 7,906

Female Bangladeshi mountaineer Wasfia Nazreen crosses a ladder over a crevasse on Everest.

THE EVEREST 1996 DISASTER

Despite its formidable challenges, Everest is big business. Climbers pay up to US$25,000 in permit fees and there are many specialist companies ready to shepherd paying clients up the peak. This increasing commercialisation was at least partly responsible for the mountain's worst disaster on 11 May 1996.

That year a total of 14 separate groups swarmed around Base Camp. They included professional teams, a commercial expedition headed by New Zealander Rob Hall, and another group led by American Scott Fischer. The members of the commercial groups had paid up to US$65,000 to be guided to the summit. Though the south ridge is barely wide enough to accommodate a single climber, 33 people headed for the top on the same day. This human "traffic jam" led to tragedy as dozens of climbers were caught out by a sudden storm, high on the mountain and late in the day. Hall and Fischer were among the eight who perished, along with two clients and another guide.

The disaster became the subject of TV specials and books, most notably the bestseller *Into Thin Air* by survivor Jon Krakauer. In the aftermath there were forceful calls for a halt to the practice of taking enormous sums of money from anyone wishing to tackle Everest regardless of their expertise. However, business is business; 234 people summited in a single day in 2012.

metres (25,938ft) and set up Camp VIII. The following day Hillary and Tenzing set out on another mad dash for supplies, making a return journey over almost a vertical mile between camps IV and VIII in less than 30 hours. With all the toing and froing, by the end of the month they would, in effect, have climbed the mountain three times.

On 26 May Evans and Bourdillon headed up from Camp VIII in clear weather. They made it to the South Summit, just 100 metres (300ft) short of the highest point, but with their oxygen tanks malfunctioning and time running short they were forced to turn back. Two days later Hillary and Tenzing set out for their own attempt. By nightfall they were 8,500 metres (27,900ft) above sea level. They bivouacked at the bleak spot christened Camp IX, and the following day they continued upwards. Hillary led the way over the vertical outcrop of rock, now known as the Hillary Step, which formed the final hurdle. From there onwards it was a simple slog up the ultimate snowy incline.

Camp 1 at 6,100-metre altitude on the Manaslu.

Reaching the top

At 11.30am on 29 May 1953 Edmund Hillary and Tenzing Norgay stepped on to the summit of Everest, the highest point on the surface of the earth. "I stretched out my arm for a handshake," Hillary later wrote, "but this was not enough for Tenzing who threw his arms around my shoulders in a mighty hug."

The pair had proudly brought to a close what has been called "an Edwardian quest for the poles of the earth". Their achievement also made for an auspicious start to the new Elizabethan age as the news reached London in time for the coronation of Queen Elizabeth II on 2 June – though some have pointed out that it was fitting that the final triumph in the era of British imperial exploration belonged to a beekeeper from the furthest corner of the Commonwealth and a Sherpa from the only South Asian country that had never been part of the Raj.

Kanchenjunga – third highest

Visible in the distant mists from Darjeeling and with access from Sikkim, the history of Kanchenjunga (8,586 metres/28,169ft), like that of Everest, goes back far beyond the opening of Nepal to foreigners. This mountain is the best documented of all, having been attempted as early as 1905. It was once believed to be the highest mountain on earth.

Kanchenjunga is vast: some 13km (8 miles) in length by 8km (5 miles) wide. After an optimistic British reconnaissance in 1954, the Alpine Club and the Royal Geographical Society of

Nepal's only challenger for the high-altitude crown is Pakistan, which has the peaks of K2 (world's second highest) and Nanga Parbat, and which claims the world's greatest concentration of mountains over 7,000 metres (22,966ft).

London dispatched an expedition the following spring, led by Charles Evans. This particularly strong team included George Band, Joe Brown, Norman Hardie and Tony Streather.

After a hard struggle, plagued by avalanches and not without mishap – a young Sherpa died after falling into a crevasse – Band and Brown left for the summit, using artificial oxygen, on 25 May 1955. They had chosen a route on the southwest face and, having gained the main ridge, the top lay beyond a tower of grey-green rock. Joe Brown, acclaimed as the finest rock climber of his generation, managed to overcome this obstacle to reach the easy slope leading to the summit with George Band following close behind. Hardie and Streather reached the top the following day.

The four climbers kept a promise made to the Sikkimese not to stand on the sacred summit of the highest point so, although credited with the first ascent, Kanchenjunga remained the "Untrodden Peak".

Lhotse – fourth highest

For a long time the fourth peak, Lhotse (8,516 metres/27,940ft), had no separate identity from its dominating neighbour to the north, Mount Everest. Even its name, which translates as "South Peak", implies that it is not a mountain in its own right. Once Nepal opened its borders the error became all too clear – from the south Lhotse forms an enormous mountain wall.

Although no attempt was made until 1953, the Swiss-American mountaineer, Norman Dyhrenfurth had identified a route to the summit from the South Col of Everest. European and US assaults did not make much impact until spring 1956 when a Swiss expedition established a Base Camp beneath the Khumbu icefall. Poor weather hampered progress, but on 18 May Swiss climbers Ernest Reiss and Fritz Luchsinger reached the summit of the world's fourth highest peak.

The great Italian mountaineer Reinhold Messner had declared in 1977 that Lhotse's formidable south face "may well be impossible". But in the autumn of 1990 it was successfully climbed by a large Russian expedition consisting of 17 mountaineers and 13 Sherpas. Two Soviet members, Sergei Bershov and Vladimir Karataev, reached the summit on 16 October.

Makalu – fifth highest

Makalu (8,463 metres/27,766ft), in eastern Nepal, is the highest peak between Everest and Kanchenjunga and is a mountain of exceptional beauty. As with Annapurna I (see page 135), the French have laid claim to Makalu, although

Sherpas evacuate an injured climber.

US and New Zealand teams had explored the region earlier the same year. The French reconnaissance party headed by Jean Franco visited the mountain in 1954, returning a year later with an expedition consisting of the very best guides France could muster, among them Jean Couzy, Lionel Terray, Guido Magnone and Serge Coupé. They were also ably supported by an expedition doctor, geologists, 23 Sherpas and an army of no fewer than 315 porters.

Their route to Camp 5 on the Makalu La proved technically very difficult and required a large amount of fixed rope. From there, they were able to traverse easy slopes on the north side. A steep couloir gave on to the knife-edged ridge leading to the summit, first reached on 15

May 1955 by Couzy and Terray. In total eight Frenchmen and one Sherpa reached the summit that year.

The outstanding success of the expedition was down to a combination of a strong, well-organised and highly motivated team aided by the finest equipment and blessed with good weather. The latter is critical to success on 8,000-metre (26,250ft) mountains.

Cho Oyu – sixth highest

Cho Oyu (8,201 metres/26,906ft) rises 32km (20 miles) west of Everest. Known as the "Goddess of Turquoise", it was the third of Nepal's 8,000-metre (26,250ft) peaks to be climbed.

At the top of Cho Oyu.

The first reconnaissance took place in 1951, followed a year later by the British Cho Oyu expedition led by Eric Shipton. Once again this was an experienced team including many who would go on to take part in the first ascent of Everest. From the Nangpa La, the traditional yak trade route to Tibet, a route was spotted that looked feasible, but the north flank was out of bounds in closed Tibet.

In 1954 a Viennese author, Dr Herbert Tichy, put together an expedition which proved the exception to the rule that 8,000-metre (26,250ft) mountains demanded large-scale expeditions. With only two European companions he organised a lightweight party very much in keeping with the "small is beautiful" philosophy expounded by Tilman and Shipton. Accompanied by half a dozen Sherpas they left Namche Bazar for the Nangpa La in late September. Finding a way through the icefall they established a high camp but a storm drove them down and left Tichy with frostbitten hands.

Shortly afterwards two members of a Franco-Swiss expedition to nearby Gauri Shankar arrived at Cho Oyu Base Camp, hoping to steal a march on Tichy. The Austrians had not yet fully recovered from their earlier attempt, but spurred on by the arrival of the competition, they were driven back onto the mountain. An epic ascent followed. Unable to use his damaged hands, Tichy had to be helped over the rock band, but at 3pm on 19 October 1954 the summit was reached by Tichy, Sepp Joechler and Pasang Dawa Lama. It was the first ascent of an 8,000-metre (26,250ft) peak in Nepal without the use of artificial oxygen.

Dhaulagiri I – seventh highest

The name of this spectacular peak means, innocuously enough, the "White Mountain", but Dhaulagiri (8,167 metres/26,795ft) has come to be known as the mountain of storms and sorrows.

Dhaulagiri I was the first 8,000-metre (26,250ft) peak to be attempted by the French, who abandoned a planned attempt on Annapurna I in 1950 in order to try and climb it. They failed, and ironically Dhaulagiri I ended up as the very last 8,000-metre (26,250ft) peak in Nepal to be climbed.

> *On reaching Cho Oyu's summit, Herbert Tichy felt "a sense of complete harmony such as we had never known before, an almost unearthly sense of joy – worth far more than a few frozen fingers."*

Seven expeditions attempted Dhaulagiri, including one sponsored by President Perón of Argentina, but it was not until 1960 that a massive Swiss attempt achieved success via the northeast spur. Supplied by a small glacier plane piloted by Ernst Saxer, the expedition brought to an end the "Golden Decade" of mountaineering in Nepal by putting two

The recommended rate of ascent is 500 metres (1,650ft) per day at altitudes above 3,000 metres (10,000ft). Beyond 5,000 metres (16,500ft) more caution is required.

Europeans and two Sherpas on the summit on 23 May 1960.

Manaslu – eighth highest

Europeans lay claim to the first ascents of many of the Himalayan giants, but Manaslu (8,163 metres/26,781ft) is determinedly an Asian mountain. Not only was it first climbed by a Japanese expedition, but a high number of Nepalese, Japanese and South Korean lives have been lost on this daunting peak whose name simply means "Soul" in Sanskrit. During two days of avalanches in the spring of 1972 15 men lost their lives in the largest single death toll yet on any Nepalese peak.

The mountain itself is stunning. The highest of a cluster of glorious summits including Peak 29 (Ngadi Himal) and Himal Chuli, Manaslu stands in splendid isolation between the Annapurna Range and Ganesh Himal.

Between 1953 and 1956 the Japanese mountaineering elite served their Himalayan apprenticeship by making several attempts on Manaslu. In 1956 the venerable 62-year-old expedition leader, Yuka Maki, led an approach via the Buri Gandaki. The Japanese set about climbing the northeast face, despite some disputes with the local villagers. Toshio Imanishi and Sirdar Gyalzen Norbu Sherpa reached the rocky pinnacle of the summit at midday on 9 May.

Annapurna I – tenth highest

Annapurna I (8,091 metres/26,545ft) was the first 8,000-metre (26,250ft) mountain to be climbed when, in 1950, a strong French expedition, led by Maurice Herzog, reached the summit by the north face. Having failed to find a way up Dhaulagiri, they had turned their attention to the tenth highest peak.

The team included such notable Chamonix guides as Gaston Rebuffat, Lionel Terray and Louis Lachenal. Lachenal and Herzog reached the summit, but deteriorating weather and a series of mishaps almost turned success into

Altimeter from Mallory and Irvine's ill-fated Everest expedition.

COPING WITH ALTITUDE

Heroic feats by the world's finest mountaineers have led the way for less experienced climbers eager to test their skills in Nepal's mountains. But the impact of altitude is a serious concern even for those going no higher than Base Camp. From around 2,400 metres (8,000ft) most people begin to feel the effects of altitude. As you climb higher the impacts are complicated by the threat of a condition known as acute mountain sickness (AMS), which results when you ascend faster than your body can adjust. Headaches, nausea and tiredness are the commonest symptoms, but they can progress to pulmonary or cerebral edema. Below 5,500 metres (18,000 ft) the onset of AMS is usually slow enough to allow an easy descent to lower altitude. Above that height, the syndrome can strike with devastating speed.

What does this mean for the Himalayan trekker heading for Everest Base Camp (5,357 metres/17,575ft) or the Thorung La (5,416 metres/17,764ft)? Simply allowing adequate time to acclimatise is the single biggest measure that can be taken to prevent problems with altitude. Mountaineers aiming for the summit of Everest spend weeks in the rarefied air at the base of the mountain allowing their bodies to adjust. On a smaller scale the same approach is essential on the trail, with rest days to allow for acclimatisation, and a willingness to turn back should more severe symptoms develop.

disaster. Herzog suffered severe frostbite during an epic descent, resulting in amputations. Despite this, their success is generally credited with heralding the beginning of the "Golden Decade" of climbing on Nepal's 8,000-metre (26,250ft) mountains.

Problems at high altitude

At Mount Everest Base Camp (5,357 metres/17,575ft) the amount of oxygen in each breath is half that of sea level. At the top of Everest this has shrunk to one third of that at sea level. The tiny amount of oxygen in each breath at such altitude was at one time thought to be inadequate to support human exertion, and it was long believed – by both scientists and mountaineers – that climbing the mountain without supplemental oxygen would prove impossible.

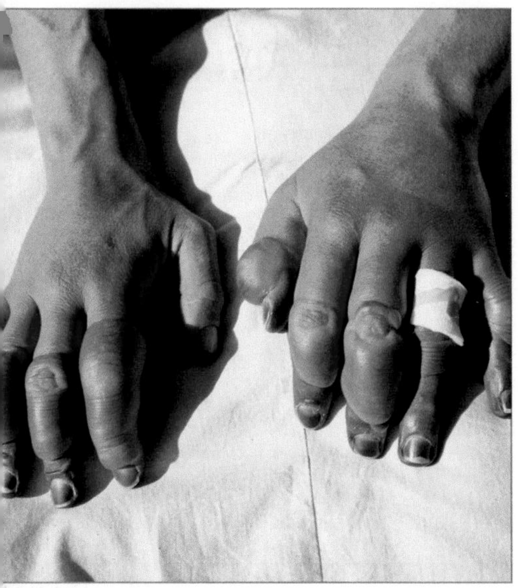

Frostbitten fingers are one of the commonest hazards to the ill-prepared mountaineer.

In 1978, however, Reinhold Messner and Peter Habeler set off from the Base Camp of Everest with no artificial oxygen and went all the way to the summit. So firmly entrenched was the notion that bottled air was essential that some people cast doubt on their claims when they came down. However, Messner definitively silenced the naysayers two years later when he left Base Camp on the Tibetan side of Everest, alone and without oxygen, and went to the summit and back in four days.

Messner himself, the first man to climb all 14 of the world's 8,000-metre (26,250ft) peaks, speaks of the environment above 8,000 metres (26,250ft) as the "death zone". At these heights the body cannot adjust; it can only slowly deteriorate. Thinking is slowed and neurologic function is impaired; simple tasks and decisions become cripplingly difficult, and hallucinations are common – some climbers have reported hearing the sound of orchestras playing. Breathing rapidly in the high dry air accelerates dehydration, and fluid must be painstakingly replaced by chopping ice, melting it on a stove, and forcing the lukewarm result past parched lips. Climbers sometimes spend up to five hours a day replacing the liquid that has been lost. Four or five days above 8,000 metres (26,250ft) is the most time that a human has spent at that height and survived.

Human beings evolved at low altitude, but the potential to adapt to even these great heights is built into our bodies. Breathing automatically accelerates; red cell production is increased to carry more oxygen, and given time, the body adjusts. If you were deposited by helicopter at the summit of Everest, without prior acclimatisation and without artificial oxygen, you would lose consciousness within minutes and die within hours. The fact that a properly acclimatised person can live and function at that height is something of a genetic miracle, and testament to the human body's astonishing capacity for adaptation.

The weather at high altitude can change abruptly. Winds can exceed 200kph (125mph) and temperatures drop far below freezing. Frostbite is a constant risk but stopping to warm frozen toes or fingers can be impossible in precarious, exposed situations. The throat and lungs become parched and coughing becomes severe and uncontrollable. Climbers have been known to break their ribs during severe coughing spells and have had to climb down unassisted with this additional pain. Avalanches too are a constant concern, and the near impossibility of effecting a rescue operation at high altitude means that a small tumble and a minor injury can prove fatal. Regardless of new technology, commercialisation on Everest, and the eye-catching stunts of cutting-edge mountaineers, climbing into the "death zone" will always be an enormous and potentially deadly undertaking.

Heroes of the Himalayas

Huge mountains attract larger-than-life figures, and the great Himalayan climbers of the last 100 years have been true giants.

The first true mountaineering celebrity was George Mallory (see page 267). Not only did he enter legend by climbing higher than anyone before him and by vanishing forever into the summit clouds on 8 June 1924; he also set a precedent for mountaineering as a literary endeavour with his erudite letters and his infamous quip: "Because it is there".

Sir Edmund Hillary

The first man to climb Everest successfully was far removed from Mallory's Cambridge sophistication. Edmund Hillary was a lanky New Zealand beekeeper. Born in Auckland in 1919, he had cut his teeth climbing in New Zealand's Southern Alps. In 1951 Hillary took part in a reconnaissance of Everest led by Eric Shipton – another pioneering giant of mountaineering – and in 1953 he and his Sherpa companion Tenzing Norgay became the first men to reach the top of the world. "We knocked the bastard off" was Hillary's summary of the achievement.

Though he went on to climb many other Himalayan mountains, in later life Hillary was best known for his charity work amongst the Sherpas of Khumbu. The organisation which he founded, the Himalayan Trust, now supports schools and hospitals throughout the region. Hillary and was made an honorary Nepalese citizen in 2003. He died in 2008.

Reinhold Messner

The brightest star of the generation that followed Hillary was the seemingly superhuman South Tyrolean Reinhold Messner. Born in 1944, Messner made his first successful attempt on a Himalayan peak in 1970, reaching the 8,126-metre (26,660ft) summit of Nanga Parbat in Pakistan. During a gruelling descent Messner lost six toes to frostbite, and his brother Günther was killed in an avalanche. However, he went on to become the first man to scale all of the world's 14 giant 8,000-metre (26,250ft) peaks, as well as the first to climb Everest without supplemental oxygen, and the first solo climber to reach the world's highest summit. Messner is widely credited with perfecting the fast, lightweight, alpine style of Himalayan mountaineering first espoused by another mighty Tyrolean, Herman Buhl (who died in 1957 on Chogolisa in the Karakoram).

Modern mountaineers

The first woman to climb Everest was Junko Tabei from Japan, who reached the summit in 1975 after a near-catastrophic avalanche lower on the mountain. She later became the first woman to scale the highest peaks of every continent, and remains a highly respected mountaineer and conservationist.

The Himalayas continue to claim victims from amongst the elite. In 2009 the 40-year-old Slovenian Tomaž Humar, regarded by many as an obvious successor to Reinhold Messner, died after falling on the South Face of Langtang Lirung. He had achieved international renown following his epic solo ascent of the south face of Dhaulagiri, one of the most dangerous climbs in the Himalayas. Amongst the current top flight of mountaineers is Britain's Kenton Cool, who has reached the summit of Everest 11 times.

Apa Sherpa.

Many Sherpas have followed in the pioneering footsteps of Tenzing Norgay to join the mountaineering elite, and many of the significant records for Everest ascents are held by Sherpas. Apa Sherpa, originally from the village of Thame on the Everest Trail, has climbed the peak a record-breaking 21 times, while Pemba Dorje Sherpa holds the record for the fastest ascent. In 2003 he climbed from Base Camp to the summit in eight hours and 10 minutes.

Nothing can compare with the adrenaline rush of running the rivers of Nepal.

RAFTING AND KAYAKING

Flowing down from the Himalayas through the country's varied landscapes, rivers offer one of the most popular and exhilarating ways of seeing Nepal.

Fed by the glaciers of the world's highest mountains and the snows of the Tibetan plateau, Nepal's feverish rivers provide exciting opportunities for whitewater rafting or kayaking in an ever-changing landscape. On their way to India's sacred Ganges, the waters surge through Himalayan gorges, traverse rugged foothills, course between tropical forests and meander across the Terai plains.

River running is one of the best and most thrilling ways to abandon the cities and experience the rural life of Nepal without investing the time and energy required for a long trek.

Whitewater history

The Himalayan rivers are considered sacred to the Nepalese. They are places for cremation, and the confluence of two rivers is usually revered as a holy site. Water brings life, but the rivers are also feared, which explains why even on the hottest days it is unusual to spot locals swimming in the cooling waters.

The first people to run Nepal's rivers were therefore foreigners. Exalting at the opportunity to test virgin waters, early pioneers set about exploring the rivers soon after Nepal opened its borders in the late 1940s. Sir Edmund Hillary attempted a journey to the source of the Sun Kosi in 1968. Various rivers were kayaked and rafted by visiting adventurers, including Michael Peissel who tried to drive a hovercraft up the Kali Gandaki in 1973.

But it was not until 1976 when American Al Read started running and charting the rapids of the Trisuli and upper Sun Kosi rivers that river running began in earnest under the guidance of foreign experts. Today local guides handle the rafts and supervise the camp staff. Kayaking, meanwhile, has burgeoned in recent years.

Enjoying all that Nepal's rapids have to offer.

Many of the major rafting companies also organise kayaking trips; there are specialist kayaking operators too, and both experienced and novice paddlers from around the world come to test their mettle in Nepal's white water.

Selecting a river

Nepal's rivers link the mountains and plains like blue veins. Tumbling out of the highlands they are sometimes violent, sometimes calm, but always beautiful. Trips are available from one to 13 days on different rivers, all offering dramatically different experiences.

The Karnali, descending from Tibet's Mount Kailas, is Nepal's mightiest river. Ten days of wilderness, excitement and exploration make this the classic Himalayan expedition. Finish with a visit to Bardia National Park (see page 295) for an unbeatable combination.

The Sun Kosi, Nepal's "River of Gold", traverses 270km (165 miles) through the beautiful Mahabharat Range. At the right flow it's an incredible combination of white water, scenery, villages and quiet, introspective evenings along what many people consider to be one of the world's definitive river journeys. An eight- or nine-day trip finishes in far eastern Nepal.

In the far east the snows of Kanchenjunga feed a challenging cousin of the Sun Kosi. The Tamur combines one of the best short Himalayan treks over a 3,000-metre (10,000ft) pass with an exhilarating river expedition.

The Trisuli, named after Shiva's trident, runs parallel to the road from Kathmandu to Mugling before joining the Gandaki river system and becoming the Narayani River. One- to three-day trips along this river can end at Chitwan National Park (see page 288).

The Annapurna and Dhaulagiri mountains feed the Kali Gandaki west of Pokhara. This is known as the river of the goddess Kali, and at the confluence of tributaries there are temples and cremation sights in abundance. A three-day trip is a good wilderness alternative to the Trisuli.

The Marsyangdi is one of the most challenging whitewater runs in the world. A five-day trip combines a short trek with demanding rafting and stunning scenery.

The Bhote Kosi, three hours from Kathmandu on the road to Tibet, is a turbulent mountain stream offering the steepest rafting in Nepal. An overnight stay at one of the luxurious resorts on the banks can include bungee jumping, canyoning or trekking.

The Seti is an excellent two- to three-day trip in an isolated area with easy rapids and can be combined with trekking and jungle safaris, while the Bheri, in western Nepal, is a trip with great jungle scenery and lots of wildlife. This is one of the best fishing rivers and can be combined with a visit to Bardia National Park.

The Arun River from Tumlingtar makes an excellent three-day wilderness trip, although getting to the starting point is rather complicated and time-consuming.

Seasons and expeditions

Late September to mid-December and March through to early May are the best times to run rivers in Nepal, avoiding both cold and rain. The water temperature is only 6–10°C (43–50°F) but the air is clear and warm.

Most rafting trips let passengers partake in the paddling; others allow you to relax and enjoy the fun while the guide controls the boat using centre-mounted oars. Either way, rafting combines tranquillity and thrills.

Many of Nepal's rivers are remote and unpredictable and a responsible rafting company is vital to ensure safety. The best outfitters provide all the essentials for a safe and fun trip: fully trained staff, self-bailing rafts and safety kayakers on more difficult rivers, rescue equipment, high-buoyancy lifejackets and helmets, first-aid and raft-repair kits, tents and transport.

An Ultimate Descents raft.

On longer trips, time is set aside for hiking into side canyons, visiting nearby villages and swimming in the river or lazing on beaches. River rafting is an exceptional experience anywhere, but with Nepal's unique topography, cheerful people and traditional culture it is all the more rewarding.

Himalayan rivers can fluctuate dramatically and as a general rule the higher the flows the more challenging the rafting will be.

Mountain biking

Nepal's dirt roads provide the perfect surface for mountain biking, from the tortuous trails of the mountains to the lowland plains of the Terai.

Mountain biking arrived in Nepal in the mid-1980s with a few of the more adventurous expatriates who would set out of a weekend to explore the network of trails that crisscross the slopes and trace the ridges of the Kathmandu Valley. Intrigued children in distant villages would run up shouting "*Gearwallas Aayo*! – the people of the geared bikes have come!" For the current generation of village children a flash of colour and a rattle of gears as a party of mountain bikers whizzes past is as much a part of the everyday scene as birdsong and buffaloes.

Biking in the Kathmandu Valley

The Kathmandu Valley remains the premier venue for mountain biking, with a wide range of routes offering everything from a sedate meander through the rice fields, to a thrilling downhill run. Plenty of agencies in Kathmandu rent bikes, and some people choose to head out on their own to explore the valley independently. There are large-scale maps of the valley available from bookshops in Thamel, some with specific biking routes marked. Once beyond the congested ring road the air freshens up quickly, and getting away from traffic and tarmac is remarkably easy.

There are also many Kathmandu-based companies offering guided biking trips around the valley. These range from half-day tours to three- or four-day trips around the valley rim. The so-called "Scar Road" in the Shivapuri National Park (see page 199) is a popular and rugged single-track route, and the other trails that thread their way through the thick green forest of the park offer multiple variations.

The route from the heights of Nagarkot all the way down to Kathmandu is a popular downhill run, and multi-day trips include the route from Kakani to Mulkharka, Chispopani and Nagarkot. Biking companies often lead less experienced groups on easy-going trips around Tokha, due north of the city.

Cross-country routes

Further afield, the 12-day Kathmandu to Pokhara route traces the old trading route through the hills (see page 211). Another long-haul biking trail follows the old Raj Path down to the Terai at Chitwan National Park. There are also plenty of opportunities for biking from Pokhara.

More ambitious trips go from Pokhara to Bardia National Park in the far west, or from Kathmandu to the Arun Valley in the east. Some cyclists even set out to complete the Annapurna Circuit or Everest Base Camp trek by bike – though inevitably there will always be significant uphill sections on any route such as this.

Mountain biking on the Annapurna Trail.

Amongst the well-established biking companies offering high-quality equipment and experienced guides is Himalayan Mountain Bikes (www.bikeasia.info), located in Chaksibari Marg in Thamel. They set up classic routes and offer trip advice, as well as exciting combination adventures that team up biking with canyoning, hot springs, rock climbing, paragliding, rafting, monastery tours or jungle treks. Dawn till Dusk (www.nepalbiking.com) is another reliable outfit that offers good rates on valley and country tours.

ADVENTURE SPORTS: FROM PEAK TO JUNGLE

From hunting to rafting and paragliding, few countries in the world offer the range of sporting opportunities available in Nepal.

Anyone with a taste for adventure and a certain level of fitness will find something to thrill them within Nepal's varied landscape.

Commercial river rafting got under way in 1976 when the company Himalayan River Exploration started plying the Seti and Trisuli rivers, floating visitors down to Chitwan National Park. Today it is one of the country's most popular sports. Adventurous kayakers regularly shoot the rapids as well, and many rafting companies also arrange kayak rentals. For more a sedate waterborne activity, row boats are readily available on Pokhara's Phewa Lake; when the afternoon winds pick up, search out a sailboat for hire.

Spring and autumn are the best seasons for sport fishing in lowland lakes and rivers. Trout-like species make the best eating and the large *mahseer* provide the most exciting sport.

In the 19th century Nepal was a favoured ground for hunting big game, a privilege granted only to invitees of the ruling Rana regime. However, the rhinos and tigers of Chitwan are now strictly protected and hunting is only permitted with a licensed guide in designated areas.

Modern mountaineering has become a test of ingenuity using high-tech gadgetry, and other forms of lightweight, ultra-modern sports equipment have found niches in the Himalayas, particularly mountain bikes.

Canyoning, rock climbing and bungee jumping are all ways to take advantage of the vertiginous landscapes of Nepal.

A paraglider untangling himself after a flight at Pokhara.

A view from above of the Peace Pagoda in the Pokhara Valley, enjoyed in a microlight aircraft.

Climbers ascend an ice wall.

An elephant safari in the jungle.

AIRBORNE NEPAL

The Himalayan thermals that rise between the ridges of Nepal's mountains – not to mention the stunning scenery over which they circulate – have made the country popular for aerial sports. Pokhara is the hub for airborne adventures, with a daily deluge of paragliders descending from the heights of Sarangkot. Avia Club Nepal (www.aviaclubnepal.com) runs microlight flights over the Pokhara Valley and beyond, as well as organising paragliding trips. The spectacular Zip-flyer Nepal, stretching down from Sarangkot 1.8km (1 mile) to the valley floor, offers a chance to fly while still safely connected to the ground.

A number of serious adventurers have recently taken paragliding to new heights – quite literally – in combining mountaineering ascents with airborne descents. In 1988 the French mountaineer Jean-Marc Boivin completed the first paragliding descent of Everest – having first had to haul his gear all the way up the summit. A small but growing number of BASE jumpers have started executing spectacular free-fall leaps at altitude. In 2013, 60 years after Tenzing and Hillary climbed Everest, Russian Valery Rozov jumped from 7,220 metres (23,687ft) up on the North Face.

Sports such as paragliding combine high-tech equipment with nature's most spectacular views.

Mountain bikes are ideal on Nepal's labyrinth of dirt roads, pedalling around the Kathmandu Valley or venturing into the mountains.

Nepal's whitewater thrills are divided among five commercially operable rivers and attract thousands of tourists every year.

Spectacular views on the Annapurna Trail.

An ancient woodland trail in the Langtang-Gosainkund region.

A rhino at the Chitwan National Park in the Terai.

On the steps of Nyatapola Temple in Bhaktapur.

PLACES

A detailed guide to the country, with principal sites clearly cross-referenced by number to the maps.

Lohan Chowk in Bhaktapur.

Nepal is defined by the Himalayas. They rise in a mighty ridge of rock and ice, in clear view from the windows of aeroplanes banking in for the final approach to Kathmandu. There is much more to the country than snowy summits, however. The heartland of Nepal has always been the Middle Hills. Deep within this mesh of beetling green ridges is the fulcrum of the country, the Kathmandu Valley, a 570-sq km (220-sq mile) pocket of level land more laden with treasures than a maharaja's jewel box.

A visit to Nepal generally begins in the capital, with a wide-eyed wander through the medieval cityscape of Durbar Square. These historic quarters may fray away into an edgy modernity, but the past is still writ large in the neighbouring royal cities of Patan and Bhaktapur, and a little further afield the valley offers a seemingly endless procession of temples, slow-paced Newari villages and epic ridge-top views.

A stunning mountainous landscape.

It would be easy to devote an entire visit to Nepal to the Kathmandu Valley, but there is much else to see. West through the knots of the Middle Hills lies Pokhara, with its serene lakeside setting and its glittering mountain backdrop, and other quiet hill towns dot the country's midriff – Gorkha, Bandipur and Tansen, all worthy of a detour. The other side of Nepal lies to the south in the Terai, a belt of low-lying tropical land between the hills and the Indian border. The tiger-haunted national parks at Chitwan and Bardia are the major attractions here, along with fabled historical sites including Lumbini, the birthplace of the Buddha.

And then, of course, there are the mountains, an unavoidable presence in the north. Most visitors head for one of three mountain areas – the Annapurna region with its long-established trails, the Everest area, or the Langtang-Gosainkund-Helambu region due north of Kathmandu. But beyond these is a vast array of untrammelled outlands for the adventurous traveller to explore: Manaslu, Kanchenjunga, Mustang and more.

NEPAL
INDIA
HIMALAYA
Gangdisê Shan
Karnali
Seti
Mahakali
Bheri
Rapti
Dhaulagiri
Lumbini
Mahabharat Range
Siwalik (Churia) Range
Khaptad National Park
Rara National Park
Shey-Phoksundo National Park
Sukla Phanta National Park
Bardia National Park
Dhorpatan Hunting Reserve
Kanti Himal
Gautam Himal
Dhaulagiri Himal
Nanda Devi 7817
Nanda kot 7010
Api 7132
Saipal 7031
Kapchuli 6850
Chhunsadaha 6108
Gorakh Himal 6088
Chanla Pass 5293
Namia Pass 4968
Kanjiroba 6883
Sanla Pass 5584
Sanda Bhanjyang 5124
Dhaulagiri I 8167
Annapurna I 8091
Machhapuchhre 6993
Guerla Mandatashan 7728
Lucknow
Kanpur
Allahabad
Gorakhpur
Bahraich
Faizabad
Ayodhya
Jaunpur
Pokhara
Bhairahawa (Siddharthanagar)
Nepalganj
Dhangarhi
Mahendranagar
Jumla
Simkot
Darchula
Dipayal
Tanakpur
Birendranagar
Tulsipur
Ghorahi
Butwal
Tansen
Baglung
Kushma
Jomsom
Gonda
Sultanpur
Rae Bareli
Fatehpur
Azamgarh
Deoria
Basti
Tanda
Ghazipur
Unnao
Sitapur
Hardoi
Shahjahanpur
Lakhimpur
Balrampur
Nanpara
Burang
Khojarnath
Darma
Kolti
Chainpur
Silgarhi
Sanphebagar
Mangalsen
Baitadi
Patan
Dandeldhura
Jajarkot
Dunai
Ringmo
Kaigau
Jaglungompa
Khanigau
Tsarang
Chhusang
Muktinath
Tukuche
Annapurna
Ghorapani
Lumle
Behani
Waling
Tamghas
Piuthan
Libang
Sallyan
Chhinyu
Kohalpur
Bhaluban
Patharkot
Bartun
Taulihawa
Pakri
Nautanwa
Nichlaul
Siswa Bazar
Padrauna
Karnali
Seti
Ghaghara
Sarda
Babai
Rapti
Tila
Sama
Ganga (Ganges)
Yamuna
Humla Karnali
Mugu Karnali
Chamliya Khola
Barban Khola
Mapam Yumco
La'nga Co
Konggyü Co
Palung Co
Chemayungdung

Nepal
0 50 km
0 50 miles
N
CHINA
Tibet
NEPAL
INDIA
BANGLADESH
HIMALAYA
Nyainqentanglha Shan
Tsieri Range
Burtra Range
Ladakh Range
Mahabharat Range
Siwalik (Churia) Range
Langtang Himal
Phurbichyachu Himal
Khumbu Himal
Chamlan Himal
Umbak Himal
Janak Himal
Zhari Namco
Tangra Numco
Ngangze Co
Monco Bunnyi
Xuru Co
Daggyai Co
Paikü Co
Cogen Zangbo
Zangbo Jiang
Raka Zangbo
Nigapring Kyim
Como Chamling
Amzhong
Budarongding
Patsakuh
Nyugu
Liasi
Gyagya
Lage
Gyatro
Sangsang
Rutog
Linkuo
Quinglag
Linkakuoka
Yagmo
Pabai Dzong
Kaika
Tatzu
Zhonka Zhong
Baruduksun
Zongga
Nyima
Siling
Mainpu
Chamuta
Xegar
Mabja
Dinggye
Dobzha
Quxar
Sa'gya
Silong
Lhasa
Yati
Xixabangma Feng 8013
Tashihkang
Changmu
Niehen
Dashingha
Manaslu 8163
Himal Chuli 7893
Lapsang Karbo 7150
Lukuwa
Cho Oyu 8201
Mount Everest 8850
8501 Lhotse
Makalu 8463
Kangchenjunga 8586
Langtang National Park
Sagarmatha National Park
Shivapuri National Park
Makalu-Barun National Park
Chitwan National Park
Parsa Wildlife Reserve
Koshi Tappu Wildlife Reserve
Gandaki
Bagmati
Narayani
Kosi
Mechi
Janakpur
Sagarmatha
Besi Sahar
Buri Gandaki
Marsyangdi
Gorkha
Dumre
Dhabe
Manakamana
Mugling
Dhunche
Yala
Trisuli
Trisuli Bazaar
Melamchigaun
Sermathang
Mahakal
Bhote Kosi
Barabise
Kathmandu
Patan
Bhaktapur
Pharping
Dhulikhel
Panauti
Lele
Hetauda
Charikot
Tama
Jiri
Chhule
Namche Bazar
Lukla
Ringmo
Najin
Uwa
Thudham
Helok
Dobhan
Kerun
Okhaldhunga
Sun Kosi
Lamidanda
Sindhulimadi
Bhojpur
Arun
Tamur
Terhathum
Phidim
Dhankuta
Ilam
Kannem
Darjeeling
Cart Road
Amlekhganj
Phatalaia
Simra
Birganj
Raxaul
Patharkot
Sonbarsa
Katari
Dhalkebar
Janakpur
Madhwapur
Jaynagar
Khutauna
Rajbiraj
Mahendranagar
Dharan
Madhumalla
Birtamod
Bhadrapur
Bhantabari
Biratnagar
Birpur
Bettiah
Sagauli
Motihari
Bairgania
Sitamarhi
Belsand
Depura
Madhubani
Ihanjharpur
Nirmali
Forbesganj
Gopalpur
Gopalganj
Deoria
Maharajganj
Muzaffarpur
Darbhanga
Sapta Koshi
Supaul
Raiganj
Basantpur
Dalkola
Laiganj
Samastipur
Saharsa
Chhapra
Rusera
Purnia
Kishanganj
Dinapur
Patna
Arrah
Teghra
Katihar

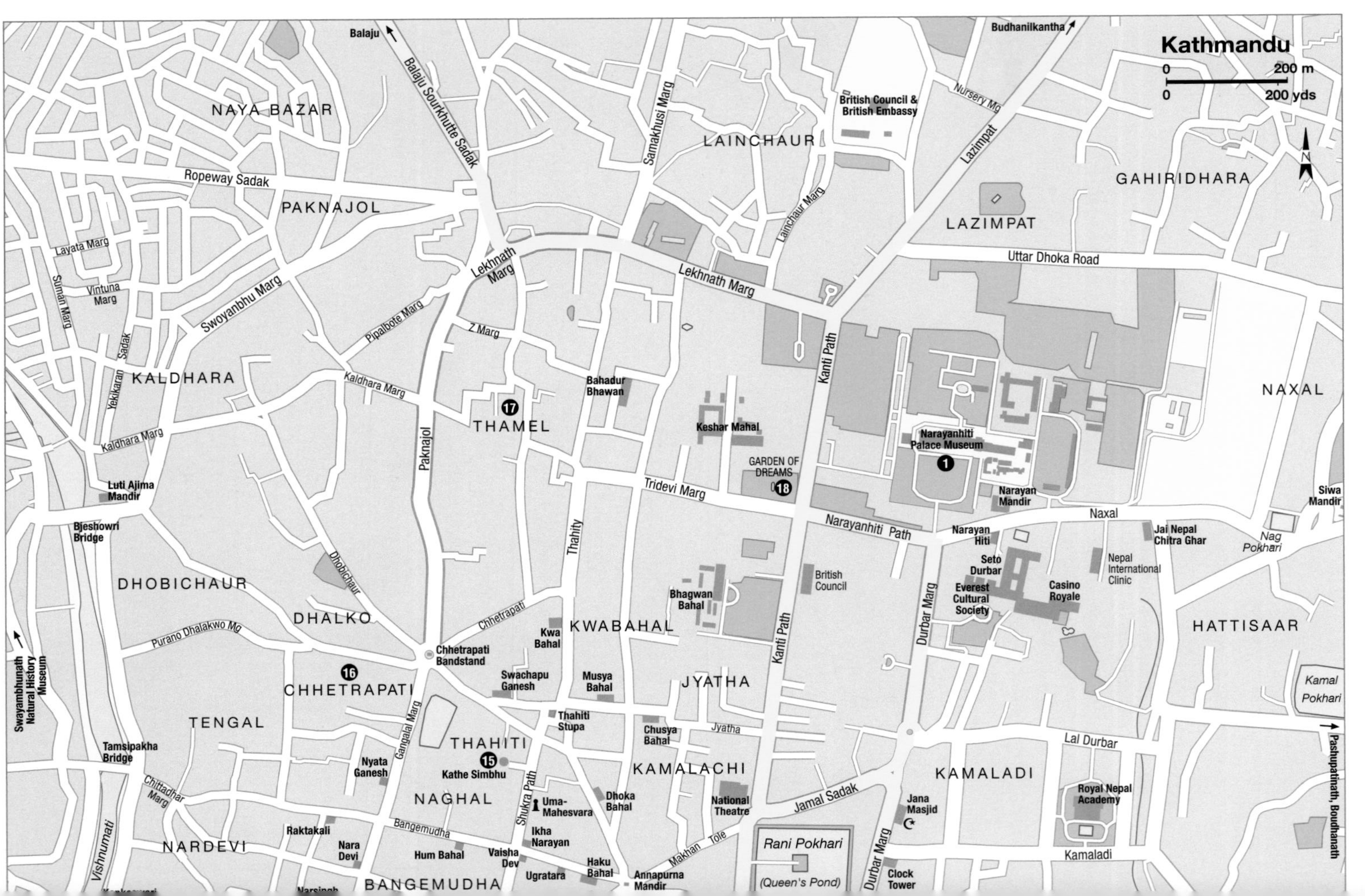
Kathmandu
0 200 m
0 200 yds
N
Balaju
Balaju Sourkhutte Sadak
Budhanilkantha
British Council & British Embassy
Nursery Mg
Lazimpat
NAYA BAZAR
Samakhusi Marg
LAINCHAUR
GAHIRIDHARA
Ropeway Sadak
PAKNAJOL
Lainchaur Marg
LAZIMPAT
Layata Marg
Lekhnath Marg
Uttar Dhoka Road
Suman Marg
Vintuna Marg
Swoyanbhu Marg
Pipalbote Marg
Z Marg
Kanti Path
Sadak
Yekikaran
KALDHARA
Kaldhara Marg
Bahadur Bhawan
NAXAL
THAMEL
Keshar Mahal
Kaldhara Marg
Paknajol
Narayanhiti Palace Museum
GARDEN OF DREAMS
Tridevi Marg
Luti Ajima Mandir
Narayan Mandir
Naxal
Siwa Mandir
Bjeshowri Bridge
Narayanhiti Path
Narayan Hiti
Jai Nepal Chitra Ghar
Nag Pokhari
Thahity
Seto Durbar
Nepal International Clinic
British Council
Dhobichaur
DHOBICHAUR
Bhagwan Bahal
Everest Cultural Society
Casino Royale
Durbar Marg
Chhetrapati
DHALKO
Kwa Bahal
KWABAHAL
HATTISAAR
Purano Dhalakwo Mg
Kanti Path
Chhetrapati Bandstand
Swayambhunath Natural History Museum
Kamal Pokhari
Swachapu Ganesh
Musya Bahal
JYATHA
CHHETRAPATI
Thahiti Stupa
Jyatha
TENGAL
Gangalal Marg
Chusya Bahal
Lal Durbar
Pashupatinath, Boudhanath
Tamsipakha Bridge
THAHITI
Kathe Simbhu
Nyata Ganesh
KAMALACHI
KAMALADI
Shukra Path
Royal Nepal Academy
Chittadhar Marg
NAGHAL
Uma-Mahesvara
Dhoka Bahal
National Theatre
Jamal Sadak
Jana Masjid
Raktakali
Bangemudha
Ikha Narayan
Rani Pokhari
Vishnumati
NARDEVI
Nara Devi
Hum Bahal
Vaisha Dev
Makhan Tole
Durbar Marg
Kamaladi
Haku Bahal
Ugratara
Annapurna Mandir
(Queen's Pond)
Clock Tower
BANGEMUDHA

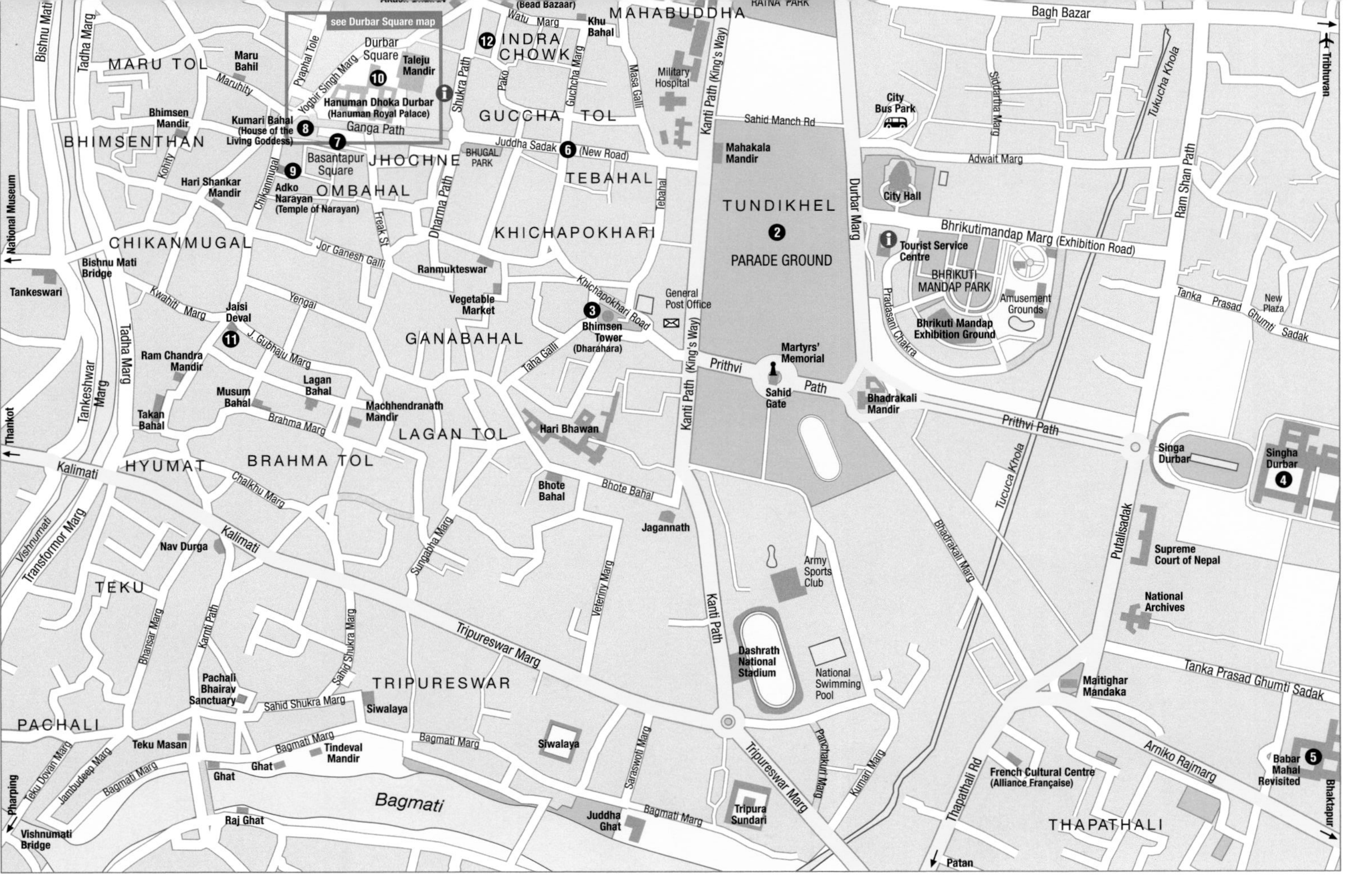
see Durbar Square map
(Bead Bazaar)
Watu Marg
Khu Bahal
MAHABUDDHA
RATNA PARK
Bagh Bazar
Tribhuvan
Bishnu Mati
Tadha Marg
MARU TOL
Maru Bahil
Maruhity
Pyaphal Tole
Yogbir Singh Marg
Durbar Square
Taleju Mandir
Hanuman Dhoka Durbar (Hanuman Royal Palace)
Ganga Path
Shukra Path
Pako
INDRA CHOWK
Guchcha Marg
GUCCHA TOL
Masa Galli
Military Hospital
Kanti Path (King's Way)
Sahid Manch Rd
City Bus Park
Siddartha Marg
Tukucha Khola
Bhimsen Mandir
Kumari Bahal (House of the Living Goddess)
BHIMSENTHAN
Basantapur Square
JHOCHNE
BHUGAL PARK
Juddha Sadak
(New Road)
TEBAHAL
Tebahal
Mahakala Mandir
Adwait Marg
Ram Shah Path
Kohity
Hari Shankar Mandir
Chikanmugal
Adko Narayan (Temple of Narayan)
OMBAHAL
Freak St
Dharma Path
KHICHAPOKHARI
TUNDIKHEL
PARADE GROUND
Durbar Marg
City Hall
Bhrikutimandap Marg (Exhibition Road)
Tourist Service Centre
BHRIKUTI MANDAP PARK
Amusement Grounds
Bhrikuti Mandap Exhibition Ground
Pradasani Chakra
Tanka Prasad Ghumti Sadak
New Plaza
National Museum
CHIKANMUGAL
Jor Ganesh Galli
Ranmukteswar
Bishnu Mati Bridge
Tankeswari
Kwahiti Marg
Yengai
Vegetable Market
Khichapokhari Road
General Post Office
Jaisi Deval
J. Gubhaju Marg
GANABAHAL
Bhimsen Tower (Dharahara)
Taha Galli
Prithvi Path
Martyrs' Memorial
Sahid Gate
Bhadrakali Mandir
Prithvi Path
Ram Chandra Mandir
Tadha Marg
Tankeshwar Marg
Lagan Bahal
Musum Bahal
Brahma Marg
Machhendranath Mandir
Takan Bahal
LAGAN TOL
Hari Bhawan
Kanti Path (King's Way)
Singa Durbar
Singha Durbar
Thankot
Kalimati
HYUMAT
BRAHMA TOL
Chalkhu Marg
Bhote Bahal
Bhote Bahal
Tucuca Khola
Vishnumati
Transformor Marg
Nav Durga
Kalimati
Sungabha Marg
Jagannath
Bhadrakali Marg
Putalisadak
Army Sports Club
Supreme Court of Nepal
TEKU
Veteriny Marg
Kanti Path
National Archives
Bhansar Marg
Kanti Path
Sahid Shukra Marg
Tripureswar Marg
Dashrath National Stadium
National Swimming Pool
Tanka Prasad Ghumti Sadak
Maitighar Mandaka
Pachali Bhairav Sanctuary
TRIPURESWAR
Sahid Shukra Marg
Siwalaya
PACHALI
Teku Masan
Bagmati Marg
Tindeval Mandir
Bagmati Marg
Siwalaya
Saraswoti Marg
Tripureswar Marg
Panchakuri Marg
Kumari Marg
Thapathali Rd
French Cultural Centre (Alliance Française)
Arniko Rajmarg
Babar Mahal Revisited
Teku Dovan Marg
Jambudeep Marg
Bagmati Marg
Ghat
Ghat
Bagmati
Juddha Ghat
Bagmati Marg
Tripura Sundari
THAPATHALI
Pharping
Vishnumati Bridge
Raj Ghat
Patan
Bhaktapur
1
2
3
4
5
6
7
8
9
10
11
12

Shopping on Asan Tol.

KATHMANDU

Nepal's capital is swiftly becoming a bustling metropolis, but ancient rhythms of trade and worship endure, and within its narrow streets are myriad monuments of great beauty and significance.

Main Attractions

- Views from Bhimsen Tower
- Hanuman Dhoka Durbar
- Taleju Mandir
- Asan Tol
- Garden of Dreams

The founding of Kathmandu, the capital of Nepal and its only large city, is estimated to have taken place during the Licchavi period, beginning in about AD 300, although recent archaeological excavations at Hadigaon indicate even earlier settlements. However, it was not until the time of the Mallas, from the 13th century onwards, that the city began to develop in earnest, together with neighbouring Patan and Bhaktapur. During the golden age of these Malla city-states, their splendid Durbar squares vied for artistic ascendancy. Today, Kathmandu forms the hub of the surrounding valley, its atmospheric temples and shrines holding their own amid the growing urban sprawl, clamouring traffic and increasing pollution that is the modern legacy.

The centre of Kathmandu's old city and the structure from which it derives its name, is the Kasthamandap or "House of Wood". This impressively large pavilion was built in the 12th century at the crossroads of two important trade routes and was originally used as a community centre for trade and barter. The city developed in radial fashion from this hub, the old Royal Palace and Durbar Square being constructed soon afterwards.

With the unification of the valley in the 14th century, King Jayasthiti Malla selected Kathmandu as his capital. Considerable expansion took place from this time, with the main activity focusing on the palace complex itself, which also served as the administrative headquarters. Nevertheless, the diagonal trade route running from the Kasthamandap through Asan Tol maintained its commercial importance, as indeed it still does today as a thriving bazaar.

Modern Kathmandu

During the late 19th century Kathmandu began to expand rapidly, and

Durbar Square from above.

the traditional Newari concept of a tightly knit city preserving every square metre of precious arable land was lost. By the 1960s Western-style dwellings of concrete and glass began appearing on the outskirts of the city. In the past two decades Kathmandu's growing pains have multiplied considerably with explosive urbanisation. Precious rice-growing land is being lost to brick factories, and private houses are built on every available terrace.

The rapid development has been matched by the pace of political change, starkly illustrated at the modern **Narayanhiti Palace Museum** ❶ (Thu–Mon 11am–3pm; charge). This was long the seat of the ruling Shah dynasty, but when parliament voted to abolish the monarchy in 2006 the last king, Gyanendra, was evicted and the palace was opened to the public. The current building dates from 1970, and was built to replace an earlier, earthquake-damaged structure.

Two main thoroughfares run south from the palace. Kanti Path, which begins life as Lazimpat in the embassy district further north, skirts the tourist area of Thamel, with its backpacker guesthouses and restaurants. Parallel to Kanti Path to the east is **Durbar Marg**, the main artery of the modern, commercial part of town with its banks, travel agencies and restaurants.

Durbar Marg and Kanthi Path run either side of the **Tundikhel** ❷, the long open expanse of grassland used as the central parade ground that separates the old medieval city to the west from the expanding eastern part with its mushrooming modern buildings. Traffic flows clockwise around the Tundikhel – or, more and more frequently nowadays, becomes snarled in enormous honking traffic jams. At the northern end is **Rani Pokhari**, a tank (artificial lake) with a small white shrine in the centre, built by Pratap Malla for his queen in memory of their dead son. The southern end is marked by the Martyrs' Memorial and the white landmark of the **Bhimsen Tower** ❸ (daily 8am–7pm; charge). Also known as Dharahara, this slender,

Singha Durbar, home of parliament and government ministries.

minaret-style structure was originally built in 1832 as a watchtower, but it was largely destroyed by an earthquake in 1934 and was subsequently rebuilt. From the top, 62 metres (203ft) up, there are sweeping views across the city.

Victorian palaces

Traditional Nepalese architecture generally changed very little throughout the centuries. When damaged by age or earthquakes, temples would customarily be replaced in the same form as the old building. This changed dramatically in the mid-19th century with the introduction of European neoclassical styles by the Rana rulers. The contrast with Nepalese architecture was striking. Jung Bahadur, the founder of the Rana regime, returned in 1850 from a visit to France and England with visions of grandeur. Ladies were encouraged to adapt their styles to Victorian fashions, and anything European was admired.

The sumptuous Rana palaces of Jung Bahadur and his family numbered several hundred throughout the valley. They boasted elaborate plasterwork and imposing columns and were entirely furnished from Europe, with crystal chandeliers and gilt furniture. Many still survive, though generally in a rather tarnished condition. Taken over by the government or private organisations for offices or schools, today they are mere shadows of their former selves.

The culmination of this architectural vogue was the grand palace of **Singha Durbar** ❹, which now houses Nepal's parliament. A building of gigantic proportions, it consisted of 17 courtyards and as many as 1,700 rooms and was reputed to be the largest palace in Asia. It was built over a period of only 11 months in 1901. In 1973, much of it was damaged by a mysterious fire but several courtyards were rebuilt and the imposing white facade restored.

Another example of fine architecture can be seen in the city's most elegant shopping venue, **Babar Mahal Revisited** ❺. Stables, cowsheds and outbuildings of an old Rana palace have been restored and converted into

A museum guard.

Nepalese flags for sale.

smart boutiques, bars and restaurants. Treasures range from colourful Indian handicrafts to hand-woven silks, exquisite thangkas, sturdy old brass and fine Tibetan carpets. Babar Mahal lies just south of Singha Durbar, in the neighbourhood of Maitighar.

New Road

The old city of Kathmandu has remained intact through the centuries, except for **Juddha Sadak** (known as **New Road**) ❻, so called as it was rebuilt after the major earthquake of 1934. This wide street runs west from the Tundikhel, where an arch spans the road adjacent to the Nepal Airlines Building, notable for the bronze sculpture of a yeti bearing a tray. Further west the road becomes known as Ganga Path.

This major commercial axis is the hub of the new consumer society that has flourished since Nepal opened up to the West. Electronic goods, imported clothes, cameras, watches and jewellery are all available here. Halfway up on the left, shoeshine boys congregate beneath a spreading pipal tree where men gather to peruse the morning newspapers.

At the statue of Juddha Shamsher Rana, under whose direction the street was built, is the cavernous supermarket of Bishal Bazaar. But the area's modern image is only skin-deep. Branching off from here, narrow side lanes thrust between rows of traditional houses. Many of these alleys end in squares with corner central *chaityas* and shrines.

The Old City

To enter the Durbar Square area, you have to pay a fee at any of its five main entrances. This money is used for heritage conservation and tourism promotion. The ticket includes entry to the Hanuman Dhoka Durbar.

The first lane off to the left after the southeastern ticket booth is **Freak Street**, the famous 1960s haunt of long-haired hippies. Today's young world travellers favour the laid-back atmosphere of the lake at Pokhara (see page 218), and the lodges of Thamel in the northern part of Kathmandu. The hippies have long since gone

Shopping opportunities on Freak Street.

– King Birendra's coronation in 1975 initially prompted their departure and today's visa laws discourage dalliance.

The open brick platform at the top of New Road on the left is **Basantapur Square** ❼, formerly a vegetable market and, before that, the home of the royal elephants. Souvenir and trinket vendors display their wares on long tables lined with red cloth. The Hanuman Dhoka (see page 162) looms on the right and the graceful temple silhouettes beckon visitors into the Kathmandu Durbar Square.

Kumari Bahal (House of the Living Goddess) ❽ is the 18th-century stucco temple with intricately carved windows on the far (west) side of the square. Members of the public can only go as far as the elaborately carved inner courtyard, where the resident *Kumari* or "living goddess" herself may occasionally be glimpsed.

As you leave the *bahal*, the **Adko Narayan (Temple of Narayan)** ❾ is on your immediate left. The triple-roofed structure on a five-tiered plinth was built in 1670 and provides an excellent vantage point during festivals. On ordinary days the plinths are thronged with traders hawking their wares, farmers resting with their burdens and people chatting or simply enjoying the atmosphere.

Durbar Square

Kathmandu's **Durbar Square** ❿ (charge; fee includes entry to the Hanuman Dhoka Durbar), with more than 50 temples and monuments packed into its compact area, is at the heart of the Old City and top of the list on most people's sightseeing itineraries. Start at the western end to enjoy the most complete view of the square, and then walk into the beginning of the small street called Maru Tol to find the famed **Kasthamandap (House of Wood)** Ⓐ which represents the very centre of the city. One of the oldest buildings in the valley, it dates from the 12th century and supposedly gave Kathmandu its name. The Kasthamandap was originally a community centre, and was later turned into a temple dedicated to Gorakhnath. The god sits in the centre of the platform in a

TIP

The Durbar Square ticket is valid for one day, but it can be exchanged for a visitor's pass valid for the entire duration of your stay in Nepal at the Site Office on the southern edge of Basantapur Square. To do this, you'll need to take your passport and a photo. The process only takes a few minutes and the office is open 8am–7pm.

A stallholder selling Nepalese crafts.

Khukris for sale at Basantapur Square.

wooden enclosure. A pair of bronze lions guard the entrance and carvings along the first-storey cornice depict Hindu epic literature.

Hidden behind the Kasthamandap is the small but very important golden shrine of **Ashok Binayak** **B**, also known as Maru Ganesh. A constant flow of worshippers here offers devotions to the obliging elephant-headed god; in particular those departing on a journey pay a visit beforehand to ensure a safe trip. The number of visitors increases noticeably on Tuesdays and Saturdays, unlucky days dedicated to Ganesh. Opposite the temple is a gilt image of Ganesh's mount, the rat.

Returning to the square, the large Maju Deval Shiva Temple dominates the left side, its three roofs towering over a steep plinth. Note the **Shiva-Parvati Temple** **C** on the left, named for the folksy images of Shiva and Parvati, gazing benignly down from the central window of the upper balcony.

A statue of King Pratap Malla is set on a column at the entrance of the second part of the square. He faces the inner sanctum of his private prayer room on the third floor of the **Degutale Mandir** **D** dedicated to the royal deity. Opposite the entrance to Hanuman Dhoka Durbar stands the small octagonal **Krishna Mandir** **E**. On the right a large wooden lattice screen hides the huge gilded face of the Seto Bhairav, a fierce figure who is revealed only during the Indra Jatra festival between August and September. At that time he is showered with rice and flowers, and *chhang* (rice beer) flows out of his mouth, poured from a tank above to refresh the crowd.

Hanuman Dhoka Durbar

The Durbar Square is dominated by **Hanuman Dhoka Durbar (Hanuman Royal Palace)** **F**, the former seat of power (daily except government holidays Apr–Oct 10.30am–4pm, Nov–Mar 10.30am–3pm (until 2pm on Fri); entrance included in Durbar Square ticket fee; no cameras allowed). It is flanked by a 1672 statue of the monkey-god Hanuman, smeared with red paste and shaded by an umbrella.

THE LIVING GODDESS

The *Kumari* is Kathmandu's living goddess, a young girl cosseted inside the Kumari Bahal at the heart of the city, and worshipped by kings and commoners alike. Except for the religious festival of Indra Jatra she never leaves her *bahal*, and custom dictates her feet must never touch the ground. The practice of worshipping *Kumaris* – regarded as incarnations of Durga – is thought to have begun during the reign of the last Malla kings, and there are several more of these divine infants in the Kathmandu Valley. But it is Kathmandu's "Royal Kumari" that remains best known.

The living goddess is chosen from a selection of girls of four or five years of age, all belonging to the Buddhist Sakya clan of Newar goldsmiths and silversmiths. The *Kumari's* body bears 32 distinctive signs. After enduring tests, she confirms her selection to the attendant priests by choosing the clothing and ornaments of the previous *Kumari* from among a large collection of similar items. Once her horoscope is confirmed as auspicious she is settled into the *bahal*, which is her home until she reaches puberty or otherwise loses blood through an accident. When the term of the *Kumari* comes to an end, the girl leaves richly endowed and free to marry. Recent *Kumaris* have returned to a normal life, albeit one tainted by the common belief that the ex-goddess brings bad luck to a household and early death to her husband.

A sadhu in Durbar Square.

The palace gate is colourfully painted and guarded by soldiers in the black-and-white Malla uniform.

On the immediate left as you enter is a sculpture of Narsingh, an incarnation of Vishnu as a man-lion tearing apart the demon Hiranya-Kashipu. The first courtyard is Nassal Chowk where important royal ceremonies and festivals, including coronations, took place. *Nassal* means "the dancing one". In the corner of the courtyard are the five round roofs of a temple dedicated to the five-faced deity Pancha Mukhi Hanuman.

The palace complex is a series of 14 courtyards whose main structure was built by the Mallas, though its origins are Licchavi. The superb woodcarvings for which it is renowned testify to the Mallas' artistry. The construction began in the north with the two courtyards, Mohan Chowk and Sundari Chowk, built for King Pratap Malla in the 16th century, and progressed south. King Prithvi Narayan Shah renovated and added to the palace complex after his conquest of the valley in 1769. He is responsible for the nine-storey Basantapur Tower and the smaller towers of Kirtipur, Patan and Bhaktapur. All four are set around the Lohan Chowk and are said to have been contributed by citizens of the towns after which they are named.

Climb up the steep staircase of Basantapur Tower for superb views of the city spread out below, ringed by snowy mountains, and admire the erotic carvings on the base of the struts of the tower.

After the Ranas came to power in 1846, further changes were made and the white stucco western wing with the neoclassical facade was added. Hanuman Dhoka Durbar was extensively restored by a Unesco programme prior to King Birendra's coronation in 1975.

The north of the square

Returning to the square, there are more erotic carvings on the struts of the two-tiered 17th-century **Jagannath Mandir** Ⓖ, the oldest structure in this area. Next to this temple is **Gopinath Mandir** Ⓗ with three roofs

Stone lions in front of Shiva-Parvati Temple.

The mighty Maju Deval Shiva Temple.

FACT

The Hanuman statue's evil eye is said to deter the entrance of malign spirits, while the thick sindhur paste protects innocent devotees from coming to harm.

and a three-stepped plinth. Nearby, the terrifying **Black** (**Kala**) **Bhairav** relief is a masterpiece, highly admired and revered as a form of Shiva. This fierce god wears a garland of skulls and has eight arms, carrying six swords, an axe and a shield. He tramples a corpse, the symbol of human ignorance. He is never without offerings of the faithful, placed in his skull bowl. The Black Bhairav is believed to punish anyone who tells lies in front of him by causing them to bleed to death. In the past, criminals were dragged before the image and forced to swear their innocence while touching its feet. Conveniently, the image is located directly across from the city's main police station.

This northeastern end of Durbar Square is dominated by the magnificent three-tiered gilded **Taleju Mandir** ❶, Kathmandu's largest temple, built on a huge stepped platform and dedicated to the royal deity, the goddess Taleju Bhawani. The walled precinct is considered so sacred that it is off-limits to all but royalty and certain priests; ordinary Hindus are allowed access once a year during the Durga Puja of the Dasain festival (see page 90). The Taleju Bhawani is a South Indian goddess who was brought to Nepal in the 14th century and enshrined as the ruling family's special deity – shrines to her were also erected in Bhaktapur and Patan. The temple was built in 1562 by King Mahendra Malla and, according to legend, human sacrifices used to be performed here until the goddess became displeased with such practices. Human sacrifices were outlawed in 1780.

At the northwestern end of Durbar Square is an open courtyard called the **Kot** ❶ or "armoury". Now part of police quarters and army barracks, this is the site of the terrible "Kot Massacre" in which the young army officer Jung Bahadur Rana murdered almost all the Nepal aristocracy and his political rivals, enabling him to establish the Rana regime in 1846 (see page 26).

South of Durbar Square

South of Durbar Square the frenetic bustle subsides into quieter residential

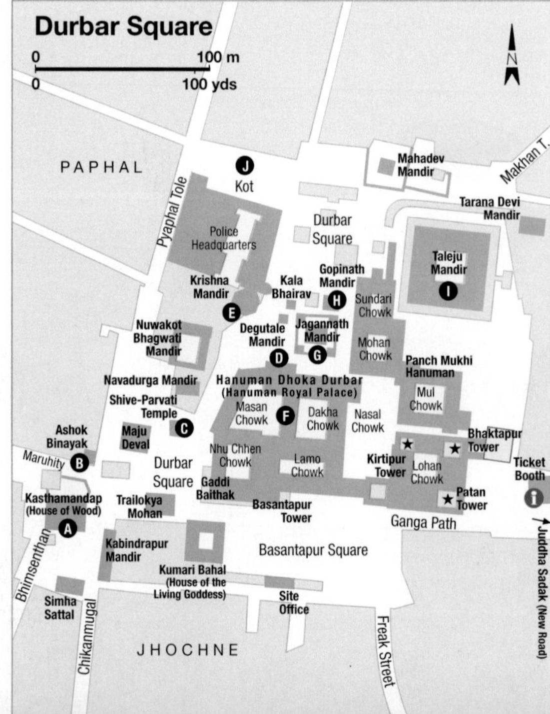

Nassal Chowk in the royal palace.

streets. From the southwestern corner of the square head along Chikanmugal, a cobbled street lined with shops selling traditional sweets.

Jaisi Deval ⓫ is the main temple in this area. Built in 1692 and dedicated to Shiva, it rises in three tiers above a quiet intersection. A statue of the bull Nandi stands at the base of the steps, and across the way an upended slab of natural rock is worshiped as a Shiva *lingam*. Beyond Jaisi Deval there are more small temples tucked away in quiet courtyards.

At the busy Tripureshwar Marg the Old City gives way to chaotic modern development once more. This is an area of Kathmandu far removed from the action of Durbar Square, and further still from the tourist comforts of Thamel. Amidst the broken roads, the slums and the oozing black waters of the Bagmati River, the enormous developmental challenges facing modern Nepal are plain to see. But there are interesting and little-visited sites amongst the decay. The **Pachali Bhairav Sanctuary** is dedicated to a fearsome manifestation of Shiva, and houses a reclining brass image of his companion, Betal. Animal sacrifices are made here on Tuesdays and Saturdays. Nearby, the crumbling **Tindeval Mandir** (daily 9am–3pm) has a trio of unusual Indian-style towers presiding over a quiet courtyard.

The bazaars

Leaving Durbar Square, a *garuda* statue lies half-buried in the street. Cast a glance at the little Tarana Devi Mandir hidden behind the Taleju Mandir before getting swallowed up in the activity of the Makhan Tol bazaar. There are many temples and courtyards of interest and it is worth detouring as you explore the old bazaar areas on foot.

Indra Chowk ⓬ is an animated and picturesque junction of six streets. The gilded griffins rearing their bodies up in front of the rambling shrine to Akash Bhairav are particularly distinctive. This temple houses a deity said to have fallen magically from the sky. The image of the deity is displayed in public only once a year, during the

FACT

The striking statue of Vishnu disembowelling a demon in the Nasal Chowk of Hanuman Dhoka Durbar was built by Pratap Malla in 1673 as an act of penance after he was inadvertently possessed by the god during a dance performance.

Hanuman Dhoka Durbar dominates the square.

A religious idol in Durbar Square, adorned with floral offerings.

lively eight-day Indra Jatra festival – one of Kathmandu's most important celebrations (see page 89).

This area traditionally sells blankets and textiles, including the soft wool pashmina shawls that are popular in the West (see page 85). Shop carefully, however, as cheaper acrylic substitutes abound.

Tucked behind an old building through a narrow entrance is the glittering magic of the **Potey Pasaal**, or "Bead Bazaar", where every day is like Christmas. Cross-legged merchants sit in tiny stalls, presiding over colourful displays of glass beads imported from as far afield as Europe and Japan. Combinations can be pieced together while you wait into any item you wish – earrings, necklaces, bracelets or belts. Nepalese women prefer red or green beads, often adorned with a single faceted gold bead or *tilhari* that symbolises marriage.

Khel Tol ⓭, which is beyond Indra Chowk, is the oldest trading segment of the bazaar and there is a constant coming and going of traders, pedestrians and vehicles. All manner of goods can be bought in the shops, ranging from bangles, saris and the red yarn tassels that women braid into their hair, to the large copper pots for festival feasts.

Turn left into a courtyard marked by a tall, carved pillar and enter one of the most venerated shrines in Kathmandu. The **Seto Machhendranath Temple** ⓮ is a beautiful structure standing in the middle of a monastic courtyard. The shrine is dedicated to Machhendra, the guardian deity of the valley, who is worshiped here by Buddhists as a form of Avalokiteshvara and by Hindus as an incarnation of Shiva. This white *(seto)* god is pulled in a huge chariot through the streets of Kathmandu during the lively four-day Seto Machhendra festival held annually between March and April (see page 92). The entrance to the temple is guarded by magnificent brass lions. Within the courtyard there is rich ornamentation and decoration, most of it dating from the 17th century, though the complex almost certainly has earlier origins.

Asan Tol is always teeming with people.

It could be said that **Asan Tol** is the real heart of the Old City. Traditionally a grain market and a place to hire porters, this crossroads is constantly thronged with people. It also features several temples. Most notable among these is the elaborately decorated little Annapurna Temple, dedicated to the goddess of plenty, here represented by an overflowing pot or *purna kalash* which symbolises abundance. Devotees often toss in offerings of a few coins to bring good fortune. Produce sellers line the streets feeding into Asan, providing fresh vegetables daily for Kathmandu's downtown residents.

Two roads lead east from Asan Tol, both emerging on Kanti Path, opposite Rani Pokhari. Beyond this fenced-in lake the solid white clocktower of the **Trichandra College** is visible, built by the Ranas. To the right is the open expanse of the Tundikhel.

To see more of the Old City take the road leading directly north from Indra Chowk, which passes several shrines, stupas and courtyards worth exploring. In the Bangemudha neighbourhood look for the "Toothache Shrine", a nail-studded chunk of wood. Toothache sufferers transfer their pain by hammering in a nail around the tiny gilded image of Vaisha Dev, the "god of toothache". Nearby dentists, with their window displays of dentures, take a more worldly approach.

A few steps further is the striking white Buddhist stupa of **Kathe Simbhu** ⓯, built as a replica of Swayambhunath as a convenience for those who are physically unable to climb up the steep steps to that hilltop shrine (see page 171). Across the road, look for a beautiful 9th-century sculpture of Shiva and Parvati, also known as Uma-Mahesvara. Shops in this area specialise in cloth from neighbouring countries, from brilliant Chinese brocades to Bhutanese striped cottons and bolts of Tibetan prayer flags. The white stupa of Thahiti, ringed with prayer wheels, marks the transition from old town into new.

The tourist quarter

The narrow streets north of here take on a distinctly Western air as you

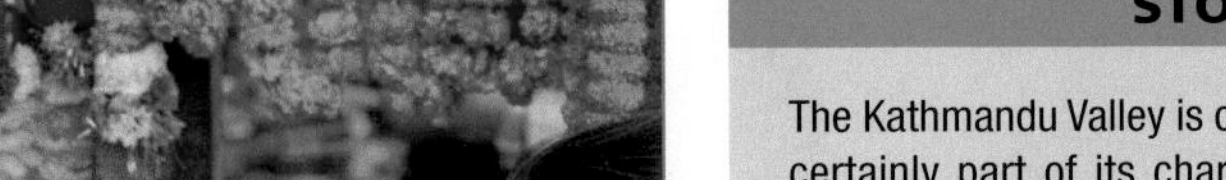

Creating floral garlands for offerings.

STOLEN RELICS

The Kathmandu Valley is often called an "open-air museum" and certainly part of its charm comes from the great quantity of ancient art found all over in temple courtyards and riverside fields. Sadly, organised art trafficking has moved in to despoil this heritage, fuelled in recent years by the desire of private collectors for "chic" Asian images. Even holy relics are not exempt: several years ago a sacred artefact said to be a piece of the Buddha's bone, donated to Nepal by Sri Lanka, was dug up from its site in Swayambhunath. Artist and historian Lain Singh Bangdel documents this cultural plunder in his book *The Stolen Images of Nepal*. Page after page of ancient stone sculptures are depicted, alongside photos of their now-vacant settings. The overall effect is heartbreaking. Images may be wrenched out of their settings or sawn off at the feet. If the head alone is considered valuable enough, the figure may be decapitated. Local people have sought to protect remaining images by caging them behind elaborate metalwork, as with the grilles enclosing Kathmandu's Seto Machhendranath Temple or encasing two gilt Tara images at Swayambhunath, although clumsy efforts to cement stone images to their setting have predictably diminished the beauty of the sculptures.

TIP

While virtually every restaurant in Thamel offers wireless internet access, a tranquil alternative is the Garden of Dreams. Wi-fi is available throughout the garden for Rs50 per hour, and there are few more charming spots to check your email.

reach the tourist areas of **Chhetrapati** ⓰ and eventually **Thamel** ⓱. Favoured by world travellers and cost-conscious trekkers, Thamel is a jumble of budget lodges, restaurants and increasingly upmarket hotels. This is the place to buy T-shirts, turquoise-encrusted silver jewellery, English-language paperbacks, chocolate cake and any number of souvenirs and fake antiques proffered by vendors. More illicit items such as hashish are also plentiful, as hissing street salesman will soon inform you. Thamel is a world in itself, a budget paradise or hell, depending on your perspective. Its international flavour and bargains are intriguing, and though there is little authentically "Nepalese" about the place, in its own way it is as much a part of Kathmandu as the ancient temples or modern middle-class districts.

The name "Thamel" encompasses a number of smaller neighbourhoods, but the heart of the action is focused in the area around the Kathmandu Guesthouse. Several blocks east, Tridevi Marg runs into Kanti Path and Narayanhiti Palace Museum.

At the intersection is the tranquil **Garden of Dreams** ⓲ (daily 9am–10pm; charge). Keshar Shumsher, the Europhile son of a Rana prime minister, built the garden in the 1920s, with a neoclassical pavilion for each of Nepal's six seasons, inscriptions from the Rubaiyat of Omar Khayam, and Latinate statues of Hindu goddesses. After his death in 1964 the garden fell into disrepair, but it has now been restored, creating a cool and shady oasis in the heart of the city. There are plenty of quiet corners, along with an upmarket restaurant and bar.

To the west of Thamel, more traditional old Newar neighbourhoods such as Dhalko and Dhobichaur stretch down to the Vishnumati River. Both the Luti Ajima Temple on the river's near bank and the Shobha Bhagwati Temple on the far bank are well-patronised local shrines, interspersed with cremation sites. Further on is the Hotel Vajra, with its art gallery, library and cultural events.

Thamel caters to all backpackers' needs.

Chasing pigeons in Durbar Square.

Swayambhunath's great stupa.

AROUND KATHMANDU

In the course of one day, visitors to Kathmandu can journey around the outskirts of the city and take in three of the most impressive temples in Nepal, revered by both Buddhists and Hindus.

Main Attractions
Swayambhunath
Boudhanath
Pashupatinath
Gokarna Mahadev

The area around **Kathmandu** ❶ has long been the cultural and political hub of Nepal, and history lies in deep layers here. The various spiritual traditions that have influenced the region have left their mark here too, and the area is extraordinarily rich in places to visit. Three of Nepal's finest temples, Swayambhunath, Boudhanath and Pashupatinath, lie within easy striking distance of the capital and are places of pilgrimage for the country's Hindus and Buddhists. There are also countless smaller shrines of both faiths in the region.

Ancient Swayambhunath

Atop a green hillock on the western edge of Kathmandu stands the great stupa of **Swayambhunath** ❷ (daily 6am–sunset; charge), a site more than 2,500 years old marking the point where the legendary patriarch Manjushri discovered the lotus of the ancient valley lake. For centuries an important centre of Buddhist learning, the painted eyes of the Buddha gaze out from all four sides of this spectacular monument.

Constructed to specific rules, each with a symbolic meaning, the stupa of Swayambhunath is a model of its kind. Its dazzling white hemispherical mound represents creation, inset by statues of meditating Buddhas representing the four elements of earth, fire, air and water. The 13 gilded rings of the spire are the 13 degrees of knowledge required to ascend the path to enlightenment and nirvana, itself symbolised by the umbrella on top. The whole is hung with multi-coloured prayer flags whose every flutter releases prayers heavenwards. The faithful circumambulate the stupa clockwise, turning the banks of prayer wheels as they go, and even prostrating full-length in reverence.

Temples on Pashupatinath's hill.

TIP

You can reach Swayambhunath by taxi from central Kathmandu, but a pleasant alternative is to walk, taking in the backstreet scenes along the way. Head west from the Asan Tol area until you cross the Vishnumati River and the stupa comes into view ahead.

The pilgrims' approach to the shrine is through a wooded park up a steep flight of 300 stone steps, lined with stone sculptures of animals and birds – vehicles of the gods. Cars can drive part-way up the rear side of the hill and park near one of the Tibetan monasteries. Legend relates how Manjushri had his hair cut at Swayambhunath, each hair becoming a tree, and the lice becoming monkeys – the rhesus macaques that live around the temple are appropriately persistent, and care should be taken to avoid getting too close. Banks of new prayer wheels and stupas have recently been constructed around the base of the hill.

Statues of the Buddha repose in richly decorated niches at the four cardinal points of the stupa. Statues of the goddesses Ganga and Jamuna, masterpieces of Newari bronze art, guard the eternal flame in a gilded cage behind the stupa. On the surrounding terrace are many *chaityas*, small stupas, two *shikhara*-style temples and a huge *vajra* (symbolic thunderbolt). An adjacent *gompa* (Buddhist monastery) conducts daily services in the light of flickering butter lamps, overlooked by its vast Buddha statue. The local communities have organised cleaners and guardians to regularly maintain the heavily visited shrine areas.

Prayer flags adorn the stupa.

If you begin to feel slightly overwhelmed by all the religious fervour, turn around and look out, instead, across the spectacular scenery of the valley. This is the best place to get an overview of the ever-growing sprawl of Kathmandu. Away to the southeast you should be able to pick out the Bhimsen Tower (see page 158) on the far side of the Old City. There are a number of simple restaurants around the temple, and a multitude of stalls selling drinks, offerings and trinkets.

About 15 minutes' walk south of Swayambhunath, the National Museum in Chhauni (Wed–Mon 10.30am–4pm (winter to 3pm); charge) features local treasures, including ancient stone sculptures, paintings, woodwork and metal sculpture. Medieval treasures include images of Buddhist deities.

Boudhanath

The largest stupa in the whole of Nepal is **Boudhanath** ❸ (Open 24 hours; charge dawn–sunset), located on flat land 5km (3 miles) northeast of Kathmandu and encircled by pastel-painted facades of houses and monasteries.

Boudhanath (also known as Bhoudha) shelters the single largest community of the 16,000 Tibetans who have made Nepal their home since 1959 (see page 48). The many new monasteries and the *rinpoches* (high ranking lamas) who reside here have established this as one of the most flourishing centres of Tibetan Buddhism in the world, and there are few places, outside Tibet itself, that offer such an insight into their culture.

The huge white dome is surmounted by penetrating red, yellow and blue painted all-seeing eyes of the primordial Buddha and is set on concentric, ascending terraces in the powerful pattern of a mandala. Around the base of this enormous and strikingly simple stupa is a ring of 108 images of Buddhist deities and 147 insets containing prayer wheels. Boudhanath is more accessible than Swayambhunath – it is possible to climb up onto the base of the stupa and join the monks and pilgrims on the kora, the ritual clockwise circuit of the dome.

Poles are hung with prayer flags, renewed and blessed with fragrant juniper incense at the Losar Tibetan New Year festival between February and March. As hundreds of Tibetans gather in their best clothes and jewellery, a portrait of their spiritual leader, the Dalai Lama, is paraded under silk umbrellas accompanied by the growls of horns. Masked dancing completes the celebrations on this most happy and picturesque day in the valley (see page 91).

The area around the stupa is always bustling: pilgrims and tourists mingling amidst stands of butter candles and souvenir stalls, against a soundtrack of Tibetan music emanating from the surrounding buildings.

Pashupatinath

Shiva is both the Destroyer and Creator, at once the end of old things and the beginning of new ones. Among his many incarnations, he appears as Bhairav "The Cruel", Mahadeva "The Great God" and Pashupati "Lord of the Beasts". Shiva is usually represented as a light-skinned man with a blue throat, five faces, four arms and three eyes. He typically holds a *damura* (drum) and a *trisula* (trident) as a symbol of his threefold identity – creator, keeper and destroyer. His vehicle, the bull Nandi, is an ancient symbol of fecundity. Together with his elephant-headed son, Ganesh, he is the most helpful god in the valley – and also the most awesome.

Sometimes Shiva is seen as an ascetic holy man, and many of his sadhu (holy man) followers, covered with sackcloth, dust and ashes, swarm to **Pashupatinath** ❹ (charge) between February and March to celebrate his birthday. Shivaratri is one of the great Hindu festivals of the valley (see page 91), attracting thousands of pilgrims to what is regarded across South Asia as one of the *Paadal Petra Sthalams*, or sacred abodes of Shiva.

Throughout the year, Shiva is worshipped at Pashupatinath as a *lingam* (phallus) in his incarnation as the Lord Pashupati. Don't be too taken in by the dreadlocked sadhus that surround the temple – while some are undoubtedly genuine, many are fakes dressed up to earn money from the relentless tourist photographs.

The great temple complex is 5km (3 miles) east of central Kathmandu, close to the airport. The easiest way to reach it is by taxi or bicycle. It is also possible to walk along quiet roads between Pashupatinath and nearby Boudhanath.

Entrance to the inner temple precinct is forbidden to non-Hindus, but visitors can get a glimpse of the action inside from the slope behind the

The view west from Swayambhunath.

Prayer wheels surround Swayambhunath's stupa.

TIP

There are several Tibetan Buddhist gompas (monasteries) around Boudhanath, all of which welcome respectful visitors. The Guru Lakhang Gompa offers particularly fine views of the stupa.

compound. The best overview of the whole complex is from the terrace on the wooded hill across the river. The large, gilded, triple-roofed temple was built in 1696, though 300 years earlier there was already a structure on this site. The Bagmati River is lined with *dharmsalas* (pilgrim resthouses) and cremation ghats, including a royal ghat reserved exclusively for members of the royal family. There is usually a cremation in progress on one of the platforms by the river. The ashes will be scattered in the river, regarded as holy as it flows into the sacred Ganges, despite its polluted water and seasonal low flows. If you have the stomach for it, tourists are free to watch cremations from above, but photography is generally discouraged as a sign of respect.

The tradition of *sati*, when wives burned themselves alive on their husband's funeral pyre, has not been permitted since the early 20th century, but many married couples still bathe together in the water in the belief that this will lead to their reunification in the next life. There are also many other occasions when the faithful take ritual purificatory baths in the river. One of the most colourful is the three-day women's festival of Teej between August and September when, dressed in their finest red and gold saris, hundreds of women, laughing and singing, converge on Pashupatinath. At other times of the year, the ghats are a mixture of the devout washing, and laughing children splashing about irreverently in the water.

Around Pashupatinath

If you continue up the hill, the path leads through the trees to the brick structure of the Gorakhnath Shikhara, flanked by the brass trident of Shiva and surrounded by resthouses and *lingas* on a wide platform.

Down the hill on the other side is the Guhyeshwari Temple dedicated to Shiva's *shakti* (consort) in her manifestation as Kali. Female Hindu deities sometimes take on ferocious, fierce and bloodthirsty appearances. One of the most important goddesses is the dominating and sexual *shakti*

A body is readied for cremation on the high-caste ghat.

HOLY SMOKE

Around Pashupatinath you'll often spot sadhus smoking *ganja* (cannabis) through their *chillums* (conical clay pipes). For devotees of Shiva this is an act of worship rather than recreation, as the god is generally credited with having invented the drug.

Cannabis is mentioned in the ancient Hindu Vedas as one of the "five sacred plants", and is often presented as an offering at Shiva temples, particularly during the Shivaratri festival, and for many Shaivite sadhus smoking the substance is a means of communing with the god.

As a consequence of this long-established cultural practice there is a tacit toleration by the Nepalese authorities of ritual consumption of the drug – though not of its recreational use.

Maha Devi. She can take thousands of names and incarnations. She is the black goddess Kali "the Dark One" and Durga "The Terrible of Many Names". She is forever giving birth but her stomach can never be filled and her craving for blood is insatiable. Animal sacrifices are a particularly popular characteristic of her worship in Nepal.

This riverside shrine is, like so many others, forbidden to non-Hindus, although Buddhists also revere this as a sacred site and the seed from which the Swayambhunath lotus grew.

The ancient stupa of **Chabahil** ❺ is at a busy crossroads north of Pashupatinath and marks an early Licchavi settlement. It is a relatively primitive stupa but does have some interesting early sculptures and *chaityas*. The Chandra Binayak is in the middle of the village of Chabahil, 200 metres (650ft) behind the stupa. This small Ganesh shrine features rich brasswork and is believed to cure diseases and external bodily injuries.

Gokarna Mahadev and Tika Bhairav

Beyond Pashupatinath, past the Hyatt Regency Hotel and Boudhanath, take the road left for 4km (2.5 miles) to the important Shiva shrine, the **Gokarna Mahadev** ❻, on the banks of the Bagmati River in the small village of Gokarna.

The ochre-coloured three-roofed temple was built in 1582. The fine woodcarvings around the doors and roof have been restored to their original pure beauty and the golden roofs glisten in the sun, framed against the dark forest across the river.

Again, the interior of the temple is off-limits to non-Hindus. Irregular stone steps descend the river bank, where Shiva lies on a stone bed of cobras. In August and September at Gokarna Aunshi, or Fathers' Day, those whose fathers have died during the previous year must come and ritually bathe here (see page 89).

Early sculptures surround this scenic shrine, including one of Brahma, but none are more beautiful than the 8th-century statue of Parvati, the oldest image at Gokarna, now protected by clothes inside a small shrine, set between the main temple and the road.

Tika Bhairav shrine

A Shiva shrine of an altogether different register is located at Tika Bhairav near Lele, where Shiva is portrayed in his terrible form as Bhairav. To reach this unusual shrine, you have to travel outside the Kathmandu Valley towards the adjoining Lele Valley, to the south of the capital, and turn sharply left, descending to the confluence of the rivers. Do not look out for a conventional temple, however. This monumental, multi-coloured fresco is an abstract close-up of Bhairav's face painted on a huge brick wall, under the spartan shelter provided by a tin roof. For those travellers who are keen on cycling among beautiful unspoiled scenery, this also makes for a very pleasant mountain-biking route.

Monkeys at Pashupatinath.

You will see many sadhus in this area.

The Moghul-inspired Krishna Mandir.

PATAN

One of the Kathmandu Valley's three ancient capitals, Patan is rich in temples and traditional architecture, as well as being the centre of Nepal's thriving carpet industry.

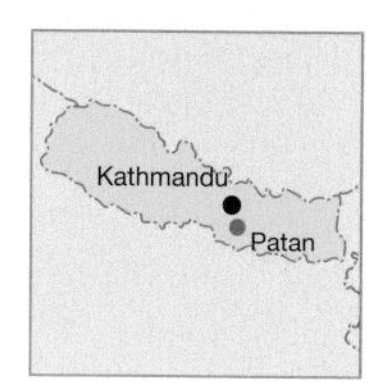

South of the Bagmati River Kathmandu makes way for **Patan** ❼, second of the three rival city-states that once tussled for dominance of the valley. Buddhism sets the tone in Patan, and according to local myth the city was founded by the mighty Buddhist Emperor Ashoka in the 3rd century BC – though there is no historical proof of this. The city has long been famed for the superb craftsmanship of its artisans – a reputation that rightly endures today. Patan is also known as Lalitpur, "The Beautiful City".

Four main roads radiate from Patan's **Durbar Square** to the four allegedly Ashokan stupas, brick and grass mounds that mark the boundaries of the city. Patan first developed as a major settlement under the Licchavis, and **Mangal Bazaar**, an area adjoining the Durbar Square, may have been the site of King Manadeva's palace in the 5th century. However, the city's greatest building period took place under the Mallas from the 16th to 18th centuries. Most of the monuments seen today were built or rebuilt at that time. With no fewer than 136 *bahals* or courtyards and 55 major temples, Patan is a cradle of arts and architecture, a great centre both of the Newari Buddhist religion and of traditional crafts (see page 79).

Many of the historic buildings have been restored in recent years, and a fee (Rs500; valid for the duration of your stay in Nepal) is now levied upon entering the square.

The Royal Palace

As in the other cities of the valley, the heart of Patan is its Durbar Square. A spectacular example of Newari architecture, the **Royal Palace** Ⓐ, with its walled gardens on the eastern side of the square, is faced by a dozen temples of various sizes and styles.

Main Attractions

Patan Museum
Krishna Mandir
Kwa Bahal
Kumbeshwar Mandir
Mahabuddha

Amidst the columns of Patan's Durbar Square.

The palace consists of three main *chowks* or courtyards that open onto the square. The southernmost and smallest is the Sundari Chowk, which has in its centre a masterpiece of stone architecture and carving, the sunken royal bath called Tusha Hiti. Created around 1670, the walls of the bath are decorated with a double row of statuettes representing the eight Ashta Matrikas, the eight Bhairavs and the eight Nagas. Many of these are now missing. Two stone snakes *(nagas)* girdle the top of the basin into which water flows through a spout gilded with metal. The three-storey buildings around the *chowk* contain a corner temple and have wonderfully carved windows and grilles in metal and ivory. Stone images of Ganesh, Hanuman and Narsingh guard the outside of this courtyard.

The oldest courtyard is the central Mul Chowk, built in 1666 for Srinivasa Malla. The low two-storey residence of the Patan royal family encloses a courtyard with a small gilded central shrine, the Bidya Mandir. The Shrine of Taleju is guarded by two fine brass images of Ganga on a tortoise and Jamuna on a mythical crocodile-like figure.

Towering over this part of the palace, in the northeast corner of the Mul Chowk is the triple-roofed octagonal tower of the **Taleju Bhawani Mandir**, built in about 1666 and housing the royal deity. A third, northern courtyard, the Mani Keshab Narayan Chowk, is entered from the main square via the much admired "Golden Gate". The beautifully restored building here now houses the **Patan Museum** **B** (daily except public holidays 10.30am–5.30pm; charge). This is probably Nepal's best museum, with a sensitively displayed and intelligently labelled collection of Hindu and Buddhist art. The window seats on the upper level are a fine place to watch the action in the square, and the small open-air restaurant is a pleasant place for lunch. Between this and the central *chowk* is the temple of Degutale, the personal deity of the Malla kings. Surmounted with a four-roof tower and originally built in 1640, the kings once performed their sacred Tantric rites here.

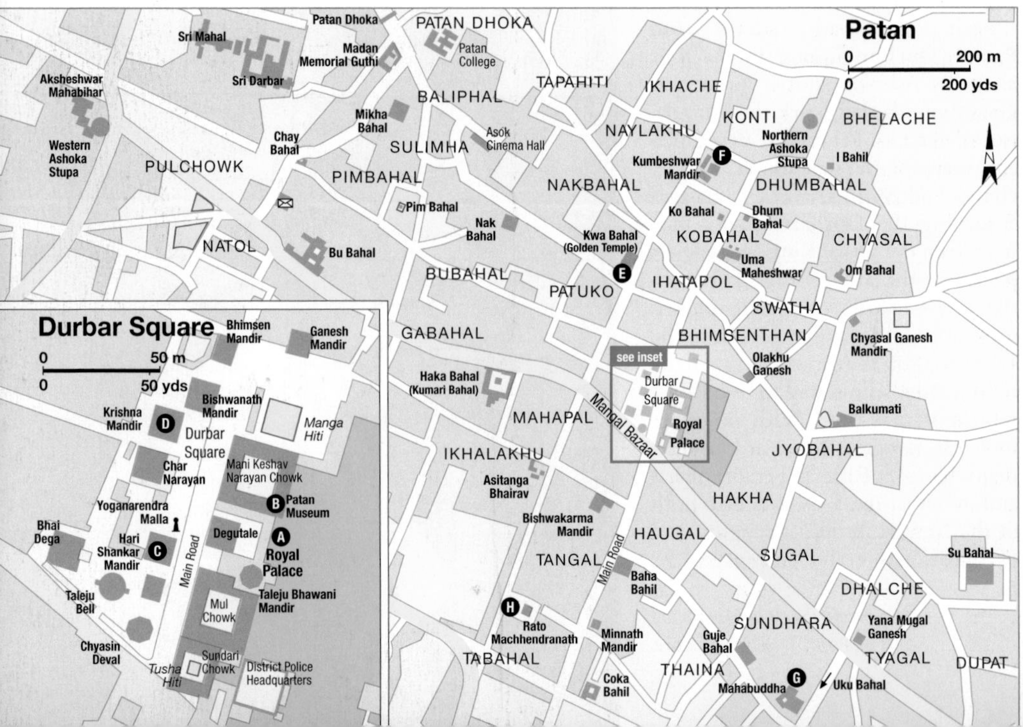

Temples on the square

Facing the Sundari Chowk at the southern end of the square is the Chyasin Deval, an octagonal stone *shikhara*-style building raised by the daughter of an 18th-century king in memory of the eight wives who followed her father onto his funeral pyre. To the west is the Bhai Dega with a Shiva *lingam* within.

To the north a huge bell hangs between two pillars; nearby is the triple-roofed 17th-century **Hari Shankar Mandir** Ⓒ, with its carved roof struts and guardian stone elephants. Just north, a gilded statue of King Yoganarendra Malla prays atop a pillar, shaded by the hood of a royal cobra. The stone *shikhara* behind dates from 1590. Beyond is a small Narayan temple that is probably the oldest surviving temple in the square, built for the god Char Narayan in 1565.

Opposite the northern courtyard of the palace is the striking **Krishna Mandir** Ⓓ. Built in 1637 at the command of King Siddhi Narsingh Malla, its airy colonnades clearly show that the architectural influence of the Muslim Mughal rulers of north India had reached Nepal by this stage. The first two storeys comprise a series of pavilions in smooth black stone. Encircling these are carved friezes depicting scenes from two Hindu epics, the *Mahabharata* and the *Ramayana*, with explanations etched in Newari. A slender *shikhara* emerges from the top. A gilt statue of Garuda mounted on a high pillar faces this elegant shrine.

The next temple is the **Bishwanath Mandir**, a profusely decorated double-roofed pagoda. The building collapsed in the 1990 monsoon but has been reconstructed. The last temple is the highly venerated **Bhimsen Mandir** dedicated to Bhimsen, the god of traders, and decorated in silver and gold. This brick structure was erected in the late 17th century but the marble facade dates from Rana times. At the corner of the northern *chowk* is the lotus-shaped, recessed **Manga Hiti** with three carved water spouts in the shape of crocodile heads.

Northern Patan

On leaving Durbar Square there is a maze of small streets, rich in monuments of great interest. Patan is known for its *bahals*, two-storey Newari Buddhist monasteries built around courtyards, and the less elaborate *bahils*. The most renowned of these is the **Kwa Bahal** Ⓔ, known as the "Golden Temple", a few minutes' walk north of Durbar Square.

This is an ancient sanctuary and legend connects its origins with a 12th-century queen. The entrance is guarded by a pair of lions, and the inner courtyard houses a spectacular rectangular building with three roofs and a facade richly embossed with gilded copper. The long metal streamer descending from the roof to the courtyard is the *pataka*, the ladder by which the deities can descend upon the temple from the heavens. The metalwork throughout the building shows great craftsmanship and the central shrine is lavishly embellished.

The statue of King Yoganarendra Malla.

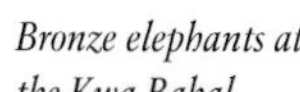

Bronze elephants at the Kwa Bahal.

Erotic carvings at Jagat Narayan Temple.

Up a wooden staircase is a Tibetan Buddhist shrine, decorated with frescoes and rafters painted with sacred mantra. The whole complex is still an active Buddhist monastery.

A little further north, the towering **Kumbeshwar Mandir** Ⓕ dominates an area of residential streets. The Kumbeshwar, the Nyatapola in Bhaktapur and Panch Mukhi Hanuman in Hanuman Dhoka Palace are the only temples in the valley with five roofs. Founded in 1392, the Kumbeshwar is the oldest surviving temple in Patan. Its precincts are scattered with rare early sculptures and its struts, cornices and door frames are intricately carved. Two ponds in the courtyard are believed to be fed from the holy Gosainkund Lakes (see page 245). Dedicated to Shiva in his form of "Lord of the Water Pot", the Kumbeshwar is the focus of the Janai Purnima festival, when pilgrims pay homage to a silver and gold *lingam* in the middle of the tank (see page 89).

Patan's northern Ashoka Stupa lies a few minutes beyond Kumbeshwar in a secluded courtyard. The hemispheric mound, topped with mysterious painted eyes, is the most impressive of the city's four stupas. The road continues through fertile fields to the banks of the Bagmati River. The shrine of Sankhamul Ghat is a fascinating collection of crumbling courtyards and temples. Most notable is the brick *shikhara* of Jagat Narayan, encircled by terracotta *nagas*.

Southern Patan

Down a narrow street southeast of Durbar Square is the architectural masterpiece of **Mahabuddha** Ⓖ, "Temple of the Thousand Buddhas". The entrance is well marked down a lane to the right and curio shops line the route.

Mahabuddha stands in a cramped courtyard and is a tall *shikhara* structure entirely covered by terracotta plaques depicting the Buddha. The best view is from the roof terrace of an adjacent house. Built at the end of the 16th century, the monument was damaged and rebuilt after the 1934 earthquake. The spare parts "left over" from the restoration were used to construct a smaller *shikhara* dedicated to Maya Devi, the mother of the Buddha.

THE LOST WAX TECHNIQUE

Patan has for many years been a centre of metalwork, and the efforts of its craftsmen were exported to monasteries, temples and palaces in India, China and Tibet in past centuries. Today the craft continues, and while much of the work now ends up in tourist boutiques, the traditional methods of *repoussé* (embossing sheet metal from the reverse) and the "lost wax technique" are still practised.

The complex lost wax technique, known locally as *thajya*, has been used in the Patan area for at least 1,500 years. In the first stage a precise model of the planned metal image is moulded from a mixture of beeswax, oil and sap from the sal tree. A high degree of artisanship is required to craft the wax, with separate elements carefully heated and set in place.

Once the wax model is complete it is coated in thick layers of clay and cow dung; exit channels are left in the coating, and the whole thing is then gently heated. The wax melts and escapes, leaving a perfect reverse image inside. The resulting mould is then filled with molten copper, bronze or brass, cooled, and broken open to reveal the final version of the desired image. The work is not finished at this stage, however, for the excess metal must be filed off, the surfaces cold-forged, and the more delicate details chased into the surface. Finally, the most prized images are gilded with gold.

Metal workers at SRS Handicraft in Patan.

Further south is another monastery, the Uku Bahal, with gilded roofs and animal sculptures. The carved wooden struts on the courtyard's rear wall date from the 13th century, and written records of the monastery go back to AD 1117, but most of the current structure was built in the 19th century.

Double back west through the metalworking neighbourhood of Thaina, where craftsmen make the air ring with their hammers on metal, then turn south at the Mangal Bazaar road to visit the brightly painted shrine of Minnath, a minor local deity known as the "son" or "daughter" of the famous **Rato Machhendranath** H nearby. Rato ("Red") Machhendranath dwells across the street in a three-storey temple set in a grassy compound. A local form of the Buddhist deity Avalokiteshvara, he is venerated as Shiva by Hindus and is worshipped by all as the guardian of the valley and the god of rain and plenty. The present temple was built in 1673 and is a fine example of Newari architecture. A row of prayer wheels lines the base, while carved roof struts show the tortures of condemned souls in hell.

The painted idol of Rato Machhendra is taken out of his shrine every summer and paraded through Patan in a chariot for several weeks. This is Patan's biggest festival, designed to ensure plentiful monsoon rains (see page 88). It culminates in the Bhoto Jatra festival when the sacred bejewelled waistcoat *(bhoto)* of the serpent king is displayed. Following this ritual, the chariot is dismantled. However, every 12 years the chariot is dragged all the way to Bungamati (see page 205), a village 6km (4 miles) south of Patan where the deity spends the winter.

The southern neighbourhood of **Jawalakhel** is home to Nepal's only zoo (Tue–Sun 10am–4pm; charge). It is also a major centre of the carpet industry. The Tibetan Refugee Camp established here in the 1960s promoted a craft that has now become Nepal's biggest export and the largest employer in the valley. Visitors are welcome to watch the manufacturing process at the **Tibetan Handicraft Centre**. Weavers knot wool into traditional patterns in the main hall, chatting and singing all the while.

TIP

Patan will delight souvenir hunters. Handicraft shops line many of the backstreets, offering block-printed fabrics, quilted cushion covers, pottery, paintings and a wide range of metalwork.

Traditionally dressed women dance at a festival.

Bhairavnath Mandir.

Maps on pages 184, 198

BHAKTAPUR

Now protected as a Unesco World Heritage Site, this former capital of the Kathmandu Valley is the best-preserved medieval town in Nepal, rich in temples and traditional architecture.

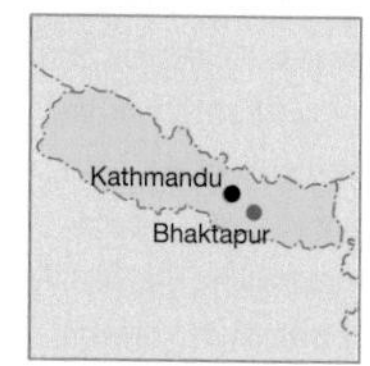

With its skyline of ancient temple roofs set against the white peaks of the Himalayas, the city of **Bhaktapur ❽**, also known as Bhadgaon, is one of the highlights of any visit to Nepal. It is said to have been founded in the shape of Vishnu's conch shell by King Ananda Malla in the 9th century. Once the most powerful of the valley's trio of Malla city-states and a flourishing marketplace on the trade route to Tibet, Bhaktapur has preserved its traditional character far better than Kathmandu and Patan, in part due to its more isolated location, slotted up against the surrounding hills. The Old City has been comprehensively restored and is regarded as a classic showcase of "medieval" Nepalese town life. This is a place where cars and concrete have yet to dominate; the narrow streets are richly atmospheric, and traditional life continues apace amidst a flourishing tourist trade.

The town, with over 70,000 inhabitants, 98 percent of them Newar, is also the most self-contained and self-sufficient of the valley's major urban settlements. Its farmers supply food from the surrounding fields, the craftsmen are still able to restore and decorate the ancient houses and temples, and its people have maintained their religious and cultural traditions. An entrance fee (valid for one week) is collected from tourists by the municipality and used to maintain a clean urban environment and for the conservation of historic and religious monuments. Visitors who wish to stay more than a week should apply for a free pass at the tourist information counter near the main gate. A photocopy of visa and passport, and two passport-size photos are required. Bhaktapur lies 16 km (10 miles) east of Kathmandu along the busy road to Banepa, Dhulikhel and the Chinese border. A more interesting alternative

Main Attractions

- Sun Dhoka
- Batsala Durga
- Taumadhi Tol
- Potters' Square
- Dattatraya Square

Souvenir shops in Taumadhi Tol.

TIP

Bhaktapur makes an excellent alternative base to Kathmandu, and an overnight stay is the best way to take in the remarkable traditional atmosphere. The Old City is dotted with pleasant budget lodges, and a number of boutique guesthouses.

route north of the main highway takes you through the small town of Thimi, famous for its terracotta pottery and delicate papier-mâché masks and dolls. The settlement takes its name from the Newari word *chhemi*, meaning "capable people", and the streets are lined with shops selling the wares of local artisans.

Durbar Square

The traditional approach road from Kathmandu passes a grove of pine trees on a hillock and the recently restored **Siddhi Pokhari**, the largest of the city's network of historic water tanks.

Follow the road through narrow streets to the **Durbar Square**. This part of town was originally outside the boundaries of the city, which was centred further east around Dattatraya Square. Between the 14th and 16th centuries, when Bhaktapur was capital of Kathmandu Valley, the centre moved west to Taumadhi Tol. Durbar Square became integrated during the reign of King Bupathindra Malla around the beginning of the 18th century.

Entering Durbar Square through a 19th-century gate, the sparseness of the temples is immediately apparent, compared to the profusion in the Durbar squares of Kathmandu and Patan. The devastating 1934 earthquake destroyed many of the highly decorated buildings of all shapes and sizes that once crowded the square. Legend claims there were 99 courtyards here, though this is hard to believe. Today, by contrast, the brick-paved square has a pleasant, open feeling.

On the left a pair of very fine stone statues represent Durga with her 18 arms and Bhairav with 12, both guarding the entrance to a lost part of the palace. Buildings on the southern side have been restored by local craftsmen, and house offices and a restaurant. Nearby is the Rameshwar Temple dedicated to Shiva and a brick *shikhara*-style temple dedicated to Durga with images of Hanuman and Narsingh. The most striking feature ahead of you as you enter the square is the exquisite gilded statue of King Bupathindra Malla, seated on a tall stone pillar.

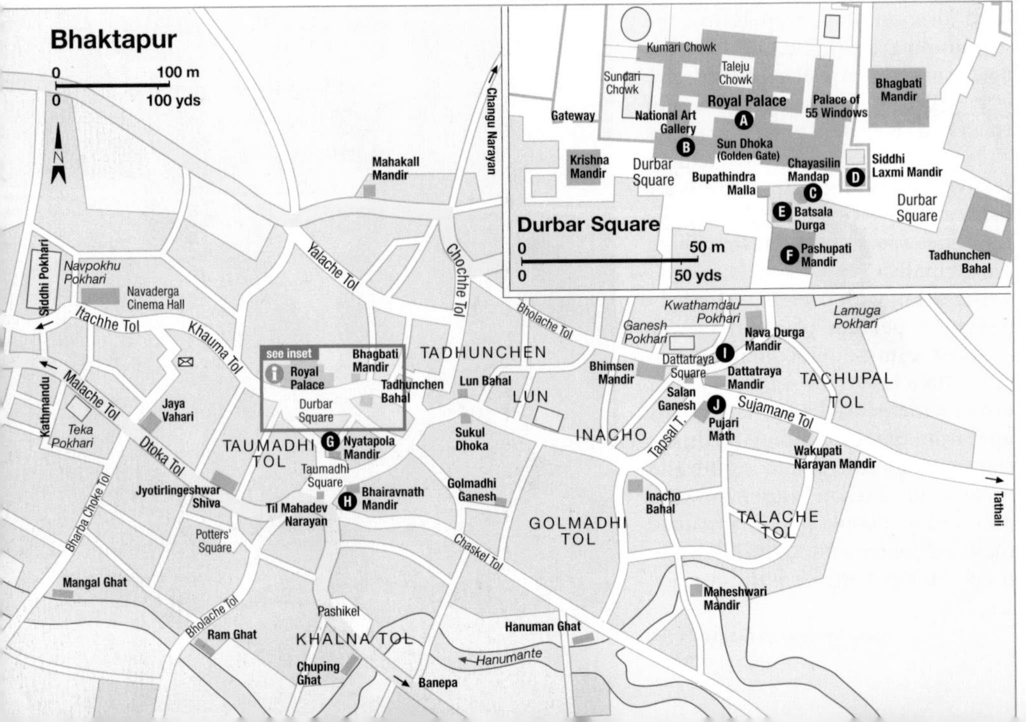

The Royal Palace

The entrance to the Royal Palace is marked by the superb **Sun Dhoka** or "Golden Gate", one of the greatest architectural masterpieces of the valley. Created in 1753 by Jaya Ranjit Malla, it is a monument to the skill and artistry of the craftsmen who produced it. In gilded copper the doorframe illustrates many divinities and the gate itself, set in brickwork, is capped with a gilded roof with finials of elephants and lions.

Standing back from the Sun Dhoka, what remains of the former **Royal Palace** Ⓐ can be seen, though it was much damaged in the 1934 earthquake. The 18th-century Palace of 55 Windows is on the right, built of brick with an upper floor of carved wooden windows.

Walk through the Sun Dhoka into the religious and ritual courtyards of the royal palace. Pass under a couple of low doorways across small courtyards and wind your way around to the back where the elaborately carved entrance to the Taleju Chowk is on the left. This is as far as non-Hindu visitors may go as the two *chowks* of the Taleju and Kumari are sacrosanct. However, the guards may allow you a glimpse into the courtyard containing the Taleju God-house with its rich carving and decoration.

To the left of the Sun Dhoka is a plastered and whitewashed section of the palace built in the early 19th century. It now houses the **National Art Gallery** Ⓑ (Wed–Sun 10am–5pm, Mon 10am–3pm; charge; ticket also covers entry to the bronze and woodcarving museums), with its collection of fine artworks and *paubha scroll* paintings. The entrance is flanked by Hanuman, the monkey god, and Narsingh, the man-lion.

Nearby is the Sundari Chowk, the ritual bathing courtyard of the Bhaktapur kings. Unlike other courtyards it is no longer surrounded by buildings, but the tank has some stone divinities and is unusually large. From the centre of the tank rises a magnificent *naga* or sacred serpent.

Although no longer complete, the Bhaktapur palace is a place to linger a while and contemplate the beauties contained in what must have once

A carved door at the Royal Palace.

Batsala Durga.

Carvings in Taumadhi Tol.

been the most impressive of all the Durbar squares in the valley.

Temples on the square

Return to the Durbar Square. Ahead is the **Chayasilin Mandap** Ⓒ, an octagonal pavilion destroyed by the 1934 earthquake but entirely reconstructed between 1987 and 1990 with German funding. Note the fine woodcarving with hardly a difference between the new and original pieces, and the interior steel girders, ensuring a longer life than that of the previous building. Great effort has gone into detecting and integrating original timber components from the period.

Turn to the eastern plaza and pass on the left the fine stone *shikhara* of **Siddhi Laxmi Mandir** Ⓓ, known locally as *Lohan Dega* or "Stone Temple", with animal guardians and a pair of nobles at the bottom, each dragging a naked child and a dog. A two-storey arcaded building frames this corner of the main square. Up a lane to the east is an intimate and unusual Buddhist monastery called Tadhunchen Bahal, restored with great care by the municipality in 1999.

Reorient yourself by the pillar of Bupathindra and note the big bell that was erected in the 18th century. Next to the bell, the stone *shikhara* of **Batsala Durga** Ⓔ is a symphony of pillars and arches with divinities represented by stone carvings. The *shikhara* is surmounted by copper pinnacles and wind bells. A sunken stone *hiti* or water fountain is behind, with a delightfully carved spout.

Further on is the large, two-roofed **Pashupati Mandir** Ⓕ, one of the oldest temples in the valley, dating from the 15th century. Beyond, a narrow lane, Baha Tol, lined with inviting shops and small restaurants, leads down to the lower square.

Taumadhi Tol

Locked in the heart of the Old City and presided over by two spectacular temples, Taumadhi Tol is the most atmospheric part of Bhaktapur. The buildings here were restored in the 1990s with revenue from tourist entrance fees.

The **Nyatapola Mandir** Ⓖ is Nepal's tallest temple, standing more

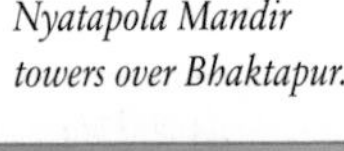

Nyatapola Mandir towers over Bhaktapur.

than 30 metres (98ft) with a total of five storeys (*nyata* in Nepali means "five-stepped"). Carved wooden columns support the tapering roofs and form a balcony around the sanctum. The temple is balanced superbly upon five receding square plinths, and the steep central stairway is flanked by huge stone guardians on each plinth. Each pair is believed to have ten times the strength of the pair on the plinth immediately below. The two famous Malla wrestlers at the bottom of the stairway are ten times as strong as ordinary people, and the elephants above them ten times as strong as the wrestlers, and so on. The list extends with lions, griffins, and the goddesses Baghini and Singhini. Metaphysical power culminates at the top of the steps in the closed chamber housing Nyatapola's secret deity, Siddhi Lakshmi, a Tantric goddess to whom her patron-king, Bupathindra Malla, dedicated the temple in 1702. Exactly 108 painted wooden struts supporting the roofs show the goddess in her different forms. Despite this looming manifestation of Tantric power, no ordinary Bhaktapurian has ever seen the goddess. Only priests are allowed into the inner sanctum to attend to her hidden idol. The huge steps provide perfect seating for the first day of the New Year festival, when they are crowded with spectators.

The **Bhairavnath Mandir** H is set at right angles to the Nyatapola and is a perfect architectural foil to its spire-like lines. The rectangular base rests directly onto the square and its three-tiered roof gives a massive, solid appearance. Dedicated to the city's patron god Bhairav, his awesome powers also counterbalance those of the Tantric goddess, portraying a peculiar Newar perception of the balance of spiritual terror.

The image of Bhairav is taken out for chariot processions across the town during the week-long Bisket Jatra New Year celebrations. Consisting of only a head, it resides in an upstairs room on a brass platform and is barely 30 centimetres (1ft) in height. The real entrance to the temple is from behind, through the small neighbouring Betal house. Betal, the God of chaos, rides

Boys playing in Bhaktapur's streets.

TIP

Bhaktapur is famous for its "king curd". Known locally as *juju dhau*, and available from small shops near Durbar Square, this very superior yoghurt is made from creamy buffalo milk and a small amount of sugar, and set into earthenware dishes.

on the front of the chariot as a figurehead during Bisket Jatra. Outside of the festival period the huge wooden pieces of the dismantled chariot are usually stacked against the wall of the Bhairavnath Mandir.

The Nyatapola Café and Sunny Restaurant are pleasant places to overlook the square and watch the constant activity.

Potters' Square and the ghats

From the southwest corner of Taumadhi Tol a narrow street winds downhill to the potters' quarter, where hundreds of pots dry in an open square. The pots are made in open-fronted workshops on the southern side of this small square. Fresh clay is mixed from a huge mound on the right, and then spun into jugs, cups and bowls on treadle wheels, or moulded by hand into various trinkets. Behind the wheels the completed pieces are fired under huge mounds of straw, buried beneath layers of dusty sand. The finished work is on sale at various stalls around the square, and Ganesh, the elephant-headed patron of potters, presides from the nearby Jeth Ganesh Temple, built by a successful artisan in 1646.

Follow the narrow lanes heading west out of the pottery market to several interesting temples, courtyards and *bahals*. A lane to the south leads downhill to the Hanumante River and the Ram Ghat, one of the bathing and cremation places serving the western part of the city.

Southeast from Taumadhi Tol, the steep flagstoned lane marks the processional route taken by the chariots of Bhairav and his goddess Bhadrakali during the annual Bisket Jatra festival on their way down to a square near the river (see page 87). Thousands of people gather for this most boisterous of valley festivals, which marks the New Year in April with the raising of a 25-metre (82ft) *lingam* pole.

To the south at **Chuping Ghat** a serene riverside temple compound houses the Music Department of Kathmandu University. Here both foreign and local musicians study the traditional music of Nepal and learn its various instruments and dance forms.

BHAKTAPUR'S REBIRTH

On the afternoon of 15 January 1934 a catastrophic earthquake rocked Nepal and north India. Across the region tens of thousands of people died; whole towns were razed to the ground, and the shocks were felt in far-off Mumbai. In the Kathmandu Valley, meanwhile, temples toppled from their plinths and many historic buildings were left in ruins.

Some of the worst damage was in Bhaktapur, where much of the Old City was destroyed. Bhaktapur had already slumped into obscurity since the rise of Kathmandu as the modern capital, and after the quake the decline continued. All that changed in the 1970s, however, when the German government began to fund restoration work.

The Bhaktapur Development Project was launched in 1974. The project, which ran for 17 years, originally focused on the rebuilding of temples and monuments. However, following complaints from the inhabitants of what was then a desperately poor city, attention shifted to improving the lot of the people of Bhaktapur, while at the same time maintaining traditional architecture and culture.

A modern sewerage system was installed beneath medieval streets, mains water was piped to private homes, and hundreds of jobs were created in the process. Since 1991 the municipal government has taken over the continuing maintenance and restoration, and the entrance fee paid by tourists is used to fund the work.

Potters' Square in Bhaktapur.

Special short courses can be arranged for interested visitors.

Across the Hanumante Bridge, a stretch of Nepal's traditional main route to Tibet still exists as a pleasant country walk upstream to the confluence at Hanuman Ghat. This is Bhaktapur's major cremation site with a profusion of shrines and ancient statuary under huge pipal trees.

Uphill to the north is the oldest part of Bhaktapur and the narrow lanes are a maze of passages, courtyards and old houses.

Dattatraya Square

To the east of Durbar Square, Tachupal Tol was once the centre of ancient Bhaktapur. The area is also known as **Dattatraya Square** ❶, after its commanding Dattatraya Temple. The temple was originally a community centre and dates from 1427. This is the only temple in the valley dedicated to Dattatraya, who is worshipped by followers of both Shiva and Vishnu as well as Buddhists who consider the god to be a cousin of the Lord Buddha.

At the opposite lower end of the square is the two-storey Bhimsen Mandir, which was erected in 1605 in front of a deeply recessed water fountain. The **Pujari Math** ❸ next to Dattatraya is the oldest and most important of 13 such *maths* or pilgrim hostels in Bhaktapur, this one also serving as the residence for the Dattatraya priests. It now houses the restored woodcarving museum on one floor – don't miss the exquisite wood adornments in the courtyard and the windows. Round the corner down a narrow lane is the much-acclaimed Peacock Window. On the north side of the Tachupal Tol is the little Salan Ganesh, erected in 1654 in a lavishly decorated temple, and in another *math* the bronze and brass museum.

The road east out of the square passes the temple courtyard of Wakupati Narayan on the right, and leaves the city northeast to join the main road past an army encampment to the hilltop village of Nagarkot (see page 201).

Southwest from Dattatraya Square the main bazaar road leads directly back to the Taumadhi and Durbar squares.

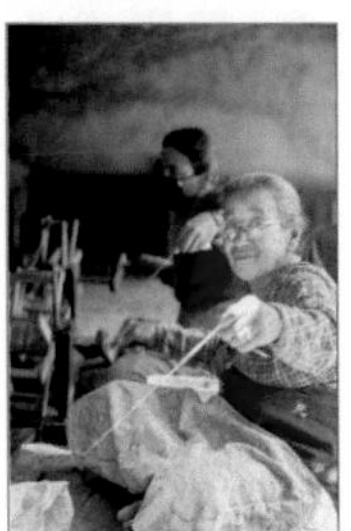

Women weaving.

Dattatraya Temple.

NEPAL'S WORLD HERITAGE SITES

Four separate regions around Nepal have been declared Unesco World Heritage Sites; two as outstanding cultural sites and two as natural treasures.

The Kathmandu Valley has been called a "living museum", a place where history rubs shoulders with tourists and shoppers in the bustling bazaars and temple compounds. In 1979 the whole area was named by Unesco, the United Nations Educational, Scientific and Cultural Organisation, as a World Heritage Site, with seven separate locations within the valley identified under the designation: the Durbar squares of Kathmandu, Patan and Bhaktapur; the great stupas at Swayambhunath and Boudhanath; and the Hindu sites at Pashupatinath and Changu Narayan.

According to Unesco these seven sites represent "an exceptional testimony to the traditional civilisation of the Kathmandu Valley", displaying the complex melange of Hinduism, Buddhism and the myriad architectural influences that have flowed into the region over the centuries.

Beyond the Kathmandu Valley, the birthplace of the Buddha at Lumbini was gazetted as a World Heritage Site in 1997, for both its archaeological importance as an early centre of pilgrimage, and for its overwhelming spiritual significance for millions of Buddhists worldwide.

Nepal's other World Heritage Sites are a fitting testament to its incredible ecological and geographical diversity. In the snowy heights of the Himalayas, the Sagarmatha National Park, centred on Everest, was recognised by Unesco in 1979. Far to the south, meanwhile, the steamy forests of Chitwan received their own recognition in 1984 as a major refuge for endangered species.

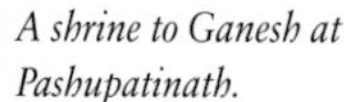

A shrine to Ganesh at Pashupatinath.

Kathmandu's Durbar Square contains 60 important individual structures, the great majority of which date from th 17th and 18th centuries.

Safaris in Royal Chitwan National Park offer the chance to se one-horned rhinoceros', barking deer, leopards and crocodiles.

Religious text engraved in stone.

CULTURAL CONSERVATION

Following the early success of German-backed restoration work in Bhaktapur (see page 188), World Heritage status has brought more attention to the ancient sites of the Kathmandu Valley. Work began in Kathmandu's Durbar Square under Unesco auspices in 1973, and renovation and preservation continues across the valley today.

Unesco funding for conservation work is dependent on carefully considered management, and for all the political turmoil of recent decades, Nepal has largely kept on track when it comes to the preservation of its past. Funding from private foundations such as the Kathmandu Valley Preservation Trust and the American Himalayan Foundation has also helped to restore and conserve various individual sites.

Patan's museum, a former Malla palace, was restored with Unesco guidance as a joint Austrian-Nepalese project, and a number of traditional homes in the town have been restored and turned into boutique hotels and restaurants with Unesco advice. There is much work still to do, however, as the crumbling temples that dot the southern edge of Kathmandu clearly show, but Unesco recognition has placed the valley's past on a firm footing.

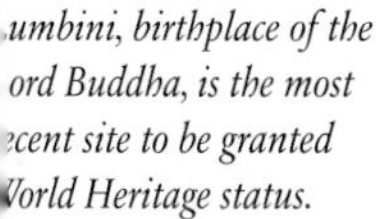

umbini, birthplace of the ord Buddha, is the most ecent site to be granted Vorld Heritage status.

This stupa rises in stepped terraces to a giant whitewashed hemisphere, topped by the "all-seeing" eyes of the Buddha.

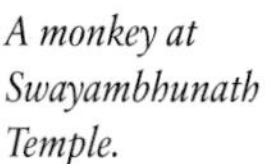

A monkey at Swayambhunath Temple.

Enjoying mountain views from Sarangkot.

FOUNDERS

KATHMANDU VALLEY

Once a mighty lake, the Kathmandu Valley today offers a plethora of sights, from ancient temples to ridge-top viewpoints, all within easy striking distance of the capital.

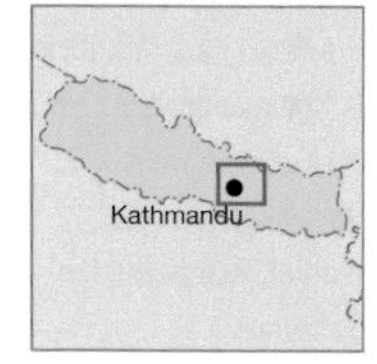

Main Attractions

- Budhanilkantha
- Changu Narayan
- Sankhu
- Views and walks around Nagarkot
- Pharping
- Shivapuri National Park

The Kathmandu Valley has always been the fulcrum of Nepal, and its rich green levels are studded with relics of the country's long and lavish history. Successive dynasties have left their mark in the stupendous palaces, temples, sculptures and carvings to be found tucked away amongst the rice terraces.

According to local tradition, the valley was created when the god Manjushri cut a cleft in the surrounding hills and drained the waters of the sacred lake; the mark of his mighty sword can still be seen in the form of the Chobhar Gorge, where the Bagmati River leaves the valley and heads south to join the Ganges.

The valley is compact and relatively flat, almost as broad as it is long and covering an area of some 570 sq km (220 sq miles). Set at an altitude of between 1,200 and 1,500 metres (4,000–5,000ft) above sea level in the midlands of Nepal's Mahabharat Range, the valley is remarkably fertile, with wheat grown through the winter, and rice planted in the same terraces in spring.

It is sometimes claimed that there are more gods than people in the Kathmandu Valley; besides the grand temples of the royal cities, there are myriad small shrines dotted along the waysides and out amongst the fields. Flower petals, vermilion powder and rice are offered on brass trays at these sacred spots each day, and there are many small local festivals in the villages of the valley, which you may chance upon as you travel the back roads.

Perhaps nowhere else on earth has such a concentration of important monuments that are still active and part of everyday life. There are beautiful shrines, both Buddhist and Hindu, and it is easy to get off the beaten track to explore the more remote temples, traditional villages and pilgrimage sites. This cultural wonderland is set

Terraces at Dhulikhel.

TIP

To reach Kirtipur, hire a taxi or catch a bus from the Ratna Park bus stand in Kathmandu. It is then a 10-minute walk up to the village from the marketplace where the bus stops.

against a backdrop of rural tranquillity. The fertile green hills offer wonderful trekking opportunities, and for the more adventurous visitor the best way to explore is on foot or bicycle. Within minutes of leaving the main roads, you can still find the enduring atmosphere of the old Nepal, where villagers tend their terraced fields, and scarlet chillies dry in the sun. A permanent presence to the north, meanwhile, is the mighty mass of the Himalayas, rising in a long ethereal line above a foreground of fresh green rice shoots.

Kirtipur

The rocky ridgetop city of **Kirtipur** ❾, lying to the west of the Bagmati River, is a magnificent exception to the usual Newari settlements that are built on plateaux. Perched on twin hillocks and clinging to a saddle about 5km (3 miles) southwest of Kathmandu, Kirtipur has two satellite hamlets of Panga and Nagaon, located to the south.

First established as a kind of outpost of Patan in the 12th century, it became an independent kingdom and was the last stronghold of the Mallas, only falling to King Prithvi Narayan Shah in 1769, after a prolonged and terrible siege. After the conquest it is said the vengeful Gorkha ruler had the noses and lips of all the men in the town cut off, sparing only players of wind instruments. A folk memory of this brutality endures, and the residents of Kirtipur still forbid members of the Nepalese monarchy from entering their village. Remains of the fortified wall and part of the original 12 gates can still be seen.

Most of the inhabitants of Kirtipur are farmers (the nearby campus of the Tribhuvan University occupies portions of Kirtipur's former farmlands), and merchants, while other locals commute daily to office jobs in Kathmandu. The traditional occupation of spinning and weaving produces handloom fabric for sale in Kathmandu. The thud of the looms in the houses can be heard when walking down the narrow streets.

New houses and a few monasteries are growing up around Kirtipur, but

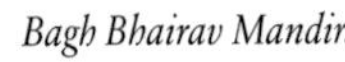

Bagh Bhairav Mandir.

the old centre has a neglected feel, and to visit this area is almost like stepping back in time. The brick-built homes are set on stepped terraces linked by steep paths, milling with villagers, cows and dogs. A long flight of steps leads up to Kirtipur from the valley floor and a road switchbacks halfway up the hill, although no cars are able to drive into the village itself.

The southern hill is surmounted by the **Chilanchu Vihar**, a central stupa surrounded by four similar stupas at cardinal directions. The paved area of this former monastery is still used for drying crops. The higher northern hill is inhabited by Hindus who worship at the **Uma Maheshwar Mandir**. The approach up stone steps is flanked by a pair of fine stone elephants; from the temples there is a stunning view of Kathmandu and the striking patchwork of the valley and the mountains beyond.

In the middle of Kirtipur, where the two hills meet north of the tank, stands the famous **Bagh Bhairav Mandir**. This three-roofed temple is enclosed within a courtyard and contains an image of Bhairav in his tiger form. The shields and swords were presented by the Newar troops after Prithvi Narayan Shah's conquest of the valley. In an upper room is an image of the goddess Indrayani, who is paraded through the streets during the village's largest festival between November and December (see page 91).

Ichangu Narayan and Budhanilkantha

Part of the great Hindu trinity along with Brahma and Shiva, Vishnu is revered by many Hindus as the highest deity, creator and keeper of the world. He is a god with a thousand names, and comes in a variety of forms or incarnations *(avataras)*. As the god Narayana he is most often depicted resting atop a bed of snakes afloat in the cosmic ocean; as Krishna he is a youthful god frolicking with *gopis* (milkmaids). Once a year, in either October or November, a day's pilgrimage requires devotees to visit the four great Narayan shrines; no mean feat as they lie far apart. In addition to Changu Narayan (see page 199), the other three are found in rural village settings.

TIP

While there are public buses and minibuses running around the Kathmandu Valley, private transport allows you to explore the side roads, and to get far from the beaten track. Cars with driver can be hired from agencies in Kathmandu, as can motorbikes for those confident in Asian traffic.

Kirtipur women relaxing.

Kathmandu
Patan
Bhaktapur (Bhadgaon)
Kathmandu Valley
Shivapuri National Park
Shivapuri Lekh
Borlang Danda
Tare Danda
Ahale Danda
Maiya Ban
Nagarjun Ban
Swayambhunath
Boudhanath
Chabahil Stupa
Pashupatinath
Guhyeshwari Mandir
Chandra Binayak
Gokarna Mahadev
Gokarna Forest Reserve
Budhanilkantha
Changu Narayan
Ichangu Narayan
Kakani
Kirtipur
Bagh Bhairav Mandir
Chilanhu Vihar Stupa
Tribhuvan University
National Museum
Rani Bhawan
Tribhuvan
Chobhar Gorge
Adinath Lokeswar
Karya Binayak
Bishankhu Narayan
Vajra Varahi Mandir
Royal Botanical Garden
Godavari Kunda
Shekh Narayan Mandir
Astura (Gorakhnath)
Dakshinkali Mandir
Tika Bhairav
Lele
Phulchoki 2762
Southern Stupa
Eastern Stupa
Zoo
Taudaha Lake
Hatiban
Chaukel Danda
Risal Danda
Chibau Danda
Bagmati
Manohara
Hanumante
Bidur
Mugling
Thamel
Thimi
Kirtipur
Godavari

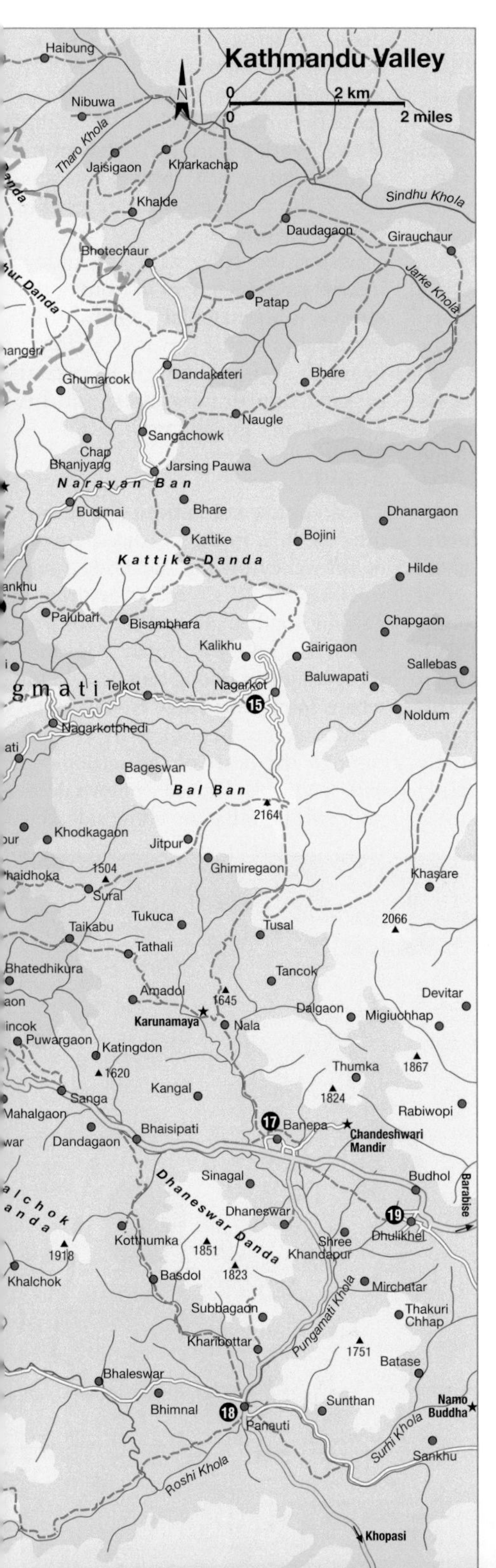

Worshippers start at **Ichangu Narayan** ❿, an ancient site thought to have been founded by King Hari Datta in the 6th century AD. The little temple complex is set in a clump of trees just beyond the village of Ichangu, a pleasant half-hour walk west from the ring road crossroads opposite the temple of Swayambhunath (see page 171).

To the northwest, the "Queen's Forest" reserve of **Nagarjun Ban** ⓫ (daily 7am–10pm; charge) is a beautiful walled hill topped with a Buddhist *chaitya*, where the Lord Buddha is believed to have meditated, and it is a favoured place for joggers, walkers and picnickers. There are two sacred caves, and pheasant, deer and monkeys can still sometimes be seen here, along with spectacular views of the valley and the Langtang region. The main entrance gate into the forest is just to the north of **Balaju**. In Balaju itself is a Sleeping Vishnu statue, which dates from the same period as the larger and more famous image at Budhanilkantha. The Balaju Vishnu reclines in a shady park known as the Water Garden, a popular weekend picnic spot. In the same park are the 22 carved stone water spouts of the Balaju Hiti, a traditional bathing place and an oasis amid the surrounding urban sprawl and the "Balaju Industrial Estate".

Budhanilkantha ⓬, 9km (6 miles) north of Kathmandu, with its monumental reclining Vishnu, is a modest village on the north side of the valley near an early Licchavi settlement. It nestles at the foot of the 2,732-metre (8,963ft) Shivapuri Peak, the summit of Shivapuri National Park (see page 106), a favourite trekking, birdwatching and picnicking area. A small fee is charged at the entrance of the park. The massive black statue of the reclining Vishnu lies comfortably half-submerged in the primeval ocean, resting on a bed of snakes.

Nowhere else have the Licchavi sculptors translated the ancient image into stone so powerfully or so literally. Some 1,500 years ago craftsmen dragged the five-metre (16ft) rock from outside the valley and placed the "creator of life" in this small pond at the foot of the Shivapuri Hills. Worshippers cover the sleeping Vishnu with offerings of flower petals and rice. Budhanilkantha was a taboo spot for Nepal's kings, for it was said that a royal would face a swift demise after looking upon the statue.

Changu Narayan

Since the 14th century, the successive rulers of Nepal have been considered incarnations of Vishnu. Every former royal palace has its Vishnu shrine and there are many more scattered throughout the valley. None is richer in spectacular Licchavi sculpture than the hilltop temple of **Changu Narayan** ⓭ (daily dawn–dusk; charge).

The road access to Changu Narayan, 12km (7 miles) east of Kathmandu, is from the north side of Bhaktapur. Alternatively the temple can be reached by a 45-minute walk up from the Sankhu road, across the Manohara River, using the old pilgrim's route; or a pleasant half-day hike along the ridge from Nagarkot on the eastern valley rim. Local guides from the village are available.

The lavishly decorated two-tiered temple was rebuilt after a fire in 1702, but the earliest inscription in the valley dated AD 464 testifies to the considerable talents of the Licchavi king Manadeva I, Nepal's first great historical figure. The temple stands in a spacious courtyard, littered with priceless stone sculptures dating from the 4th to the 9th centuries AD. This golden age of classical Newari art produced masterpieces that were entirely religious in character. Note especially the lion-headed Vishnu Narasimha, dismembering the king of the demons; Vishnu with 10 heads and 10 arms going through the different layers of the universe; Vishnu Vikrantha, a dwarf with six arms. A 5th-century stone sculpture of Vishnu is also kept inside the temple but is accessible only to the priests.

Beside the stele with the oldest inscription, which is set in front of the temple, is an image of a Garuda, the mythical bird that serves as Vishnu's heavenly vehicle. Graceful statues of King Bupathindra Malla and his queen sit in a gilded cage.

Sankhu

The sleepy town of **Sankhu** ⓮ is tucked into the hills in the northeast corner of the valley on the old trade route to Helambu. It is reached by driving beyond Boudhanath and the Gokarna Forest Golf Resort. Today Sankhu's prosperous past is long forgotten, but it retains some remarkable Newari architecture. A brick-cobbled street runs through the heart of the settlement, with spectacular latticed windows decorating the buildings on either side. Few

Reading local notices pasted on a wall.

tourists visit, and the place has a wonderfully authentic feel. Old women sell vegetables on the pavement, young girls watch the world passing from upstairs balconies, and chickens and cows dodge the passing bicycles.

Trees above Sankhu hide an important temple to the Tantric goddess, Bajra Jogini. Follow the wide stone path north of the village and climb up the steps to the temple, flanked with smaller shrines, stupas and statues. The main structure dates from the 17th century and has a fine golden *torana* above the door. Behind the temple you will find various other shrines and sculptures.

Views from the valley rim

Amongst the crowded alleyways and teeming temple compounds of the cities, and in the lush, semi-tropical greenery of the lower Kathmandu Valley, the mountains for which Nepal is best known can seem a world away. However, there's no need to commit to a lengthy trek to take in the Himalayan landscapes: you only need to go as far as the upper reaches of the valley. For the non-trekker, there are a number of viewpoints on the valley rim with clean and comfortable accommodation and easy day trips to interesting villages or historic and sacred sites. Up here the sedentary connoisseur of fine mountain scenery can enjoy it all from the comfort of a deckchair, while those with a little more energy can tackle any number of pleasant day hikes.

The settlement of **Nagarkot** ⓯ clings to a 1,985-metre (6,512ft) hilltop, far removed from noise and traffic pollution. A one-hour drive up the winding road from Bhaktapur leads to what is one of the best close-range Himalayan vantage points anywhere on the Kathmandu Valley rim. From the Annapurnas to Everest, the peaks seem no more than a day's walk away. There is a large and increasingly sophisticated range of accommodation at Nagarkot for those who wish to see the sun rise and set over the mountains. Tourist buses run daily between Thamel and Nagarkot, and there are good walking routes back down to towards Bhaktapur. Mountain bikers can enjoy a fun, zigzag descent towards Sankhu on a dirt road.

On the opposite, western rim of the Kathmandu Valley, the road northwest to Trisuli and the fort at Nuwakot (see page 212) leaves the valley near the viewpoint village of **Kakani** ⓰, at a height of 2,073 metres (6,801ft). An old retreat of the British envoys to Nepal since the mid-19th century, a delightful Raj-style cottage at Kakani still belongs to British ambassadors to Nepal. There are several hotels here, most with sweeping views out over the Ganesh Himal and Langtang Lirung, with Annapurna II and Himal Chuli, Lenpogang (Great White Peak) and Gauri Shankar stretching out to the west and east. Several day hikes and valley rim treks begin or end at Kakani. Nearby is the bungalow built and used by the British Gurkhas and a well-maintained park built to commemorate victims of a 1992 plane crash in the area.

A detail of Uma Maheshwar Mandir.

Uma Maheshwar Mandir.

FACT

Garuda, the eagle-like vehicle of Vishnu, is also revered by Buddhists. The Brahminy kites – large birds of prey which you will see circling over the Kathmandu Valley – are regarded as a manifestation of Garuda.

Banepa Valley and Panauti

The "Chinese Road" or Arniko Highway skirts Bhaktapur, then climbs towards the rim of the Kathmandu Valley, passing a huge modern statue of Shiva on the way, before descending to the Banepa Valley. The busy and charmless trading town of **Banepa** ⓱ was once the capital of a 14th-century kingdom which boasted diplomatic relations with China's Ming emperors. Turn right at the Tribhuvan statue to reach Panauti. To the northwest of Banepa a track runs through terraced rice fields to Nala, another former outpost of Bhaktapur. Seldom visited by tourists, this Newari settlement retains a medieval atmosphere. In the centre of the village is a beautifully proportioned temple dedicated to the great goddess Bhagvati, built in 1647.

A treasure trove of art and architecture, **Panauti** ⓲ is set south of Banepa at the confluence of the Pungamati and Roshi rivers. Once an important staging post on the Tibet trade route, Panauti boasts one of the only two known pre-Malla structures, the Indreshwar Mahadev Temple. Contemporary with the 12th-century Kasthamandap and of the finest proportions with exquisite woodcarvings – especially the beautiful roof struts – this important temple was badly damaged by an earthquake in 1988, but has been restored with French assistance.

At the confluence itself is a pleasing jumble of small temples, shrines, *lingas* and a cremation ghat. Across the river is the 17th-century Brahmayani Temple with superb Newari paintings or *paubha*. Apart from these attractions, it's a pleasure simply to wander the town's brick-paved streets, admiring the finely carved resthouses, stupas and stone water taps, perhaps stopping to observe a traditional gold- or silversmith at work.

Over the rim of the valley from Banepa is the **Chandeshwari Mandir**. A track leads northeast past the Adventist Hospital to the temple on the bank of a forested gorge. Legend says that this entire valley was once crowded with demons. The temple is dedicated to Parvati, whom the inhabitants called upon to slay Chand, the most fearsome of these demons. It

Looking out over the Indreshwar Mahadev Temple.

thus became known as Chandeshwari, "The Slayer of Chand". The main attraction is a remarkable fresco of Bhairav, painted on the western wall of the main structure. The *torana* and struts of the three-tiered temple are richly carved with the eight Astha Matrikas, or "Mother Goddesses", as well as eight Bhairavs.

Dhulikhel

East from Banepa on the Arniko Highway is the town of **Dhulikhel** ⓳. Set on a hilltop, Dhulikhel was an important trade post and duty collected on gold and riches destined for the *rajas* of Kathmandu financed the elegant woodcarvings on some of its handsome buildings. Its strategic importance continues as the new Sindhuli highway to the Terai leads from here to Janakpur (see page 284). It is also home to Kathmandu University's main campus.

Dhulikhel is central to a number of day excursions, beginning with an early morning 30-minute hike up to the Bhagvati Temple for an unforgettable sunrise over the Himalayas. Trails leading along the ridge north of town are easy to follow, though local schoolchildren eager to practise their English will set you on your way if you go astray. There are several peaceful hotels and resorts on the hillsides around Dhulikhel, and the views north across the foothills to the long white rampart of the Himalayas are spectacular.

South of Dhulikhel, the **Namo Buddha** (meaning "Hail to the Buddha") is a sacred site which for untold centuries has drawn reverent pilgrims. Legend tells that the Buddha sacrificed his body here in order to feed a starving tigress and her cubs. A carved stone slab on the top of the hill depicts the moving story, a lesson in compassion and selfless giving. Clustered around the main stupa are tea shops selling *chiya*, *alu daam* and *chiura* (tea, potato curry and beaten rice), a simple lodge and a huge prayer wheel; on the hilltop above are several Buddhist retreats and monasteries, ringed with prayer flags and a line of nine white stupas.

A dirt road travelled by increasing numbers of vehicles reaches Namo Buddha from Dhulikhel via Kavre, and

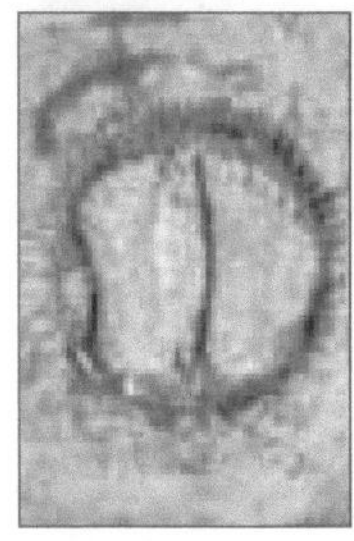

A detail of the Indreshwar Mahadev Temple.

Terraced fields by Panauti.

An Indreshwar Mahadev Temple fresco.

is a pleasant round-trip walk of eight hours. From the stupa another road drops west downhill through a sacred forest and across a wide valley for a two-hour walk or a half-hour drive to Panauti. Check the road conditions before you attempt to drive. This road is often only open to bikes and walkers. The main road continues to the Chinese border and eventually to Lhasa, the Tibetan capital, provided it is not obstructed by snow or landslides.

Patan to Pharping and Dakshinkali

South of Patan (see page 177), various roads and trails link settlements and sacred sites to the one-time capital. There is a road to Pharping and Dakshinkali, another to Lele via Chapagaon, and another leads through some pretty villages to the botanical gardens at Godavari.

The road to Pharping follows the serpentine twists and turns of the Bagmati River, passing one of the most celebrated natural sites of the valley, the **Chobhar Gorge ⓴**. This is where, according to legend, the patriarch Manjushri released the waters of the lake that once filled Kathmandu Valley with his mighty sword, and the Chobhar Hill is indeed sliced in two by the waters of the Bagmati River. Now much disfigured by a massive cement factory, this sacred spot is marked with the Adinath Lokeshwar Temple on the top of the Chobhar Hill. This temple, built in 1640, is decorated with household utensils left as offerings by newly wed couples in the hope of a successful marriage.

A labourer near Dhulikhel.

Those seeking strength of character go to worship Ganesh at **Jal Binayak**, just beyond the Chobhar Gorge. A beautiful brass rat, the vehicle of Ganesh, faces the rock that represents the elephant-headed god in this restored triple-roofed temple, which was originally constructed in 1602. A steel suspension bridge imported from Scotland in 1903 crosses the river near the Jal Binayak shrine. Just beyond the gorge is the pretty and sacred Taudaha Lake, which, according to legend, was created by Manjushri himself for the *nagas* (serpents) who were stranded when the valley lake was drained.

En route to Pharping, the road passes through the pine forest of **Hatiban**, which shelters the pleasant Hatiban Himalayan Heights Resort. There are stunning views across the valley from part of the way up Champa Devi Hill, which rises to the right, as well as from the resort terrace.

Pharping ㉑ is the largest village in this historic corner of the Kathmandu Valley and an important centre for Tibetan Buddhism. The 17th-century Tantric Bajra Jogini Temple is still closed to foreigners, but next to the temple steps lead up the hill to the **Astura Cave**. The cave is sacred to the great Tibetan saint Guru Rinpoche (Padmasambhava), as Buddhists believe that the rocks here bear the marks of his head- and hand-prints, although Hindus attribute these to Gorakhnath. The tiny cave has become an important pilgrimage site, and has encouraged the spread of new monasteries and

Map on page 198

meditation centres around Pharping, which attract foreign and local Buddhists. Nearby is the **Shekh Narayan Mandir**, dedicated to an incarnation of Vishnu as the dwarf Vamana. Adjacent to the temple is another important Buddhist cave, known as Yanglesho, where Guru Rinpoche is said to have turned a group of *nagas* (snakes) to stone. He is also believed to have attained his realisation of the Mahamudra teachings at this spot.

Located in a dark valley at the confluence of two streams, **Dakshinkali** ㉒ is renowned for its twice-weekly sacrifices on Tuesdays and Saturdays. This sinister shrine is the most spectacular of all the Kali temples attracting hundreds of thousands of visitors annually. Only male animals are sacrificed in Nepal, usually buffaloes, goats, ducks or chickens. Women line up on one side and men on the other, carrying their animals to the priest who will ritually decapitate them with a *khukri* knife and bathe the black stone image of Kali in blood. Despite the ritual bloodshed, this is also one of the valley's most popular picnic spots; there are cooking facilities in the managed park area of the shrine.

Patan to Lele

The twin villages of **Khokana** and **Bungamati** date from the 16th century and are located down a road dotted with *chaityas*, appropriate for an ancient processionary route. Bungamati is famous as the winter home of the Rato Machhendranath, god of Patan, who resides every winter in a *shikhara*-style temple. Walking in the Bungamati area is now less pleasant because of new brick kilns and heavy trucks. Khokana is slightly bigger than Bungamati and is known for its manufacture of mustard-oil. The oil presses can be seen in operation in the houses of the village. Unesco has now identified these two ancient villages as being of both historic and architectural importance worthy of restoration.

The shrine of **Karya Binayak** ㉓ is located between Khokana and Bungamati, in a forest reserve. From the road linking the hamlets, a path leads up to a beautiful clearing and the walled compound of the shrine.

TIP

Several of the Tibetan Buddhist monasteries around Pharping have guest accommodation in their compounds for interested visitors. The Manjushri De-Chen Buddhist Learning Centre at the top of the town has comfortable carpeted rooms with hot water.

Misty mountains near Dhulikhel.

After a sacrifice at Dakshinkali.

Carrying a rooster at Dakshinkali, which is known for its sacrifices.

Here Ganesh is the centrepiece of the shrine and is believed to help complete difficult tasks.

The road from Patan to Lele passes some beautiful countryside with terraced mustard fields and bamboo stands drenched in sunlight. Drive through the 16th-century brick-built towns of **Sunakothi** and **Thecho**, with fine examples of Newari temple architecture. A short distance to the south of Sunakothi, a path leads west to Bungamati and the shrine at Karya Binayak. Just before you reach Chapagaon, where the surfaced road comes to an end, take the path east to the important Tantric temple of Vajra Varahi, located in a sacred grove of trees. Although built in 1665, the site itself is much older and various natural sculpted stones are regarded as images of Ganesh, Bhairav and the Ashta Matrikas. The **Vajra Varahi** is a Tantric manifestation of Kali; the stone statue of the deity is a replacement for the ancient image which was stolen. It has since been recovered and is on display at the National Museum in Chhauni (see page 172).

There is a *kunda* (sacred pool) in the dusty Lele Valley, a bumpy trip south only made by the more intrepid tourists. Leaving the Kathmandu Valley, the track winds its way steeply downhill through intricately terraced fields and reddish-brown soil to the ancient Licchavi village of **Lele** ㉔. The Saraswati *kunda* is beyond the village and marked by a shrine built in 1668 and other temples. Turn right before Lele and the park commemorating the 1992 crash of a Pakistan Airlines jet, to the confluence village of **Tika Bhairav** famed for its painted fresco beside the river (see page 175). Unfortunately there is a large quarry nearby, and heavy lorries can make the road rather noisy and dusty. Further on down this rough road is the lovely Malla Alpine Resort with commanding views, while the minor tracks heading into the hills south of the Lele Valley are popular with trekkers and mountain bikers.

Godavari and Phulchoki

The tree-lined road running southeast to Godavari from Kathmandu passes through the pleasant country towns of Harisiddhi, Thaiba and Bandegaon, where the road branches to **Bishankhu Narayan** ㉕, one of the most celebrated Vishnu shrines in the valley. This cave temple marks the site where Vishnu is believed to have thwarted the evil intentions of the demon Bhamasur. Those able to squeeze through the narrow rock fissure to reach the shrine, marked with statues of Vishnu and Hanuman, are claimed to have been freed from all past sin.

The verdant village of **Godavari** ㉖ lies further to the south. St Xavier's School is located here; run by the Jesuits, this was the first Catholic school to open in Nepal following the expulsion of missionaries in 1768. The Royal Botanical Garden (daily 10am–4pm; charge), with its Department of Medicinal Plants, is to the north. This is a pleasant spot with its rushing streams and shady meadows and is popular for picnics and as a location for the filming of Hindi film sequences. A greenhouse on the hill above has a collection of orchids and ferns. From here a quiet path leads on to the Godavari *kunda*, where the waters of the Godavari River pour from the mountains. Beyond this is a Buddhist stupa, a government fish farm and a small deer park.

Phulchoki ㉗ the "flower-covered hill", is the highest point on the valley rim at 2,762 metres (9,062ft) and a rewarding area for hikers and birdwatchers. The triple-peaked hill is 20km (13 miles) southeast of Kathmandu, and a road winds its way to the top where a small shrine has been built to the "Mother of the Forest", Phulchoki Mai. Another small Phulchoki shrine is found at the bottom of the hill, near the disfiguring marble quarry. Spring is a spectacular time to see the flowers – rhododendrons, orchids and morning glories, as well as many beautiful butterflies. Several excellent walks start from here (see page 209), with tremendous views of the Kathmandu Valley and the Himalayan peaks beyond.

A road leads southeast from Patan to the villages of Sanagaon and Lubhu, from where a track can be followed all the way to Panauti (see page 202), a rewarding trip for mountain bikers.

Winnowing grain in the streets of Bungamati.

Hikes in Kathmandu Valley

During the winter months when the high passes are blocked with snow, the Kathmandu Valley itself makes for a fine trekking destination.

The Kathmandu Valley is threaded with a multitude of trails, tracing the ridges of the surrounding hills, or descending from high viewpoints to quiet villages and road-heads. There are many enjoyable day hikes or mini-treks that offer an introduction to Nepalese hill life and dramatic mountain views, and it is even possible to make a full circuit of the valley rim. Decent large-scale valley maps are available from bookshops in Kathmandu, and most trails can be walked independently. However, a guide can be valuable in the more remote areas.

Routes from Nagarkot

Commanding the eastern rim, Nagarkot (1,985 metres/6,512ft) is a good place to begin several day hikes or a longer northern rim trek. A three-hour walk descends westward to Changu Narayan (1,541 metres/5,055ft), passing through terraced fields and thatched-roof villages, crossing the road at a sharp bend and heading along the ridge to the temple's gilded roofs.

Another dirt road winds downhill from Nagarkot to the charming little village of Kattike, where a few simple cafés serve snacks and drinks. A track continues southwest from here to Sankhu. This route is a good option for mountain bikers as well as hikers.

Descending southeast from Nagarkot to Banepa is another pleasant excursion. The trail begins below the view tower within the military area. Two tracks lead south through terraced fields past Nala, an old village with splendid temples, to reach Banepa in five to six hours.

To Shivapuri

A multi-day trek from Nagarkot along the valley rim continues west beyond Kattike to the village of Jarsingpauwa. From here head uphill along a paved road for a few kilometres to the hamlet of Chauki Bhanjyang, where food and lodging is available. From the village a dirt track heads uphill towards the forests of the Shivapuri National Park. Once inside the park there are various options – north to Chisopani, or south to Mulkharka and Sundarijal. A guide is recommended for walks inside the park.

From Chisopani it is possible to continue west to Shivapuri Peak through forests, before mounting the final knoll (2,732 metres/8,963ft) for a

Trekking is a great way to explore the Kathmandu Valley.

360-degree view of the Himalayas and Kathmandu Valley. You can stay in the Shivapuri Village Resort on the north side of the valley rim. The walk is three to four hours from the summit down forested slopes, but arrange a guide from the lodge.

For a longer, six-hour walk, retrace your steps east from the summit for one hour and descend to the right, down to the Buddhist monastery and retreat of Nagi Gompa, then further to the loop road. Turn left, head through Tamang villages, and follow the Thana Dara ridge that overlooks Phulbari and Kopan monasteries and Boudhanath (see page 172) before angling east to the Shivaite temple, Gokarneswar.

The Rim Trek

The onward rim trek continues west from Shivapuri, reaching Kakani (2,073 metres/6,801ft) in eight to ten hours. The westward path off the summit meets the dirt loop road and you can take either the south or north path. With a guide you can follow a forest ridge trail, crossing the Kathmandu to Likkhu Khola trail (a possible campsite) and continuing toward two hills from where Kakani's white lodge is visible. A bus to Kathmandu can be stopped on the Trisuli road. Otherwise, continue the following day towards the northwest of the valley for an easy half-day hike along the hillside above the Kakani road, using Nagarjun's white stupa as a landmark. Meet the road at Teenpeepli where you can catch a bus to Kathmandu.

Nagarjun

The forested hill west of Kathmandu is Nagarjun, also called Jamacho. An entry fee is payable at the main gate, 1 km (half a mile) up the Trisuli road from Balaju. A dirt road winds to the top (2,096 metres/6,877ft), while hikers can walk for two hours on a footpath. At the top is a Buddhist stupa and a view of Ganesh Himal, Langtang and the Kathmandu Valley. A return trail descends southwest to Ichangu Narayan. There is no easy route in this area. A few Nepali phrases or a guide will help.

Routes from Thankot

From the Thankot police checkpost you can walk local trails that link Bagwati, Shiva, Matatirtha and Maccha Narayan temples en route to Kirtipur (see page 196). South of Kirtipur the Chandragiri Ridge runs parallel to the Kathmandu–Pokhara highway, as far as the Nagdhunga Pass. Champa Devi (2,278 metres/7,474ft), the highest peak on the ridge, affords a panoramic view of the valley.

Day hikes to Champa Devi also start from Pikhel, on the Chobhar–Dakshinkali road. A road leads up through Hatiban (Elephant's Forest) to the Himalayan Heights Resort, with good views. The easy grade turns steep and the path peters out, leaving a scramble up the rocky slope to a white stupa and a Hindu shrine marking the Champa Devi summit. Several return routes are possible; close to the ridge continuing west a trail descends from the second saddle to Kirtipur. From the third saddle the trail reaches Kisipidi.

To Phulchoki and beyond

There is no main trail connecting Chobhar or Pharping to Phulchoki, the highest hill on the valley rim (2,762 metres/9,062ft). An easier approach is from Godavari. Two trails lead to the top in about four hours, one climbing up from the temple across from the marble quarry, the other ascending along the next ridge north. Both enjoy rhododendron forests and breathtaking views: Himal Chuli, Everest, Kathmandu Valley and the Terai.

The last leg of the perimeter trek links Phulchoki to Panauti. It is not an easy descent to the Roshi Khola, but once there a trail follows the stream most of the way. From Panauti it is four hours to Dhulikhel with its comfortable lodges, or six hours via the Buddhist site of Namo Buddha.

Trekkers climb to the top of Shivapuri along a path lined with prayer flags.

Carrying a heavy load near Bandipur.

KATHMANDU TO POKHARA

Historic fortresses, ancient temples and striking mountain views make the journey from Kathmandu to Pokhara memorable, whether travelling on foot or by road.

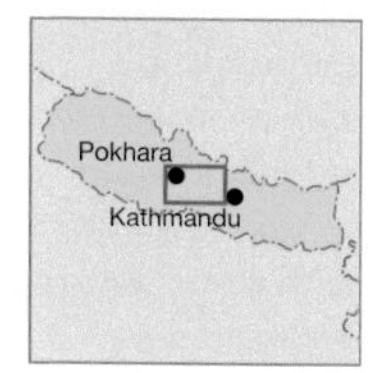

Main Attractions
- Nuwakot
- Daman
- Gorkha
- Manakamana cable car
- Bandipur

In the 1960s, just getting from Kathmandu to Pokhara was an expedition in its own right. Those who could afford the fare went by air; everyone else had to tackle the week-long journey through the Middle Hills on foot, along deep valleys and steep hillsides. Everything changed in 1974 when the 200km (124-mile) Prithvi Highway was completed with Chinese funding. Today cars and buses make the trip in around six hours. There are a number of fascinating stops on either side of the main road, however, and it is worth breaking the journey to explore the pleasant hill towns that are bypassed by most travellers. Those with yet more time to spare, meanwhile, can still tackle the journey the old-fashioned way, along a network of walking trails through the hills north of the main highway.

The Pokhara Trail

The eight- to nine-day walk along the old pedestrian "highway" is an excellent introduction to trekking in Nepal, with relatively low passes – a maximum of 1,300 metres (4,250ft) – teahouses for accommodation and several exit spots should the experience prove tiring. Few foreigners tackle this route, however, and it offers a fine insight to Nepalese life away from the tourist traps, as the trail passes through villages where old men sit cross-legged sucking tobacco smoke through hookahs (water pipes), and women weave on looms stretched taut across their backs. In clear weather there are superb views of the central Himalayas: Ganesh Himal, Himal Chuli, Ngadi Chuli, Manaslu and the Annapurnas. A side trip can be made to the pleasant bazaar town of Ampipal, with its project hospital and primary school. Newars, Brahmans, Chhetris, Tamangs, Gurungs and Magars populate this corridor of ruggedly beautiful country. It is best to do

A Ramkot grandfather on his porch.

TIP

Try to get a seat on the right side of the bus when heading to Pokhara – you'll get the best views down over the Trisuli River, and if the weather is clear you should catch a few glimpses of the mighty snow peaks to the north.

the trek in winter; during the summer months the heat can be unpleasant and the humidity high.

The trail begins at Trisuli, at the end of a twisting 80km (50-mile) road from Kathmandu. Prithvi Narayan Shah's old fortress of **Nuwakot** ❶ stands an hour's climb above this little bazaar town. The warrior prince captured Nuwakot in 1744, cutting off one of the Kathmandu Valley's primary supply routes, and allowing him to launch his heroic siege, which culminated in the defeat of the Malla kings. The restored seven-storey fortified palace (Wed–Mon; charge) stands largely intact, and the surrounding town is rich in traditional Newari architecture.

The opposite end of the trail, meanwhile, is at the peaceful lake of Begnas Tal in the Pokhara Valley, from where buses run to Pokhara itself (see page 217). If you would like to tackle this route at a slightly faster pace, it is also possible to travel by mountain bike, and a number of Kathmandu-based companies run organised biking trips in the area

Along the Prithvi Highway

Most travellers get their first glimpse of Nepal outside the Kathmandu Valley from a bus window as they hurtle along the Prithvi Highway. Depending on road conditions and traffic, it's a five- to eight-hour journey.

The highway climbs out of the Kathmandu Valley to Thankot, then drops in a series of spectacular hairpin curves down to Naubise, passing some remarkable agricultural terracing along the way. From here on the road follows the course of the Trisuli River, the most popular stretch of whitewater rafting in Nepal (see page 140). In the middle part of the route, the valley narrows sharply, and the road clings to the steep hillside south of the river. Look out for the precarious zip-wire and basket contraptions that locals use to get across the unbridged sections of the river. Buses usually stop for a lunch break at **Mugling**, locally known as "Dal Bhat Bazaar" for the quantity of local eateries lined up along the highway. Mugling marks the journey's halfway

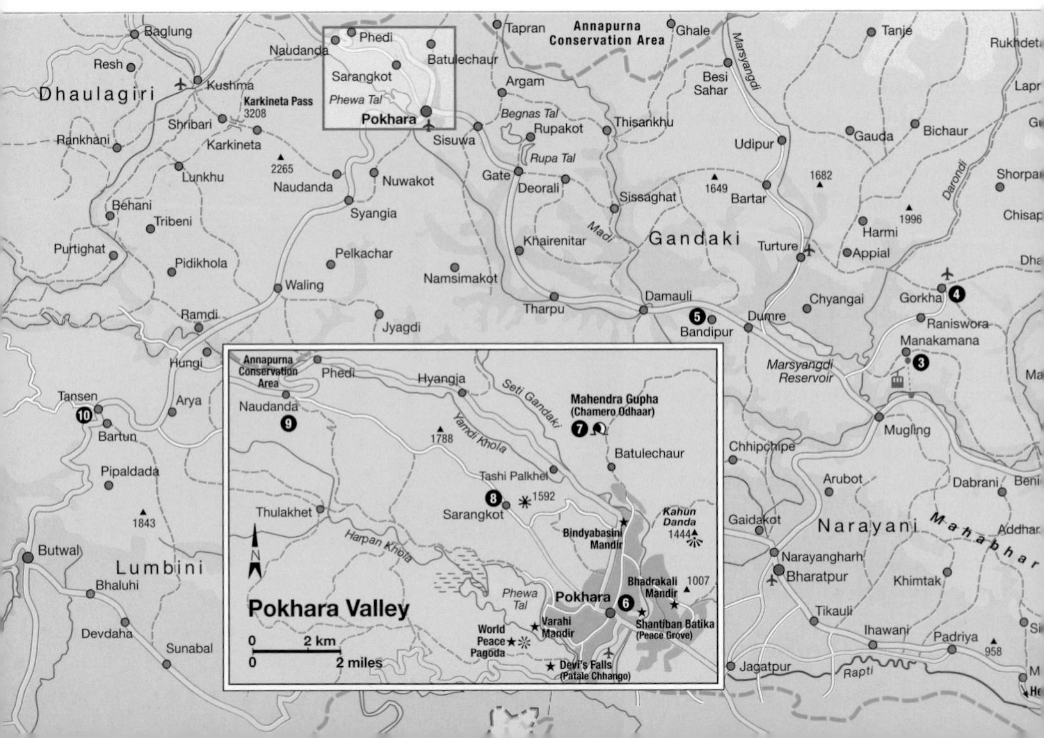

Map on page 212

point. Shortly after is the small town of Abu Khaireni, and the turn-off to Gorkha. A little further on is **Dumre**, a dusty roadside stop marking the turn-off for the Manang trek and the eastern side of the Annapurna Circuit. In the final stages of the journey the hills fall back; level rice fields line the road, and the suburbs of Pokhara come into view.

Daman's mountain views

The Tribhuvan Raj Path, Nepal's first road link to India, branches off from the main highway near Naubise and leads to the town of **Daman** ❷. Daman is a favourite of hardcore mountain bikers who come to tackle the 2,100-metre (6,900ft) climb from nearby Hetauda. But the town also offers probably the broadest Himalayan panorama anywhere in Nepal. From its 2,400-metre (7,874ft) vantage point, enhanced by a circular view tower, a full 400km (250 miles) of snow-clad peaks are visible, from Dhaulagiri to Everest and beyond.

From Daman's often windy, pine-forested hill, the lovely Palung Valley with its jigsaw-patterned terraces, stretches to the north and west. A small Buddhist gompa tended by monks and nuns from Bhutan can be reached in an hour's walk from the tower, down a marked trail through the forest.

Despite the spectacular views and pleasant surroundings, relatively few tourists make it to Daman. However, the Everest Panorama Resort offers excellent tourist accommodation, while the town itself, a mainly Sherpa community, remains a tiny huddle of shops and tea stalls serving as an overnight halt for lorry drivers who ply the Tribhuvan Raj Path between Kathmandu and Birganj on the Indian border. Buses run daily from Kathmandu and Hetauda, or you can hire a private car and driver in Kathmandu for the winding three-hour drive. Travellers en route to or from Chitwan National Park by private vehicle can also take this longer route as an alternative to the more direct road via Mugling.

Back on the main Prithvi Highway, the little village of Cheres, between

Cable car to Manakamana and the Bhagwati Mandir.

A devotee makes offerings at Manakamana Temple.

Kuringhat and Mugling, is the starting point for a spectacular cable car ride to the famous wish-fulfilling temple at **Manakamana** ❸ (1,713 metres/5,620ft), one of Nepal's most popular shrines. The cable car carries pilgrims and sightseers up to the **Bhagwati Mandir**, where the devout pray for male offspring or before setting out on any major venture – physical, spiritual or commercial. It is customary for pilgrims to offer an animal sacrifice when praying here, and the sacrificial courtyard at the temple is a thoroughly gory place.

Gorkha's royal palace

Only 22km (14 miles) off the main highway, the historic town of **Gorkha** ❹ was the ancestral home of the mighty Prithvi Narayan Shah who launched himself from here to unify Nepal in the 18th century. Gorkha's old bazaar is a typical hill centre purveying a jumble of rice, gold, pots, pans and bangles. The town is dominated by the spectacular old Shah palace, **Upallo Durbar** (daily; charge), perched some 300 metres (1,000ft) above. It's a long climb up a stone stairway, but the crest rewards with lovely views of Baudha, Himal Chuli and Manaslu. The palace itself has been impeccably restored, and its stone-block construction and detailed woodwork are exceptional even by Nepalese standards. The inner sanctum, guarded by soldiers, contains a Kali image which demands a prodigious number of animal sacrifices, particularly during the 10-day nationwide festival of Dasain (Sept–Oct), when the compound runs red with the blood of hundreds of buffaloes, goats and chickens. There is some reasonable budget and mid-range accommodation in the town, and a number of treks begin from here (see page 241).

In Upallo Durbar.

Bandipur

A short way beyond Dumre, a 7km (4-mile) side road branches off south to the beautiful Newar hill town of **Bandipur** ❺. This was once a major trading centre on the old Kathmandu–Pokhara Trail, and though it fell into decline after the opening of the Prithvi Highway it is still home to a remarkable collection of traditional Newari architecture. The town enjoys a spectacular location, and there are many opportunities for day hikes out into the surrounding hills, which are dotted with natural caves. There are a number of nearby temples, including the Thani Mai Temple, a steep climb from the centre of the bazaar. The long, flat ridge above the town is known as the Tundikhel. Flanked with sacred trees, this was once the main trading place; today it offers spectacular views at sunrise.

Sustainable tourism has been developed in Bandipur in recent years. The main streets have been repaved, and buildings renovated, and there are now a number of attractive cafés and places to stay in the town. The Old Inn Bandipur (see page 316) offers the best accommodation.

Gurkhas

Nepal's most famous export is its soldiers, and across the globe the word "Gurkha" is synonymous with formidable fighting skills and near-superhuman bravery in battle.

Contrary to a common misconception the Gurkhas are not an ethnic group. Their name is drawn from that of the hill state of Gorkha, and the first so-called Gurkhas were the mixed Thakuri, Magar, and Gurung troops who helped sweep Prithvi Narayan Shah to power in 1769, and who then set about expanding the boundaries of the new Nepalese state. This expansionism brought Nepal into conflict with another rising power in South Asia, the British, and between 1814 and 1816 European soldiers clashed violently with the Gurkhas.

A martial race

Although the British eventually won a rather equivocal victory, it had been a bruising fight, and so impressed were the colonial officers by the tenacity of their *khukri-* (knife) wielding opponents, that they began to recruit them for the East India Company Army. The men were mainly drawn from amongst the Magar and Gurung, but also from the Rais, Limbus, Sunuwars and Khasas. However, the British characterised all these disparate hill peoples as a single "martial race".

Over the years a genuine respect for Gurkha prowess developed, particularly after Gurkha regiments remained loyal during the 1857 uprising by Indian troops against the British. Over the next 50 years Gurkhas fought all over Asia, from Afghanistan to Malaya and more than 114,000 Gurkhas saw service in Europe and the Middle East during World War I. After, this, two of their number – Kulbir Thapa and Karna Bahadur Rana – were awarded the Victoria Cross for gallantry; a further 10 Victoria Crosses were awarded to Gurkhas during World War II.

As the Gurkhas were recruited from territory that had never been under British control, their units were preserved when India gained independence in 1947 – six regiments became the Indian Gurkha Rifles, while four regiments remained the British Brigade of Gurkhas. Both Britain and India continue to recruit troops from Nepal today, and Gurkhas also serve in the security forces of Singapore and Brunei.

Gurkhas today

The legend of Gurkha bravery is still routinely bolstered by the comments of those who have served with them, and by occasionally apocryphal tales from the battlefield. One senior Indian Army officer famously said that "If a man says he is not afraid of dying, he is either lying or is a Gurkha", and during the Falklands War it was claimed that Argentinian troops abandoned their positions and fled the moment they heard that Gurkha troops were approaching. British Gurkha units have seen recent service in Afghanistan against the Taliban Pashtuns – also dubbed a "martial race" in the days of the Raj.

For all their renown, however, the Gurkhas have not always been treated as equals by the British Army, and it was only in 2009, after a series of campaigns, that it was announced that all Gurkhas with at least four years' service would be given the right to settle in the UK. All Gurkhas who signed up since 1997 now also receive the same pension as their British counterparts. Being a Gurkha soldier is still a position of great status in Nepal, and hundreds of young men sign up for the gruelling recruitment process each year. Their salaries and pensions make a significant contribution to the national economy.

Gurkha police.

Boats to rent on Phewa Tal.

POKHARA AND POKHARA VALLEY

The traditional staging post for treks into the Annapurnas, Pokhara is also a destination in its own right, with a peaceful lakeside setting and sublime mountain views.

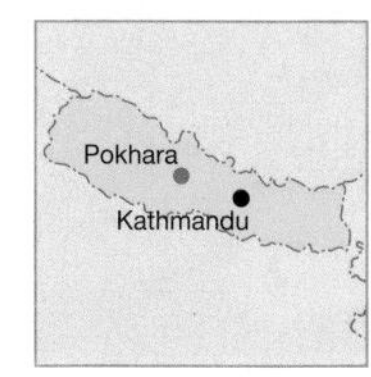

Main Attractions
Lakeside
World Peace Pagoda
International Mountain Museum
Views from Sarangkot
Tansen

Nestled beneath the snow-crested Annapurna Massif 200km (125 miles) west of Kathmandu, the lush Pokhara Valley has been quietly winning the hearts of travellers for decades. While the Lakeside tourist area is becoming more crowded, Pokhara is always redeemed by its setting, and many visitors find that their most lasting impression of Nepal is Machhapuchhre's razor-edged "Fish Tail" peak piercing the skyline or reflected in the still waters of Phewa Tal. Closer at hand there are forested foothills and any number of trails for day hikes, and you don't have to walk too far before the guesthouses and souvenir shops give way to fields and farmhouses.

Pokhara Valley

Pokhara ❻ is Nepal's second most popular tourist destination, and many visitors make their way here en route for the trekking trails of the Annapurnas (see page 227), or to enjoy a relaxing holiday at the very foot of the Himalayas. The 124-sq km (48-sq mile) valley remains largely farmland, its fields an intensely vivid green during the monsoon. Lazy water buffalo amble down back lanes, followed by women carrying fodder.

Pokhara's lush natural beauty contrasts with mountain views of epic proportions. The main Himalayan peaks are closer here than in the Kathmandu Valley: Annapurna I lies 48 km (30 miles) from Pokhara; Machhapuchhre, looming over the valley, is just 30 km (19 miles) away, and yet the summits of these mountains stand around 7,000 metres (23,500ft) higher than the town.

Pokhara sits at about 900 metres (3,000ft) above sea level, significantly lower than Kathmandu and generally several degrees warmer. The mild climate and annual rainfall of 4000mm (157 inches) produce a subtropical

Taking in the panorama.

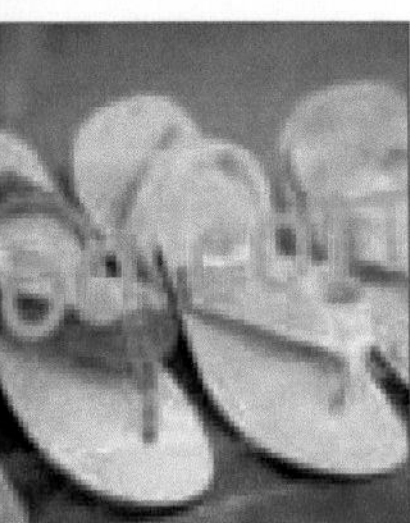

Sandals for sale at Pokhara's Lakeside.

landscape in the lower reaches of the valley. Flowering cacti, poinsettias, citrus and banana trees line the rice and mustard fields; garden walls are hedged with thorny spurge spiked with red blossoms and the gnarled roots of pipal and banyan trees burst from stone chautaras (resting platforms). A lakeside forest of mixed oak and evergreen conifers borders the extensively cultivated Mahabharat Hills to the south.

Located in the geographical centre of Nepal on a main highway from Kathmandu, Pokhara is accessible by tourist bus or private taxi via a five-toeight-hour drive through a scenic cross-section of Nepal's Middle Hills. Like most Nepalese highways this one suffers annual damage from monsoon rains. There are also regular flights shuttling passengers from Kathmandu, with panoramic views of the Annapurnas and the Central Himalayas along the way.

A trip to Pokhara can easily be combined with visits to other Nepalese attractions: Chitwan National Park, Lumbini and Tansen are all accessible by road from here, as are several whitewater rafting runs, including the popular float down the relatively calm Trisuli River (see page 140).

The Old Town

A generation ago Pokhara was a quiet Newar and Gurung farming community which came alive only during winter when caravans from Mustang – announced by the jingle of mule bells – and heavily laden porters from Butwal congregated at the lakeside to exchange goods. The wheel was not yet in use in Nepal when the first aeroplane landed at Pokhara in 1952. Six years later, the first jeep was flown in by plane even before the primitive wooden bullock cart arrived by the same means in 1961. The eradication of malaria in the late 1950s, the commissioning of hydroelectric power in 1968 and the completion of the Kathmandu–Pokhara and Pokhara–Sonauli highways in the early 1970s abruptly shunted Pokhara into the 20th century – but without much planning.

Modern Pokhara is an important regional centre of government, education and commerce, but it retains its laid-back feel. The town sprawls over a surprisingly large area. To the north is the Old Town, known as Bagar, a clutter of small shops selling traditional goods. In the heart of this area is the small, two-storey **Bhimsen Mandir** Ⓐ, while a little further north, the hilltop **Bindyabasini Mandir** Ⓑ is dedicated to a form of the goddess Bhagvati and is frequented by devotees dragging up goats and chickens for sacrifice. East of here is Prithvi Narayan Campus, where the **Annapurna Regional Museum** Ⓒ Sun–Thu 9am–5pm, Fri 9am–noon; free) displays exhibits on local flora and fauna, including an extensive butterfly collection.

Lakeside

Southwest of the Old Town is the beautiful Phewa Tal, the largest of the Pokhara Valley's eight lakes, and the hub of its thriving tourist industry. The first foreigners to home in on this serene location were overland travellers looking to extend the Hippie Trail one stage beyond Kathmandu. Today the budget lodges and bamboo cafés of old are giving way to a far more sophisticated scene, with a long strip of modern hotels, restaurants and travel agencies lining the old road through **Lakeside** (Baidam) **D** and the slightly quieter **Damside** (Pardi) **E**. At times the area can look like an offshoot of Kathmandu's Thamel, but for all the bustle and commercialism the setting is still sublime; the streets are still relatively quiet, and there's still a relaxed, easy-going ambiance. The best lake views come at the southern end of the main drag, around Gaurighat.

Lazy Pokhara life is best experienced with a serene float on the placid waters of the 2.5km (1-mile) -long Phewa Tal. Brightly painted rowing boats can be rented at several locations (around Rs350 for a half-day), and agencies on the main road hire out kayaks. The pretty **Golden Temple of Varahi** **F** on a tiny shaded island draws pilgrims and romantics. Just opposite is the winter palace of the former Nepalese royals, an unobtrusive building slotted onto the shoreline. The lake's western shore is also worth exploring. The hills drop steeply down to the water here, and a few simple restaurants and several resorts are dotted around the slopes. Steep trails lead from the shore up to the ridge top, crowned with a Japanese-built Buddhist monastery, the so-called **World Peace Pagoda**. Damside is an easy paddle to the south.

Museums and waterfalls

A long, paved road leads east from Lakeside through the modern bazaar area around Mahendra Phul and down to the airport and the local Bus Park at the eastern entrance to the town. The **Pokhara Regional Museum** (Wed–Thu, Sat–Sun 10am–5pm, Mon and Fri 10am–3pm; charge) displays costumes, implements and ritual items of the many ethnic groups inhabiting the region around Pokhara, with a special exhibit on Upper Mustang. Close to the airport is a government **Tourist Information Centre**, as well as several

FACT

Pokhara takes its name from *pokhari*, meaning "pool" or "lake" – an apt moniker for a place defined by its principal body of water.

Enjoying an aerial view of Phewa Tal.

TIP

There is now a spectacular zipline operated by High Ground Adventures from Sarangkot. A run on the 1.8km (1.1-mile) -long line costs Rs5890, including transfer from the company's Lakeside office (tel: 061-466349; www.highgroundnepal.com).

hotels and trekking agencies. The **International Mountain Museum** G (daily 9am–5pm; charge) is a huge barn of a building set in a vast garden. The displays cover every aspect of mountains, from culture to climbing, and from geology to mythology. The focus is on the Himalayas, but the ranges of Europe and Taiwan get a showing too. There's a rather sorry looking stuffed snow leopard in a glass case in a corner, and an amusing model of a yeti.

Around 2km (1 mile) west from the museum along the Siddhartha Highway is **Devi's Falls** H (daily; charge) where the Pardi Khola River drops dramatically into a deep sinkhole. According to a modern legend the falls are named after a foreign tourist called David – mispronounced "Devi" by the locals – who plunged to his death in the churning waters of the sinkhole. The torrent is impressive in the rainy season but it dries to a meagre trickle in winter. It's a popular spot with domestic tourists, and friendly vendors sell tourist trinkets and souvenirs with their own particular brand of aggressive Tibetan charm.

Across the road from Devi's Falls is the Tibetan settlement of Tashi Ling, one of three former refugee camps in the Pokhara Valley. Carpets and Tibetan souvenirs are on sale here, and there is a modern Buddhist monastery. A bigger, more impressive Tibetan settlement is at Tashi Palkhel near Hyangja, 4km (2 miles) west of town along the Baglung Highway. The whitewashed houses strung with fluttering prayer flags house around 1,000 Tibetans, many employed in the local carpet factory. Cottage industries abound here and a small monastery, a few simple restaurants and a basic guesthouse can all be found on the grounds.

At the village of Batulechaur, north of Pokhara Bazaar, ancient subsurface lakes have left limestone caverns large enough to walk through at **Mahendra Gupha** 7. There is a small admission fee to the cave, which is dimly lit by a generator. For a few more rupees, young boys with flashlights will provide a guided tour pointing

The World Peace Pagoda.

WORLD PEACE PAGODA

South of Phewa Tal, the bone-white World Peace Pagoda, built in 1999, is an unmissable Pokhara landmark, part of a global network of monuments to world peace built by the monks of the Japanese Nipponzan-Myohoji Buddhist sect. The movement was founded by Nichidatsu Fujii, who oversaw the building of the first peace pagodas at Hiroshima and Nagasaki after World War II. Fujii died in 1985, but his followers have continued his work, and there are now some 80 peace pagodas worldwide.

The Pokhara monument features Buddha statues from four different countries – Nepal, Sri Lanka, Thailand and Japan – as a symbol of international unity. Boatmen will ferry you across to the foot of the hill from Lakeside (around Rs700 return); it's a stiff 40-minute climb to the pagoda.

out stalactite and stalagmite features, which locals interpret as images of deities. The local name for the cavern is Chamero Odhaar, "House of Bats".

The Pokhara region's fascinating geology is also visible at the deep gorge of the Seti Gandaki, visible from the Mahendra Phul bridge near the airport. Here the river rushes 30 metres (100ft) below in a 9-metre (30ft) -wide gap in the earth, carved as the river winds its way through the valley's soft soil.

Most of the remaining seven lakes of the Pokhara Valley are small, but the twin lakes of Rupa and Begnas Tal make a pleasant destination for a day hike or a picnic. They are located about 15km (9 miles) east of Pokhara by road. Begnas Tal, with its long line of rowing boats for rent, is tucked behind the village of Sisuwa, with its extensive fisheries project and a few simple tourist lodges. The forested ridge of Panchbhaiya Danda divides Begnas Tal from Rupa Tal. An hour-long hike up the ridge to the viewpoint of Sundari Danda rewards with sweeping views of peaks and lakes.

Excursions from Pokhara

Numerous trails lead into the hills surrounding Pokhara, making it a superb trekking headquarters. A day hike to the hilltop viewpoint of **Sarangkot** ❽, at 1,592 metres (5,271ft), is popular despite the steep ascent of two to four hours. Climbers are rewarded with stunning mountain and lake views, while several restaurants and lodges at the top cater to visitors. Try to take the walk in the early morning to watch the sun rise slowly over the mountains, changing their colours from pink to gold. For non-hikers or those with less time, a road leads up to a cluster of tea stalls some 15 minutes below the summit. From Sarangkot a quiet road leads westward along the ridge to the old fortress of Kaski and follows on to the village of **Naudanda** ❾, now on the Pokhara–Baglung Highway and another base for treks into the Annapurnas.

On the east side of Pokhara, the slightly lower vantage point of Kahun Danda (1,443 metres/4,778ft) is a shorter, easier and less crowded option

Sunset from Sarangkot.

Machhapuchhre's "Fish Tail".

TIP

Tansen's tourist information centre is run by a local NGO, GETUP (Group for Environmental & Tourism Upgrading Palpa, tel: 075-521341), which offers excellent advice on treks and hikes in the area.

for drinking in mountain views. The Manangi Gompa at the foot of the hill, sponsored by wealthy Buddhists from the eastern Annapurna region of Manang, displays typical Buddhist artefacts in a modern setting.

Another scenic excursion involves a drive west along the Siddhartha Highway to the Kubhinde Pass for a spectacular sunrise over the Annapurna Massif. Like the fortress ruins site at Sarangkot, Nuwakot, located 15km (9 miles) south of Pokhara, served as a lookout for Kaski kings prior to conquest by Prithvi Narayan Shah (see page 212). The 72km (45-mile) highway joining Pokhara with Baglung to the west has improved access to the area. It's a pleasant two-hour drive to the roadside tea stalls at Naya Phul, the jumping-off point for many treks, including up the Kali Gandaki River to Jomsom. The pretty riverside town of Birethanti is only a half-hour walk from here.

Travel agents in Pokhara also arrange pony treks along the lakes and river-rafting trips in the region include a moderate float on the Seti Gandaki from Damauli to Narayangharh, the Kali Gandaki and the Marsyangdi. Some companies hold kayaking clinics, beginning with an easy day on Phewa Tal and concluding with a whitewater passage down the Seti Gandaki (see page 140). **The Himalayan Golf Course** (tel: 061-521882; www.himalayangolfcourse.com) at Majeri Patan, 7km (4.5 miles) outside Pokhara, offers a wonderful opportunity to tee off in the shadow of the Himalayas. For the more adventurous, Frontiers Paragliding offers paragliding trips over the valley (tel: 061-466044; www.nepal-paragliding.com).

Tansen

A half-day's drive from Pokhara along the bumpy Siddhartha Highway linking Pokhara and Butwal reaches the enchanting trading town of **Tansen** ⑩, at an elevation of 1,400 metres (4,600ft). Daily flights from Kathmandu to Bhairahawa (Siddharthanagar) shorten this trip to less than two hours.

Few tourists have discovered Tansen's secluded serenity, and the

Crowds take in the mountain vista from Sarangkot at dawn.

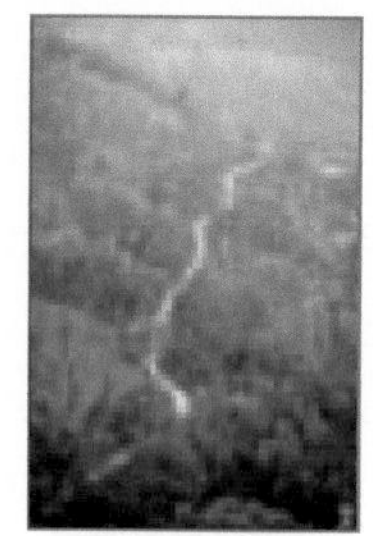

Sarangkot is popular for the views that reward those who hike to the top.

atmosphere only adds to the simple pleasures of a visit here. A huddle of red-brick houses perched on a steep hillside, Tansen is an old Newari trading settlement, one of the largest of many such places scattered across Nepal's central hills. This town of 16,000 people was once the capital of the powerful independent kingdom of Tanahun until its eventual subjugation by the Shah kings in 1806. Many people, however, still refer to the town by its old royal name of Palpa.

Steep, old cobbled streets lead up through small bazaars famed for their colourful *topis* (traditional men's hats) and handcrafted metalware. The clack of wooden looms reminds the visitor that handwoven *dhaka* cloth is a local speciality. Other sights include Baggi Dhokha, the northern gate to rambling old **Tansen Durbar**, a former residence for Rana governors, which now houses government offices. The 19th-century **Amar Narayan Temple** on the eastern side of town has a glittering facade of beaten metal. Nearby is the town's parade ground or Tundikhel, overlooking the green Madi Valley far below.

From the wooded hilltop viewpoint of Srinagar Danda rising up behind the town, the Himalayas are visible from Dhaulagiri to Gauri Shankar. To the south, the Tinau River cuts through the Mahabharat Range; beyond, the Siwalik Hills rise from the Terai. On winter mornings the valleys are swathed in white mist.

The countryside surrounding Tansen offers lovely destinations for day hikes, such as the Magar village of Chilangdi, an hour's walk from town, or the potters' village of Ghorabanda Bazaar, 3km (2 miles) north off the highway. **Ridi Bazaar**, a Newari settlement with an important Vishnu temple, lies 10km (6 miles) down an unpaved road with a minibus service. Most intriguing is the 14km (8-mile) hike up the Kali Gandaki to the crumbling riverside palace of Rani Ghat, an imposing Rana-era edifice. Longer trips include a Pokhara–Dhorpatan–Tansen circuit, a four-day hike along the Kali Gandaki to Beni, or a week's walk along Panchase Lekh to Pokhara.

In the woods above Tansen.

The Annapurna Massif.

In a pine forest below the massif.

TREKKING IN THE ANNAPURNAS

Rising in a great hulk of rock and ice, the Annapurna region is the most popular trekking destination in Nepal, and offers a variety of routes for all abilities.

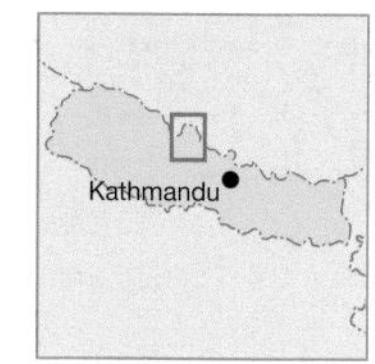

The mighty Annapurna Massif rises to 8,091 metres (26,545ft), a huge and icy presence to the north of Pokhara. The spine of this range marks the apex of the main Himalayan chain itself, and the fulcrum of the continental divide. South of the Annapurnas there are alpine meadows, pine forests, musk deer and monkeys; but to the north of the massif the valleys are bleak and bare, scorched by a dry wind and deep beneath the trans-Himalayan rainshadow. This is part of a high, dry geographic and climatic zone that extends into Tibet and beyond.

The region's human geography reflects this transitional nature too. Seven ethnic groups live side by side here, each revering different deities and speaking different languages. In the lower southern valleys Hindus dominate, but the villages higher up are peopled by Gurungs, Magars and Thakalis, who follow the Buddhist doctrine or a syncretism of Hinduism and Buddhism. Still further north, towards the border, are peoples more recently migrated from Tibet, such as the Lopa of Kagbeni, who practise the pre-Buddhist Bön religion, and the Buddhist Manangis, whose career as skilled traders began in the 18th century with a royal edict exempting them from customs regulations.

While roads have been slowly creeping into the region in recent years, nibbling away at its sense of timelessness and isolation, the mountain communities are still a world away from Kathmandu or Pokhara, and a journey here will take you into the heart of what many people regard as "the real Nepal".

The Annapurna Massif

Tens of thousands of trekkers visit the Annapurna region each year to tackle its trails and passes, and

Main Attractions

- Upper Manang Valley
- Crossing the Thorung La
- Mustang
- New trails in Thak Khola
- Sunrise at Poon Hill
- The Annapurna Sanctuary

Yaks on the Annapurna Trail.

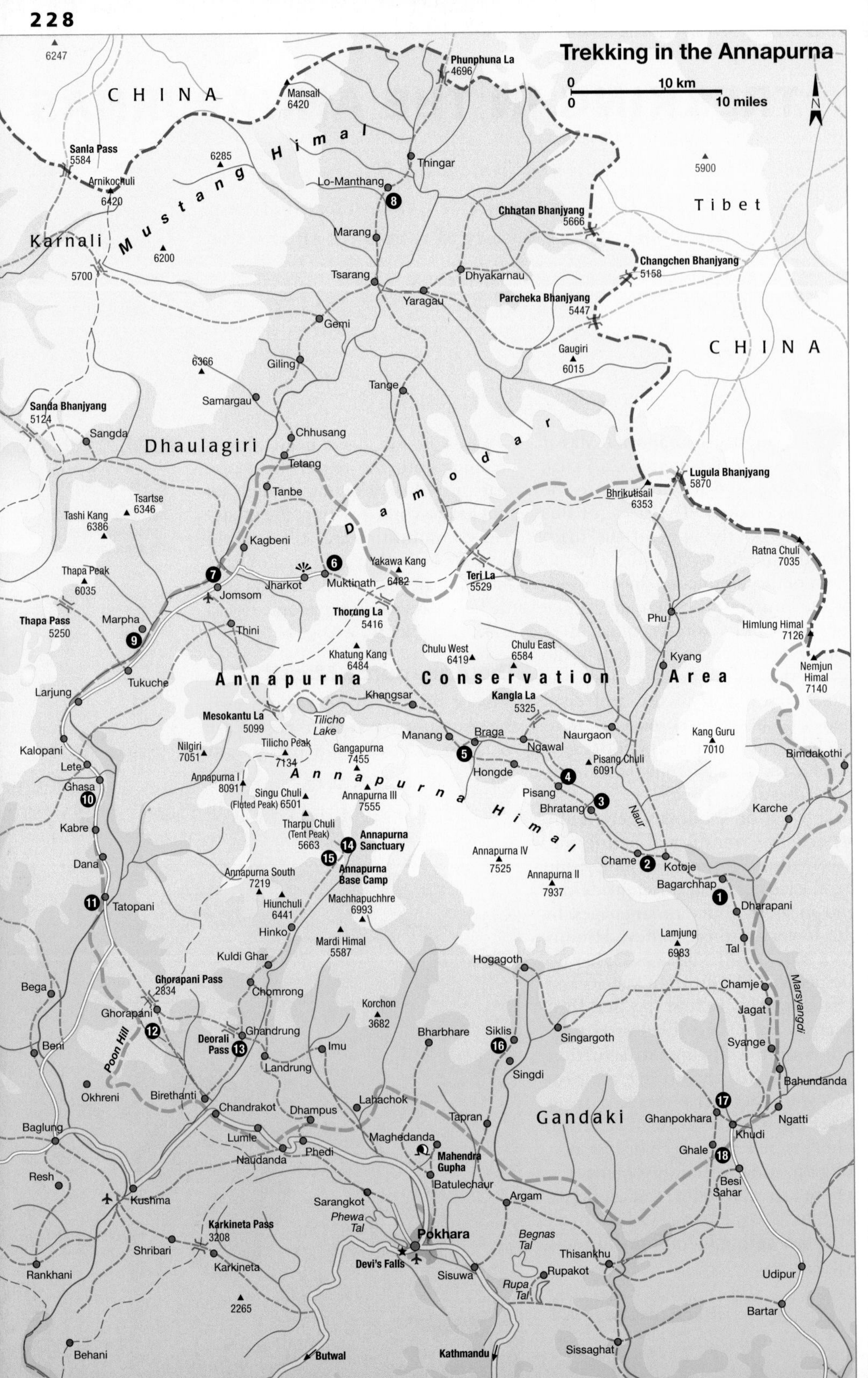
Trekking in the Annapurna
0 10 km
0 10 miles
N
CHINA
Tibet
CHINA
Mustang Himal
Karnali
Dhaulagiri
Damodar
Annapurna Conservation Area
Annapurna Himal
Gandaki
Phunphuna La 4696
Mansail 6420
Sanla Pass 5584
Arnikochuli 6420
6285
6247
6200
5700
5900
Thingar
Lo-Manthang
Marang
Tsarang
Chhatan Bhanjyang 5666
Changchen Bhanjyang 5158
Dhyakarnau
Yaragau
Parcheka Bhanjyang 5447
Gemi
Gaugiri 6015
6366
Giling
Tange
Samargau
Sanda Bhanjyang 5124
Sangda
Chhusang
Tetang
Tanbe
Lugula Bhanjyang 5870
Bhrikutisail 6353
Tsartse 6346
Tashi Kang 6386
Kagbeni
Ratna Chuli 7035
Yakawa Kang 6482
Thapa Peak 6035
Jomsom
Jharkot
Muktinath
Teri La 5529
Thapa Pass 5250
Marpha
Thini
Thorung La 5416
Phu
Himlung Himal 7126
Khatung Kang 6484
Chulu West 6419
Chulu East 6584
Kyang
Nemjun Himal 7140
Tukuche
Larjung
Khangsar
Kangla La 5325
Mesokantu La 5099
Tilicho Lake
Kalopani
Nilgiri 7051
Tilicho Peak 7134
Gangapurna 7455
Manang
Braga
Ngawal
Naurgaon
Kang Guru 7010
Bimdakothi
Lete
Ghasa
Annapurna I 8091
Singu Chuli (Fluted Peak) 6501
Annapurna III 7555
Hongde
Pisang Chuli 6091
Pisang
Bhratang
Naur
Karche
Kabre
Tharpu Chuli (Tent Peak) 5663
Annapurna Sanctuary
Annapurna Base Camp
Annapurna IV 7525
Annapurna II 7937
Chame
Kotoje
Bagarchhap
Dana
Annapurna South 7219
Hiunchuli 6441
Machhapuchhre 6993
Tatopani
Dharapani
Hinko
Mardi Himal 5587
Lamjung 6983
Tal
Kuldi Ghar
Hogagoth
Bega
Ghorapani Pass 2834
Chomrong
Chamje
Marsyangdi
Jagat
Korchon 3682
Ghorapani
Poon Hill
Deorali Pass
Ghandrung
Bharbhare
Siklis
Singargoth
Syange
Beni
Imu
Landrung
Singdi
Bahundanda
Okhreni
Birethanti
Lahachok
Chandrakot
Dhampus
Tapran
Ghanpokhara
Ngatti
Baglung
Lumle
Maghedanda
Khudi
Phedi
Naudanda
Mahendra Gupha
Ghale
Resh
Batulechaur
Besi Sahar
Kushma
Sarangkot
Argam
Phewa Tal
Karkineta Pass 3208
Pokhara
Begnas Tal
Shribari
Devi's Falls
Thisankhu
Rankhani
Karkineta
Sisuwa
Rupakot
Udipur
Rupa Tal
2265
Bartar
Behani
Butwal
Kathmandu
Sissaghat

Map on page 228

to take advantage of its excellent and long-established facilities. This influx, combined with a growing local population, has obviously resulted in a range of environmental problems such as deforestation, poor sanitation, littering and water pollution. However, since 1986, the NGO Annapurna Conservation Area Project (ACAP), which manages the region on behalf of the authorities, has been fostering sustainable resource management and community development programmes. The results are inspiring. There is an entrance fee (Rs2,000), which all visitors to the Annapurna Conservation Area must pay, and which goes to fund the work of ACAP.

The biggest factor affecting the Annapurna region today is the progress of road-building work. Jeep tracks have snaked their way all the way up the Thak Kola to Jomsom and beyond, and even on the more rugged eastern side of the range, what were once mule trails are slowly turning into dirt roads. Tarmac will eventually follow, and one day a surfaced road will loop the entire Annapurna Massif – though this is still many years away. The arrival of the roads has obviously brought better access for locals to health care, education and markets, but it has also had a negative impact on tourism – trekkers come to hike wild mountain trails, not to walk along roads. As these roads appear, however, ACAP is creating new alternative trails through quieter parts of the same valleys, and while the true wilderness character of the region may eventually disappear, trekking will always have a future in the Annapurnas.

The Annapurna Circuit

While the **Annapurna Circuit** of old – a committed three-week hike right the way around the massif – is no more thanks to the advance of the roads, the best part of the route is still as it always was. New alternative trails in the lower reaches, meanwhile, mean that you can still spend the best part of a month in a slow orbit of these mighty mountains, and the circuit as it exists today is still widely considered to be the classic Nepal trek. The route takes in the Annapurna and Lamjung himals (6,983 metres/22,910ft), including **Annapurna I** (8,091 metres/26,545ft), the tenth-highest peak in the world, **Annapurna II** (7,937 metres/26,040ft), **Annapurna III** (7,555 metres/24,787ft), **Annapurna IV** (7,525 metres/24,688ft) and **Gangapurna** (7,455 metres/24,458ft). On the eastern front, it traces the Marsyangdi River up and over the Thorung La pass (5,416 metres/17,769ft) then descends the long gorge of the Kali Gandaki River to the west. The trek can also be done in reverse but this involves a much more rapid rate of ascent without sufficient time to acclimatise and so is not generally recommended. Lodges line the entire length of the trail, making this one of the best routes for independent trekkers not wishing to carry food and camping equipment.

Mountain goat herder.

A tumbling waterfall on the Annapurna trail.

The route to the trailhead branches off the main Pokhara–Kathmandu highway at Dumre (see page 213). Traditionally trekkers hit the trail at Besi Sahar, and it is still possible to start walking from here. However, there is now a motorable road up the valley beyond Bhulbule, and some choose to start their walk there. Starting from Besi Sahar, the first day's walk up the Marsyangdi River affords wonderful and ever-changing views of the high Himalayas. To the north and west loom **Machhapuchhre** (6,993 metres/22,937ft) and Annapurna II to IV. Dominating the eastern skyline are Manaslu (8,163 metres/26,781ft), the world's eighth highest peak, **Himal Chuli** (7,893 metres/25,895ft), Peak 29 (7,835 metres/25,705ft) and Baudha Himal (6,672 metres/21,890ft).

The trail climbs gently through banana palms and rice fields, shaded by welcome *chautaras* (roofless structures intended as resting places) beneath the sprawling limbs of aged pipal and banyan trees. Sometimes the two types of trees are joined, symbolising a male–female union. At Bahundanda (1,310 metres/4,300ft), Hindu communities give way to Gurung and Magar villages. Typical two-toned ochre and whitewashed houses mirror the amalgamation of two cultures and ecological zones. Here, the wide valley squeezes into a rock-bound cleft, millet replaces rice, and rhododendrons cover the slopes.

At the little settlement of Tal, the first village of the Manang district, there is a cluster of decent tourist inns. The large bazaar village of **Bagarchhap** ❶, a half-day's walk further, suffered a massive landslide in 1995, which destroyed much of the settlement. Today, however, it a bustling place once more with decent lodgings. Here the valley swerves due west to enter the 24km (15-mile) -long Manang Valley. A new trail blasted out of solid rock avoids a section once considered too dangerous even for pack animals. In earlier times, the only southern entry into the Marsyangdi Gorge was a high trail over the treacherous Namun Bhanjyang pass (4,890 metres/16,039ft) to

Manang village, nestled in the Manang Valley.

Map on page 228

Ghanpokhara, Khudi or west to the Modi Khola.

As the climate cools, forests turn to pine. **Chame** ❷ (2,655 metres/8,710ft) is the district headquarters and checkpost for Manang, with electricity and natural hot springs (as at Bahundanda). A side valley branches north here into the Naur-phu region. The people of the **Naur** and **Phu** villages were originally from Tibet and, like those of Dolpo (see page 304), remain largely isolated. A six- or seven-day detour leads up the Naur Valley to Phu, returning to the main trail near Manang via the **Kang La** (5,320m/17,454ft).

Back on the main trail, 1km (half a mile) beyond **Bhratang** ❸, a sweeping rock face of dark limestone spans two promontory points some 1,650 metres (5,413ft) above the river. Known as "Ghost Rock", it represents the arduous route to heaven for local Gurungs. The main trail continues up through thinning pine forest and enters the broad valley of Nyeshang, or upper Manang.

Upper Manang Valley

With their clusters of flat-roofed stone buildings huddled against crumbling cliffs and with the *mani* walls – banks of stones inscribed with Buddhist mantras – lining the approach, the villages of **Pisang** ❹ and **Braga** ❺ show that you are now well within the cultural sphere of Greater Tibet. Buddhist prayer flags adorn the settlements and the northern flanks of Annapurna II, IV and, further up, Annapurna III, Gangapurna, Tarkekang (7,193 metres/23,599ft) and Tilicho Peak (7,134 metres/23,405ft) rise above. A high trail connects Pisang to Braga through the traditional villages of Ghyaru and Ngawal. This route is longer but more interesting, offering mountain views of Pisang Chuli (6,091 metres/19,983ft), Chulu East (6,584 metres/21,601ft), and Chulu West (6,419 metres/21,060ft). There is much to see in the upper valley warranting a rest-day at Braga or Manang if time allows. This will also help acclimatisation for the high country ahead.

Braga's 500-year-old gompa is one of the cultural highlights of the valley. Terracotta statues of the Kargyu lama lineage lines its walls, which are painted with vivid frescoes. **Manang** village (3,535 metres/11,600ft), the largest and last significant settlement in the valley, has its own, simpler monastery. The region's most active Buddhist centre is Bodzo Gompa, perched on a ridgetop between the two villages. It is customary to make a small donation to help with its upkeep.

There are various attractive day hikes to higher elevations from this part of the valley, all of which help with acclimatisation. One trip reaches a forested plateau overlooking the glacier-fed Gangapurna Lake. Another ascends to **Khangsar**, a Tibetan-influenced village along the difficult 18km (11-mile) track to the remote and scenic area of Tilicho Lake (4,919 metres/16,138ft).

FACT

Annapurna is named for Annapurna Devi, the Hindu goddess of plenty and an incarnation of Shiva's consort, Parvati. Machhapuchhre meanwhile is named rather more prosaically for its appearance – it simply means "fish tail".

An Upper Pisang villager manages a heavy load.

The village of Braga is culturally Tibetan.

Several hundred trekkers pass through Manang every day during peak season and flights from Pokhara to the tiny airstrip at Hongde, south of Braga, bring others not so well acclimatised. The Himalayan Rescue Association (HRA) Trekkers' Aid Post, which is seasonally staffed by volunteer Western physicians, treats trekkers and villagers. The Manang Mountaineering School offers summer classes in climbing techniques and safety.

Across the Thorung La

Proceeding slowly up from Manang, a night at Yak Kharkha and another at Phedi (4,404 metres/14,449ft) will prepare you well for crossing the Thorung La (5,416 metres/17,764ft), the highest point on the circuit. The first part of the pass is the steepest, levelling off in a series of false summits before the top, which is unmistakably marked with stone cairns, wind-whipped prayer flags and, in season, the world's highest teahouse. Magnificent views unfold all around. The icy trail descends to Muktinath (3,810 metres/12,500ft), completing an exhausting eight- to ten-hour hike from Phedi.

Trekking through the snow on the Thorung La Pass.

Along with Pashupatinath Temple in the Kathmandu Valley, **Muktinath** ❻ is the most sacred Hindu site in Nepal. Pilgrims come to bathe in the pure spring waters that gush from 108 water spouts shaped as cows' heads. Buddhists come to the nearby Dhola Mebar Gompa to pay homage at a shrine enclosing a blue flame of natural gas which burns eternally above a trickle of water. Ammonite fossils called *shaligrams* – evidence of the Himalaya's former position beneath the Tethys Sea – are revered as embodiments of Vishnu. Full moon is a propitious time to visit Muktinath, and, during August and September, to witness a rowdy festival called Yartung during which local Tibetans hold horse races amid much wild drinking, gambling and dancing.

The trail descends from the shrine through a lovely high valley dominated by the ruined fortress of Jharkot. En route to Jomsom, it's well worth taking a short detour through the fascinating old citadel town of **Kagbeni**. Close-packed mud-walled houses, their flat roofs stacked with firewood, lend a medieval feeling to the narrow streets. The local monastery is open to visitors. Near Kagbeni, the trail divides in four directions: north into the fabled kingdom of Mustang; south down the Kali Gandaki, dividing the Dhaulagiri Himal from the Annapurnas; west to Dangar Dzong and Dolpo; and east from Muktinath.

After the bleak heights further east, the local administrative centre of **Jomsom** ❼ feels like a return to civilisation. This is the major settlement of the region, with a busy cluster of government offices, hotels, shops and a hospital. Nepal Airlines, Sita Air and Tara Air service the local airstrip with flights from Pokhara. The **Jomsom Eco-Museum** (daily; fee) on the town's southern outskirts features displays of local ethnic groups and geography. Many people now end their trek here, and return to Pokhara by road. However, new trails still traverse the lower valley – and there is also the tantalising possibility of a journey north into Mustang.

The Mustang Trail

Hidden within the Inner Himalayas, Mustang was only opened to foreign trekkers in 1992, and at present access is limited to group travellers who must pay substantial fees, be accompanied by an official and adhere to the strict environmental regulations. Because Mustang lies deep within the trans-Himalayan rainshadow, it has no monsoon season and can be visited during the summer.

The usual route to Mustang followed by tour groups starts in Jomsom (2,750 metres/9,020 ft) and the journey generally takes a week there and back – though most tours allow several days' exploration around the Mustang capital, Lo-Manthang. *Chortens*, prayer flags and *mani* walls show the religious importance of the route leading north. The trek leads into the land of the Lopas, a tribe whose language, religion and clothing is distinctly Tibetan. The women wear colourful aprons and the men sport plaited ponytails and heavy turquoise earrings.

Several mountain passes up to 4,300 metres (14,100ft) high cross impressive steppes and deserts with small watering holes. All around are the grand 6,000-metre (19,680ft) mountains of the Damodar Himal. Eight hours of trekking leads to a deserved halt in a Champa village at 4,100 metres (13,450ft).

The next day involves a seven-hour hike across passes of up to 4,600 metres (15,090ft) to the meadows of Pee (4,100 metres/13,450ft). The villages of Tange and Dri (3,350 metres/10,990ft) are reached the following day. From there the path leads to the 600-year-old Mustang capital of **Lo-Manthang** ❽. The flat-roofed houses and numerous art treasures of this town are surrounded by a mighty wall: the King's Palace, the ancient town temple, the giant statue of Buddha Maitreya and several monasteries are all waiting to be explored.

Thak Khola

South of Jomsom lies the upper Kali Gandaki River region, known as the Thak Khola, and home of the Thakali people whose *bhattis* (lodges) are legendary among trekkers for their cleanliness and unbeatable *dal bhat*. The turbulent river flows between incredibly high peaks, creating one of the deepest river gorges on earth. Dhaulagiri I (8,167 metres/26,795ft) and Annapurna I tower nearly 7,000 metres (23,500 ft) above the river at some points, separated by a distance of less than 20km (12 miles). A stiff wind created by the temperature differential and the deep gorge blows through here daily from late morning, gusting up to 40kmph (25mph). It is advisable to take a scarf and glasses to protect your face. The

FACT

The Annapurna Circuit traverses a huge range of wildlife habitats. In lower zones there are monkeys, jungle cats and wild boar; the alpine middle regions are home to black bear, musk deer and yellow-throated marten, while in the loftiest reaches tahr (mountain goat), bharal (blue sheep) and snow leopard dominate.

MULE TRAINS

Jingling, clopping mule trains are a tradition in the Annapurna region that dates back thousands of years. Trans-Himalayan trade of this type is described in historical records from the 4th century and no doubt predates these. For millennia people have ferried goods up and down the river valleys carved through the mountains, exchanging highland necessities for lowland ones, traditionally by barter. The old salt trade is a typical example, involving two vital goods – highland salt gathered from Tibet's vast lakes, and rice which grows in abundance on the lower slopes of the Himalayas. Traditionally, Thakali people operate the caravans of sturdy mules, a sterile hybrid of donkeys and horses. Sure-footed and calm-tempered, the mules are well built for narrow, rocky Himalayan trails. Wooden packsaddles are laden with goods that vary depending on the direction: wool, salt and turquoise from Tibet on the downward journey; Nepalese rice, cloth and cigarettes for the upward return. Modern selections have been updated to include Chinese shoes, fabric and thermos flasks. The animals are adorned with harnesses of bells and headdresses of colourful plumes. Lead mules may wear a headpiece inset with textile woven in the same fashion as Tibetan carpets. While the new road-building projects have seen trucks usurp mules on the major routes through the mountains, they continue to play a vital role in the more remote upland valleys.

The Mahindra jeep is seen all over the region.

traditional Annapurna Circuit went this way, down towards Pokhara. Today there is a road running along the old route, but ACAP has pioneered alternative trails on the east bank of the river, and new lodges have sprung up in the villages along the way. In some stretches proper bridges have yet to be built, so this new route is best done during the dry months when water levels are low.

A side trip strictly for hardy trekkers encircles the Dhaulagiri Himal, comprising Dhaulagiri I to VI all over 7,260 metres (23,800ft), through partially restricted, semi-wild territory. A month-long trek heads west from Jomsom, crossing two high passes and continuing on to Tarakot in Dolpo, returning to Pokhara via Dhorpatan. A short-cut itinerary climbs out of the Kali Gandaki and over Dhampus and French passes via Hidden Valley, then turns southeast to follow the Mayangdi Khola to Beni, west of Pokhara.

Marpha ❾ is a gastronomic delight with garden vegetables, apples, apricots and peaches sold fresh, dry and as *rakshi* (distilled liquor). Both Marpha and Tukuche (2,590 metres/8,480ft) have retained their indigenous charm despite electrification, with cobbled streets traditional buildings, and excellent lodging.

Traces of forest appear on the hillsides as the trail leaves behind the dry moonscape for wetter, lower regions. The spectacular waterfall at Rupse Chhaharo cascades into the swirling Kali Gandaki. Exploratory trips such as up the Dhaulagiri Icefall reward those with a flexible schedule and a tent. A seven-day hike up to Annapurna Base Camp and back follows the spectacular route discovered by French climbers with Maurice Herzog in 1950 (see page 135) on the first-ever ascent of an 8,000-metre (26,250ft) peak (Annapurna I).

Below the Thakali town of **Ghasa** ❿ the Kali Gandaki plunges through a narrow chasm, and the transition from pines to deciduous trees marks the lower limits of Thakali *bhattis* and Tibetan Buddhist influence. At **Tatopani** ⓫ (1,189 metres/3,900ft),

A stone structure at Jomsom.

Map on page 228

lodge-keepers capitalise on natural hot springs (the place name means "hot water" in Nepali) and a balmy, floral setting, tempting trekkers with good food and creature comforts. The long climb up through rhododendron and oak forests to Ghorapani Pass regains 1,660 metres (5,450ft), with views back to Dhaulagiri I.

Poon Hill and Ghandrung

Ghorapani ⓬ ("horse water"), a jumble of trekker lodges literally carved out of a denuded landscape, is an easy destination for trekkers, with glorious views of Annapurna South (7,219 metres/23,684ft), Hiunchuli (6,441 metres/21,130ft) and from the top of **Poon Hill** (approximately 3,200 metres/10,500ft) an unforgettable sunrise over Machhapuchhre. Lodgekeepers have installed fuel-efficient stoves and composting toilets, and have removed lodges from Poon Hill itself (named for a Magar clan), establishing it as a protected area.

From Ghorapani there are two main return routes to Pokhara. One follows the steep descent down some 3,700 steps from Ulleri to Tirkhedhunga (1,577 metres/5,175ft) and on to Birethanti's riverside lodges in a long day. The roadside stop of Naya Phul on the Pokhara–Baglung Highway is an easy half-hour walk from here. The older and significantly less trafficked trail continues up to Chandrakot and continues through Lumle where it meets the highway again near Khare and Naudanda. An alternative skirts to the next ridge south via Jhobang and Bhadauri before descending to the Harpan Khola flowing out of Phewa Tal. The journey culminates with a boat ride across the lake into Pokhara.

Many trekkers make a six- to eight-day Pokhara–Ghorapani–Ghandruk loop, beginning at Naya Phul and ascending up to Poon Hill for mountain views. This loop has the advantage of low altitude, which makes it less challenging than many and also feasible even in winter months. The walk from Ghorapani (2,853 metres/9,360ft) to **Ghandrung** ⓭ – also known as Ghandruk – tunnels through virgin forest and lush jungle. During March and April, these parts of the lower Annapurna range are ablaze with flowering rhododendrons with ivory, rose, apricot and crimson bouquets. The little settlement of Tadapani (not to be confused with the earlier Tatopani) provides food and lodging along the route, although it's possible to hike from Ghorapani to Ghandrung in a single long day. Ghandrung's sprawling split-level town is one of the biggest Gurung settlements in Nepal. A day is well spent roaming its maze of stone-paved paths among handsome slate-roofed houses. The community prospers, as do others in the region, from its young men serving in Gurkha regiments.

The Annapurna Conservation Area headquarters, with a museum and informative staff, sits on a promontory behind the health post. The

TIP

If you fly or take a bus to Jomsom to tackle the main Annapurna route in reverse you should be very wary of the risk of altitude sickness, and spend a couple of days acclimatising before tackling the Thorung La.

A sadhu at Muktinath, Nepal's most holy Hindu site.

The forbidden kingdom of Mustang

Long forbidden to foreign travellers and home to an enduring Tibetan heritage, the remote kingdom of Mustang has a powerful allure.

Deep beneath the trans-Himalayan rainshadow, Mustang is far removed from the fertile valleys south of the mountains. Culturally and geographically it has long had far more in common with Tibet than with the rest of Nepal, and indeed it was only properly brought into the Nepalese fold after the fall of the Rana regime in the 1950s. This is a land of rolling, dun-coloured hills, mud-walled villages, bitter winds, bone-white *chortens* and the scent of butter tea – and for a few fee-paying trekkers it is one of Nepal's most prized travel destinations.

The land of Lo

Mustang has always been known to its inhabitants as Lo, and straddling ancient trading routes it was closely linked to the fiefdoms of western Tibet. According to local tradition Mustang came into being as an independent kingdom in 1380 when a leader by the name of Ame Pal united the warring villages along the course of the upper Kali Gandaki River. His descendants ruled the region for 25 generations, and the current Raja of Mustang, Jigme Palbar Bista, still occupies a mud-walled palace in the capital Lo-Manthang, which stands some 3,779 metres (12,400ft) above sea level.

Most of Mustang's 7,000 inhabitants follow the Sakya school of Tibetan Buddhism, introduced to the region in the 15th century by Ngorchen Kunga Sangpo. In subsequent years, the kingdom became a renowned centre for Buddhist learning and art.

Mustang was invaded by Prithvi Narayan Shah's Gorkha armies in the late 18th century. It was so far from Kathmandu, however, that there was little prospect of formal annexation, so the raja was left in place as a notional Nepalese vassal – a state of affairs that continued until the 20th century.

A Tibetan woman washes clothes in the river at Mustang.

Centre of resistance

After China's invasion of Tibet in the 1950s Mustang became the base for guerrilla fighters resisting Chinese rule. Secretly trained and armed by the CIA, they ran cross-border raids into their former homeland. China formally closed the border in 1960, and eventually both Nepal and the USA bowed to political pressure; support for the guerrillas was withdrawn, and in an effort to hamper any further attempts at political contact across the frontier, Mustang was essentially locked away from the outside world for 31 years. The old trans-Himalayan trade routes that had brought wealth to the kingdom were definitively cut, and the region slipped into obscurity, with many locals leaving home to seek a better life south of the mountains.

Only in 1992 were the tightly isolationist restrictions lifted and a handful of trekkers willing to pay steep permit fees allowed into the kingdom. Today around 3,000 foreigners travel to Mustang each year; all must come as part of an organised tour.

Change is coming to Mustang. In 2008 the raja was stripped of his official royal status in line with the abolition of Nepal's own monarchy. There has been some local disquiet over a perceived failure of the central government to channel revenues from trekking fees into the area, and a new road is creeping towards the capital to link Mustang to the rest of the country. But for now this remains a remarkable land, richly redolent of the ancient mystique of the Tibetan world, and as far from the clamour of the 21st century as it is possible to travel.

Map on page 228

site provides an unbeatable photo opportunity taking in Annapurna South, Hiunchuli, Machhapuchhre and the steep-sided Modi Khola valley leading into the Annapurna Sanctuary.

The Annapurna Sanctuary

Long before trekkers came flocking to the Himalayas, Deothal, as the Gurungs know it, was a place of refuge and spiritual renewal, where nothing should be slaughtered nor meat eaten. Colonel Jimmy Roberts christened this frozen amphitheatre of rock and ice the **Annapurna Sanctuary** ⓮ during his unsuccessful 1956 attempt to climb Machhapuchhre, itself a sacred summit that is now closed to expeditions.

Surrounded by 11 peaks over 6,400 metres (21,000ft), the Sanctuary affords trekkers a natural high usually reserved for mountaineers. **Annapurna Base Camp** ⓯ (4,070 metres/13,550ft), a large snow-covered meadow with several small lodges, is only a week's walk from Pokhara, through Dhampus and Landrung in one direction and Ghandrung and Itinku in the other.

Along the trail's lower reaches, teahouses provide excellent lodging. No fires are allowed in the sanctuary; kerosene can be bought and stoves rented in the idyllic little village of Chomrong. While the route to the sanctuary is straightforward, following the Modi Khola River, the weather is fickle and the Modi Valley gorge is susceptible to avalanches and early snow. Non-expedition climbers can try out Tharpu Chuli (Tent Peak, 5,663 metres/18,550ft) with a permit.

The Southeastern Annapurna Hills

Siklis ⓰, one of the early southern Gurung settlements, retains an aura of olden times where traditions run strong. The local *jhankri* (shaman) and *lama* (priest) each have a revered place in the Buddhist community and village elders oversee an effective forest management system whereby the entire year's wood supply is cut

Balancing supplies on the Annapurna Trail.

Manang Valley, bathed in bright sunlight.

Oxen at work.

in just three days, culminating in a celebration.

Built on an east-facing slope above the Modi Khola at 1,981 metres (6,500ft), Siklis looks north onto Annapurna IV and east to Annapurna II and Lamjung Himal. From Pokhara, a two-day trek to Siklis continues west to the Piper Pheasant Reserve where hunting is permitted. A seven- to 10-day trek returns along the Modi Khola southeast from Siklis, climbs to Kalikathan and Syaglung on a ridge running parallel to the east–west Annapurna Himal, and descends to the lakes of Rupa Tal and Begnas Tal in the Pokhara Valley.

The Annapurna Hills are alive with tales of battles between rival kings from the days of fierce trade feuds and territorial skirmishes. The faded glory of **Ghanpokhara** ⓱ tells its story as controller of the Marsyangdi salt trade. A prominent hilltop position (2,165 metres/7,100ft) grants it sweeping views of Lamjung, Manaslu and Gorkha himals. Stone ramparts of the old Lamjung Durbar royal fort residence of **Ghale** ⓲ remain from this lineage which in 1559 conquered Gorkha, and from there went on to found the kingdom of Nepal. Today's Gurungs raise sheep and goats for wool, which the women weave into striped blankets (*baakhu*), shawls and jackets.

Trekking peaks in the Annapurna region

The Annapurna Massif is the focal point of two distinct groups of trekking peaks: those of the Annapurna Sanctuary and those of the Manang Himal. Within the Annapurna Sanctuary there are four trekking peaks.

Mardi Himal (5,587 metres/18,330ft) is only 24km (15 miles) north of Pokhara and is somewhat overshadowed by Machhapuchhre. It forms a distinct knot of arêtes and glaciers on its southwest ridge. First identified by Basil Goodfellow in 1953, it was not climbed until 1961, when Jimmy Roberts reached the summit via the east flank. Mardi Himal is seldom climbed today.

Hiunchuli (6,441 metres/21,132ft) is a difficult mountain, despite its

A revitalising cup of tea on the Thorung La Pass.

Map on page 228

apparently accessible location. A guardian at the entrance to the Sanctuary, it looms due north of Chomrong. All of its approaches are challenging, protected by rock slabs and hanging ice. First climbed in 1971 by an American Peace Corps Expedition, it has seen few ascents since.

Tharpu Chuli (**Tent Peak**) (5,663 metres/18,580ft) was named by Jimmy Roberts for obvious reasons. The peak stands opposite the lodges near the Annapurna South Base Camp on the north side of the South Annapurna Glacier. Several routes have been done on the mountain but the normal route is the northwest ridge, first climbed in 1965 by Gunter Hauser and party. **Singu Chuli** (**Fluted Peak**) (6,501 metres/21,329ft) rises north of Tent Peak and is part of the same ridgeline. First climbed in 1957 by Wilfred Noyce and David Cox, following a route on the northeast face, the mountain has resisted most later attempts.

The arid landscape of Manang lies north of the Great Himalayan Range at the head of the Marsyangdi Valley and was first explored by Tilman and Roberts in 1950. North of the Manang Valley is a line of jagged peaks. **Pisang Chuli** (6,091 metres/19,983ft) is popular with trekking groups and rises from the meadows above Pisang. First climbed by J. Wellenkamp in 1955 by the southwest face and ridge, this route remains the only reported climb on the mountain, despite it having a striking west flank. **Chulu East** (6,584 metres/21,601ft) lies north of Ongre at the head of the Chegagji Khola, where it forms an icy pyramid. It was first climbed by the German Annapurna Expedition in 1955, probably by the south ridge. The northeast ridge, however, provides a route of moderate difficulty, first climbed by Isherwood and Noble in 1979. **Chulu West** (6,419 metres/21,060ft) is along the main crest of the Manang Himal and southeast is **Chulu Central** (6,555 metres/21,505ft). Both can be climbed on the same permit. Chulu West was first climbed in 1978 by Larry Zaroff and Peter Lev via the northwest ridge.

FACT

Prince Charles hiked in the Siklis area in 1980, calling on Gurkha recruits' home hamlets. A four-day "Royal Trek" retracing his route takes in village life and striking mountain panoramas.

The dramatic landscape.

Loading up a donkey in the Langtang Valley.

TREKKING IN LANGTANG-GOSAINKUND-HELAMBU

Due north of Kathmandu are the beautiful mountain regions of Langtang, Gosainkund and Helambu, where a network of trails offer excellent trekking for both novices and experienced hikers.

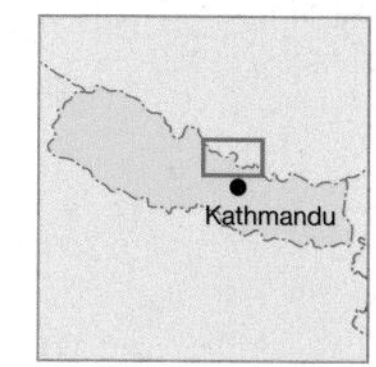

The high peaks of Langtang-Gosainkund-Helambu lie within view of the Kathmandu Valley, yet the area receives far fewer trekkers than the Annapurna or Everest regions, despite its fantastic scenery, easy access and extensive network of trails. While the northernmost valleys have plenty of epic upland vistas, perhaps the greatest attraction of this region is its enduring culture, with trekking routes traversing welcoming Tamang and Gurung villages far less sullied by tourism than the mountain communities in more popular parts of Nepal. The recently pioneered Tamang Heritage Trail in particular is an excellent introduction to the traditional culture of these wild uplands. Adjoining areas are even more unspoiled: few trekking agencies promote the Manaslu, Ganesh or Jugal Himal, which flank the Langtang Range west and east, but groups or independent trekkers willing to camp or to sleep in smoky village homes and to carry a few days' supply of food will discover an environment unchanged in centuries.

Gorkha treks

The little hill town of **Gorkha** (see page 214) is a place with a pivotal role in the history of Nepal. It was from this humble fiefdom – just one of the dozens of petty principalities that speckled the Middle Hills – that the mighty Prithvi Narayan Shah rose in the 18th century to conquer the Kathmandu Valley and found the state of Nepal.

Today Gorkha is a sleepy backwater once more, but it is also the starting point for a number of short and long treks making concentric loops into the Himalayas and ending at Dumre on the Prithvi Highway or on the Gorkha access road. From almost any point it is possible to see the vast ramparts of Manaslu (8,163 metres/26,781ft),

Main Attractions
- The Tamang Heritage Trail
- Treks from Gorkha
- The Langtang Valley
- Gosainkund Lakes
- Gosainkund–Helambu Trek

Trekking on a rhododendron-lined path.

Himal Chuli (7,893 metres/25,895ft), Baudha (6,672 metres/21,890ft) and Ganesh Himal (7,406 metres/24,298ft). After the half-day drive from Kathmandu, most trekkers stay in Gorkha itself or camp nearby.

The main trekking path out of Gorkha descends west to the Darondi Khola down a slippery, forested hillside, where a trail sets off to the northeast, hugging a corrugated ridgeline between the Darondi and Buri Gandaki rivers. By day three on this route, the lush millet terraces are left behind and camp is made in the forest on top of bulky Darchya (3,048 metres/10,000ft), from where the Himalayas appear in all their snowy finery.

The route then splits in three directions. The eastward trail descends to the village of **Laprak** ❶, facing a waterfall plummeting to a tributary stream of the Buri Gandaki. The westward route winds down through rhododendron forests to the pleasant Gurung town of Barpak, with its flagstone walkways and smells of freshly distilled millet *rakshi*. Continuing westward, a steep descent into the valley meets a pedestrian highway that runs parallel to the gentle Darondi Khola down to Khoplang and back to Gorkha, completing a week-long trek.

The northern path leads to Rupina La (4,600 metres/15,100ft), which connects the headwaters of the Darondi and Buri Gandaki rivers. Beyond the cairn-marked summit, a sketchy trail skirts the Chhuling Glacier and eventually joins the Buri Gandaki at Ngyak.

Around Manaslu

A challenging trek reaches north of the main Himalayan range, circling the Manaslu-Himal Chuli-Baudha Massif via Larkya La (5,135 metres/16,846ft). The 18- to 21-day trip can begin from either **Besi Sahar** on the early stages of the Annapurna Circuit (see page 229), or from Gorkha. From Thonche, above the Marsyangdi River, to Nyak in the upper Buri Gandaki, travel is permitted only to holders of trekking or expedition permits organised through trekking agencies. A guide, tents and food for at least a week are also essential.

A traditionally dressed local man in Thulo Syabru.

THE TAMANG HERITAGE TRAIL

The Langtang region is home to one of the newest trekking routes in Nepal, a trail that focuses on traditional villages rather than high peaks and passes, and that was established for the benefit of local communities.

The Tamang Heritage Trail was originally developed by the Nepalese government in 2004 as part of the Tourism for Rural Poverty Alleviation Programme. The project aimed to set up a network of village homestays that would benefit entire communities, with a portion of takings from tourism spent on social welfare, and village funding. The official oversight of the trail has now come to an end, and the system is in the hands of locals, with trekkers bringing new incomes to isolated and impoverished villages.

The trail begins in Syabrubesi and loops its way through the valleys and ridges west of the Bhote Kosi River. The usual first stop is the village of Gatlang, a typical Tamang community, while subsequent days take in Tatopani, named for its hot springs, Timure and Briddhim. Most trekkers take a week to complete the route, though there are plenty of opportunities for excursions and variations deeper into the hills. While the mountain scenery along the way may not match the longer established routes, the Heritage Trail is one of the very best treks for those wishing to experience mountain life and cultures.

Larkya La ❷, guarded by the northern flanks of **Manaslu** and **Larkya Himal**, is within 10km (6 miles) of the Tibetan border. On the east side, descendants of Tibetan immigrants have settled in hamlets such as Sama and Lho. Stone images of Milarepa, an 11th-century Tibetan poet and teacher of Buddhism, record his visits to the region for meditation. At Ngyak, the Buri Gandaki heads south through a gorge to Arughat (488 metres/1,601ft), after which the route climbs westward onto the ridge via Khanchok to Gorkha.

The 16- to 18-day Gorkha-to-Trisuli trek traverses undulating ridges at the base of Ganesh Himal. From the upper Buri Gandaki the route heads northeast to Tirudanda, ending either at **Betrawati** ❸ on the Trisuli River or at Syabrubesi, where the Langtang River enters the Bhote Kosi valley giving birth to the mighty Trisuli River. The valleys and hillsides here are mainly occupied by Tamangs, the predominant hill people across much of Nepal. Their Tibetan heritage is evident in their features and their Buddhist culture.

The Langtang Valley

From downtown Kathmandu, the massif of Langtang Himal, crowned by the snow-capped **Langtang Lirung** (7,246 metres/23,771ft), can be seen on a clear day, jutting above the green hills of the Shivapuri National Park. Some 30km (19 miles) away, the long glaciated valley known as Langtang divides the northern range from **Gosainkund Lekh** (4,590 metres/15,060ft) and the Jugal Himal.

Langtang is easily accessible from Kathmandu: a tarmac road connects the capital to **Dhunche**, entrance to **Langtang National Park** ❹, and Syabrubesi, the take-off points for treks into Langtang and to the sacred Gosainkund Lakes.

It is a long and bumpy journey of around nine hours from Kathmandu's Machha Pokhari Bus Stand, and there is a Rs1,000 entrance fee to the National Park, but the landscapes and village scenes that lie beyond the trailheads make it all worthwhile. There is

TIP

You can pay the entrance fee to the Langtang National Park at the main checkpoint just before Dhunche, but it is also possible to pay the fee in advance at the Tourist Service Centre in Kathmandu while obtaining the necessary TIMS card for your trek. The permit is checked at various army posts along the Langtang Valley.

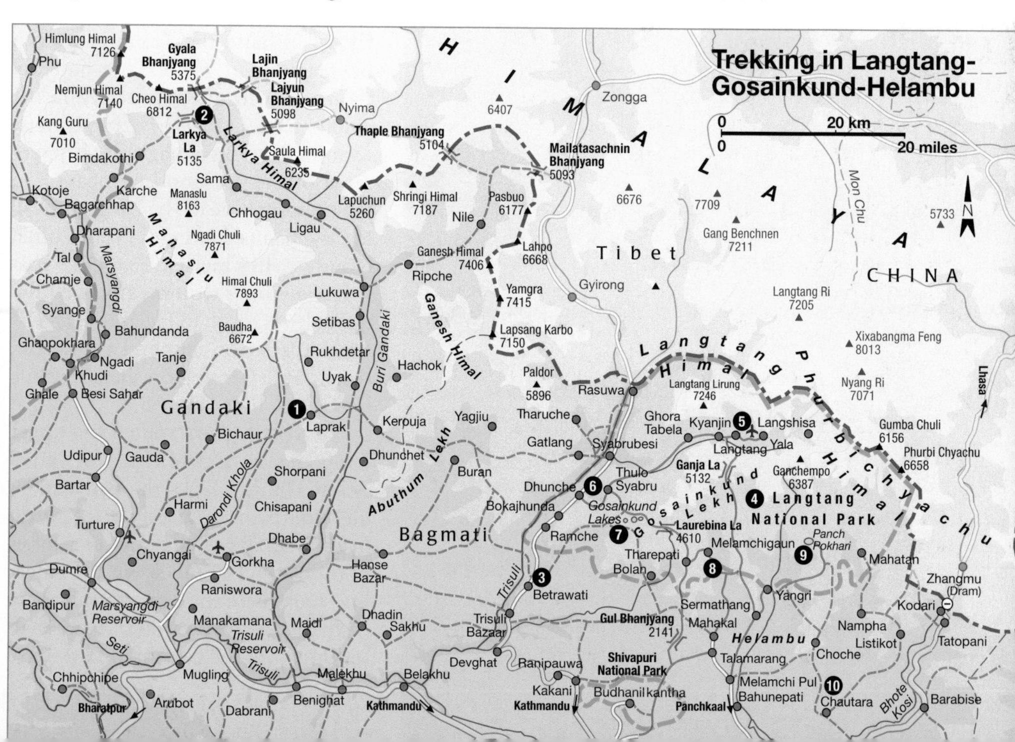

FACT

Legend tells that the upper Langtang Valley was discovered by a man in search of his yak, hence the name which means "in pursuit of a yak". The people are thought to be descendants of immigrant Tibetans who intermingled with Tamangs from Helambu. They are mainly sheep and yak herders, but grow buckwheat, potatoes and barley as well.

plenty of lodge-style accommodation along the trekking routes here, but there are few of the crowds that clog the Annapurna Circuit or other high-profile trails, making the area an excellent option for independent trekkers looking to stray a little way from the beaten track.

In 1976, Langtang became Nepal's second largest national park (see page 106). The extensive forests of rhododendron, fir, birch, and blue and chir pine here are a heartening contrast to the heavily cultivated hillsides elsewhere in the region. Wildlife of the park includes leopard, musk deer, Himalayan black bear, rhesus and langur monkeys and the endangered red panda. The Bhote Kosi-Trisuli River is an important migratory route for birds travelling between India and Tibet. There is information about the region's ecology at the national park information centre in Dhunche.

Two main tracks enter the Langtang Valley from Syabrubesi (1,470 metres/4,822ft). The longer route follows the steep, dry hills of the north side of the valley, which contrast starkly with the thick forests on the opposite side. At Ghora Tabela ("Horse Stable"), high cliffs rim the meadows.

Langtang village (3,300 metres/10,850ft) is the largest and last permanent settlement, with a cluster of stone houses, trekking lodges, and a bakery. Two or three hours further up the valley is **Kyanjin ❺**, a cluster of stone huts surrounded by potato and turnip fields, with a small Buddhist gompa and a cheese factory which was originally set up with Swiss funding in the 1950s. Curd and cheese made from local milk can be bought here. The walk from Syabrubesi to Kyanjin can be covered in three long days, but at 3,750 metres (12,300ft) a slower ascent is advised. This is as far as most trekkers go, but several day hikes are possible to the upper reaches of the valley. For the self-sufficient hiker, there are possibilities for exploring eastwards as far as Langshisa (4,080 metres/13,400ft) and Tilman's Col – a difficult crossing (named after Bill Tilman, the first Westerner to visit Langtang in 1949), which leads east to Panch Pokhari. Closer at hand the Tsona Lakes can be reached in a pleasant half-day return trip from Kyanjin, while the 4,600-metre (15,091ft) viewpoint at Kyanjin Ri offers a magnificent panorama of the surrounding peaks. On the opposite side of the Langtang Valley, the Ganja La, a snowy and often cloudy 5,132-metre (16,833ft) pass that sometimes requires alpine equipment, leads south to Helambu. Hikers with experience, tents and a guide can reach Tarke Ghyang on the other side in three to four days.

The easiest return route from upper Langtang is back down the valley. Below Ghora Tabela, the path scrambles south up a landslide to **Thulo Syabru ❻**, its single row of timber houses stretched far down the ridgeline. From here you can return directly to the road at Syabrubesi, or branch south to join the Gosainkund trek.

Trek porters in the forest.

Map on page 243

The Gosainkund–Helambu Trek

Langtang National Park also includes the sacred **Gosainkund Lakes** ❼, a pilgrimage site for thousands of Shiva devotees during the July–August full-moon festival of Janai Purnima. Hindus throng to bathe in the lakes' holy waters; males change a string worn around one shoulder renewing their devotion to Shiva, god of reproduction and destruction. *Jhankris* (shamans) dance in an induced trance to all-night singing and drum-beating. According to legend, Shiva formed the lakes by thrusting his *trisul* (trident) into the mountainside, creating three gushing springs and giving the Trisuli River its name.

The trail to **Gosainkund** (4,312 metres/14,144ft) climbs from either Dhunche or Syabrubesi through lush rhododendron hillsides to Sing Gompa, where there is another cheese factory. The 2,400-metre (7,800ft) elevation gain from Dhunche requires three days for proper acclimatisation. Food and lodging are available at the lakes during trekking season.

East of the lakes Laurebina La (4,609 metres/15,124ft) leads to the **Helambu** region. Scores of rock piles left by pilgrims seeking good fortune dot the treeless landscape. From the pass, the path descends through Gopte to a cluster of shepherds' huts and trekking lodges at Tharepati, where it divides into two return routes to Kathmandu. The shorter way rides the ridge south through cool rhododendron forests (crawling with leeches during monsoon season) passing several Tamang villages before entering the Shivapuri National Park and cresting the Kathmandu Valley rim at Burlang Bhanjyang, some 1,100 metres (3,600ft) above Sundarijal. This ridge forms the divide between two of Nepal's major river systems – the Gandaki, which extends west to Dhaulagiri, and the Sapt Kosi whose tributaries extend east to Kanchenjunga on the border with Sikkim. The end of the trail at Sundarijal is just a short drive from Kathmandu.

The other trail from Tharepati climbs east and then plunges 1,000 metres (3,300ft) to a tributary of the

Locally made yak's cheese.

An aerial view of Kyanjin.

TIP

If visiting the Helambu in late summer, be sure to try the local apples, which are a real treat, as is the region's spring flower show of *laligurans* (rhododendrons) and purple irises.

Melamchi Khola and above it the village of **Melamchigaun** ❽. Stone houses lie scattered across the terraced fields above an old gompa dressed with tall prayer flags. The people of Helambu call themselves Sherpas but their link with the Sherpas of Solu Khumbu is distant, underlined by different dialects, clothes and recorded ancestry. Inside the heavy timber homes of Tarkeghyang and Sermathang, rows of polished copper cauldrons and brass plates line the sitting rooms. These lavish arrays of kitchenware are the traditional way of displaying a family's wealth throughout the Tibetan-influenced areas of Asia. A gompa set on the ridge above Tarkeghyang commands excellent views of the Himalayas, looking north towards the Ganja La and Dorje Lakpa (6,990 metres/22,927ft) and a cluster of peaks over 6,000 metres (20,000ft). This area is also associated with the Tibetan poet-sage Milarepa, who, according to local legend, visited during the 11th century.

The trail descends into the Melamchi Khola valley and leads to the village of Talamarang and the rice paddies of Melamchi Pul from where the route to Kathmandu follows the dirt road south to Panchkaal. A more scenic alternative climbs west from Talamarang back up to 1,890 metres (6,200ft) via Pati Bhanjyang on the way to Sundarijal.

Sacred lakes

The Nepalese invest sacred meaning in nature, particularly water and high points, expressed by strings of prayer flags and *mani* stone piles. Many high lakes are important places of pilgrimage.

Dudh Pokhari (Milk Lake) lies at 4,270 metres (14,000ft) on the ridge west of the Darondi, a two-week trek north from Gorkha via Darchya and Barpak. Far from permanent settlements, only shepherds and pilgrims are encountered on the trail. This trek should be attempted only with the help of a guide and staff to carry supplies. The return route stays high along Sirandanda ridge and exits east to the Gorkha road or west via the Chepe Khola to Dumre.

Crossing a river on a suspension bridge.

A five-day round trip to Bara Pokhari (3,110 metres/10,200ft) trails east from Phalesangu and Ngadi on the lower Marsyangdi. Paths also connect with Sirandanda, three to four days away. The lake often has snow until spring.

Another set of sacred lakes in the east of Langtang National Park called **Panch Pokhari** ❾ (Five Lakes) introduces trekkers to the saw-toothed Jugal Himal. The trek from Tarkeghyang crosses the Indrawati Khola, brown with the hills' red clay which it carries to the Sun Kosi, and mounts a 3,600-metre (12,000ft) ridge to the lakes. The shortest exit route heads straight down the ridge to **Chautara** ❿, a large bazaar connected to the Kathmandu–Kodari road by jeep or bus.

Trekking Peaks of Langtang, Jugal and Ganesh Himal

Langtang and Jugal lie just 50km (30 miles) north of Kathmandu and are readily accessible to visitors. However, despite the vast number of mountains in the area, there is only one established trekking peak. Formerly known as Ganja La Chuli, Naya Kanga (5,844 metres/19,180ft) is west of the Ganja La pass which separates the Langtang Valley from Helambu.

The normal route climbs from Kyanjin Gompa towards the Ganja La and ascends the northeast face and north ridge. No record of a first ascent has been traced. South side routes have been made but are more difficult.

Further west from Langtang, the icy pyramids of the Ganesh Himal make a stunning panorama from the Kathmandu Valley. Set between the Buri Gandaki and the Bhote Kosi, they provide an enjoyable trekking peak climb for able mountaineers. Paldor (5,896 metres/19,344ft) can be approached from the Trisuli Valley and thence from the Chilime Khola to Gatlang. Base Camp is best placed at the head of the Mailung Khola from where several small peaks offer training climbs. The northeast ridge, known as Tilman's Ridge, provides a fine route of ascent.

An alpine stream.

Porters gather rocks for use at camp.

The road to Tibet

For all Nepal's own mystique, as far as many travellers are concerned, the land that lies beyond its northern borders is the ultimate adventurous destination.

Few places on earth have such an enduring grip on the world's imagination as Tibet. This high-altitude former theocracy has been subjected to the full force of Orientalist fantasy and imperial geopolitics – not to mention more than half a century of often oppressive Chinese rule – but has somehow always retained its allure.

The forbidden land

Tibet's geography alone has been enough to ensure its long isolation from the rest of the world. The entire region lies at an average altitude of almost 5,000 metres (16,400ft), and early explorers were often thwarted by the terrain long before they were baffled by the suspicious Tibetan authorities. This remoteness earned Tibet a pronounced status during the heyday of European exploration – a status which has endured into the 21st century. The exotic glamour of the local brand of Buddhism, meanwhile, has only heightened its appeal.

That the mystical Tibet of typical Western imaginings was – and is – often far removed from the bleak reality of life on the trans-Himalayan plateau is beside the point, and the tantalising prospect of an overland journey to this forbidden land is still an abiding ambition for many.

Tibet had a complex relationship with China for many centuries, slipping in and out of the shadow of its huge neighbour as imperial power in Beijing waxed and waned. But in 1951 the People's Republic invaded and Tibet has been a restive region of the Chinese state ever since. Since the invasion the Chinese government has worked hard to bring Tibet into the fold, through a mix of tight control of traditional Tibetan institutions, firm responses to internal dissent, the construction of roads and railways to the very heart of the region and the influx of huge numbers of Han Chinese migrants.

Over the years thousands of Tibetan refugees have fled south across the border and, while the exiled spiritual leader, the Dalai Lama, based himself in India, many others have settled in Nepal. Chinese rule and the occasional outbursts of resistance have added further complications for would-be travellers, but when the situation is stable it is still possible to make the epic journey to "the roof of the world".

Portrait of a young Tibetan boy.

Travelling to Tibet

The 1,000km (600-mile) overland journey from Kathmandu across the Tibetan border is one of the most spectacular road trips on earth, wending its way through Nepal's lush green hills to the barren windswept plains of the Tibetan Plateau. When the border is open, travel agencies in Kathmandu arrange organised tours to the Tibetan capital, Lhasa. These agencies generally organise the necessary Chinese visas and travel permits for their guests, and a typical seven- or eight-day tour costs around US$1,500. The trip is possible year-round, but the border is generally closed from late February to the end of March around the anniversary of the Dalai Lama's 1959 flight to India.

The 114km (70-mile) Arniko Raj Marg, also known as the Friendship Highway, was built with Chinese assistance in the 1960s and follows the course of the ancient Kathmandu–Lhasa trade route. The most spectacular scenery begins on the far side of the Tibetan border.

The route begins by climbing eastward over the rim of the Kathmandu Valley, passing Bhaktapur

 Map on page 243

(see page 183) and the tourist resort of Dhulikhel (see page 203). Dropping into the severely deforested Panchkaal Valley, it crosses the braided strands of the Indrawati Khola at Dolalghat. This riverside village is the lowest and hottest point of the trip, at only 634 metres (2,080ft) altitude.

From Dolalghat the highway swings north to follow the course of the Sun Kosi, the "River of Gold". As the road climbs, the river gorge deepens and the scenery becomes increasingly dramatic – a taste of what's to come. The turn-off to Jiri, trailhead for the Solu-Khumbu region, is 78km (48 miles) from Kathmandu. Soon after this is Lamosangu, a sprawling roadside town with a mineral-processing plant. The little village of Barabise lies 8km (5 miles) further. Monsoon landslides regularly wipe out sections of road in this region.

The small town of Tatopani, 23km (14 miles) past Barabise, is the end of the road for many. Its name comes from its natural hot springs, now channelled through a cement tap-stand that locals favour as a laundry facility. Nepalese customs and immigration is a few kilometres down the road at the tiny settlement of Kodari.

Into Tibet

A concrete "Friendship Bridge" spanning the Bhote Kosi marks the border between Nepal and China. Chinese customs and immigration is at **Zhangmu**, a large town visible high up on the hillside some 8km (5 miles) away. Also known as Khasa or Dram, it's a bustling settlement where Tibetan, Chinese and Nepalese influences and goods mingle. Nepalese can travel up to this point without a passport or permit; many come to purchase Chinese cloth, thermos flasks, shoes and milk powder.

From Zhangmu the landscape begins its incredible transition, as the road winds its way up a narrow river gorge. Travellers usually stop off at the village of Nyalam (4,100 metres/13,450ft), which marks the dividing point between forest and bare plains. After a few more hours of ascent, the road crests at the 5,050-metre (16,570ft) Lalung La Pass, to emerge onto the Tibetan Plateau, a high, dry and wild realm quite unlike anywhere else on earth.

The North Face of Mount Everest is visible slightly further down the road en route for the farming town of Gyangtse. The magnificent, multiroomed Kumbum stupa here was created in the 15th century by Newar craftsmen, who endowed it with a wealth of beautiful frescoes and images.

The next location along the route is Shigatse, Tibet's second largest city. At the centre of town is the great monastery of Tashilunpo, an impressive collection of ochre buildings roofed in glittering gold. Beyond Shigatse the road continues to Lhasa itself.

The road to Tibet, with Everest in view.

The Everest mountain range at dawn, from left: Nuptse, Everest, Lhotse, Ama Dablam, Dablam.

Tshola Tsho Lake.

THE EVEREST REGION

Mount Everest, the highest mountain on earth, is Nepal's ultimate icon; the surrounding region is also fascinating for its enduring village life and remarkable religious traditions.

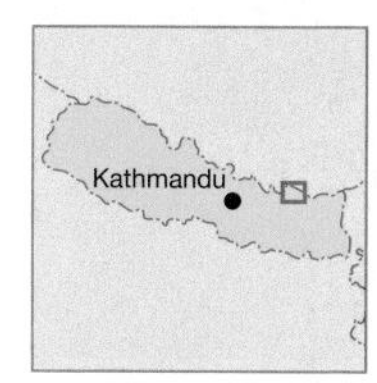

Eastern Nepal epitomises the original Sanskrit meaning of the name Himalaya: "Abode of Snows". Five of the world's 10 highest peaks, including Mount Everest at 8,850 metres (29,035ft) – known as Sagarmatha to the Nepalese and Chomolungma to the Tibetans – preside over a region of enormous geographical and cultural contrasts. In ancient Tibetan literature, valleys such as Khumbu and Rolwaling are sanctified as *beyuls*, hidden places of refuge for troubled times. Because the annual monsoon rains arrive earlier and stay later, the region as a whole is greener and lusher than other mountainous areas of Nepal. It is also friendly, relaxed and relatively prosperous.

The Sherpa homeland

Eastern Nepal is home to at least a dozen ethnic hill peoples including the celebrated Sherpas of mountaineering fame (see page 53). The Sherpas, whose name, "people from the east", denotes their original home in the Eastern Tibetan province of Kham, settled in the Everest region in the 16th century. They kept their connection to their homeland by continuing to trade over the Nangpa La pass, bringing salt, wool, carpets, Tibetan artefacts and mastiff dogs south from Tibet, and carrying grains, raw iron, paper, cotton cloth and *dzo* (a cross-breed of cattle and yak) north from the lowlands. By the time trans-Himalayan trade subsided in the early 1960s, the Sherpas had already proven adept as mountain guides and high-altitude porters. Turning their energies to the new trekking business, they have prospered from tourism more than any other ethnic group, both as lodge-keepers in Khumbu and through employment in the Kathmandu-based trekking industry. Sherpa life has changed with the influx of visitors and money, but most observers agree they have managed to

Main Attractions

- Solu
- Thyangboche
- The Everest Base Camp Trek
- Gokyo
- Island Peak
- Rolwaling Valley

Porters in the Everest region.

A mountain flight helicopter.

maintain the core of their identity, successfully combining new-found prosperity with traditional values.

Trekking in eastern Nepal offers a wide range of wilderness and cultural encounters. Most first-timers choose to live out their dreams of standing at the foot of Mount Everest, though Upper Khumbu offers a number of other routes. Others prefer less-trammelled areas east of Khumbu, including the Kanchenjunga region (see page 274). A middle-altitude region such as Solu rewards with pleasant walking and a moderate climate year round.

Solu

The region of Solu, or Sho Rung as the Sherpas know it, lies between 2,600 and 3,200 metres (8,500–10,500ft) elevation, extending from Jiri east to the Dudh Kosi (Milk River). It is a land blessed with a temperate climate, well-watered forests and pastures, and rolling farmlands cultivated in maize, wheat, barley and apples. Buddhist monks and nuns led by *rinpoches* serve the predominantly Sherpa communities from *gompas* (monasteries) patterned after those built by their ancestors in Tibet.

While most trekkers bound for the Everest region fly straight in to Lukla from Kathmandu, the journey up through Solu's land of milk and honey is much more than a mere path to Khumbu's high country. The area invites a leisurely pace. The standard itinerary through Solu to Lukla takes six days, but there are plenty of opportunities for side trips. Detour for a retreat at the fascinating Thupten Choling Monastery a few hours' walk above Junbesi. Relocated from Rongbuk Monastery on the Tibetan side of Mount Everest, this gompa is the focal point of a large community of monastic and lay practitioners. Chiwong Gompa near Phaplu is another vibrant Buddhist community: ritual Mani Rimdu dances are performed here every autumn. Trekkers come also to photograph the spring rhododendron and magnolia blooms, which are more profuse in Solu's forests than almost anywhere in Nepal.

A wilderness trek north from Junbesi to the pilgrimage site of Dudh Kunda reaches the base of Numbur

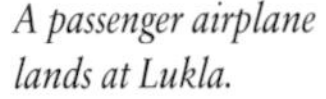

A passenger airplane lands at Lukla.

(6,957 metres/22,829ft), Solu's sacred peak, locally known as Shorung Yul Lha. Everest and the Khumbu range rise to the east, while Gauri Shanker (7,146 metres/23,444ft) and Menlungtse (7,181 metres/23,560ft) tower to the north.

Most treks through Solu follow the route used by early Everest expeditions. Nowadays the trail begins at the roadhead town of **Shivalaya** ❶ at 1,767 metres (5,797ft), a long day's bus ride from Kathmandu, cutting several days off the old trail from Lamosangu. Solu's moderate elevation does not signal an easy trek, however, for the terrain is relentlessly up and down.

Trekking in Khumbu

Khumbu is too beautiful and too friendly a place to hurry through. Besides, at such elevations, it can be dangerous to trek too high too fast (see page 136). Fortunately for trekkers, there are two medical stations in Khumbu staffed by Western doctors during the trekking seasons: a small hospital at Kunde developed with assistance from Sir Edmund Hillary's Himalayan Trust, and the Trekkers' Aid Post at Pheriche, which operates under the auspices of the Himalayan Rescue Association. The Trust has assisted in building numerous schools, health posts, bridges, roads and water pipelines throughout Solu-Khumbu.

For visitors with limited time, the best way to approach Khumbu is to fly to **Lukla** ❷ (2,866 metres/9,403ft). The 40-minute flight gives a thrill of a lifetime as the little plane descends below the peaks into the Dudh Kosi gorge to the runway that ends in a mountain face. Fifty years ago Lukla was the "sheep place" its name implies; today it is a bustling community of lodges and restaurants serving cinnamon rolls and coffee to trekkers awaiting their morning flight.

From Lukla, the trail climbs gradually up the steep-sided Dudh Kosi Valley, weaving from side to side as it passes through forests of blue pine, fir, juniper, rhododendron, birch and oak. Many villages, particularly Phakding, the standard first night's stop, cater to trekkers with Western food and dormitory lodging.

TIP

Lukla Airport has often been described as "the most dangerous airport in the world" due to its extreme location and short, angled runway. In practice huge numbers of flights wing their way in without incident, but fickle mountain weather and poor visibility lead to frequent cancellations and enormous backlogs of stranded trekkers – so be sure to allow plenty of leeway in any itinerary here.

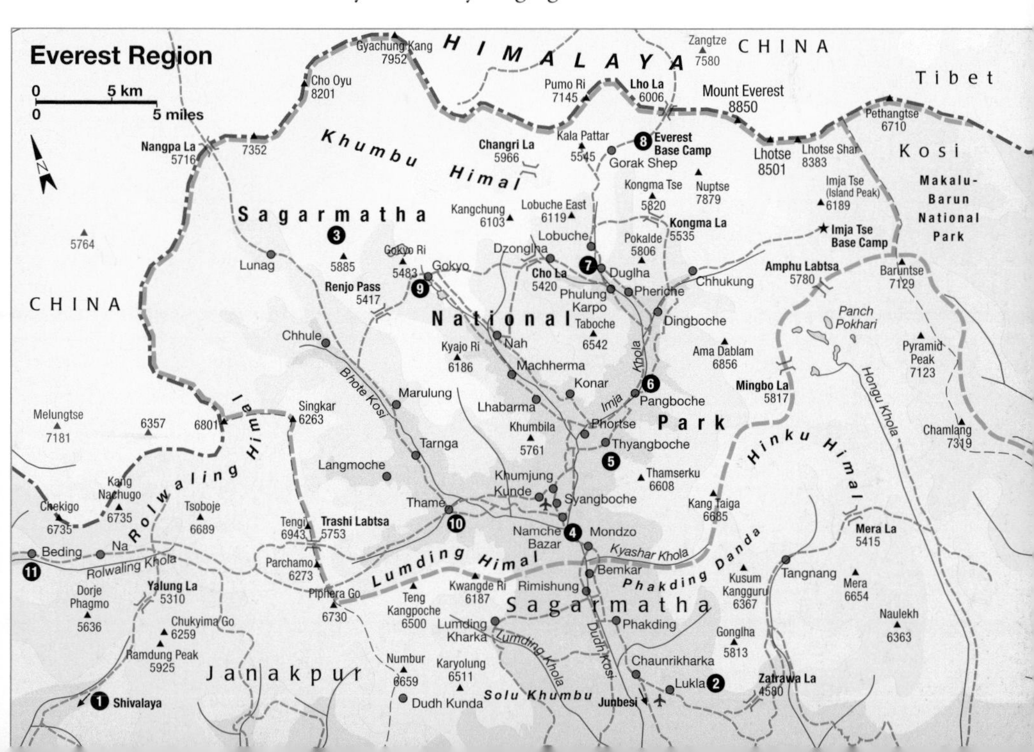

TIP

Atop a hill east of Namche Bazar, the Visitor's Centre at Sagarmatha National Park headquarters offers informative displays on local customs, flora and fauna, as well as stunning mountain views up the valley.

Narrow bench-lands are cultivated in wheat, potatoes, spinach, onions and radishes. Piled stone walls and huge boulders are carved with the Buddhist mantra "*Om mani padme hum*". On Fridays, hundreds of barefoot porters line the trail, toting food and wares up the mountainside to Namche Bazar's market.

All of Khumbu falls within **Sagarmatha National Park ❸**, established with help from the government of New Zealand, Sir Edmund Hillary's native country. In 1979 Khumbu was recognised as an Unesco World Heritage Site. The entrance fee for the park can be paid at Mondzo (2,845 metres/9,332ft).

Namche Bazar

At the confluence of the Dudh Kosi and Bhote Kosi, the trail crosses a high, sturdy bridge and begins a gruelling ascent to Namche Bazar (3,446 metres/11,300ft). On the way, the first glimpses of Everest and Lhotse (8,501 metres/27,890ft) are revealed. The Bhote Kosi leads northwest to Thame, and trails cross the Nangpa La (5,716 metres/18,753ft) to Tibet.

The prosperous town of **Namche Bazar ❹**, with its two- and three-storey houses-cum-lodges, a bank and post office, sits in a U-shaped, west-facing valley, with the sacred mountain Khumbila (5,761 metres/18,900ft) to the north, Thamserku (6,608 metres/21,680ft) to the east and Kwangde Ri (6,187 metres/20,298ft) to the west. Stone-paved lanes are lined with shops filled with an amazing selection of mountaineering equipment and gourmet expedition food. Swiss chocolate and French pâté stand alongside Russian sardines and Italian sausage; other shops rent crampons, mountaineering boots and sleeping bags, or sell paperbacks and Tibetan jewellery imported via Kathmandu.

High-quality lodges proffer nightly DVD showings, hot showers and fresh-baked pastries. Namche's weekly Saturday market or *haat bajaar* is a fascinating example of this local means of trade typical of Nepal's eastern hills. Porters, merchants and locals gather together for a busy morning of commerce; afterwards, they filter into local

The thriving town of Namche Bazar.

Map on page 255

tea- and *chhang*-shops to exchange the week's gossip.

Above Namche, the hamlet of Syangboche clusters around an airstrip serving the deluxe Japanese-operated Hotel Everest View. Tucked into a lovely valley a half-hour walk beyond, the two traditional villages of Khumjung and Kunde provide a counterpoint to Namche's commercial excess. Dry-stone walls separate potato fields where entire families can be seen digging or ploughing in season. The introduction of the potato in the 18th century revolutionised Khumbu's economy, allowing the barren terrain to support a much higher population.

The trail to Everest Base Camp

By far the most travelled trail in Khumbu leads to Everest Base Camp. Most trekkers take at least six days from Namche Bazar, including acclimatisation time. But with side trips and days simply to soak in the mountains' wonders, two, or preferably three, weeks are needed to see this area of Khumbu without rushing.

The monastery of **Thyangboche** ❺, rebuilt after a fire destroyed the original buildings in 1989, is one of Khumbu's most important and beautiful cultural centres. Thanks to donations from the Sherpa and international communities, the monastery has been rebuilt in an almost identical style to its predecessor. The monastery is perched on a forested promontory at 3,867 metres (12,684ft). From here Ama Dablam (6,856 metres/22,493ft), Everest, Nuptse (7,879 metres/25,850ft) and Lhotse (8,501 metres/27,890ft) create a perfect tableau to the north. A Sherpa Eco Centre, with informative displays explaining the religious and home lives of Sherpas, and several lodges share the meadow site – a popular campsite for group treks. The Thyangboche Development Project has developed the area's infrastructure, installing hydropower and telephone connections..

Thyangboche is the best-known location of the Mani Rimdu festival, a dance-drama in which monks dressed in painted masks and silk robes perform ritual dances depicting Buddhism's subjugation of the ancient Bön religion.

Mani stone carvings (prayer rocks) at Namche Bazar.

Selecting eggs at Namche Bazar's Saturday market.

Prayer wheels and rocks are often seen around the Everest region.

The forest surrounding Thyangboche is considered sacred and species such as the "fanged" musk deer and iridescent *danphe* (Himalayan monal pheasant) thrive here. The trail wanders down through the forest and crosses the Imja Khola's seething waters on a plank bridge. The climb to **Pangboche 6**, site of Khumbu's oldest gompa, passes by skilfully etched *mani* stones and the last scattered trees below the timber line.

Soon the canyon widens into alpine meadows, and the river and trail divide. The Imja Khola leads east toward the high, uncommercialised settlements of Dingboche and Chhukung. The mountain viewpoint of Chukkung Ri (5,043 metres/16,588ft) provides superb views of the ice-draped southern face of the Lhotse-Nuptse Massif. At Chhukung (4,753 metres/15,594ft), five glaciers descend; a path edging Imja and Lhotse glaciers passes a lake on the way to Island Peak (Imja Tse) Base Camp. To the south, the Amphu Labtsa Pass (5,780 metres/18,963ft) leads to the wild and rugged Hongu Basin. Within this huge glacial cirque nestle five small lakes (Panch Pokhari) amid a number of peaks over 6,000 metres (19,685ft). Hongu can also be reached via the Mingbo La (5,817 metres/19,084ft) on the southeast ridge of Ama Dablam, the high but gentle Mera La (5,415 metres/17,766ft), accessed from Lukla or from the Salpa Pass trail leading into Khumbu from the east.

From the confluence of the Imja and Lobuche Kholas, the left-hand trail climbs gradually to Pheriche, an unimpressive settlement with tea shops and a trekkers' medical post midway up a windswept valley. Yak trains carrying goods whose prices increase incrementally with elevation plod up the eroded slope to **Duglha 7** and over the crest where a line of stone *chortens* commemorate climbers killed on Everest.

Lobuche's clustered lodges, set at the edge of the Khumbu Glacier (4,930 metres/16,171ft), are the staging ground for higher forays to Kala Pattar (Black Rock), Everest Base Camp and climbs on the trekking peak Lobuche Peak. A two-hour hike through a morass of boulders reaches Gorak Shep, where there are a few small lodges.

Sherpas carry heavy loads for climbing expeditions in the Everest region.

The climb to Kala Pattar (5,545 metres/18,192ft) takes one to two further hours and is worth every step for the views of Everest's distinctive black triangle. During winter, high-level winds from the west blast all snow off Everest's towering face producing the characteristic plume from its summit. Summer winds from the east leave its white mantle intact.

Pumo Ri (7,145 metres/23,442ft) looms immediately to the rear of Kala Pattar, while Nuptse shows its vast marbled face directly in front. Base Camp and the unforgiving Khumbu Icefall stretch across the foreground, while less than 6km (3.5 miles) away across the **Lho La** (6,006 metres/19,704ft) lies the Rongbuk Glacier and Tibet.

Base Camp

Most trekkers visit **Everest Base Camp** ❽ (5,357 metres/17,575ft) as a day trip from Gorak Shep. The trail crosses the glacier amid ice seracs, some topped with boulders. Many visitors are disappointed with Base Camp, from where Everest itself is not even visible. This is the hub of the heavily commercialised mountaineering industry and sees hundreds of paying climbers guided up the world's highest peak each season. While the chronic garbage problem of past years has been somewhat mitigated by concerted clean-up efforts, and by the "garbage deposit" that each expedition must now pay in Kathmandu, Base Camp is still no pristine wilderness.

The effects of mountain tourism on the local environment, both social and natural, are hard to overlook in Khumbu. Much of the area's forest had disappeared by the time national-park regulations stopped tree-cutting for fuel and construction use, and it takes 60 years at such elevations for trees to grow back. Now trekking agencies are required to be self-sufficient in kerosene for their clients' cooking needs. Individual trekkers stay in Sherpa lodges, where the cooking hearth has traditionally been a congenial gathering spot, and large amounts of wood are needed to feed hungry foreigners. Recent innovations to save firewood include a "back boiler" system that heats water via a pipe through the hearth. Mini-hydroelectric projects are becoming more common,

FACT

Every two years the Everest region plays host to the world's highest marathon. First tackled by hardy runners in 1987, the Everest Marathon follows the downhill route between Gorak Shep and Namche Bazar. All profits from entry fees go to the Everest Marathon Fund, which supports development projects in the region.

Hardy yaks are vital to high mountain life.

Everest dates

The epic saga of mankind's relationship with Mount Everest has been a long one, punctuated by triumph and tragedy and marked by any number of unforgettable landmarks in mountaineering achievement.

16th century: The first Sherpa settlers move into the valleys south of the mountain known to Tibetans as Chomolungma.

1847: Surveyors from the British Great Trigonometrical Survey of India first spot a distant summit rearing 225km (140 miles) behind Kanchenjunga. They record it as "Peak B".

1852–4: An Indian mathematician, Radhanath Sikdar, computes a mass of surveying data and concludes that "Peak B" is 8,840 metres (29,002ft) high – just 33ft short of the modern estimate – and the mountain is recognised as the highest on earth.

1865: The British Royal Geographical Society officially adopts the name "Mount Everest", in recognition of a former surveyor-general of India, Sir George Everest.

The successful 1953 British expedition to scale Mount Everest.

1921: The first expedition, headed by C.K. Howard-Bury, surveys the North Face. Seven Sherpas die in an avalanche, the first fatalities recorded on Everest.

1922: The first attempt to climb the peak takes places from the northern side. George Mallory, Howard Somervell and Edward Norton are the first mountaineers to ascend beyond 8,000 metres (26,250ft).

1924: During the third British expedition Andrew Irvine and George Mallory are last seen at 8,500 metres (27,900ft).

1950: Nepal opens its borders to foreigners, and Bill Tilman pioneers the southern approach through Solu Khumbu.

1953: Edmund Hillary and Tenzing Norgay Sherpa become the first to reach the summit, via the South Ridge.

1963: Americans Willi Unsoeld and Tom Hornbein, guided by N. Oyrenfurth, become the first to ascend by one route (West Ridge) and descend by another (Southeast Ridge).

1975: Junko Tabei is the first woman to reach the summit by the southern approach.

1978: Everest is scaled for the first time without the use of artificial oxygen by Reinhold Messner and Peter Habeler, by the southern approach.

1979: A Yugoslavian group is the first to ascend and descend by the West Ridge – still the most difficult route today.

1980: Leszek Cichy and Krzystof Wielcki of Poland make the first winter ascent; Messner makes the first solo ascent, without bottled oxygen, and, in August, the first summer ascent.

1988: A huge Chinese-Japanese-Nepalese group scales the first north–south and south–north traverses simultaneously.

1988: Marc Betard of France sets a speed record in an ascent of 22.5 hours up the Southeast Ridge.

1996: Nine climbers perish in a blizzard during the so-called "Everest Disaster" which raises serious questions about commercialisation of mountaineering on the peak.

1999: George Mallory's body is discovered.

2003: Sibusiso Vilane from Swaziland is the first black African to reach the summit.

2004: Pemba Dorje Sherpa climbs Everest in a record-busting 8 hours 10 minutes.

2008: Edmund Hillary dies aged 88.

2010: Thirteen-year-old American Jordan Romero becomes the youngest person to scale Everest.

2011: Apa Sherpa tops the mountain for the 21st time.

but these primarily provide power for lighting, not cooking. And whereas Khumbu Sherpas have certainly benefited economically from the popularity of trekking, ever-increasing contact with Westerners undeniably accelerates cultural change, which penetrates even the most remote villages of the region.

The Gokyo Valley

The return trip to Namche Bazar can be accomplished much more quickly by following the same route, but hardy trekkers take the time to explore side valleys such as **Gokyo ❾**. Churning with glaciers that melt into turquoise lakes, and rimmed with savage mountain scenery, the Gokyo Valley is many veteran trekkers' favourite side of Khumbu. Trails cling to both sides of the steep Dudh Kosi gorge, joining at the toe of the giant Ngozumpa Glacier, and continuing up its lateral moraine past half-frozen lakes to a cluster of lodges at the small lake of Gokyo. The western trail passes lodges at Dole, Lhabarma, Luza and Machherma. The opposite trail is unpopulated except for a single tea shop at Thare. For proper acclimatisation, the whole journey from Namche or Khumjung should take four half-days (or three full days with one day's rest).

Himalayan tahr are often seen grazing on narrow ledges in the lower reaches, their long golden-brown hair barely visible against similarly coloured grasses. Below Dole, the trail winds up through rhododendron, poplar and birch, its thin smooth bark, like brown mylar, peeling off layers at a time.

The entire Gokyo Valley is sparsely populated, with shelter found only at summer yak-herding settlements where trekking lodges have also been established. There is no food or lodging from Machherma to Gokyo. This altitude is well above the tree line, and only scrub rhododendron, azalea and hardy grasses can survive. Around the lakes, the ground is snow-covered for much of the year, except during the monsoon when buttercups, asters, edelweiss and gentians bloom.

Gokyo, with several surprisingly comfortable lodges, sits on the shore of the third lake, Dudh Pokhari, at 4,750 metres (15,580ft). Rising above

Gokyo is a small hamlet of stone houses and stone-walled pastures.

A porter on the Everest Trail.

it is the easily climbable Gokyo Ri (5,483 metres/17,984ft). From the top, a panoply of peaks stretches out in all directions. To the north, **Cho Oyu**, at 8,201 metres (26,906ft), the sixth highest in the world, and Gyachung Kang (7,952 metres/25,991ft) grow out of the corrugated ice folds which tumble to the glacier. Pumo Ri, **Changtse**, Everest, Nuptse, Makalu (at 8,463 metres/27,766ft, the world's fifth highest), Ama Dablam and Thamserku stretch to the east and south. Beyond a 5,900-metre (19,360ft) ridge to the west lies the Bhote Kosi valley leading to the Nangpa La.

Day hikes from Gokyo along the lateral moraine lead past several more lakes and the mountaineering touchpoint of Cho Oyu Base Camp. For those combining Gokyo with a trip to Everest Base Camp, it's possible to save two days' walk by taking a shortcut crossing Cho La (5,420 metres/17,782ft). The eastern side skirts the small mountain lake of Tshola Tsho and crosses the moraines between Cholatse and Taboche (6,542 metres/21,462ft), emerging above the village of Pheriche. Another shortcut from Gokyo can be done without a tent: trekkers can stay overnight with Sherpas in Dragnag (4,680 metres/15,351ft) further down the valley and travel in one long day (12–14 hours) to Lobuche.

Locals walk from Gokyo down to Namche on the Machherma–Dole Trail in a single day, but a more moderate pace requires two to three days. If heading to Pangboche, the Dudh Kosi's eastern trail via Phortse offers an unparalleled perspective on Khumbila, Thamserku, Kang Taiga (6,685 metres/21,932ft) and Ama Dablam. Set above a steep ravine facing Thyangboche to the west, Phortse is a peaceful farming community. Potato fields stretch to the cliff's edge, marked by 300-year-old stone *chortens* and a fringe of birch forest. The three-hour walk to Pangboche is memorable for its vantage over the Imja Khola.

Thame

A relatively easy three- to four-hour walk up the Bhote Kosi from Namche Bazar reaches the settlement of **Thame** ⑩. Its mud-walled, Sherpa-style houses

Porters scramble alongside the Dudh Kosi River.

surrounded by potato fields show few signs of the 21st century. Here is the perfect antidote to noisy trekker lodges. Thame's monastery clings to the ridge above, with views of waterfalls cascading down Kwangde Ri. The *gompa* looks up the valley toward Nangpa La leading into Tibet, territory that is closed to trekkers. Guests at the monastery may be offered a cup of Tibetan butter tea – a mild black tea churned in a wooden cylinder with yak butter and salt, which is something of an acquired taste.

Crowning the tributary valley west of Thame is the infamous Trashi Labtsa Pass (5,753 metres/18,875ft) leading into the Rolwaling Valley. Trekkers have died from rock falls and sudden avalanches on this extremely rugged route, now restricted to organised groups. Ice axe, crampons, rope and a blessing from the Thame lama are advised. Most mountaineering expeditions in Khumbu follow the Sherpa practice of making a *puja*, an offering, to the mountain deities before beginning a climb.

Khumbu trekking peaks

Home of the world's highest mountains, the Khumbu region provides a profusion of lesser peaks accessible to serious mountaineers who may not be ready for an ascent of one of its true giants.

Island Peak (Imja Tse) (6,189 metres/20,305ft) is the most popular and one of the more accessible trekking peaks, lying between the Imja and Lhotse Glaciers up the Chhukung Valley. It is dwarfed by the massive south face of Lhotse, Baruntse and Ama Dablam. Its south face rears up as a rocky black triangle, the end of a truncated ridge thrown down from Lhotse Shar, from which it is separated by a snowy col at 5,700 metres (18,700ft). Its name comes from a 1952 expedition led by Eric Shipton, who described an isolated mountain "resembling an island in a sea of ice". Island Peak was first climbed in 1953 by a party that included Tenzing Norgay. Their initial route, from a camp at Pareshaya Gyab up the southeast flank and the south ridge, remains the standard route.

Pokalde (Dolma Ri) (5,806 metres/19,049ft) is a relatively undistinguished peak, the culmination of a rocky ridge beyond the huge lateral moraines of Pheriche. In many ways it can be regarded as the final bony knuckle on the long-fingered ridge that extends southward from Nuptse, flanking the east bank of the Khumbu Glacier. To the Sherpas, Pokalde is immensely important as the home of a major deity and the object of a monsoon pilgrimage during which the devout walk clockwise around the mountain. The straightforward route from the east was probably pioneered by Sherpas to place prayer flags on the summit. The first Western ascent was recorded in 1953 by a group from the Everest Expedition that included John Hunt, Wilfred Noyce, Tom Bourdillon and Mike Ward. They climbed the north ridge direct from the Kongma La.

Pokalde is best approached from the lodges of Lobuche and can be climbed in a day. A well-marked trail leads

Island Peak (Imja Tse) is one of the most popular trekking peaks.

across the Khumbu Glacier and climbs to the pass in about three hours. The cluster of tiny lakes on the east side provides an ideal high camp.

Kongma Tse (5,820 metres/19,094ft) was originally listed as Mehra Peak but was renamed to avoid confusion with Mera Peak further south. Twinned with Pokalde, Kongma Tse rises to the north of the Kongma La. *Kongma* is the Sherpa word for the snow cock, a large bird found in great numbers in this area. Viewed from Gorak Shep, the mountain sports fine glaciers that hang suspended above the west face. The normal route is from the lakes below the Kongma La via the south-face glacier.

Lobuche East (6,119 metres/20,075ft), west of the town, has a rocky east face which stands sentinel over the route to Everest Base Camp. Named after a Sherpa god, the true summit has proved an elusive goal. The rocky outliers of the peak were first climbed by the Swiss in 1952. Numerous subsequent attempts have fallen short of the actual summit, which rises above a deep notch at the far end of a long aligned ridge. It is possible the first ascent was not until April 1984, when the south ridge was climbed to the main ridge. The east face of the mountain, easily accessible from Lobuche village, has attracted strong teams. Jeff Lowe, a pioneer on many trekking peaks, led a difficult route up an icy couloir, while the obvious but still difficult east ridge was climbed by Todd Biblier and Catherine Freer. A host of challenging possible lines remain.

Kwangde Ri (6,187 metres/20,298ft) is a stunning peak visible from Namche Bazar, forming a long east–west ridge bounding the Bhote Kosi. Although within Khumbu, Kwangde is actually the northern limit of the Lumding Himal. Kwangde has several summits, all of which are included on a single permit. The main summit, Kwangde Lho, has a formidable north face that was first climbed in 1982.

Far less formidable from the north is the curving main ridge thrown towards the Bhote Kosi from Kwangde Shar. This fine northeast ridge offers a less difficult route and was first climbed Alpine-style in 1978 by Lindsay Griffin and Roger Everett.

Trekking here rewards hikers with spectacular views.

More exacting, and perhaps more interesting, is the approach to Kwangde from the south. The high, uninhabited Lumding Valley was first explored by Jimmy Roberts and Sen Tenzing in 1953. A year later, American Fred Becky entered the valley, crossing the Moro La from the east before going on to discover the Lumding Tsho Teng, one of the highest lakes in the world. The south ridge of Kwangde Lho has become the normal, albeit difficult, ascent and was first climbed in 1975 by a Nepalese team.

Kusum Kanguru (6,367 metres/ 20,889ft), more than any of the other trekking peaks, epitomises the dilemma inherent in the name. As its Tibetan name implies, this shapely citadel of rock and ice has "three snowy summits" that have provided a difficult and adventurous challenge. Found at the southern end of Charpati Himal, Kusum Kangguru rises between the Dudh Kosi and the uninhabited river drainage of Hinku Drangka. Rising close to Lukla, it is perhaps the easiest trekking peak to approach but the hardest to climb. Kusum Kangguru offers nothing for the incompetent and little for the merely skilful. Even by its easiest route, the east face above the Lungsamba Glacier, the mountain is technically demanding. The peak has attracted the elite of the mountaineering world and boasts more routes than any other peak on the list. Of the many climbs on its numerous faces and ridges, perhaps the most daring exploit was that of New Zealander Bill Denz who in 1981 completed a solo traverse of the mountain.

Mera Peak (6,654 metres/21,830ft) is the highest of the trekking peaks, It forms a heavily glaciated mass between the Hinku and Hongu valleys, east of Lukla and almost due south of Everest. First climbed in 1953 by Jimmy Roberts and Sen Tenzing, it has in the last few years become one of the most frequently climbed mountains on the list. Its popularity is undoubtedly due to both its altitude and technical simplicity. As there are no lodges in either the Hinku or Hongu valleys, parties need to be self-contained, which makes it even more attractive to those in search of a mountaineering adventure.

The quickest approach is the Zatrawa La, east of Lukla. Parties approaching from Jiri can reach the mountain from the south via the Hindu Drangka and Pangkongma. The normal route of ascent is via the Mera La and the wide, gently sloping glaciers that fall from the summit's north face.

The bloom of a bright mountain flower.

The Rolwaling Valley

The Rolwaling Valley is believed by Tibetan Buddhists to be a *beyul*, one of the sacred mountain refuges blessed by the 8th-century sage Guru Rinpoche. As a consequence, Buddhism is taken very seriously here, and the hunting and killing of animals is still forbidden in the valley. The valley's northern flank is dominated by Gauri Shankar (7,146 metres/23,439ft), once thought to be the highest peak in the world. It resisted all mountaineering attempts until a Nepalese-American team scaled it in 1979. Three smaller peaks in this region are open as trekking peaks.

Porters trekking in the snow.

Ama Dablam, a sheer wall of rock.

Trekking access to Rolwaling is from Charikot (1,998 metres/6,554ft) on the Lamosangu–Jiri road. Several days' walk up the Bhote Kosi is Simigaon (2,019 metres/6,623ft), where the Rolwaling Khola enters from the east. **Beding** ⓫ (3,693 metres/12,113ft) the last permanent settlement in upper Rolwaling, is grey and barren save for the brightly painted window shutters of the stone houses and a gompa. Beyond is the summer yak herders' settlement of Na (4,183 metres/13,720ft), and, still further, the stark beauty of glaciers and glazed ice slopes. To trek this far and return down the valley is worthwhile for the high-altitude experience and the serenity of a silent white world.

From the lower Bhote Kosi, an alternative trail heads west up the Sangawa Khola and climbs to Bigu Gompa (2,512 metres/8,240ft) with its sheltered convent tucked in a juniper forest. The path continues upward beyond all habitation, passing numerous potential campsites, to cross Tinsang La (3,319 metres/10,890ft) and descend to the roadside town of Barabise. Another follows the ridge north past Deodunga ("God's Rock") almost to the Tibetan border, where the trail turns west to meet the Kodari–Kathmandu road.

Rolwaling offers several trekking peaks. **Ramdung** (5,925 metres/19,439ft) is one of several appealing small peaks south of Na, best approached by crossing the Yalung La. These peaks were first climbed in 1952 by the Scottish Himalayan Expedition led by W.H. Murray. Although not a high peak, the approach is quite long and for most parties two camps above Kyiduk will be required. A second high camp on the Ramdung Glacier is usual if climbing the normal route, the north-east face from the Yalung La. In recent years groups have favoured an approach around the west side of the mountain.

Parchamo (6,273 metres/20,580ft) is a lovely glacier peak at the eastern end of the Rolwaling Himal. Shipton, Gregory and Evans first attempted it in 1951, following the north ridge until they were stopped by difficult terrain and lack of crampons. Parchamo was not climbed until 1955, when Dennis Davis and Phil Boultbee finished the north ridge.

High camp on Mera Peak.

The legend of Mallory and Irvine

The sad story of two ill-fated explorers who tried to tackle Mount Everest three decades before Hillary and Tenzing has an enduring grip on popular imagination.

On 8 June 1924 high on the Tibetan side of Mount Everest two tiny figures were spotted, inching their way towards the summit. Then the heavy mists of the coming monsoon rolled in and the pair vanished forever into the realm of legend. Their names were George Mallory and Andrew Irvine.

Because it is there

Mallory, at the age of 37, was the brightest light of British mountaineering. He belonged to a remarkable generation – the educated and cultured young men who had come of age at the high-watermark of the British Empire but had had their worldview irreparably altered by the horrors of World War I. Handsome, talented and mercurial, his response to the question of why anyone should climb Everest has become the ultimate encapsulation of human endeavour: "Because it is there". Andrew Irvine, meanwhile, was just 22 and much less experienced, but he was selected by Mallory to accompany him on the push for the summit.

Mallory and Irvine climbed clad only in layers of tweed, shoed in hobnailed boots, encumbered with heavy metal oxygen cylinders and strung together with lengths of coarse hemp rope. Their disappearance embedded their legend into public consciousness – not least given the mystery which still surrounds the question of whether they actually reached the summit.

The great mystery

The pair were last spotted by the expedition geologist near the notorious "Second Step", a formidable rock ledge on the north side of the summit. Over the decades champions and detractors have tussled over the question of whether Mallory and Irvine could possibly have climbed the Second Step.

No bodies were recovered from the mountain in the aftermath of the disappearance, but in 1975 a Chinese climber – who subsequently died in an accident himself – reported spotting an "English dead" in vintage clothes on the North Face. It was not until 1999, however, that a research team finally discovered Mallory's remains, some 600 metres (2,000ft) below the summit. His right leg was badly broken and the rope tied around his waist had snapped, and many now believe that he and Irvine – whose body has yet to be recovered – fell while descending the ridge. Whether they had already reached the top or had turned back defeated remains a mystery. Some point out that while a watch and a bundle of letters were found on Mallory's body, there was no sign of the photograph of his wife, which he had promised to leave at the summit. Others, such as the veteran mountaineer Reinhold Messner, insist that he could never have tackled the Second Step.

In 2007 the American climber Conrad Anker, the man who actually found Mallory's body in 1999, successfully free-climbed the Second Step. Anker subsequently declared that Mallory and Irvine could, with favourable conditions, have reached the summit. However, he still believes it unlikely.

Ultimately none of this matters, for the tragic story of these two men still inspires the world's greatest mountaineers. "I regard Mallory as the man of Everest of all generations," said Sir Edmund Hillary. "He was the man who really brought Everest to the public mind."

Mallory and Irvine's 1924 expedition camp.

SHERPA MONASTERIES AND GOMPAS

Gompas are the spiritual centres of the Sherpa communities of Solu Khumbu and serve as the focus for religious and cultural activities.

Sherpas follow the Mahayana Buddhist practice known as Nyingma, and worship in prayer halls known as gompas. The first gompas at Pangboche and Thame were established by Lama Sanga Dorje between 300 and 400 years ago. In 1916 the first celibate monastery was established for religious study.

Inside the gompa there are usually three statues at the front: the central figure is the Buddha, who taught a means for developing spiritual potential; to the right is Guru Rinpoche, the Indian mystic who established Buddhism in Tibet in the 8th century AD; to the left is usually the god embodying compassion.

The gompa community

Villagers take turns as the gompa custodian while lamas and celibate monks fill the religious roles. Monks devote their lives to studying, teaching and performing religious rites for the Sherpa community but they may also be stewards, custodians, artists or prayer leaders. Monks and nuns are supported by their relatives, who consider it an honour to the family. Both are free to leave and return to lay life without discredit.

Students enter monastery schools at age seven. They study the Tibetan language, religion, history, grammar, psychology and medicine. Students may take vows of commitment to monastic life but to take the final Gelung vows, a man must be celibate and at least 20 years old.

A monk contemplates his prayers at Thyangboche Gompa.

The Mani Rimdu festival takes place in the autumn, a spectacular masked dance event *(see page 90).*

Colourful Tibetan prayer books.

As well as religious, artistic and scientific studies, student monks take part in the monastery's communal life, including kitchen chores.

Many gompas, such as Thyangboche in the Khumbu Region, are located high in the Himalayas.

Studying holy manuscripts.

LAMAS: RELIGIOUS TEACHERS

The title "lama" is reserved for religious teachers, whether or not they have taken vows of celibacy and become monks. They can read the scriptures, perform rituals and teach Buddhist principles.

A lama who has attained the highest level of spiritual achievement is called Rinpoche, meaning "precious one." He may earn this respected title through study and wisdom attained in this lifetime or by being recognised as the incarnation of a previous lama. The identity of a reincarnate lama is determined when as a child he exhibits the characteristics of the late Rinpoche and identifies certain key belongings of his previous incarnation. The young lama is then raised in the monastery and given a religious and secular education. The Dalai Lama is the world's most famous reincarnate lama, but the heads of many orders and individual gompas across the Tibetan-influenced world are chosen in the same way.

Previously, students of higher level Buddhist teachings went to Tibet to study with the most respected *ripoches*. Today a spiritual education is more accessible, in Nepal and India as well as the West.

Lamas are Tibetan Buddhism's religious teachers.

Portrait of a Nepalese woman, with Makalu visible in the distance.

EAST OF EVEREST

Far less visited than the Everest region, the east of Nepal is dominated by the mighty face of Kanchenjunga, the world's third highest mountain, and typified by the rich cultures of its people.

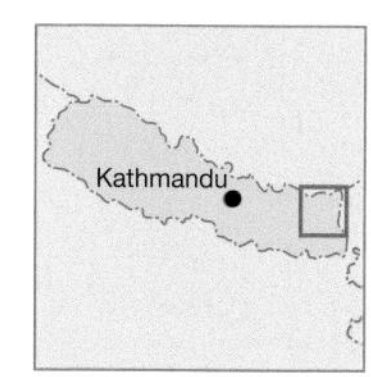

Main Attractions

The Arun Valley
Chainpur
Makalu Base Camp
Kanchenjunga

Like Nepal's far west, the region to the east of Everest is seldom visited by foreigners, but the similarities stop there. The east is far more densely populated than the west, in part due to a wetter climate; it is also narrower from north to south, is more accessible and its people are generally better off, having benefited from geography as well as participation in the Gurkha regiments. This is a fascinating area in which to trek, enlivened by open-air markets attracting a carnival of costumed peoples. Naturalists rate the eastern Himalayas highly, especially birdwatchers who can rack up scores of new sightings.

The Arun Valley

The mighty Arun Kosi, one of Nepal's two largest rivers, flows from Tibet through a narrow gorge that is thought to pre-date the rise of the Himalayan massif. At its uppermost reaches within Nepal the river receives meltwaters from the Barun Glacier off the slopes of Baruntse (7,129 metres/23,389ft), Makalu and Lhotse Shar (8,383 metres/27,503ft), and then heads south to join the Sapt Kosi.

A little-known trail on which you can leave the crowds of Khumbu behind follows an up and down trade route east over Salpa Pass (3,414 metres/11,200ft). This seven- to eight-day trek from Kharte on the Dudh Kosi to **Tumlingtar** ❶ on the Arun crosses three ridges and two main rivers, the Hinku and Hongu Kholas. Trails connect to the bazaar towns of Hille and Dhankuta north of Biratnagar. Food and shelter are sporadically available at Sherpa and Rai villages along the Salpa trail but trekkers are advised to take food for a few days and a knowledgeable guide. This trail also provides southern access into the upper Hongu Basin where well-equipped trekkers might venture. Another approach to the Arun is via

Looking over the Arun Valley.

Bhojpur, famed for its hardened steel *khukri* knives wielded by the Gurkhas. The Tumlingtar airstrip or the Hille border crossing are the most convenient entry points to the Arun Valley.

The people of Tumlingtar are mostly *Kumals*, a tribe of potters who live in elevated bamboo houses and cultivate dry crops such as black lentils and sesame. Bulbous clay pots like those sold nearby at Khandbari are used for carrying water or storing millet as it ferments into *tongba*. This tasty brew is made by pouring boiling water into a bamboo or wooden cylinder filled with fermented millet, and is popular throughout eastern Nepal and Sikkim. The liquid is drunk through a straw sieved to keep out the millet kernels. The Sherpas and Bhotias of colder climes appreciate *tongba's* warming effects. *Suntala*, similar to mandarin oranges, are another speciality of the east savoured on warm days from October to March.

The ridge-top bazaar town of **Chainpur** ❷, east of Tumlingtar, is well worth a visit, especially for the Friday market. People of the surrounding hills come to sell a variety of goods: tobacco; grains; vegetables; cloth; and good quality brassware. Tamang porters stop on the trail to rest their loads on wooden T-sticks. Women dressed in brightly flowered skirts, burgundy velveteen blouses and hefty coin necklaces gather in the tea shops and share the week's news while Newar businessmen display their *dhaka*-patterned *topis* (hats) made of handwoven cotton in geometric designs. Chainpur is a pleasant stop at any time with its flagstone walkways and shops overflowing with brass pots (sold with a great mark-up in Kathmandu).

Trekking to Makalu Base Camp

Standing in the scorching sunlight on Tumlingtar's red clay airfield at 390 metres (1,280ft) above sea level, the idea of climbing nearly 4,500 metres (14,800ft) to the base of Makalu is daunting. This is a remote and underdeveloped region, with few facilities and difficult access, and trekking into the upper Arun Valley is almost an expedition-like undertaking, requiring four

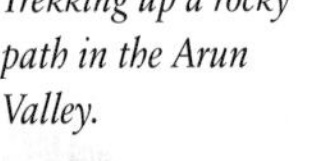

Trekking up a rocky path in the Arun Valley.

SACRED KANCHENJUNGA

Though it lies in inaccessible border regions, Kanchenjunga, the world's third highest mountain, is far more readily glimpsed than its taller counterparts, standing proud over the eastern Himalayas. It can be easily seen from Darjeeling, and as a consequence it was once believed to be the highest mountain on earth.

The mountain's name is thought to be a corruption of the Tibetan for "five treasures of the high snow", and it has long been sacred for the people of the surrounding hills. The first successful ascent was in 1955, when British mountaineers Joe Brown and George Band climbed from the Yalung Glacier. They stopped just short of the true summit in respect for its sacred nature, and subsequent expeditions have adhered to this tradition.

weeks (if the weather cooperates) to and from **Makalu Base Camp** ❸ (5,000 metres/16,400ft). A vast range in temperatures is confronted, from steamy in the lowlands to serious snow storms at high altitudes, which can block the route if ill-timed. Weather alone deters most trekkers from the Arun, and dictates others' schedule to a narrow window in March or October to November.

From Tumlingtar, the trail runs parallel to the river along a ridge to the east, passing through Brahman and Chhetri, then Rai, Limbu, Gurung and Newar villages. Oak and rhododendron forests here teem with bird and animal life. Precursory views of **Makalu** (8,463 metres/27,766ft), Baruntse (7,129 metres/23,389ft), Chamlang (7,290 metres/23,917ft) and the Khumbu peaks open to the west; and Milke Danda, one of the longest ridges in Nepal, rises to the east.

At Num, the trail crosses the Arun and starts up the Kasuwa Khola toward Makalu Base Camp in the upper Barun Valley. This is wild country and should only be attempted with an experienced guide, food for at least 16 days and snow gear. There are no settlements beyond the Sherpa village of Tashigaon, and for nine to ten days the path crosses rugged terrain rising to three passes, including Barun La (4,250 metres/13,940ft). From the high points there are panoramic views of the eastern Himalayas from Everest to Kanchenjunga and north into Tibet. Camping is possible among alpine meadows and at the base of Makalu's pink face as it reflects dusk's light off the surrounding peaks. Day hikes up the glacier offer more spectacular views. On the way down, the dank, mossy forests make an abrupt contrast to the upper horizons of ice and rock.

The return to Tumlingtar can be routed along the west side of the Arun, sharing a forested trail with chattering rhesus monkeys and swimming holes with equally boisterous children. Trekkers with a special permit can continue up the Arun from Num into remote reaches populated with Lhomis, most of whom practise the pre-Buddhist Bön religion.

In the early 1990s it appeared that much of the Arun Valley was set to be

Kanchenjunga guards Nepal's eastern frontier.

irrevocably changed by the installation of a hydroelectric facility, but the project never went ahead. Parts of the the Barun and Arun watersheds are now protected as the Makalu-Barun National Park and Conservation Area (Rs1,000 entrance fee), which was established in 1992. The area is home to snow leopards and blue sheep, and there are strict regulations on the collection of firewood.

Kanchenjunga

The area around Kanchenjunga, hard on the Indian and Tibetan borders, has been open to foreign trekkers since 1988, but with the area still restricted to permit-holding organised groups, it remains far removed from the bustle of the more popular teahouse routes further west. With support from the WWF, the Kanchenjunga Conservation Area, managed not by central government but by the local communities themselves, is successfully protecting this pristine region, which is one of the few remaining habitats for the snow leopard and red panda. Individual trekkers have no access to the Kanchenjunga area – all foreigners must go through a registered trekking agency, which guarantees to be self-sufficient in food and fuel and to not litter or pollute the area.

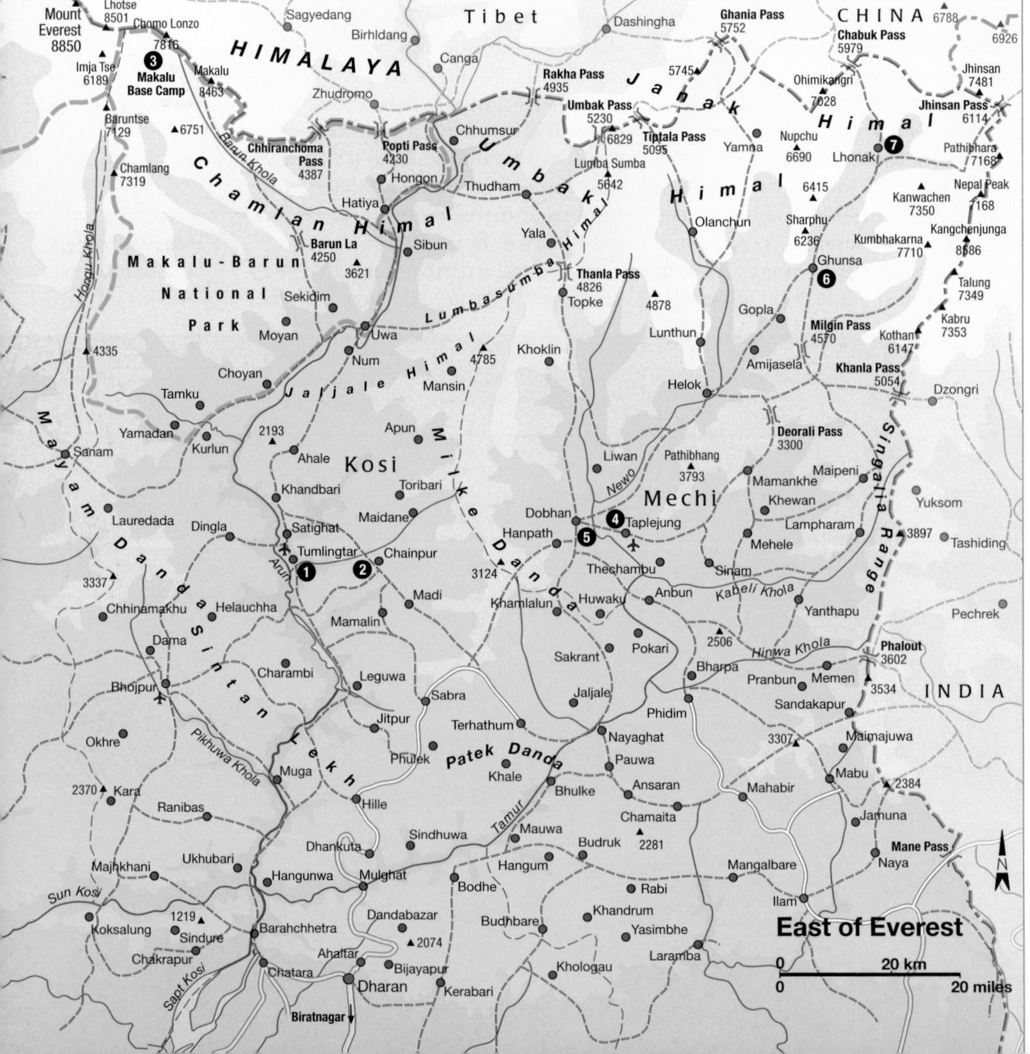

The Kanchenjunga trekking region, roughly defined as the Tamur Kosi watershed which drains the west side of Kanchenjunga (8,586 metres/ 28,169ft), the world's third highest peak, has received more attention than Dolpo, which was opened to foreigners at the same time, being relatively easier to get to and topographically more hospitable.

Still, a Kanchenjunga trek requires a minimum of three to four weeks' hiking on rough trails crossing ridge and gully to visit the mountain's base either south or north. Pangpema, at close to 5,000 metres (16,000ft), Base Camp for Kanchenjunga's northern face, sits on a glacier within 10km (6 miles) of the Tibet border surrounded by peaks upward of 6,500 metres (21,300ft). It is a long way from emergency treatment and many trekkers have had to turn back just days short of Base Camp for lack of acclimatisation time.

Flying in and out of the Suketar airstrip near **Taplejung** ❹ saves considerable driving time from Kathmandu (16–20 hours) but as with all mountain airstrips flights are prone to frequent cancellations in poor weather. A compromise solution is to fly to and from Biratnagar and drive four to six hours to trailheads at Basantpur (1,790 metres/5,871ft) via the Dharan/Dhankuta road, or Phidim (1,311 metres/4,300ft) north of Ilam. Hille, south of Basantpur, holds a lively weekly market on Thursdays and is another good place to start out. Phidim is at the end of a dirt road that traverses Ilam's young tea estates.

Heading northeast out of Hille, the trail climbs through settlements of migrants from the Walungchung region who were traditionally trans-Himalayan yak drivers. Gupha Pokhari (3,150 metres/10,300ft), the second night's rest, is a lake set on a ridge looking east at the Kanchenjunga Massif and west at Makalu and the Khumbu Himal. From here, a shorter trek follows the **Milke Danda** ridge, climbing to 4,700 metres (15,400ft) into the **Jaljale Himal**, a remote area dotted with lakes and inhabited by Tibetan mountain people. The trail up Milke Danda ridge finds little water and a rocky way often covered

FACT

The first serious attempt to climb Kanchenjunga was led in 1905 by the British climber Aleister Crowley. Today Crowley is best remembered for his later involvement in the occult – he dubbed himself "The Great Beast" and founded the Thelema cult – but in his youth he was a talented mountaineer, taking part in a daring attempt on K2 in 1902, and climbing to around 6,500 metres (21,325ft) on Kanchenjunga before being thwarted by the threat of avalanche.

Prayer flags framed by the world's highest peaks.

The mountain of Makalu is the fifth highest in the world.

in cloud. With a guide who knows the area, the return route can descend east to the Mewa Khola (Papaya River) and on to Taplejung's airfield (two weeks' walk from Hille), or head back down the ridge and turn west via Nundhaki to Chainpur and Tumlingtar.

The main Kanchenjunga Trail crosses the Mewa Khola at **Dobhan** ❺, and follows the Tamur Kosi, skirting steep valley walls. The hills are densely forested with rhododendron, oak and pine and waterfalls testify that this area receives heavy monsoon rains. At **Ghunsa** ❻ (3,350 metres/10,988ft), a Tibetan village marked with prayer flags and a gompa, two trails from Kanchenjunga's southern flanks join the northbound route.

Now close to 3,500 metres (11,500ft), full days of trekking may gain elevation too fast. The last three days to Pangpema are increasingly cold but spectacular as mountains close in from both sides of the valley. A small stone hut defines **Lhonak** ❼ and a level snowy pad is Pangpema, where expedition teams spend months as lead climbers make camps far above. Day hikes onto the glacier and higher ground for views of Kanchenjunga can delay departure.

For another perspective on Kanchenjunga and the face of Jannu (7,710 metres/25,300ft) a 30-day trek visits the southern Yalung Glacier on the return to Pangpema. Two trails head south from Ghunsa. The easterly route scrambles over snow-covered rock to cross higher Lapsang La (5,050 metres/16,564ft) while the lower alternative traverses three passes, the highest being Sinion La at nearly 4,800 metres (15,750ft). Both routes require at least a one-night stay at high altitude. Above Ramze Lake, a trail skirts the massive Yalung Glacier up to Oktang for views of Jannu and peaks dividing Nepal and Sikkim.

Starting down the Simbua Khola, the preferred descent diverts south through Yamphudin then either west to Taplejung or south to the subtropical **Kabeli Khola** valley. Like the Arun and other far-reaching areas, the Kanchenjunga trek tackles a vast range of elevations and temperatures, and is best planned for October–November or March–April. Snowfall is possible in any season.

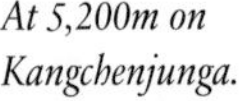

At 5,200m on Kangchenjunga.

Mountain flight

A short mountain flight over the Himalayas is the quickest and easiest way to see these spectacular mountains at close range.

Most of Nepal's domestic airlines run daily hour-long mountain flights east from Kathmandu to see Mount Everest and the other craggy peaks that define the central and eastern Himalayan range. Flying at altitudes of approximately 7,500 to 8,500 metres (25,000 to 28,000ft) – eye level with the peaks at some 22km (14 miles) distance – passengers get a magnificent close-up perspective. The flight route runs parallel to the mountains for 160km (100 miles) east of Kathmandu, and then turns around to give the view to both sides.

Practicalities

Amongst the airlines offering this one-hour "fly past" of the world's greatest peaks are Buddha Air, Yeti Airlines, Simrik Airlines and Agni Air. Various aircraft are used for the route, but only the window seats are sold, ensuring that all passengers get to enjoy uninterrupted views. There is little variation in price between airlines, with flights generally costing around US$180, including a breakfast served onboard.

All flights take place in the morning, when the weather is most likely to be clear. Boarding is at the Domestic Terminal of Tribhuvan Airport, with daily departure times ranging from 6.30 to 9am depending on the season. All the carriers run the flight year-round, but the best time for prime views is from late September to mid-December, after the rains, but before the winter fog and the haze of the pre-monsoon season.

During the busy autumn season flights are sometimes booked up months in advance, though last minute discounted deals are sometimes available at quieter times. If the weather is not suitable for flying, all airlines give full refunds or fly you the next day.

Alternative views

Flights can also be chartered for the eastern range or the Annapurna area on Buddha Air. The Annapurna flight covers five magnificent peaks over 7,000 metres (23,000ft). Helicopter tours of the Everest area, Langtang, Helambu, the Annapurnas and Muktinath are also very popular and can be arranged through travel agencies in Kathmandu and Pokhara. Tours last from 90 minutes to over two hours at an altitude of 4,800m (16,000ft).

Almost as spectacular as the awesome white mountain peaks are the Middle Hills of Nepal with their intricate cobwebs of green and yellow terraces and fairytale villages clinging to ridge tops, bisected by the great grey-green rivers that snake through their narrow valleys. Lofty views of the earth's own textures extend far north onto the Tibetan plateau and far to the south over the Terai and the plains of northern India.

The sheer magnitude of the Himalayas is intimidating but, in addition to the well-known giants such as Everest and the Annapurna Range, there are a large number of other peaks – most of them considerably higher than any of the summits of Europe or the Americas – which march range after range across the northern reaches of this small nation. Indeed, Nepal's base camps at the foot of a mountain generally lie at about 5,500 metres (18,000ft) elevation, higher than any mountain in Europe. The time and effort expended just trekking to reach them is for most people a once-in-a-lifetime adventure. But a mountain flight is an equally thrilling opportunity to see them at close range.

Pilot guiding a plane into Lukla airport.

Boarding a train to the Indian border.

On elephant safari in Chitwan National Park.

THE TERAI

Lying in a long green strip along the southern flank of the country, the Terai is a radical counterpoint to Nepal's mountain core – a place of deep jungles and South Asian colour.

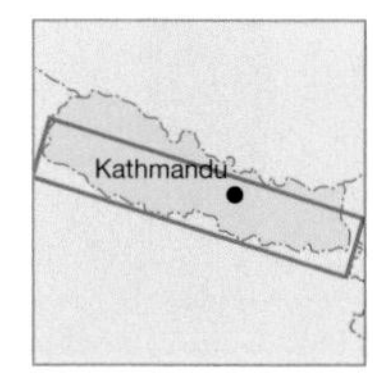

Main Attractions
- Ilam's tea gardens
- Koshi Tappu Wildlife Reserve
- Janaki Mandir, Janakpur
- Chitwan National Park
- Lumbini
- Bardia National Park

Nepal's low-slung underbelly is far removed from most travellers' image of this Himalayan nation. The far north of the country may fade out on to the Tibetan Plateau, but down here amongst the tropical forests and bustling bazaars it is the Indian subcontinent that sets the tone. The Terai's level terrain is deceptive, however, for this was long a natural barrier in its own right, almost as formidable a stumbling block for would-be invaders as the Himalayas: the swamps and jungles here harboured a particularly virulent strain of malaria which could cut swathes through parties of trespassing outsiders. While eradication programmes in recent decades have made low-altitude Nepal a much healthier place, and while these fertile plains are home to around half of the country's population, the Terai still has the feel of being an "other" land, beyond the pale of the national mainstream.

The Terai environment

The lowest outlier of the main Himalayan range, the Siwalik Hills (also known as the Churia), form the Terai's northern boundary. Where the hills divide, smaller Inner Terai valleys such as Chitwan, Dang, Deokhuri and Surkhet abut foothills covered with giant sal trees *(Shorea robusta)*. Tumbling streams feed into the slow, meandering rivers of the plains, and swamp and forest merge to create the Terai's beautiful, serene landscape and its deep pockets of wild country.

During winter, large rivers recede to reveal great stretches of white sand and the climate is pleasant albeit cold at night; in December, morning mist shrouds the landscape. From April to June mosquitoes invade the towns and a scorching, dusty wind blows from the south. The summer monsoon follows, sending water racing into old

Cutting wheat near Sauraha.

Tharu people make their home in the Terai.

and new river beds and raising the Terai's colour scheme to a livid green.

Decent roads have now been built across the Terai, forging stronger trade links with neighbouring India and paving the way for industrial development. Population has increased, and the once vast swathes of jungle have been clipped and cut into scattered fragments. The biggest of these – the national parks at Chitwan and Bardia – remain the major draw for tourists in the Terai, but there is much else to explore in these colourful lowlands.

The far east

With a population of more than 200,000, **Biratnagar** ❶ is the second largest city in Nepal. Its geographical position near the Indian border has traditionally kept it at the forefront of the country's industrial development – Nepal's very first modern industrial operation, Biratnagar Jute Mills, was established here in 1936. The Nepalese-Indian enterprise prospered with the rise of jute prices following World War II; more mills were opened and jute remains a significant export, although prices have declined in recent years. Biratnagar's other industries include sugar mills, textile factories and manufacturing of stainless-steel kitchenware.

From a tourist perspective, however, there is little to see here and most visitors use the city as a stopping-off point – Buddha Air, Yeti Airlines and Nepal Airlines fly between Biratnagar and Kathmandu about 15 times a day. Of more interest is the eastern Jhapa District, which has a rich mixture of ethnic groups and an equally varied physical look: wooden houses elevated on high poles stand juxtaposed to charmless concrete structures. At the weekly market of Damak, the ethnic and cultural diversity of the Terai is on full display in the dress of the shoppers and traders, such as the Dhimal women wearing handwoven black sarongs tied with red belts.

North of Biratnagar, where the outer ridges of the Himalayas rise steadily from the plains, the pleasant hill-style bazaar of Dharan has a refreshing climate and a neat, prosperous ambiance. Until 1989 this was the headquarters of the British Army's Gurkha recruitment in Nepal. Operations have now moved to Kathmandu and the British Gurkha cantonment has been turned into a major hospital, but the money and international experience earned

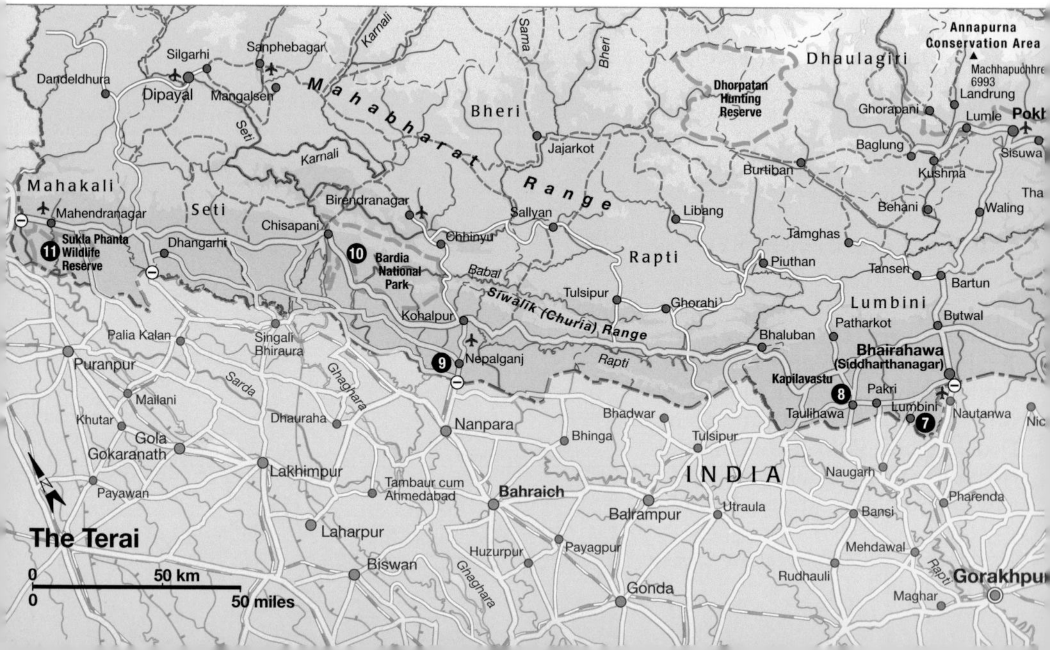

The Terai

by locally recruited soldiers still makes Dharan a sophisticated place. A British-built road winds from Dharan up into the hills to Dhankuta and Hille, the starting point for Kanchenjunga and many of the other east Nepal treks (see page 274). Further east, where the lush green foothills begin their steady rise towards Kanchenjunga, the little town of **Ilam** is the hub of Nepal's nascent tea trade. As in the better known tea-growing areas across the Indian border around Darjeeling, the slopes here are shrouded in a mantle of manicured tea bushes.

Commercial tea cultivation was first introduced into the Indian subcontinent by the British, in an effort to break the Chinese monopoly of what was already becoming an international commodity. The bushes grew well on the damp, monsoonal outer ramparts of the Himalayas, and soon regions like Darjeeling and Assam became synonymous with the high quality brews they produced. The tea trade in India was long dominated by European planters, and despite its abundance of suitable settings, Nepal's location beyond the bounds of the Raj meant that the industry got off to a much slower start here. A cup of sweet, milky *chiya* (masala tea) might have become akin to a national drink in Nepal, but much of the leaf had to be imported from India. Since the 1980s, however, tea cultivation has increased considerably, with the Nepal Tea Development Corporation coming into being in 1996 and a significant export market developing.

Ilam remains the major tea-growing area of the country, and there are fine views out across the cultivated hills where brightly clad women trim the tender tips of the bushes for drying and fermentation. Visitors can see the full production process in action at the Kanyam Tea Factory, south of town, where the plucked leaves are dried, rolled, fermented and graded.

Beyond Ilam the main highway continues to the border town of **Kakarbhitta**. It's a hot and dusty place, and while there are places to stay and eat, most travellers coming this way press on across the frontier to the Indian hill-station of Darjeeling and the mountainous region of Sikkim.

Koshi Tappu Wildlife Reserve

Beyond the Koshi River Bridge is Itahari, an unremarkable crossroads town

FACT

The word Terai simply means "foothills" or "low-lying country on the edge of the mountains". While various ethnic groups make up the population of the Terai, they are often collectively known as Madheshis by the people of Kathmandu and the Middle Hills, a term denoting their cultural and linguistic links with the populations across the Indian border.

FACT

Aside from its industry, Biratnagar is known as a political centre, having produced four of Nepal's prime ministers.

midway between Dharan at the foot of the Siwalik Hills and Biratnagar, just 6km (4 miles) from the Indian border. But it is worth continuing west for about one hour along the Mahendra Highway, through scrub jungle, to reach the **Koshi Tappu Wildlife Reserve ❷**. On the floodplain of the Sapt Kosi River, the forests here are famous for their birdlife and wild buffaloes. The reserve is bounded on the east and west by the river embankments and on the south by the barrage (dam) that forms the border with India. The reserve headquarters is at Kusaha and the nearest hotel accommodation is in Biratnagar. Many visitors, however, choose to stay in the upmarket tented camps on the edge of the reserve.

Koshi Tappu's name means "river islands", and its watery landscape is a haven for a superb concentration of waterfowl during the winter months. A total of 280 species of birds have been recorded, including 20 different sorts of ducks and the rare swamp partridge *(Francolinus gularis)*. The migratory birds can be seen between November and March resting at the Koshi barrage and on the main channel. The trail along the east embankment provides a good vantage point. While there are no tigers or rhinos, Koshi Tappu harbours the only remaining wild buffaloes *(Bubalus bubalis)* in Nepal, a population of only about 200. There are also spotted deer, blue bulls (nilgai), wild elephants and wild pigs. The reserve covers a total area of 175 sq km (68 sq miles), and sees only a tiny fraction of the tourists who flock to Chitwan, further west. This is a serene and uncommercialised spot, and river trips and elephant rides here offer glimpses into an authentic wilderness area.

Janakpur: birthplace of Sita

Continuing west again along the Mahendra Highway, past Lahan, brings you to Dhalkebar (Lalbiti) bazaar. Here a road leads 20km (12 miles) south to the sacred settlement of **Janakpur ❸**, an interesting detour into history and one of the most colourful towns of the Terai.

Janakpur's entrance arches.

Walking along the narrow dusty lanes of Janakpur it is hard to imagine that this town was once Videha, the capital of the fabled kingdom of Mithila that stretches across much of what are now India's northern state of Bihar and the Terai from the Sapt Kosi to the Gandaki. The Maithili language is today spoken by about two million people in India and southern Nepal. Traditional Maithili paintings, passed down from generations of Mithila women, have remained unchanged for centuries with their distinctive styles and colours. They can be found all over the town: on the walls of homes, on pottery and today even on fabric. Some of the women earn money for their paintings as part of a rural development programme at the Janakpur Women's Development Centre (Kuwa village; Sun–Fri 10am–5pm; free).

There has been a major settlement on the site for many centuries, but past incarnations of Janakpur have risen and fallen, with long periods of obscurity in between. Much of the town was razed by Muslim invaders from northern India in the 15th century, and the town as it appears today dates mostly from the 19th century. Given its *Ramayana*-linked fame, however, Janakpur has remained an important pilgrimage site since at least the 16th century when artefacts – holy images of Sita and Ram and a piece of Shiva's sacred bow – were reportedly discovered in the jungle by ascetics. In 1911, the main temple, the **Janaki Mandir**, was constructed over the spot where Sita's image was found and where she is believed to have lived. It is a spectacular building, showing the distinctive influence of India's Muslim Mughal culture in its cupolas, blind arches and latticework. This was a style that dominated north Indian architecture for centuries, and that was adopted by non-Muslim maharajas, by the designers of Sikh *gurdwaras*, and that was even incorporated by the British in the Indo-Saracenic style of many colonial buildings. Nepal, however, isolated from the rest of the subcontinent, remained largely immune to the Mughal influence, and along with Patan's Krishna Mandir and a handful of Rana mansions the Janaki Mandir

Selling spices outside Ram Mandir.

Visiting the stunning Janaki Mandir.

Monkeys are regarded as sacred in Hinduism.

is one of its few Mughal-style buildings. Try to visit early in the morning or in the evening, to watch the devotees chant "Sita Ram" while the priests perform their rituals.

Nearby stands the Ram Mandir. Built in 1882 and set in a stone-walled courtyard, this Rama temple has a much more recognisably Nepalese style than the neighbouring Janaki Mandir, with a pagoda roof of a style familiar from Kathmandu's Durbar Square and the other royal cities of the Kathmandu Valley.

Two annual festivals in Janakpur attract hundreds of thousands of devotees to bathe in the city's 24 man-made *sagars* (sacred ponds). The most important celebration is Ram Nawami, Ram's birthday, in April. December marks the festival of Biha Panchami, re-enacting Ram and Sita's marriage in a procession of elephants, horses and chariots accompanied by musicians beating on their drums.

In addition to its religious and historic significance, Janakpur is a modern developing town with a thriving cigarette-manufacturing industry – the Soviet-built factory still churns out "Yak" and other brands of Nepalese cigarettes. The plains around Janakpur have also earned a reputation for aquaculture and supply much of the freshwater fish for the Kathmandu market. Beyond the boundaries of the town, however, traditional Terai life endures, and this is an excellent area to explore rural landscapes and communities. Janakpur is linked to the sleepy Indian border village of Madhubani by the only railway in Nepal, via numerous small towns and villages.

The East–West Highway

Until the mid-1950s Nepal had very few motorable roads. Early visitors reached Kathmandu by foot or on horseback from Hetauda. The first road, the Tribhuvan Raj Marg, was completed in 1956 and linked Birganj to Kathmandu. It remained the only gateway to the capital city until the Siddhartha Raj Marg linking **Bhairahawa** to Pokhara and Kathmandu was completed in 1968. Today few travellers brave the hairpin

MAITHILI PAINTINGS

The Hindu women of Janakpur (formerly Mithila) have been creating their own style of artwork for almost 3,000 years, with the tradition passed down from mother to daughter over generations. Young girls are taught the distinctive art style, recognisable by its motifs and bright colours, as well as the Hindu stories behind the images, from an early age. This training culminates in courtship and marriage, when prospective husbands are wooed with paintings, and the wall of the bridal bedroom is decorated with a *kohbar*, a fresco that celebrates life and fertility with a number of symbolic images, including bamboo, birds, fish and representations of Krishna and Vishnu. The bride and groom spend four nights beneath this mural, after which it is washed away.

Visitors to Janakpur between the festival of Diwali in the autumn and New Year in April will also see numerous exterior walls in the town decorated with painted images of wealth, such as peacocks. After New Year the walls are covered over with a fresh layer of mud and the paintings thus destroyed. Tourism, however, has brought with it a demand for more permanent Maithili art and many Janakpur women now work at putting their designs, both religious and secular, on paper, to be sold in gift shops throughout Nepal.

Entering the Janaki Mandir's central temple.

bends on the road from Hetauda over Daman Pass to Naubise. There are six main entry points: Kakarbhitta, Birganj (close to the Raxaul railway line), Sonauli (also known as Belhija) close to Bhairahawa, Nepalganj, Dhangarhi and Mahendranagar, but it is advisable to check in advance before planning a border crossing as regulations are always liable to change.

Transport and communication across the Terai east to west was greatly facilitated with the completion of the 1,030km (640-mile) Mahendra Raj Marg (Mahendra Highway) in the late 1960s. Part of the Pan-Asian Highway, but more popularly known as the East–West Highway, it was constructed in several phases with assistance from the former Soviet Union, United States, United Kingdom and India. The highway is now complete, and it is possible to drive right across Nepal from east to west from Kakarbhitta to Mahendranagar in about 24 hours.

Bazaars have sprung up along the East–West Highway at truck stops and crossroads, spreading untidy rows of thatched tea shops and fruit stalls. Shiny apples, heaps of oranges and bananas displayed against the jungle backdrop of statuesque sal trees and scrubby undergrowth are one of the enduring images of a Terai journey.

Devghat ❹ is located at a sacred confluence (*tribeni*) and has great religious importance. Many believe Sita died here, and as a result many devout followers also come here to die. In January thousands gather in Devghat for the great purificatory festival of Maha Sankranti (see page 91). Dugout canoes wait to ferry visitors to the shrine, tended by a *baba*, a famous holy man whose counsel is much sought by visiting pilgrims. This is also the take-out point for many Chitwan-bound rafting trips (see page 290).

Narayangharh ❺, (also known as Narayanghat) 10km (6 miles) south of Devghat, and the adjoining town of **Bharatpur** are located five hours by car southwest of Kathmandu. The two towns mark the hub of the Terai road network and are gateways to Chitwan National Park. All vehicles,

FACT

Janakpur features in the Hindu epic *Ramayana* as "the city of King Janak". According to the epic this was the birthplace of the king's adopted daughter Sita, whom he found while tilling the soil with a golden plough. Ram, hero of the epic and an incarnation of Vishnu, won Sita in marriage by bending the great bow of Shiva, as no other man could do. The loving couple were then gloriously married in Janakpur.

Bathing with an elephant.

Axis deer in Chitwan National Park.

whatever their final destination, must pass through the mushrooming town of Bharatpur, situated on the banks of the Narayani River. There are also daily flights between Bharatpur and Kathmandu.

Narayangharh is the archetypal Terai town, with its straight grid roads, pastel-coloured concrete buildings and North Indian-style hotels and restaurants. Shops and stalls sell imported electronic products, fashions, fruit, biscuits and chocolate. Nepalese beer, Fanta and Coke are cooled in huge refrigerators or red portable freezer boxes. Windowless restaurants cooled with ceiling fans provide welcome shelter from hot and dusty streets, which throng with gaily painted rickshaws and hooting trucks. There are no obvious attractions, but plenty of colour.

Chitwan National Park

Renowned for centuries as one of the best areas for wildlife viewing in Asia, the diverse flora and fauna of the Terai national parks attract visitors from all over the world. These parks are quite different from the wide open spaces of Africa where the animals are often in plain sight. But many visitors find the excitement of a search for wildlife in the dense jungles and reed-beds, and the thrill of an unexpected encounter, every bit as rewarding.

Many of the parks started life as royal hunting reserves, where visiting dignitaries were invited to slaughter the wildlife at will. While the hunting is largely a thing of the past, today's visitors can explore these uniquely beautiful areas in similar style and considerable comfort. For those with more modest means, budget possibilities abound.

Generally the best time for wildlife viewing in the Terai parks and reserves is from February to April when the thick ground cover has retreated. By March some of the summer bird migrants have arrived while many of the winter visitors have not yet left. But some enthusiasts enjoy aspects of other seasons, and most safari outfitters remain open from October to June.

A woman making cooking stoves from clay and straw.

The most accessible of all the Terai's national parks, **Chitwan National Park** ❻ (entry fee Rs1,500) is also one of the richest wildlife areas in Asia and contains one of the last and largest remaining areas of tall grassland habitat.

The park was formerly a hunting reserve of the ruling Rana dynasty, the kings always being keen sportsmen. Every few years a great hunt would be staged during the winter months when the threat of fever was minimal. The Ranas and their guests, who included European royalty and Viceroys of India, bagged huge numbers of tigers and rhinos.

The national park occupies a lowland valley lying between the Siwalik (Churia) and Mahabharat ranges. It is drained by two major rivers, the Narayani and the Rapti. Prior to the 1950s Chitwan was only sparsely inhabited, mainly by Tharu peoples who had developed some resistance to the endemic malaria. After the eradication of malaria, Chitwan was cleared and cultivated and its population tripled in less than a decade.

A white-browed wagtail in Chitwan.

Poaching then became a problem; the rhinoceros in particular was killed for its valuable horn. In 1964 a sanctuary was declared and a large number of local people were moved out of the park area and resettled nearby. The *Gaida Gusti* or "Rhino Guards" attempted to patrol the park, but poaching continued, and by 1966 rhino numbers had slumped to less than 100 individuals from more than 1,000 just 15 years earlier. Although the population is now growing at an annual rate of nearly 4 percent and

Catching sight of a rhino while on elephant safari in the national park.

numbers about 500, poaching is still a major problem.

Only when the national park was established in 1973, with the full protection of the Royal Nepalese Army, was poaching and encroachment finally brought under control. In 1976 Royal Chitwan National Park was extended to its present size of 1,040 sq km (402 sq miles). Concessions were given to private jungle safari operators to build lodges within the park and tourism developed at a rapid pace, leading to its own set of conflicts and complications.

During the first decade of the 21st century some campaigners began to suggest that the various luxury lodges inside the park were having a detrimental effect on the environment and were placing tourism incomes above conservation. Dark rumours that some of the lodges were surreptitiously hosting visitors bent on a more traditional style of safari – with high-power rifles and trophy heads – only fuelled the furore, while those on the other side of the debate countered that such claims were being deliberately spread by the operators of resorts outside the park boundary eager to get a larger cut of the tourist dollar. In 2009 the government decided not to renew the licences of the resorts and lodges within the park, and they all stopped operating in 2012. Some operators have set up new facilities on unprotected land nearby, but the original infrastructure has largely been left in place, empty of guests and staffed by skeleton crews, while Nepal's Supreme Court continues to wrangle over the case. Some believe that the park resorts will be allowed to reopen in the future, but for now visitors must stay in the plethora of accommodation that dots the surrounding forest and farmland.

Visiting Chitwan

The large animals that live in the park are concentrated in the dense forest and tall grasslands of the floodplain. The best way to approach them is on the back of a well-trained elephant. Not only does the elephant offer the best vantage point, but the animal's scent masks that of humans. Rhinos

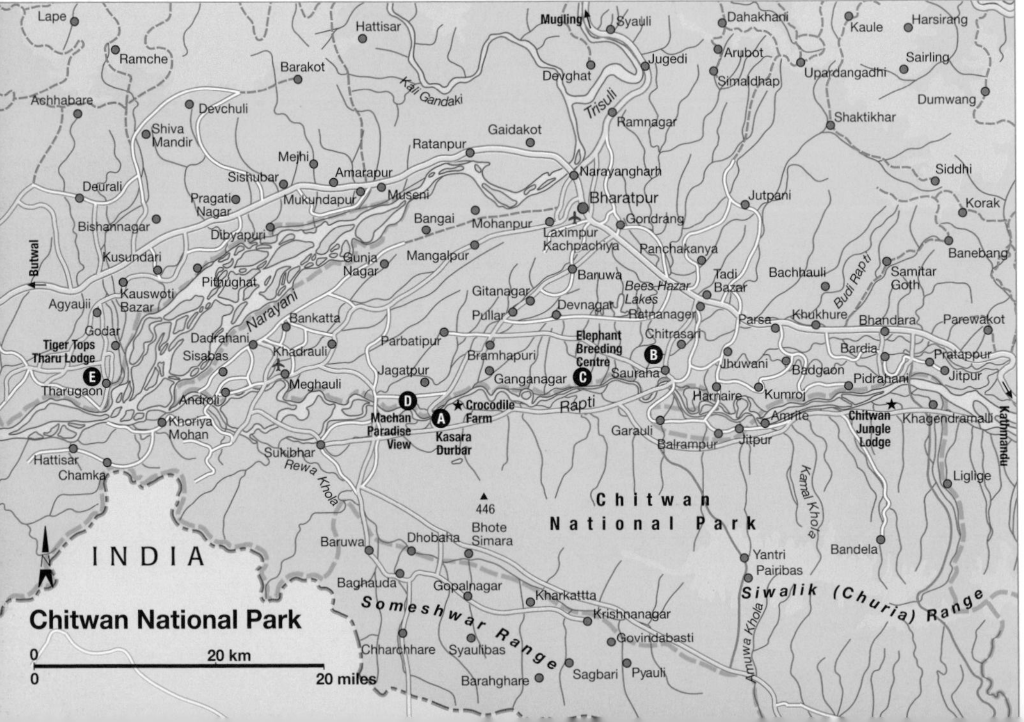

favour marshy ground and indeed some areas of prime habitat are only negotiable by elephant. This is also the safest way to view them, as well as the other large species such as tiger, gaur and sloth bear. There are government-owned elephants at the park headquarters and at Sauraha, while most lodges around the park also have privately owned elephants for carrying guests into the forest. Travelling in 4WD vehicles is another rewarding way to spot deer, wild boar, rhino, sometimes gaur and occasionally tiger, leopard and sloth bear. It is also possible to go into the park on foot accompanied by a guide. Movement around the park is not permitted after dark.

The park headquarters is at **Kasara Durbar** **A** (open daily). There is a small museum here (open daily), which includes examples of reptiles and butterflies found in the park and nearby is the Gharial Breeding Project, where batches of harmless gharial crocodile hatchlings have been raised since 1978 for restocking the Narayani River. East of Kasara is Lame Tal, a long ox-bow lake with spectacular birdlife and basking crocodiles. Other tals, such as Devi Tal, are good focal points for wildlife viewing. *Machans* (watchtowers) have been constructed overlooking tracts of grassland at Sukibhar in the west and near Dumariya in the east.

The main hub for tourist facilities on the edge of the park is further east at **Sauraha** **B**. There is a cluster of budget guesthouses and more upmarket lodges here, along with a range of restaurants, shops and travel agents. Tourist buses from Kathmandu and Pokhara end their journeys here, and there is a second park information centre on the edge of the village. The park itself lies just across the shallow waters of the Rapti River; paths and jeep tracks leading tantalisingly off into the dark shadows of the forest. An array of riverside cafés offer magnificent sunset views over the park. Small resorts stud the countryside on either side of Sauraha, and bumpy lanes lead through forest fringes and peaceful Tharu farming villages where long lines of buffalo pick their way across rice fields, elephants come lumbering

TIP

Searching out rhinos on foot is exhilarating, but it can be dangerous. Only venture into the park with an experienced guide, and do not encourage him to take you close to the animals. Alternatively, do your rhino-spotting from the safety of an elephant's back.

A crocodile basking on a Chitwan river bank.

Crossing the water at sunset.

along under the patient charge of their *mahouts* and gaggles of bright-eyed children wave eagerly to passing travellers. Hiring a bicycle from any of the travel agencies or guesthouses in Sauraha is a great way to explore the area.

Around 4km (2.5 miles) west of Sauraha is the **Elephant Breeding Centre** **C** (daily 6am–6pm; charge) where many of the elephants used for safaris in the park are kept. The best time to visit is in the late afternoon, when the animals are brought back from grazing or carrying tourists in the park to tuck into a meal of vegetation and to treat themselves to a customary dirt bath.

A number of the original luxury lodges outside the boundaries of the park itself are still operating in secluded spots away from Sauraha, including **Machan Paradise View** **D** and **Tiger Tops Tharu Lodge** **E**.

Peaceful boat or canoe trips down the Narayani River encounter migratory waterfowl, dolphin, marsh mugger and gharial crocodile as well as unrivalled views across the entire width of Nepal to the white Himalayan peaks.

One of Chitwan's greatest assets is the scope it offers for nature walks. For those with curiosity, perseverance and a certain amount of courage, walking is the most profitable way of observing birds, studying vegetation and inspecting animal tracks. Treks of two or more days are also available, which have the advantage of getting away from crowds of less ambitious tourists. But the jungle is not without a very real element of danger, so never set off without being escorted by an expert guide – visitors have been mauled by rhinos. Guides are also invaluable as both a source of information and their trained ability to listen out for wildlife and birds. Experienced guides can be hired at most lodges or at the park headquarters.

West of Chitwan

The excellent stretch of road west of Narayangharh follows the Narayani River through the Chitwan Valley, past a paper factory and the Tuborg brewery. A well-marked village road leads south to the Tiger Tops Tharu Lodge, then winds out of the Inner

Crossing the water on elephant-back.

Terai Chitwan valley and through the forested Siwalik Hills.

The highway runs between stands of leafy sal trees, complimenting the red soil and scattered golden- and cream-coloured houses. Far-reaching flatlands stretch away to the south, and young children tend water buffaloes and goats grazing alongside the deserted roads.

Located 120km (75 miles) west of Narayangharh at the base of the foothills is the pleasant crossroads town of Butwal. Gurung and Thakali people originally from the uplands make up the majority of its population. From here, a scenic road runs north through the hills to Pokhara via the viewpoint of Tansen (see page 222). Another route heads south for 20km (13 miles) to the large industrial town of Bhairahawa and the border crossing at Sonauli.

This area is full of places of historical and cultural interest. Around 20km (12 miles) west of Bhairahawa on a well-marked road is the Unesco World Heritage Site of **Lumbini** ❼, birthplace of the Lord Buddha and an important pilgrimage place for Buddhists from across Asia. The surrounding area is being developed with international funding. There are Buddhist monasteries hosting devotees from various nations, and a clutch of hotels and restaurants. The surrounding countryside is worth exploring for its peaceful agricultural scenery and hospitable, little-visited villages.

During the Buddha Jayanti festival in April or May hundreds of pilgrims descend on Lumbini to celebrate the birth of the Buddha.

Yeti Airlines and Buddha Air operate several flights a day between Bhairahawa and Kathmandu, and buses run from Kathmandu and Pokhara. Another ancient civilisation site, **Kapilavastu** ❽, lies 27km (17 miles) further west at Tilaurakot, Prince Siddhartha's childhood home and the former capital of his father's kingdom. The ruins are thought to be those of the former palace, and the place where Lord Buddha began his journey of enlightenment. Near the dam at Tribenighat, a temple marks the site of Sita's banishment, as recounted in the great *Ramayana* epic.

TIP

Cycling tours are an excellent way to explore the quiet countryside around Lumbini. The Lumbini Village Lodge, a budget guesthouse in the village near the Buddha's birthplace, organises itineraries, taking in traditional farming villages for groups of up to five people.

A smiling jungle guide.

Working the land in the Terai.

Beyond the turn-off for Luimbini the East–West Highway climbs up through the Siwalik range into the beautiful Deokhuri Valley, an Inner Terai *dun* (valley) watered by the Rapti River. This is home to the Dangaura Tharu people whose long mud houses surrounded by fertile fields can be seen from the road. The young women wear their striking black and red skirts and a distinctive headdress adorned with tassels and beads upon which they balance their loads. The Dang Valley lies further north, and is particularly popular with cyclists.

The western Terai

For many years the easiest way to reach the far west of Nepal was via India, especially during the monsoon when floods swell the rivers. However, improvements on the East–West Highway have linked the region more firmly to the rest of the country. Beyond the Deokhuri Valley, the highway penetrates the most remote part of the Terai. Here there is the true feeling of the "wild west". The four districts of Banke, Bardia, Kailali and Kanchanpur are still known as the *naya muluk*, or new territories, as they were returned to Nepal by British India as late as 1860. Before the Land Reform Act of 1964, these districts were inhabited by only Dangaura, Katharya and Rana Tharu. Migrants subsequently settled from the hills, clearing and claiming these virgin lands.

Nepalganj ❾ is the far west's largest city and is considered to be one of the hottest places in Nepal. It is also Nepal's most Muslim city, thanks to

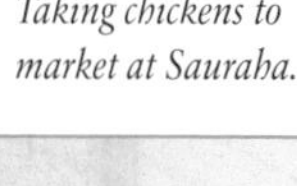

Taking chickens to market at Sauraha.

more than a century of immigration from neighbouring India – Indian-influenced Islamic architecture abounds in the city, although many of the mosques are garish, modern and closed to non-Muslims.

For centuries, Nepalganj has also been an important market town, attracting not only Indians but also Tharu and highlanders from Jumla and Tibet to its bustling bazaars north of the main square, Tribuhuwan Chowk, set out on wooden benches.

Today the population, both Indian and Nepalese, is less than 50,000; it has yet to benefit from industrialisation, although small-scale handicraft production such as silver jewellery is evident along the main street.

An important regional hub, Nepalganj is the far west's link with Kathmandu. Flights from Nepalganj airport (the country's fourth largest) connect to the hill town of Jumla and roads service the Bardia National Park and Sukla Phanta Wildlife Reserve near the western border. A good road also leads north to the fertile valley of Surkhet, now renamed Birendranagar, which was once so malarial that travellers feared to stay even one night.

Bardia National Park

Located in the remote and sparsely settled far western Terai is an untouched preserve for the more adventurous traveller keen on indigenous flora and fauna. **Bardia National Park ⑩** was first gazetted in 1976 as Royal Karnali Wildlife Reserve and the eastern extension was added in 1984, bringing the reserve to today's size of 968 sq km (374 sq miles). During the Maoist insurgency both the tourist economy and the wildlife of the park suffered badly. The area was badly affected by the political violence and visitors steered clear. Poachers, meanwhile, took advantage of the situation to infiltrate the park while government soldiers were otherwise engaged, targeting both tigers and rhinos. Now, however, the travellers have returned, and wildlife numbers are beginning to recover.

The Geruwa River, the eastern branch of the great Karnali River which diverges into two main channels studded with many small islands, forms

TIP

Despite the region's formerly insalubrious reputation, the health risks of travel in the Terai are now greatly reduced. However, this is the one part of Nepal where malaria does remain a potential threat. Around Chitwan there is minimal danger, but those travelling to more remote regions, particularly during the monsoon, should take precautions, wearing repellent and sleeping under nets – and possibly taking anti-malaria medication for extended stays.

A mother and daughter carry dung for fuel near Lumbini.

At the Unesco World Heritage Site of Lumbini.

Devotees at Lumbini's Maya Devi Temple.

the park's western boundary. The park extends east to the Nepalganj–Surkhet road and includes a large portion of the beautiful Babai River Valley, bounded by two parallel ranges of the Siwalik Hills.

There are a number of lodges clustered around the park headquarters at Thakurdwara, as well as **Tiger Tops Karnali Jungle Lodge**, set amid the fascinating Tharu villages on the edge of the forest. Most visitors fly to Nepalganj, one and a half hours from Kathmandu, then make the three-hour drive to the park. To drive all the way from Kathmandu to Bardia takes 12 hours through memorable and scenic stretches of the Terai. This inaccessibility has deterred the crowds that now flock to the more easily reached Chitwan; consequently Bardia offers a far more natural experience.

The main appeal of Bardia National Park is its reputation as one of the best places on the subcontinent to see the Royal Bengal tiger in the wild. West Nepal supports the country's second largest population of this magnificent cat after Chitwan. It is thought that around 50 breeding adults are distributed from Banke through Bardia and Kailai into Kanchanpur. A few leopards also live on the forest edges.

Trained elephants can be used to see tiger, rhinoceros and swamp deer in the Manu Tappu and Khaura Khola areas and rides can be booked at Thakurdwara. However, the park also has an excellent network of roads and driving is the best way to see the herds of deer that congregate on the open grassland. Most 4WD rides cover the west of the park, through the famous phanta grasses (see page 106) and the home of many of Bardia's wild elephant herds. The southern area of the park, also best reached by vehicle, is the roaming ground of the beautiful blackbuck antelope.

There are a number of long walks, especially along the river, which are good for birdwatching and spotting deer and monkeys. River trips by boat or dugout canoe are scenically breathtaking and excellent for seeing waterfowl, gharial and marsh mugger crocodiles, smooth-coated otters and Gangetic dolphin. This is also a great way to fish in the park's rivers; species include the huge *mahseer*, popular among sport fishers – although the fish must now be released back into the river due to a declining population. A fishing permit is required, available from the park headquarters.

Sukla Phanta Wildlife Reserve

Although small and remote, **Sukla Phanta Wildlife Reserve ⓫**, covering 155 sq km (60 sq miles), is another gem of a wildlife sanctuary, tucked into the far southwest corner of Nepal, and well worth a visit (preferably between October and April). Flights go to Mahendranagar and, more reliably, to nearby Dhangadhi.

Sukla Phanta encompasses part of the floodplain of the Sarda River, has thick sal forests and a pretty, small lake called Rani Tal. The preserve has extensive open grasslands and the largest surviving population of endangered swamp deer *(barasingha)*, numbering about 2,000. There are many deer concentrated in the open meadows and waterfowl on Rani Tal. The park has more than 450 species of birdlife, including cormorants and eagles. Other wildlife, including an estimated population of 30 tigers, can best be observed from the tall *machans* (watchtowers) or from 4WD vehicles. Entrance to the reserve on foot is not permitted unless accompanied by a guide.

Elephants also make their home in the reserve although, strangely, they are rarely seen. One particularly famous inhabitant was Thula Hatti ("Big Elephant"), believed to be the

An open-air train ride.

Images of the Buddha in Lumbini, his birthplace.

largest Asian elephant in the world, but he was killed by a mine explosion in 1993, most likely planted by a poacher.

Near the Rani Tal is a round brick compound which many believe was the fort of an ancient Tharu king, although lack of archaeological research renders this more myth than fact for the time being.

Towards India

West of Nepalganj the East–West Highway passes through the untouched forests of Bardia National Park to Chisapani, a village on the banks of the Karnali River, 350km (218 miles) west of Narayangharh. A spectacular, if somewhat incongruous, single-tower suspension bridge – reputedly the longest in the world – now links the far west to the rest of Nepal. However, very few tourists venture west of Bardia National Park, and the area remains more influenced by the Indian capital than its own.

The border town of **Dhangarhi** draws Indian shoppers in their droves with its imported goods. The challenges of a new cultural identity evident in such remote areas is also apparent in booming **Mahendranagar**, which has doubled its population in recent years and has now grown bigger than Nepalganj. Unless you're in search of Indian-style bustle, however, neither town offers much for tourists other than as bases to explore the nearby nature reserves. In contrast, nearby villages offer some of the more authentic sights of the Terai, inhabited by the native Rana Tharu and distinguished by longhouses and women wearing their colourfully embroidered traditional skirts topped with black shawls.

Although it is unlikely ever to take over from the Himalayan regions as Nepal's primary tourist attraction, the Terai certainly is a fascinating melting point of Indian and Nepalese hill traditions and a centre of burgeoning commercialism whole-heartedly embracing the 21st century. Combining this with its unequalled opportunities for viewing wildlife, a visit to the south of the country has an indisputable charm all of its own.

Farm labourers.

PEOPLE OF THE TERAI

The Terai's malarial climate has always repelled invaders, while its fertility attracted migrants. The 6th century BC saw a period of great prosperity in the region, but waves of settlers subsequently retreated and the jungle re-established itself. Only a few scattered tribal groups stubbornly remained to tend the rich land in such unhealthy conditions. The most numerous are the Tharu and small groups of the Bote, Majhi and Raji who work as fishermen and ferrymen, as well as the Kumal potters.

In the 20th century the Terai yielded to new settlers from the overpopulated Middle Hills. Cultivation accelerated following the political change of the 1950s and the eradication of malaria in the 1960s. Today nearly half of Nepal's population lives in the Terai.

The eastern Terai is the most densely populated area, particularly Jhapa District where indigenous Tharu, Rajbamsi, Dhimal and people of Indian origin have settled with the more recently arrived Rai and Limbu. In central Terai, Tharu, Kumal and Bote tribes are neighbours with hill peoples such as Brahman, Chhetri and Gurung. Until the 1970s far western Terai was heavily forested but legal and illegal settlers from the western hills, mostly Brahman and Chhetri, have joined the original Tharu tribes of Danguara, Rana and Katharya. Still, the western Terai remains sparsely populated compared to the regions further east.

Birthplace of Lord Buddha

The sacred site of Lumbini marks the historical location of the birth of the Buddha, and is the focus for devotion and pilgrimage for thousands of Buddhists from around the world.

In 543 BC at a quiet spot beside a pool in the hot levels of the Terai, a child of royal blood was born. His father was Suddhodana, king of the Kapilavastu realm, and his mother was a princess named Maya Devi. The child was named Siddhartha Gautama, but today he is best known as Buddha, the Enlightened One, and the place of his birth at Lumbini, 21km (13 miles) west of the modern town of Bhairahawa, is a major centre of pilgrimage.

The Middle Way

Siddhartha was raised in princely luxury, marrying a princess, fathering a child and enjoying all the privileges of royalty. But at the age of 29 he ventured beyond the walls of the palace for the first time, and encountered a poor man, a sick man and a corpse. He was so disturbed by this suffering that he abandoned his comfortable life to become an ascetic. This path too proved ultimately unfulfilling, and so Siddhartha instead pioneered "the Middle Way", eventually achieving spiritual enlightenment and becoming the Buddha.

After the Buddha's death, the various places across the northern subcontinent associated with his life were developed as temple complexes by his followers. At Lumbini many monasteries were built, and in 249 BC the Mauryan Emperor Ashoka visited and erected a commemorative pillar.

Lost city

However, somewhere along the line Lumbini dropped off the map. In the 4th century AD the Chinese monk, Fa-Hsien (Fa Xian), travelled to India in search of Buddhist manuscripts and found that Lumbini was already in ruins. Fa-Hsien wrote: "On the road people have to guard against elephants and lions." Beyond that point the site was lost altogether, and it was only in 1895 that Nepal's government began to search for traces. The Ashokan pillar was uncovered in 1896, and with it definitive proof that the place had once been venerated as the birthplace of the Buddha.

Since 1970 the sacred site has been protected by the Lumbini Development Trust. Excavations have been made and pottery, figurines and coins found among the ancient brick foundations. A series of monasteries, stupas and pavilions have been built in national styles by various Buddhist nations in recent years, alongside a museum, library and garden complex. The massive Ashoka pillar marks the place of Buddha's birth and the Maya Devi Temple contains a panel depicting the miraculous event.

Exploring Lumbini

Lumbini is a tranquil place. Prayer flags flutter in the hot breezes; birds chatter in the canopy of the sacred pipal tree, and pilgrims from China, Korea, Japan, Southeast Asia and beyond come to make their quiet obeisance. The monasteries are spread out over a large area of parkland; bicycle is a good mode of transport. Beyond the park the Terai rolls away in all directions, and there are quiet farm tracks to explore.

Tilaurakot, the ancient capital of Kapilavastu, is 27km (17 miles) west of Lumbini. In a lovely mango grove, excavations have revealed the brick remains of the eastern and western gates of the palace complex in which Prince Siddhartha lived with his father, King Suddhodhana. The museum in the village contains pieces dating between the 4th century BC and the 4th century AD. Near Tilaurakot are the damaged Ashoka pillars of Niglihawa and Kotihaw.

Prayer flags adorn the sacred Bodhi tree.

The Suli Gad River.

THE REMOTE WEST

Far removed from the rest of the country, western Nepal is a land apart, an untamed and sparsely populated region offering rich rewards for the hardy and determined traveller.

Main Attractions
- Jumla
- Rara Lake
- Khaptad National Park
- Phoksundo Tal
- Humla

In western Nepal the Himalayas are at their widest, unfolding as broad ridges, generally over 3,600 metres, (11,800ft) known as *lekhs*. The great Karnali River system bevels these high pasturelands into oak-pine forested valleys. Jumla, an administrative and commercial centre at 2,347 metres (7,677ft), shivers under thick snow throughout winter, while **Dipayal,** at a mere 600 metres (1,970ft) records some of the country's highest temperatures. A depleted monsoon squeezes its last drops onto the west's summer-parched farmlands in the far-reaching rainshadow of the Dhaulagiri Massif.

The Khasa Malla kings governed west Nepal and Tibet through the 14th century, when Rajput chieftains, migrating into the hills in the face of increasing Muslim dominance of north India and intermarrying with local clans, carved out petty principalities here. Occupational castes from the south followed them, settling in the valleys and low hills, while Tibetans extended their niche into the inner Himalayas, establishing an unassimilated settlement pattern that persists today. The crusade of Prithvi Narayan Shah reached Jumla in 1788 and thereafter the west answered to Kathmandu, or for a period to the northern fiefdom of Mustang.

Today, hilltop *chortens*, crude human effigies and enduring folk traditions recall the west's mixed ethnic heritage. Religious beliefs show altitudinal preferences: Buddhism in the highlands, Hinduism in the lowlands, with a form of kinship deity worship intertwined.

Trekking in the west

Trekkers bound for west Nepal enter a world far removed from the teahouses of Solu Khumbu. Only the hardy need apply – those willing to weather the difficulties for the great rewards of more isolated and rugged Nepal. Except for the Terai and silt-fed valleys, the region is agriculturally impoverished. All

Porters in the Upper Dolpo restricted area.

food and drink must be carried in as there are few opportunities to restock. Customarily ill-prepared to accommodate outsiders – peoples such as the Thakuris consider it polluting to house a foreigner and so there is no tradition of trekking lodges here – tents and camping equipment are also required. A reliable trekking guide is invaluable in finding elusive paths and dealing with non-English speaking porters.

Travel to the remote west is no easy jaunt. While the high Mugu and Limi valleys in Humla have been opened to permit-holding hikers and a number of operators offer organised trips here, facilities are almost non-existent, access is difficult, and the terrain wild. This is one of the poorest and most remote parts of Nepal, and a trek here still has many of the characteristics of a genuine expedition – thrilling, authentic and rewarding, but not to be undertaken lightly.

Jumla and Rara Lake

Jumla ❶ is where most treks begin. **Rara National Park ❷** is the far west's most popular trekking area, though it receives only a few tourists each year. Set at 2,980 metres (9,777ft), Rara Daha's (Lake) blue waters reflect a snow-clad Ghurchi Lekh fringed with evergreens. During November and April, shoreline reeds are aflutter with migrating wildfowl. The 106-sq km (41-sq mile) protected area harbours Himalayan black bear, *tahr*, musk deer, red panda, otter and monkey.

Two main trails connect Jumla to Rara, each requiring approximately six days' return journey. The more westerly route heads north from Jumla, up the valley and across grassy slopes, reaching Hada Sinja, the old Khasa Malla capital, in two days. Across the river the old palace is in ruins, but a temple to Bhagvati, goddess of justice, is worth a view. You have the choice of the longer, easier Gorosingha route or the steeper, shorter Okarpata route. Both cross the Ghurchi Mara and traverse a 3,800-metre (12,500ft) ridge overlooking Rara Lake. Forests of pine, birch and rhododendron lead to a bridge with posts carved into human likenesses, spanning the final approach to Rara Lake. It takes one full day to walk the 20km (13-mile)

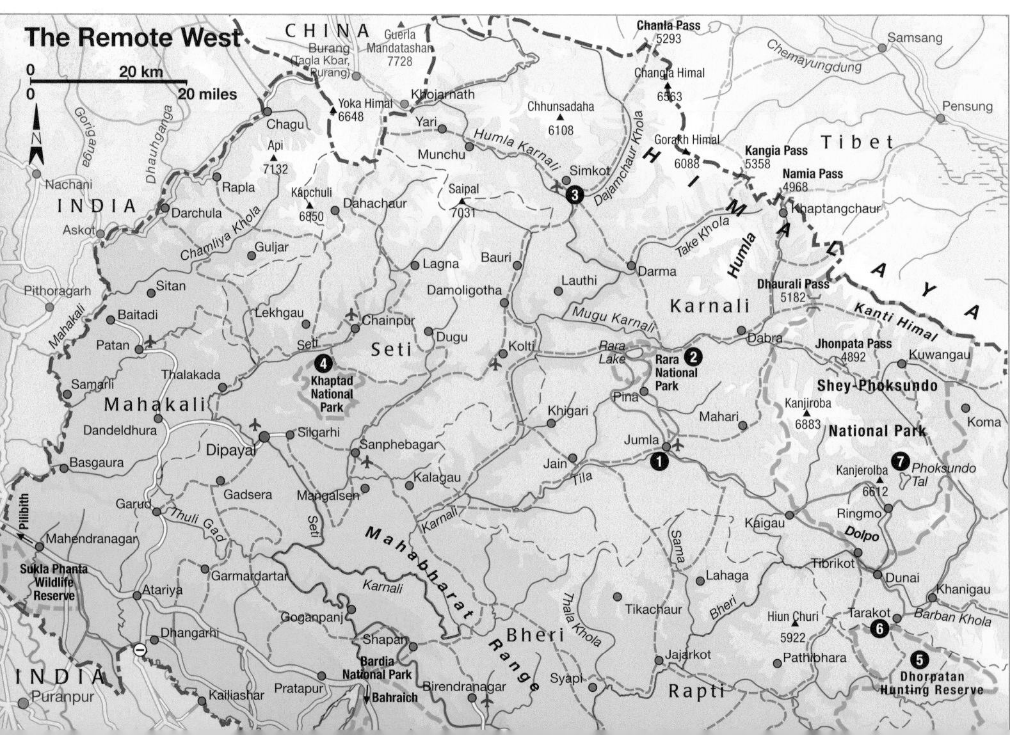

Map on page 302

trail around the largest lake in Nepal.

The return to Jumla leaves from the lake's southern rim and descends to **Pina** (2,430 metres/7,970ft). Once over Ghurchi Lagna (3,456 metres/11,340ft), the trail passes Bumra and the Lah Gad River and climbs to a meadow where it forks. The westerly branch crosses Danphya Lagna (3,658 metres/12,000ft); the easterly route descends along riverbanks. Both lead back to Jumla.

Humla

The distance from Jumla to **Humla** is far greater than the jingle in their names implies. Located 12 or more hard days' walk northwest of Jumla, Humla is visited by only a handful of Westerners and knows few of the modern world's accoutrements. Until the mid-1990s the majority of people tackling this route were pastoralist Humli farmers taking their sheep and goats along the great "salt for grain" trail to lowland Aacham. Increased supply of government salt and grain had already diminished local investment in pastoralism, but when population land pressure led Aacham to increase their grazing fees, Humlis responded by wholesaling their sheep herds and traffic on the historic trade route dropped to a trickle. However, Hindu and Buddhist pilgrims still bisect Humla en route to holy Lake Mansarovar and Mount Kailas, the centre of the world for Buddhists, in Tibet.

With the decline of their caravan lifestyle, however, other aspects of local life unravelled. Humla had a unique social system based in polyandry – with some men always off on trade or shepherding duties, the tradition of one wife to many brothers held sway for centuries. With all the men now coming home, the family seams are bursting and the economy is stunted. However, Humla has taken vigorous steps to re-invent itself. They have the national lead in forestlands owned by the community and are successfully processing non-timber forest products such as herbal oils. Humla now has several health clinics, a successful crafts exportation business and sharply increasing enrolment in school for both boys and girls.

The trail from Jumla to Humla goes west from Sinja, joining the Khater Khola, the river that drains Rara Lake,

A Tibetan nomad with his horse.

Rhododendrons are abundant at moderate altitudes in western Nepal.

following its lush riparian lands before joining the main north–south trade route below Barchya on the Karnali. From dry riverbanks, the trail rises to cross 3,800-metre (12,500ft) Munya La. Whether you follow the Karnali or fly in from Nepalganj, you will arrive at **Simkot** ❸, district headquarters of Humla. The town is located on a high ridge and has an airstrip, a clutch of government offices and a bustling market.

Humla has always lain on a major pilgrimage route to Mount Kailas, and foreign travellers are today permitted to follow this fabled trail. To reach Mount Kailas, source of the Humla Karnali and three other great rivers of Central Asia, head north out of town towards **Munchu**, the Nepal departure police checkpost two days short of the border to Tibet. It is essential that you plan ahead so that you are met at the border, otherwise the Chinese authorities will not permit you to cross. You will be driven to Taklakot, a vibrant old trade centre, pulling peoples of exotic cultures throughout the region. From here it is just 100km (60 miles) to Darchan, the first stop at the base of Mount Kailas, where at least two nights are required to acclimatise before making the four-day circuit.

Further south, the **Khaptad National Park** ❹ guards a place of religious importance as well as *lekhs* and high pastures. Five of the park's 225 sq km (89 sq miles) are sacred, sheltering shrines and streams that feed the Ganges River. Getting to Khaptad is not difficult; the four western airports (Kolti, Sanphebagar, Chainpur and Dipayal) can be reached within two to three days' walk of the park. From Chainpur in the Seti Valley, the trail mounts the 3,050-metre (10,000ft) Khaptad Lekh to the park's headquarters. An alternative return route heads south to Silgarhi, a Newar hill bazaar with stone-paved streets. Seven to ten days are needed for the trip.

Dolpo

Since 1989, the valleys leading to Dolpo's **Shey-Phoksundo National Park** have been open to organised trekking groups who are self-sufficient in food and fuel. Shey Gompa and the rest of the 1,373-sq km (531-sq mile) park above Phoksundo Lake are also accessible for organised groups with special permits. These high mountain regions were featured in Peter Matthiessen's book *The Snow Leopard.*

A three- to four-week trek into **Dolpo** requires the mindset to endure a remote and spartan landscape. There are several approach routes; from Pokhara, Jumla, or following the path up the Bheri River. Drive to Baglung on a good, paved road and start walking, or drive to Maldunga and then a further 10km (6 miles) on a very rough road to Beni.

Village tea houses are available along this corridor as far as Lumsum, from where the trail climbs steeply through pine and rhododendron forest to Jaljala Pass (3,415 metres/11,200ft). A *chautara* (tree-shaded rest stop) marks the top, where a fine camp spot looks over the Dhaulagiri and Annapurna Himals. Dhorpatan (2,760 metres/9,055ft) is reachable in seven days from Pokhara.

DOLPO'S HARDY SALT TRADERS

Sequestered from the outside world by tortuously high mountain passes and restricted entry, Dolpo has long fascinated and frustrated travellers. For centuries, a trans-Himalayan salt trade was the mainstay economy of Nepal's mountain people. Terai-grown grains brought up during winter were exchanged for the essential salt as well as wool, butter and Tibetan brick tea. Every summer, yak caravans crossed snowbound passes, well over 4,000 metres (13,200ft), sometimes enduring days without food and nights at temperatures down to –20°C (–4°F). Although the advent of iodised salt has made the value of Tibetan salt plummet, the great herds still thunder in Dolpo.

David Snellgrove first revealed the mysteries of Dolpo in his book *Himalayan Pilgrimage* (1961). More recently Eric Valle's Academy Award-nominated 1999 film *Caravan* (also known as *Himalaya*) brought Dolpo to the world's attention again. The film chronicles the salt traders' rugged life, mixed with a depiction of the classic rift between youth's urgent pride and the elders' respect for the mysterious authority of the mountain gods. *Caravan* ran for many months in local cinemas to packed audiences crackling with the excitement of Nepalese thrilled with the beauties of their own hidden culture, while DVDs of the film are widely available across Nepal.

Dhorpatan lies over a 2,930-metre (9,600ft) pass, five or six days from the trailhead. At the **Dhorpatan Hunting Reserve** ❺, blue sheep and other prized animals can be hunted with a permit. The next leg of the journey, Dhorpatan to Dunai, takes a roller-coaster track over three passes through a desolate landscape. The next stopping point is **Tarakot** ❻, known locally as Dzong for its hilltop fortress.

From Dunai, the district headquarters, two trails lead north. If the locals report it to be in good repair, take the trail up the Suli Gad River. There are lodges in Chepko and Ringmo and forest walks. After the Palam park entrance, where your entrance ticket and goods will be checked, the trail winds through a narrow gorge, passing close to a magnificent waterfall. The highest in Nepal, it tumbles 1,670 metres (5,480ft) down a series of rock shelves.

Hikers' first glimpse of **Phoksundo Tal** ❼ reveals a white glimmer of silver birch edging the lake's turquoise-blue waters, set in a cleft between rocks that rise 2,000 metres (6,500ft). Kanjiroba, at 6,883 metres (22,582ft) the highest in the region, can be seen from the tops of these surrounding peaks. Blue sheep, musk deer, goral, snow leopard, tahr and bear inhabit the park, set aside to protect an ecosystem typical of the high arid Tibetan plateau. At the southern end of the lake sits the gompa-rich hamlet of **Ringmo** (3,630 metres/ 11,900ft). According to local legend the lake was created by a vengeful demon after villagers betrayed its whereabouts to the Buddhist saint Guru Rinpoche. The demon called down a flood which inundated the valley and drowned the village in question. Its ruins are said still to lie in the depths of the lake.

Turning back down the Suli Gad and continuing west to **Tibrikot**, another fort town, the trail diverges, southward along the Bheri to Jajarkot and Surkhet, accessible by road from Nepalganj or west to Jumla. Most trekkers prefer the five- to six-day journey to Jumla, across the 3,840-metre (12,590ft) Balangra Pass and on through Rimi to Napokuna in the upper Tila Valley. The entire Pokhara or Tansen–Dolpo–Jumla trek can also be done in reverse. In either direction, weather will be a major factor.

FACT

Circumambulation around Mount Kailas is an important religious ritual, called *parikama* by Hindus and *kora* by Tibetan Buddhists. The latter believe that circuiting the mountain wipes away the sins of a lifetime.

Ancient Buddhist stupa and chortens at Shey Gompa.

Women sitting on the top level of Krishna Mandir in Patan's Durbar Square.

INSIGHT GUIDES TRAVEL TIPS
NEPAL

Transport

Accommodation

Eating Out

Activities

A – Z

Language

Further Reading

TRANSPORT

GETTING THERE AND GETTING AROUND

GETTING THERE

By air

Nepal has just one international airport – Tribhuvan (www.tiairport.com.np), about 6.5km (4 miles) from Kathmandu – and the vast majority of travellers enter the country here.

There are no direct connections to Europe or the United States, and all long-haul routes to Nepal require a transfer in Asia or the Middle East. The national carrier, Nepal Airlines, has a limited international network, mostly focusing on neighbouring countries. More useful are Gulf-based carriers including Etihad, Oman Air, Emirates and Qatar Airways, which all have connections between Nepal and the rest of the world via their Middle Eastern hubs. Jet Airways and Air India offer long-haul connections to Nepal through Delhi and Mumbai, and Southeast Asian airlines including Cathay Pacific, Thai Airways and Singapore Airlines usually offer the best routes for travel between Nepal and Australasia or America. Budget Malaysian carrier Air Asia now also flies between Kuala Lumpur and Kathmandu. Air China flies between Kathmandu and Lhasa three times a week, crossing the Himalayas on one of the most spectacular flights in the world.

Tickets to Nepal are not particularly cheap, and prices rise steeply at peak tourism seasons or during major local holidays when migrant workers return home to visit their families. All air fares must be paid in foreign currency by foreigners in Nepal. Only Nepalese and Indian nationals may pay in rupees for any flight between Nepal and India.

Individual travellers flying during the main season (October–April) should confirm their outward and return flights at the same time. It is sensible to reconfirm your international departure tickets again not less than three days before departure. Excess baggage fees at Tribhuvan International Airport are levied in foreign currency.

Flying is a good way of making journeys across Nepal.

By road

Nepal has a number of official land border crossings, and entering the country by land from India is a popular option for travellers. There are also several border crossings between Nepal and China, but only one of these is currently open for regular travel by foreigners. Check local political conditions before travelling: political crises may cause borders to close temporarily.

The main border crossings are:

Birganj (Narayani Zone) near Raxaul, India.

Kodari (Bagmati Zone) on the Nepalese-Tibetan border, open to tourists with Chinese visas and Tibet travel permits, and providing road access to Lhasa. Vehicles have to be changed at the border because Chinese vehicles are only permitted in China and Nepalese vehicles only in Nepal. Taking a private vehicle into Chinese territory is virtually impossible.

Mahendranagar (Mahakali Zone) in the far western corner of Nepal. There are good links to Delhi from here, and onward buses across the Terai to Kathmandu.

Mohana (Dhangadhi), a little-used entry point from India's Uttar Pradesh into western Nepal.

Nepalganj (Bheri Zone) with links from Lucknow in India.

Sonauli (Lumbini Zone) near Bhairawa on the road to Pokhara. This is by far the most popular entry point for travellers from India; there are good connections to and from Delhi by rail, and regular onward buses to Pokhara and Kathmandu.

Kakarbhitta (Mechi Zone) a quiet crossing from West Bengal with onward connections to Darjeeling, Sikkim and Kolkata (Calcutta).

Tourist visas for Nepal are available on arrival for most foreigners, but those heading in the opposite direction will need to obtain an Indian visa in advance. If you are entering Nepal by private car from India, be prepared to wait for several hours to get through any of the border posts. A *carnet de passage en douanes* is required for cars and motorcycles. This exempts the vehicle owner from customs duty for a period of three months. An international driving licence is also required.

By rail

In contrast with India, there is no railway network to speak of in Nepal. A 47km (29-mile) line was built in 1925 between Raxaul, India, and Amlekhganj, south of Kathmandu. Further east, a second line was built in 1940 between the Indian border and Janakpur of some 50km (31 miles). But that's all.

However, trains are still an important means of travel for those heading between India and Nepal. Combining Indian rail with Nepalese roads, it takes approximately three days from Delhi to Kathmandu via Varanasi and Patna, crossing the border at Birganj. Coming from the east, you can take the train to New Jalpaiguri from Kolkata (Calcutta), Delhi, Darjeeling or Guwahati. From there it is a one-hour taxi ride to Kakarbhitta, a Nepalese border post from where you can take a bus or taxi to Biratnagar.

International Airlines

Air China
Lazimpat
Tel: 01-444 0650
www.airchina.com
Air India
Hattisar.
Tel: 01-441 0906
www.airindia.in
Cathay Pacific
Naxal
Tel: 01-444 4820
www.cathaypacific.com
Etihad
Lazimpat
Tel: 01-400 5000
www.etihadairways.com
Jet Airways
Hattisar
Tel: 01-444 6375
www.jetairways.com
Nepal Airlines
Kantipath.
Tel: 01-422 0757
www.nepalairlines.com.np
Qatar Airways
Hattisar
Tel: 01-444 0467
www.qatarairways.com
Thai Airways
Durbar Marg
Tel: 01-422 3565
www.thaiair.com

A colourful Kathmandu bus.

GETTING AROUND

Nepal's mountainous terrain can make all forms of internal travel a challenge: monsoon rains prompt landslips in the hills that can all too easily obliterate major highways; poor visibility can see mountain flights stranded on the tarmac, and away from the main roads the going gets decidedly tough, with ancient, rattletrap buses complete with the cliché goats and chickens. However, conditions have improved greatly in recent years, and there are comfortable road options for travel between major centres, and an increasingly efficient domestic flight network. For shorter journeys around Kathmandu, meanwhile, the biggest challenge is the frenetic traffic – at rush hour walking can be the quickest option.

From the airport

There is no cultural decompression zone between Tribhuvan International Airport and the chaos of Kathmandu: the hustle and the hassle starts right at the gates. If you are not being met by your travel agent, there are pre-paid taxis available, charging around Rs600 to Thamel or other parts of central Kathmandu, but be prepared for the hard-sell on tours and alternative accommodation from the driver. The ticket booth is on the right as you exit the terminal. For the return journey from Kathmandu to the airport, taxis charge around Rs350.

Crowded city buses shuttle between the airport and the city for a few rupees. The pick-up point is on the ring road, a few minutes' walk from the airport terminal.

On departure

There are extensive security checks before all international flights leaving Nepal, and it can take a long time to clear immigration, so be sure to allow plenty of time at the airport. Facilities beyond immigration are limited, though a few small cafés sell snacks and drinks, and a couple of boutiques offer a small selection of books and souvenirs. There is no international departure tax to be paid.

By air

Given the tortuous nature of mountain roads – not to mention the fraught state of the traffic on the major highways – flying is by far the best way of moving around quickly in Nepal. There is an extensive network of airports – from large establishments capable of handling jets to the improbable mountain runways where strips of tenuous tarmac are perched on precarious ridges. Weather and technical issues do lead to frequent cancellations and schedule changes, however, so it always pays to build some slack into travel plans within Nepal.

There are a number of domestic airlines operating out of Kathmandu, with good links to the south and east of the country, and to Pokhara. Routes into the far west are less well served, and for some remote airports it is necessary to transit in Nepalganj. Domestic airports include Jumla, Mahendranagar, Nepalganj and Simikot in the west, Pokhara, Jomsom, Bhairawa, Bharatpur and Birganj in the centre, and Janakpur, Biratnagar, Tumlingtar and Lukla in the east.

There is a two-tier fare system in operation on all domestic routes: all foreigners except Indian nationals must pay for their tickets in foreign currency, and are charged around double the Nepalese price. A domestic airport tax of Rs200 is charged at Kathmandu.

The popular mountain airports at Jomsom and Lukla are major entry points for trekkers, but they are as weather-dependent as anywhere in the Himalayas. Flights sometimes take off from Kathmandu or Pokhara only to turn back as weather deteriorates en route. As the routes are only served by small aircraft enormous backlogs can build up if the clouds roll in during peak season. It is essential to reconfirm flights to and from these destinations, and while all domestic airlines offer replacements or refunds for delayed and cancelled flights, it is wise to allow several days for possible hold-ups.

Mountain flights and helicopters

Most of the domestic airlines listed below also operate one-hour mountain flights, which leave Kathmandu each morning (in clear weather only) to fly east along the Himalayas for a view of Mount Everest.

Five- and nine-seater helicopters can be chartered via travel agents and are charged per flying hour. Used during medical evacuations, they can also be hired for sightseeing flights, although there are restrictions as to where helicopters can land, especially in protected areas.

By foot

Be prepared to do a lot of walking. Taxis and cars can only take you limited distances. Even within cities many of the most interesting sites are best reached on foot, given the typical logjam of vehicles. Generally Nepalese people do not count distance by kilometres or miles, but by the number of walking hours involved in a journey.

By road

In this mountainous country with deep valleys etched between peaks and ranges, roads are vital for bringing together the various communities.

During the rainy season whole portions of existing roads are damaged and must be repaired. Maintenance on some roads is rather slow and it is best to enquire locally before setting off on a long-distance road trip.

There are six major road links. The **Tribhuvan Highway**, linking Kathmandu via Hetauda and Birganj with Raxaul at the Indian border 200km (124 miles) away, was opened in 1956 and built with Indian assistance. The **Arniko Highway** or Chinese Road leads from Kathmandu to Bhaktapur and Dhulikhel and then to the Tibetan border at Kodari (see page 248). It was built with Chinese support and opened in 1967. Some 110km (68 miles) long, it suffers from periodic landslides. Check conditions before taking a trip. Chinese engineers also helped to build the **Prithvi Highway** in 1973, which covers the 200km (124 miles) between Kathmandu and Pokhara. There are two extensions to the Pokhara road: Dumre to Gorkha and Mugling to Narayangharh. In 1970 Indian engineers completed the 188km (117-mile) extension from Pokhara via Butwal to Sonauli on the Indian border south of Bhairawa, called the **Siddhartha Highway**. The most ambitious road is the result of the cooperation of the former USSR (or its successors), the United States, Britain and India, the **Mahendra Highway**. Popularly known as the East–West Highway, this 1,000km (620-mile) lowland thoroughfare through the Terai is part of the fabled Pan-Asian Highway linking the Bosphorus with the Far East. China built the 32km (20-mile) **ring road** around Kathmandu. East of Kathmandu the Swiss-built highway from Lamosangu to Jiri stretches 110km (68 miles).A seventh road – the B.P. Koirala Highway, also known as the Sindhuli Highway, linking Kathmandu to the Terai at Janakpur – has been under construction for a decade and is approaching completion.

Away from the main highways smaller roads are creeping into the mountains along former trekking routes. For the most part these are still rough and bumpy routes, plied by uncomfortable local transport. But tarmac is inching its way into the hills, and many journeys – such as that from Kathmandu to the Langtang trailhead – can now be completed in a day, rather than as a week-long trek.

Buses

All roads are plied by local bus services, with express buses on the main routes. A ride on a local bus in Nepal is a bumpy, noisy, smelly and slow affair, but an authentic travel experience nonetheless. Some of these antediluvian beasts are mere sheet-metal boxes on wheels, but they eventually arrive at their destinations, even if passengers have to occasionally alight on the steepest climbs. No matter what, they are a cheap way of getting about inside and outside the Kathmandu Valley. They allow for a long, close look at the

Domestic Airlines

Agni Air
Shantinagar, Kathmandu
Tel: 01-410 7812
www.agniair.com.np
Buddha Air
Hattisar, Kathmandu
Tel: 01-1 554 2494
www.buddhaair.com
Fishtail Air (Helicopters)
Tinkune, Kathmandu.
Tel: 01-411 2230
www.fishtailair.com
Gorkha Airlines
Hattisar, Kathmandu.
Tel: 01-621 2096
www.gorkhaairlines.com
Sita Air
Sinamangal, Kathmandu
Tel: 01- 411 0503
www.sitaair.com.np
Yeti Airlines
Thamel, Kathmandu.
Tel: 01-446 4878
www.yetiairlines.com

A bus makes its way along a narrow mountain pass.

local folk inside the bus, if not always at the dramatic scenery outside. More modern buses – many with comfortable reclining seats and air conditioning – run along major routes. These are usually sold to travellers as "tourist buses", though they are often as widely used by wealthier locals as by foreigners. They are markedly more expensive than local buses, but much faster, cleaner and more comfortable. Virtually any hotel or travel agent in Kathmandu or Pokhara can book tickets on these buses. The highest quality tourist buses link Kathmandu, Pokhara and Chitwan. In Kathmandu most depart from the northern end of Kantipath; in Pokhara they leave from the so-called Tourist Bus Park in Damside. Tickets sold by travel agents for "tourist buses" on less well-trammelled routes often turn out to be for nothing more than regular local buses – though a pre-booked ticket will at least guarantee a seat.

Express buses run between Kathmandu and Bhaktapur – with only a few stops in between. These buses, and others for destinations around the valley, leave from Ratna Park in Kathmandu. The long-distance bus park is located at Gongabu, which is on the northern side of the ring road east of Balaju, in Kathmandu.

The most luxurious bus services are run by **Greenline Tours** (Tel: 01-425 7544; www.greenline.com.np) from their office on Tridevi Marg just east of Thamel. They have modern coaches running to Chitwan, Pokhara, Lumbini and Dhulikhel.

Cars

More reliable than any other mode of transport, private cars can be hired from any hotel, car-hire firm or travel agency. However, tourists are not permitted to drive in Nepal, so rental cars come with a professional driver. Daily rates should include driver, fuel, taxes and meals for the driver (but a gratuity is expected, depending on service). Prices vary widely depending where you're going, but a car with driver hired from a hotel would be around US$50 a day (approx. Rs5,300).

Hitchhiking

Hitchhiking is unheard of in Nepal. It is an accepted practice to flag down lifts from any passing vehicle on remote rural roads where traffic is light – trekkers branching off the trail to a road may find themselves in this situation. However, it is generally expected that you will pay the equivalent to a bus fare along the same route for your ride.

Motorbikes

While tourists are not permitted to drive cars, it is possible to rent a motorbike. Both 125cc automatic scooters and larger bikes are available from agencies in Kathmandu and Pokhara, and while Nepal's roads are not for the faint-hearted, for riders with experience of Asian traffic, a bike can be a rewarding way to get off the beaten track.

To rent a motorbike an international driving permit is required (easily available for a small fee from the Post Office in the UK), and most rental agencies will require you to deposit your passport. Check your travel insurance policy carefully before renting a motorbike – you will generally not be covered if you are not licensed to ride a bike in your home country, and riding higher powered bikes often requires additional insurance cover.

Drive on the left side of the road and be aware of people and animals on narrow roads. Accidents can lead to serious trouble, particularly when cows – which have holy status for Hindus – are involved. The accidental death of such an animal can potentially lead to a jail sentence. Petrol is surprisingly expensive in Nepal, and difficult to buy away from main roads, so plan ahead before heading into remote areas.

In Kathmandu a group of motorbike rental agencies are clustered together at Thahiti Chowk on the southern edge of Thamel. **Jay Guru Ganesh Transport Services** (Tel: 01-423 0523) has a good selection of modern bikes, including small scooters, for short or long rentals.

Mountain bikes

Many shops in tourist areas of Kathmandu and Pokhara have mountain bikes for hire along with the old-fashioned Indian and Chinese bicycles. Generally no deposit is required unless renting high-calibre equipment – a record of your hotel or passport number is enough. Make sure the bell works. Along with the brakes, this is the most important part of your bicycle as you will need it to weave through the throng.

Mountain bikes are particularly suited to the back roads of the Kathmandu Valley and further afield. **Himalayan Mountain Bikes** organise excellent escorted tours through the valley. **Dawn Till Dusk** has 50 bikes and an outlet for spares and tools in Thamel. Further information is available from Thamel at the Kathmandu Guest House.

Taxis in Kathmandu.

Dawn Till Dusk
Thamel, Kathmandu.
Tel: 01-470 0286
www.nepalbiking.com

Himalayan Mountain Bikes
Thamel, Kathmandu.
Tel: 01-421 2860
www.bikeasia.info

Taxis

Taxis are available to go to most places within the Kathmandu Valley. They have black registration plates with white numbers (private cars have white numbers on red plates). Drivers are rarely willing to use the meter, so it is always necessary to negotiate a fare before starting your journey. A relatively short ride within Kathmandu should cost around Rs200.

Kathmandu transport

Within Kathmandu, three-wheeled public scooters *(tempos)* can carry up to six passengers, always plying the same route and starting from Rani Pokhari at the edge of the Tundikhel. In an effort to reduce the capital's chronic air pollution, the old petrol *tempos* have been replaced with fleets of more environmentally friendly white electric *tempos* running on batteries, and green and yellow gas-propelled versions.

The gaudily painted, slow-moving, cycle-rickshaws are still part of the Kathmandu city scene. They are large tricycles with two seats in the back covered by a hood; the driver pedals up front. Make sure the driver understands where you are going and the price is settled before you start. Remember rickshaws should cost no more than taxis, and bear in mind that in the convoluted alleys of the Old City, you'll generally move much faster on foot.

ACCOMMODATION

HOTELS, GUEST HOUSES AND TEAHOUSES

WHERE TO STAY

Nepal has it all, from rock-bottom fleapits seemingly left over from the days of the Hippie Trail, to palace hotels redolent of the Rana regime.

Kathmandu has Nepal's greatest range of accommodation. There are plenty of luxury offerings, including international corporate hotel franchises, as well as myriad moderately priced places. Many of the large luxury hotels are clustered in the upmarket Lazimpat area, and at the northern end of Durbar Marg. Further west, the area around Thamel originally grew up as a backpackers' ghetto, replacing the older hippie hangout on Freak Street south of Durbar Square. Modern Thamel, however, is home to an increasingly sophisticated scene. While it is still possible to find ultra-cheap beds here, there are ever more mid-range places (and some excellent dining options).

Virtually all hotels in Kathmandu – including the very cheapest – offer free Wi-fi, and most make claims of 24-hour hot water, though in the cheaper places the heating is usually by solar power so there is slim chance of a steaming shower early in the morning. Power cuts are a chronic issue across Nepal. Almost all accommodation has some kind of emergency backup system, and in the more expensive places you won't even notice when the supply switches from the mains to the generator. In cheaper guesthouses, however, a battery system is often used, and while you won't be plunged into darkness, fans and power sockets customarily cut out when the mains supply gives way.

A number of luxury hotels are scattered around the Kathmandu Valley, and at viewpoints on the valley rim such as Dhulikhel and Nagarkot there are large numbers of mid-range places, aimed as much at middle-class Nepalese trippers as foreign tourists. Nepal has been surprisingly slow to catch on to the boutique hotel scene, but an increasing number of traditional Newari buildings – especially in Patan and Bhaktapur – have been converted into beautiful guesthouses in recent years. Creature comforts may not quite match those of the big chain hotels, but the experience is far more authentically Nepalese.

Outside the Kathmandu Valley the most sophisticated array of accommodation is at Pokhara. Most other mid-sized towns in the Terai and the Middle Hills have at least a few mid-range options with clean rooms and hot water. Around the national parks, meanwhile, there are budget safari lodges, and luxury jungle resorts and tented camps.

The celebrated luxury resorts within the Chitwan National Park are currently closed pending a licensing decision by Nepal's Supreme Court, but there are plenty of other comfortable places to stay on the boundaries of the park. At Bardia, meanwhile, there is a smaller selection of luxury camps and cheaper lodges.

BOOKINGS AND RATES

Thanks to the internet it is generally easy to book accommodation in Nepal from overseas – either through booking websites, or directly with the provider. Many resorts in outlying areas of the country, including the national parks, have offices in Kathmandu which are much easier to contact when making enquiries.

Most hotels add a 13 percent government tax to the bill, and many also levy a 10 percent service charge.

During peak season popular places fill up quickly. However, during quieter periods significant discounts are frequently available to those who ask.

TREKKING ACCOMMODATION

A much more humble sort of accommodation is also available in the mountains. The so-called "teahouse" is a Nepalese institution. Originally these were simply village homes that gave passing trekkers a space to sleep on the floor, but along major routes such as the Annapurna Circuit a surprising degree of comfort is now on offer, with modern bathrooms and good beds.

On the wilder trails, however, the teahouses are usually much more basic affairs, with simple dormitory-style accommodation and ice-cold showers.

Booking teahouses in advance is often impossible. Those venturing still further off the beaten track will have to come prepared for camping, or for lodging in the kind of smoky, ultra-basic teahouses more often used by local herders than by international trekkers.

KATHMANDU

Hotel de l'Annapurna
Durbar Marg
Tel: 01-422 1711
www.annapurna-hotel.com
At the upmarket end of Durbar Marg, this is the archetypal luxury hotel, with gleaming marble floors in the lobby, miles of carpeted corridors, and every conceivable comfort. The cheapest rooms are a little small for the price, but the club rooms are suitably plush with enormous TVs and a surfeit of pillows. There is a good Japanese restaurant amongst the attached eateries. **$$$$**

Hotel Courtyard
Thamel
Tel: 01-470 0476
www.hotelcourtyard.com
In a remarkably tranquil enclave close to the heart of Thamel, this imposing hotel is built of traditional brick and Newari woodwork. The lobby and corridors are a little gloomy, but the rooms are airy, with soft beds and big windows, some looking out on to the courtyard. The restaurant offers a decent breakfast. **$$**

Dwarika's Hotel
Battisputali
Tel: 01-447 0770
www.dwarikas.com
This is Kathmandu's ultimate luxury hotel, with 87 beautifully constructed rooms and suites richly endowed with traditional Newari style. Antique materials have been artfully incorporated throughout, and there are gorgeous Nepalese objects slotted into every space. The rooms all manage to feel thoroughly traditional while keeping a light touch. Service is understated and attentive, and the whole place is an oasis of calmly sophisticated tradition just a short ride from the airport, or the bustle of Pashupatinath. There are good in-house facilities, and restaurants serving Nepalese, Japanese and international cuisine. **$$$$**

Hyatt Regency Kathmandu
Boudhanath
Tel: 01-449 1234
www.kathmandu.regency.hyatt.com
Close to the great Buddhist stupa at Boudhanath, an admirable effort has been made to make this much more than just another executive chain hotel. The building has been put together in true Newari fashion, with palace architectural conventions aplenty, and its own miniature Boudhanaths in the lobby. Beneath the surface gloss the rooms are closer to the global norm, with the usual spotless bathrooms, deep-quilted beds, TVs and minibars. Here and there, however, a window allows a glimpse of the great white stupa dome and the jumble of Tibetan settlements around it, just a few hundred yards to the east. **$$$$**

International Guest House
Kaldhara
Tel: 01-425 2299
www.ighouse.com
On a quiet street a short stroll from the action of central Thamel, this long-running hotel offers excellent value. The public areas are attractively decorated with heavy traditional woodwork, and the 44 rooms are simple but well maintained with firm beds and soft lighting. There is a beautiful, bougainvillea-filled garden, and the whole place is very peaceful. **$**

Kantipur Temple House
Chusyabahal
Tel: 01-425 0131
www.kantipurtemplehouse.com
Built like a Newari mansion, this fine boutique hotel has an eco-friendly ethos and an excellent selection of traditionally decorated rooms. The open brickwork and heavy beams do make the rooms a little dark, but they are comfortable and well appointed, with plenty of earthy touches – from the handwoven bedspreads to the traditional woodwork. The whole place is a plastic-free zone, and the courtyard with its traditional roof struts and overhanging latticed windows feels like part of a living temple complex. **$$**

Kathmandu Guest House
Thamel
Tel: 01- 470 0800
www.ktmgh.com
The original guesthouse in the area and the hub around which the Thamel tourist quarter has grown, this place is a Kathmandu institution with a vast array of rooms spanning a wide gamut of prices. There is everything from ultra-basic rooms containing little more than a bed, to spacious, comfortable suites with plush furnishings and widescreen TVs. There is good food available in the restaurant at the centre of the complex, and the place has the atmosphere of a proper tourist melting pot, with everyone from the well heeled to the penurious rubbing shoulders in the public spaces. **$$**

Hotel Nepalaya
Kwabahal, Thamel

Soaltee Crowne Plaza.

Tel: 01-426 9141/3163
www.hotelnepalaya.com
In a central Thamel location, this friendly, family-run hotel is just a short walk to Durbar Square. The seven floors are topped off by a rooftop garden restaurant with spectacular views. Staff can also book and advise on treks. **$**

Potala Guest House
Thamel
Tel: 01-422 6566
www.potalaguesthouse.com
Towards the southern end of Thamel, this long-established guesthouse is a good budget option. Rooms are ranged around a narrow garden which makes for a pleasant escape from the bustling streets. The rather spartan budget rooms are nonetheless excellent value, if a little short on natural light, while the more expensive deluxe rooms are well maintained with comfortable beds and air conditioning. Staff are very helpful. **$**

Royal Penguin
Thamel
Tel: 01-421 5013
www.royalpenguinhotel.com
One of the newer options, this boutique hotel has a quirky style all of its own, eschewing any hint of traditional Nepalese design in favour of an ultra-modern minimalism. Amongst the colourful decor and Scandinavian-style fittings, however,

PRICE CATEGORIES

Price categories are per night for a double room, without breakfast, before tax.
$$$$ = more than $150
$$$ = $80–150
$$ = $40–80
$ = under $40

there are humorous touches – such as the toy animals. Everything is bright, light and airy and the staff are very welcoming. **$$$**

Soaltee Crowne Plaza
Tahachal
Tel: 01-427 3999
www.ichotelsgroup.com
Twenty minutes from city centre, the Soaltee has acres of grounds and hundreds of rooms. The standard of service is excellent; the suites are plush and expansive, and the facilities offer everything you could ask for, from a casino to a convention centre. There are several restaurants and bars, and all the standard leisure facilities. The place is thoroughly self-contained and feels decidedly insulated from the rest of the Kathmandu scene. **$$$$**

Thamel Eco Resort
Thamel
Tel: 01-426 3810
www.thamelecoresort.com
Set back from a busy Thamel street, this modern hotel has 43 rooms arranged around a small garden. There are traditional touches in the restaurant and stairwells, but the rooms are refreshingly minimalist, with white walls and linen offset by dark woodwork. The tiled bathrooms are small but spotless and the more expensive rooms have new air-conditioned units to ward off the monsoon heat. **$$**

Hotel Vajra
Bijeswari
Tel: 01-427 1545
www.hotelvajra.com
West of the city centre, this long-established hotel is a cultural experience in its own right. The brick-built Newari-style complex houses a remarkable library on the history and culture of the region, and plays host to some serious artistic organisations. There is a wide range of rooms at varying prices. All are relatively simple, but well maintained and good value, with polished woodwork and comfortable beds. There is an excellent Tibetan-style rooftop bar, good food and a lovely garden. **$$**

Hotel Yak & Yeti
Durbar Marg
Tel: 01-424 8999
www.yakandyeti.com
Built on the site of a former Rana palace, the Yak & Yeti is Kathmandu's original upmarket hotel, and it is still going strong. The formal lobby and attached bar look out onto a spacious garden, and there are some nice Nepalese touches, such as the prayer-wheel-style lightshades in the corridors. The standard rooms come with all the usual five-star fittings, but are rather soulless. The older suites are starting to look a little worn, but they have much more character, with Newari woodwork incorporated into the design. **$$$$**

AROUND KATHMANDU

Patan

Newa Chen
Kobahal Tol
Tel: 01-553 3532
www.newachen.com
Restored under the auspices of Unesco, and still run by the family that have occupied the building for generations, this boutique hotel offers a rare chance to stay in an authentic Newari home. The floors are carpeted with coir matting; there are cushioned seating areas, and the thick walls keep out the summer heat. Outside there's a pleasant garden and a small library and reading area. The rooms are remarkably good value, although traditional Newari ceilings make no allowances for Western physiques, and you may be walking with a permanent stoop by the end of your stay. **$$**

Traditional Homes Swotha
Swotha
Tel: 01-555 1184
www.traditionalhomes.com.np
In a restored traditional house just north of Durbar Square, this boutique hotel has six rooms that manage to be spacious and airy despite the original cramped form of the building. There is exposed brickwork and wooden beams, and traditional rugs on the cool floors; most rooms have miniature balconies looking out onto the alleyway below. The attached café is excellent. **$$**

A well-appointed suite at the Soaltee Crowne Plaza.

Bhaktapur

Hotel Heritage
Barahipith Gapali
Tel: 01-661 1629
www.hotelheritage.com.np
South of the river but in easy walking distance of the Old City, this is a comfortable and quirky modern hotel built of ancient elements. The rooms feature centuries-old bricks and woodwork, artfully set into new white walls; there are attractive patchwork throws on the soft beds, and slate tiling in the bathrooms. The staff are welcoming, and generous discounts are offered in the low season. **$$$**

Shiva Guesthouse
Durbar Square
Tel: 01-661 3912
www.shivaguesthouse.com
Right on the square, this is a long-standing favourite of budget travellers. Up the rickety stairs, the unpromising doors open onto small but bright and very well-maintained rooms, with comfy beds and unsurpassed views out across the heart of the city. Downstairs is a good café, and the management offer a wealth of local travel information. There's another, more modern branch just outside the square. **$**

Tagu Chhen
Itachhen
Tel: 01-661 2043
www.cosyhotel.com.np
On the approach to Durbar Square, the four apartments here offer exceptionally good value. Each has a huge bed, an airy living area with views out across the city and hills to the north, and a small kitchen. The design is modern – with tiled floors and exposed brickwork – but traditional elements, such as the latticed window shutters in the bedrooms, have been cleverly incorporated. The same management also runs the nearby Cosy Hotel. **$$**

KATHMANDU VALLEY

Budhanilkantha

Park Village Hotel and Resort
Tel: 01-470 0632
www.ktmgh.com
Run by the same management as the long-standing Kathmandu Guesthouse in Thamel, this is a tranquil spot in the upper reaches of the valley. There is a range of modern studio-type rooms, all with TV and hot water and comfortable mattresses. The most expensive accommodation is in a luxurious self-contained cottage at the far end of the expansive gardens. There is an open-air swimming pool and a range of sports and fitness facilities. **$$**

Dhulikhel

Dhulikhel Lodge Resort
Dhulikhel
Tel: 011-490114
www.dhulikhellodgeresort.com
Set on a serene hillside, with sweeping views down across the valley to the distant snows, the rooms here have private balconies and big windows for taking in the panorama. There is a comfy little restaurant, and the grounds abound with flowers. There are simpler, cheaper rooms in a block across the road. **$$**

The Himalayan Horizon
Dhulikhel
Tel: 011-490296
www.himalayanhorizon.com
This grand Newari-style hotel has traditional brickwork, and some beautiful black woodwork set into the masonry. Some of the rooms are a little worn, but they are huge and very comfortable, with big beds, tiled bathrooms, and private balconies and mountain vistas. Staff are very friendly, and there's a cosy bar with more Newari woodwork and Himalayan views. **$$**

Mirabel Resort
Dhulikhel
Tel: 011-490975
www.mirabelresorthotel.com
This quiet hotel sits on the very brink of the mountainside, with sweeping views out to the Himalayas. The rooms have a fresh feel, with crisp white paintwork and floral bedspreads, and the whole place has an atmosphere of mellow calm amid the rough stonework and plant pots. The best rooms have private balconies looking out to the mountains, and there are more fine views from the spacious upstairs restaurant. **$$**

Godavari

Godavari Village Resort
Tel: 01-556 0675
www.godavariresort.com.np
Set across a steep hillside with magnificent views out across the rice fields of the valley, this is a well-appointed resort with a wide array of facilities. The rooms are large and airy, with soft king-sized beds, comfortable chairs and polished wooden floors. The whole place is a little formal, with its conference centre, luxury restaurant and business facilities, but the setting is beautiful and the atmosphere calm. **$$$$**

Nagarkot

The Fort Resort
Tel: 01-443 2960
www.mountain-retreats.com
At the highest point of the Nagarkot Ridge, this beautiful resort has spacious and comfortable bungalows set around a large garden. The decor combines white walls and crisp linen with heavy wooden furniture, and there are spectacular views out across the hills to the northern snow peaks. **$$$**

Hotel at the End of the Universe
Tel: 01-622 6500
www.endoftheuniverse.com.np
Slotted up near the highest point of Nagarkot, with a beautiful green garden and a wide array of rooms, this is a characterful mid-range place. The rooms all have windows designed to make the most of the mountain views, and distinct decor with bright woodwork. The self-contained cottages are huge, and even the cheapest rooms are very comfortable. The restaurant has cosy, chalet-style design and decent, filling meals for the chilly mountain evenings. **$–$$**

Nagarkot Farmhouse Resort
Tel: 01-620 2022
www.nagarkotfarmhouse.com
Downhill along a rough road from the centre of Nagarkot, this wonderfully secluded eco-resort is one of the most serene places to stay on the valley fringe. The rooms have brick walls and paved floors, with rustic fabrics and wooden balconies. There are views out over the deep valleys to the north, and mountain breezes to keep away the

PRICE CATEGORIES

Price categories are per night for a double room, without breakfast, before tax.
$$$$ = more than $150
$$$ = $80–150
$$ = $40–80
$ = under $40

summer heat. Traditional Nepali dinners are served, with much of the food coming from the attached vegetable garden, and there is a meditation room on the premises. **$$**

Stupa Resort
Tel: 01-668 0199
www.stuparesort.com.np
Consisting of a variety of rooms stepped down a steep hillside, Stupa Resort is a well-run place near the centre of Nagarkot. The best rooms have exposed stonework, and sparkling bathrooms with 24-hour hot water. There are fine views down over the mountainside, and a cosy little restaurant upstairs. **$**

Shivapuri National Park

Shivapuri Village
Tel: 01-401 7725
www.shivapuri.com.np
Perched on a green ridge on the edge of the Shivapuri National Park, this beautiful, low-key eco-resort is a thoroughly tranquil spot far from hustle of the lower Kathmandu Valley. There are attractive, rustic bungalows set in a green garden, and on clear days the views across the foothills to the distant snow peaks are spectacular. **$$$$**

KATHMANDU TO POKHARA

Bandipur

Gaun Ghar
Tel: 065-520129
www.gaunghar.com
In an elegantly restored Bandipuri home, Gaun Ghar has fine Newari style and mountain views to boot. The rooms are cosy and make the best of the higgledy-piggledy form of a traditional house. Rooms open onto a cool, brick-built internal courtyard, and look out to the hills or the village. There's an excellent Newari restaurant attached. **$$$**

Old Inn Bandipur
Tel: 065-520110
In another beautifully restored house on the main street of Bandipur, this is a fine place to absorb the town's tranquil and heritage-rich atmosphere. The rooms are low-ceilinged – as befits the original design – but they have been comfortably adapted without doing away with the traditional feel. There are bare walls and plenty of rustic woodwork, as well as a fine array of Newari trinkets. There are fabulous mountain views from some of the rooms. **$$**

Darechok

Riverside Springs Resort
Tel: 056-540129
www.rsr.com.np
Midway between Kathmandu and Pokhara at Darechok, this comfortable resort is slotted neatly into the lush green folds of the Middle Hills. There are simple cabin rooms set in the garden, along with luxury tented accommodation, and the tone of the whole place is set by the surrounding forest. Also has an attractive swimming pool and a cosy lodge-style restaurant. **$$**

Pokhara

Atithi Resort and Spa
Lakeside
Tel: 061-466760
www.atithiresort.com
This new resort, set back from the main Lakeside road, has a crisp, modern design throughout, with creamy colour schemes, coir carpeting and a small but welcoming spa for post-trek indulgence. There is also a jacuzzi and a small swimming pool. The 51 rooms all have deep bathtubs, small balconies and large TVs. **$$$**

Hotel Barahi
Lakeside
Tel: 061-523017
www.barahi.com
This long-established hotel has 85 rooms built around a large swimming pool. The deluxe rooms are large and plush, with carpets and king-size beds and marble fittings in the bathrooms. Those on the upper levels have balconies looking out over either the lake or the mountains. The standard rooms are smaller, with tiled floors and less natural light, but are good value. The staff run a slick operation and the place is popular with tour groups. **$$**

Fish Tail Lodge
Lakeside
Tel: 061-465071
www.fishtail-lodge.com.np
Slotted onto a low promontory at the foot of thickly forested hills, and accessed from the main Lakeside area by a pontoon raft, this welcoming hotel has the best location in central Pokhara. The 12 deluxe rooms have balconies looking straight out towards the Annapurna range, but the 48 standard rooms have more character, with Tibetan mandalas on the walls and individual terraces opening onto a beautiful, flower-filled garden. There's a small swimming pool, and a good restaurant with more mountain views. **$$$**

Fulbari Resort Pokhara
Tel: 061-432451
www.fulbari.com
Perched dramatically above a steep gorge south of town and with the Annapurna range for a backdrop, this is a thoroughly luxurious resort. There are 165 well-appointed rooms. The cheapest

Signs for Pokhara's many guesthouses.

A hotel with a view, by Pokhara.

are nonetheless comfortable and carpeted, and face onto the garden, while the grand Landmark Suites are each themed for a different region of Nepal. There are several bars and restaurants, a golf course and a heated swimming pool. **$$$$**

Lake View Resort
Lakeside – 6 main road
Tel: 061-461477 or 463854
www.pokharahotels.com
This central lakeside hotel offers a range of bedroom options, including private bungalows, as well as extensive, flower-strewn private gardens and an excellent restaurant. The room's balconies enjoy an open view of the Himalayas as well as the lake. **$$**

Mum's Garden Resort
Lakeside
Tel: 061- 463468
www.mumsgardenresort.com
Tucked away at the end of a quiet lane, Mum's Garden has 12 bright boutique twin rooms with high white ceilings and airy balconies in a tranquil garden. This is a simple place, without TVs and there is an attractively rustic feel to the design, with exposed stone walls, traditional fabrics and slate-tiled floors, but the beds are comfortable and the welcome is warm. **$$**

Placid Valley Lodge
Lakeside
Tel: 061-465193
www.placidvalleylodge.com.np
Amongst the mushrooming modern hotels in the central Lakeside area, this family-run lodge offers excellent value. The newer rooms are particularly good, with individual balconies, a soft yellow colour scheme, wide windows to let in the light, plump pillows and small wall-mounted TVs. There is a pleasant garden, and the owners are very helpful. **$**

Sacred Valley Inn
Lakeside
Tel: 061-461792
www.sacredvalleyinn.com
With a pleasant roadside café at the front, and a relaxed ambiance, this long-standing guesthouse has simple but spotless rooms with comfortable beds and en suite bathrooms. The whole place has an unstuffy, sunlit feel; staff are helpful, and there is free Wi-fi. **$**

Hotel Splendid View
Lakeside
Tel: 061-466034
www.hotelsplendidview.com
The rooms in this multi-storey hotel in the Gaurighat area of Lakeside are a little old-fashioned, with dark carpets and heavy fittings, but they have been very well maintained, with fresh paintwork, and spotless bathrooms. The beds are comfortable; there are glimpses of the mountains from the balconies of the rooms at the back of the building, and the price is extremely good value. **$**

Temple Tree Resort and Spa
Lakeside
Tel: 061-465819
www.templetreenepal.com
Close to the heart of Lakeside, this new boutique hotel has small but very comfortable rooms with earthy terracotta colour schemes and individual balconies. The style is rustic throughout, with *pisé* walls and earthy tones. There's a swimming pool; the attached Bay Leaf restaurant serves fish from Phewa Tal, and the spa offers treatments with Himalayan herbs. **$$$**

Tiger Mountain Pokhara Lodge
Tel: 01-442 6427 (Kathmandu office)
www.tigermountainpokhara.com
On a high hilltop northeast of Pokhara, the bungalows here are slotted sensitively into the landscape. There are shady balconies looking out over the valley, slate floors, and comfortable cane chairs. There is a library stocked with a wealth of mountaineering literature, open fires in the lounge area, and the management take sustainability seriously. **$$$$**

PRICE CATEGORIES

Price categories are per night for a double room, without breakfast, before tax.
$$$$ = more than $150
$$$ = $80–150
$$ = $40–80
$ = under $40

THE ANNAPURNAS

Jomsom

Jomsom Mountain Resort
Tel: 01-200 4262 (Kathmandu office)
www.jmr.com.np
Perched above Jomsom on the key junction of the Annapurna Circuit, this rather stark luxury hotel offers very sophisticated service for such a remote spot. There is an indoor swimming pool – an easier option than the icy mountain streams nearby – and some fabulous views from the dining area. The rooms are comfortable, and well heated. The whole place is a little lacking in atmosphere, but it is well run. **$$$$**

The lights, tea houses, lodges and cafés of Namche Bazar.

LANGTANG

Arniko Highway to Tibet

The Borderland Resorts
Barabise
Tel: 01-438 1214 (Kathmandu office)
www.borderlandresorts.com
Off the highway to Tibet, just 16km (10 miles) short of the border, this fine resort is firmly focused on adventure sports. The luxury tents nestle in the forest on the banks of the Bhote Kosi River, and there is a thatch-roofed bar and restaurant area. The management lay on all manner of high-adrenaline activities, from rafting and canyoning to trekking. **$$**

The Last Resort
Barabise
Tel: 01-470 0525 (Kathmandu office)
www.thelastresort.com.np
Within striking distance of the Tibetan border and reached via a dizzying suspension bridge, this is the ultimate adventure sports venue in the upper reaches of Nepal. Home to the country's original bungee jump, other activities include rope walks and canyoning. The accommodation is provided in luxury tents with comfortable beds in a lovely garden high above the Bhote Kosi. There is a good restaurant, a spa and a swimming pool. Most people stay as part of an action-filled package, but the resort is also a fine spot to relax away from the chaos of the cities. **$$–$$$**

THE EVEREST REGION

Lukla

Everest Summit Lodge
Tel: 01-437 1537 (Kathmandu office)
www.nepalluxurytreks.com
A short stroll from the Lukla airstrip, this is the first of a string of upmarket lodges run by the same management throughout the Everest region. Solidly stone-built in the style of a Tibetan gompa, the rooms are spotless, with good heating and plentiful blankets for chilly mountain nights. The restaurant is cosy, and the garden is a fine place to relax while waiting for that little aeroplane to come winging its way in from Kathmandu. The other Everest Summit Lodges in the area are at Monjo on the way to Namche Bazar, Mende between Namche Bazar and Thame, and at Tashinga and Pangboche on the upper reaches or the trail. All offer similar service and facilities. **$$$$**

Namche Bazar

Panorama Lodge
Tel: 01-401 5665 (Kathmandu office)
www. panoramalodge.com.np
Perched above the village with a panorama all of its own, this is a welcoming and well-priced lodge. The rooms are understated and well kept, with good heating and reliable hot water. There are thick blankets and comfortably carpeted floors, and the wood-panelled restaurant area is a fine place to relax of a mountain evening. The staff are very helpful. **$$**

Hotel Sherpaland
Tel: 01-443 6952 (Kathmandu office)
www.hotelsherpaland.com
In the heart of Namche Bazar this modern hotel has been built with at least a dash of local style. The rooms are quiet and well designed, with wooden floors, rugs and plentiful blankets. The hot water is reasonably reliable in the attached bathrooms, which are kept sparkling, and the restaurant is a decent option for dinner. **$$**

Yeti Mountain Home
Tel: 01-400 0701
(Kathmandu office)
www.yetimountainhome.com
On the hillside above the village, this is part of another chain of upmarket lodges strung along the Everest trail. The rooms are clean, with wood panelling, king-size beds, and electric blankets to ward off the evening chill. The views, meanwhile, are predictably stunning and the service is excellent. The restaurant has decent food and a cosy Swiss-Tibetan decor. The other Yeti Mountain Home lodges on the trail are at Lukla, Phakding, Monjo, Thame and Kongde. **$$$**

THE TERAI

Bardia National Park

Forest Hideaway Hotel & Cottages
Tel: 01-422 5973 (Kathmandu office)
www.foresthideaway.com
With rooms in a pleasant garden in walking distance of the park headquarters, this is an excellent choice. The standard and larger deluxe rooms are simple but well kept, with mosquito nets and comfortable beds and balconies for relaxing of an evening. The restaurant is excellent, and the various tour packages on offer are good value and well run. **$**

Mango Tree Lodge
Tel: 084-402008
www.mangotreelodge.com
This family-run budget place offers excellent value and a range of quiet, comfortable rooms with *pisé* walls and mosquito nets. There is a calm, low-key atmosphere, and the budget tour packages are good value. The communal seating area is airy, and the food is simple but wholesome. **$**

Tiger Tops Karnali Lodge
Tel: 01-436 1500 (Kathmandu office)
www.tigertops.com
On the southern edge of the park, the 20 rustic thatched cottages here have recently been renovated, and are exceptionally stylish and comfortable, while maintaining a suitably rustic atmosphere. The colour schemes are cool and creamy; fittings are refreshingly simple, and there are mosquito nets and en suite bathrooms. Most people stay here on packages which include all meals from the excellent restaurant, and activities within the park. **$$$$**

Chitwan National Park

Green Mansions
Sauraha
Tel: 056-580008
Email: green@mansions.wlink.com.np
Around 5km (3 miles) from Sauraha, out amongst the rice fields and Tharu farming villages, Green Mansions is a very tranquil spot, with cottages set in a sprawling garden. The tone is rustic throughout, with rough walls, terracotta tones and patchwork bedspreads. There are attractive beaten brass shower wells in the bathrooms, and the garden resounds with birdsong. **$$**

Machan Paradise View
Tel: 01-422 50011 (Kathmandu office)
www.nepalinformation.com/mpv
Lying to the west of Sauraha in a quiet location close to the village of Jagatpur, this comfortable resort has a selection of luxury tents, and air-conditioned rooms in modern two-storey blocks. The rooms are fairly plain but well kept and comfortable; there is a lush feel to the setting, and the restaurant serves decent food. **$$$**

The Rhino Residency Resort
Sauraha
Tel: 01-4420431 (Kathmandu office)
www.rhino-residency.com
In the tourist hub of Sauraha, this long-established resort has an all-pervading green colour scheme – from the lobby to the uniforms of the staff. Rooms are airy, with high sloping ceilings, and firm beds. Some of the woodwork – green, inevitably – is a little worn, but the beds are comfortable, and there is a decent swimming pool. An appropriate safari atmosphere pervades the place. **$$$$**

Resort signposts in Sauraha.

Royal Park Hotel
Tel: 056-580061
www.royalparkhotel.com.np
Sauraha
Despite its location in the heart of Sauraha, this friendly resort makes the most of a large expanse of grounds, allowing plenty of peace and privacy, even when the place is busy. The rooms, set in thatched blocks scattered around the garden, are large and cool, with high ceilings, earthy tones, and big stone-tiled bathrooms. Most rooms have balconies, and there is a tiny swimming pool. Royal Park is popular with groups, but there is usually enough space for independent travellers to feel that they have the run of the place. **$**

Tiger Tops Tharu Lodge
Tel: 01-442 0431 (Kathmandu office)
www.tigertops.com
Lying outside the park boundaries, this was the only one of the magnificent Tiger Tops properties unaffected by the ban on accommodation inside the protected area. Set in the rolling countryside on the northwest edge of the park near the Narayani River, the resort's decidedly unusual rooms are arranged in traditional Tharu longhouses, and decorated with local crafts. While all the usual safari activities are run from here, there is also a focus on cultural tourism amongst the local village communities. **$$$$**

Koshi Tappu Wildlife Reserve

Koshi Camp
Tel: 01-442 9609 (Kathmandu office)
www.kosicamp.com
This beautiful resort on the outskirts of the reserve is a peaceful and secluded spot to find yourself away with the birds. There are 11 tented rooms, each sheltered under a thatched awning. Inside the creamy canvas structures there are carpets and comfortable beds, with an attached bathroom at the back. The place is rustic and the facilities simple, but it's an exceptionally tranquil spot, and the birdwatching opportunities start right outside your tent door. **$$$$**

Koshi Tappu Wildlife Camp
Tel: 01-422 6130 (Kathmandu office)
www.koshitappu.com
Northeast of the reserve, this charming camp has a dozen luxury en suite tents. There is a good bar and restaurant, but the whole place has a wonderfully rustic feel, and the grounds have been deliberately designed to attract birdlife. There is no mains electricity and the accommodation is lit with lamps and candles (though there is generator power available for charging electrical items). The camp management can organise boat and jeep rides, and guided bird walks. **$$$$**

Lumbini

Buddha Maya Gardens
Tel: 071-580220
www.kghhotels.com
At the southeast corner of the Lumbini Development Zone where the level plains of the Terai roll away towards India, this quiet hotel offers decent rooms with large beds, marble fittings in the bathrooms, and balconies looking out over farmland. The public areas are a little soulless, but the service is good and the location tranquil. **$$$**

Hotel Lumbini Garden
Tel: 071-680145
www.newcrystalhotels.com
Near the main gate of the temple complex, this large hotel has spartan red-brick architecture echoing the nearby ruins. The lobby and corridors are as stark as a Buddhist stupa and the service is a little clinical – this is a place aimed mainly at upscale pilgrimage tours from East Asia – but the rooms are cool and quiet with thick curtains to keep out the blazing Terai sun, firm mattresses and small but sparkling bathrooms. The prices, meanwhile, represent excellent value. **$$**

PRICE CATEGORIES

Price categories are per night for a double room, without breakfast, before tax.
$$$$ = more than $150
$$$ = $80–150
$$ = $40–80
$ = under $40

EATING OUT

RECOMMENDED RESTAURANTS

WHAT TO EAT

Plenty of visitors come away from Nepal believing that there's little more to the local cuisine than momos and *dal bhat*. It is certainly true that Nepalese cooking lacks the complexities of India or China, but there is still a great deal on offer here for adventurous gastronomes.

Most tourist restaurants carry a few token Nepalese dishes on their globe-straddling menus, but the best places to sample authentic flavours are in small, street-side local eateries, or in one of the sophisticated Newari restaurants that have opened in Kathmandu in recent years.

Itinerant hippies and hungry mountaineers first created a market for pastas and pizzas in Kathmandu and Pokhara, and today local restaurateurs make an exceptionally good job of any number of international cuisines. The typical tourist restaurants dabble in everything from Korean to Mexican, but the best places pick a speciality and stick to it. In Kathmandu's Thamel and Pokhara's Lakeside you'll find some excellent Italian, Thai and Middle Eastern restaurants. There's also a long-standing tradition of "German bakeries", with strudel, bread and chocolate cake.

Out on the trekking routes, lodge owners make a remarkable effort to emulate all this internationalism, and on the Annapurna Circuit apple pie is as much of a staple as *dal bhat*. On lesser popular routes however, you will find yourself subject to an endless round of rice and lentils.

WHERE TO EAT

Local cafés are known as *bhojanalayas*. Simple meals featuring rice, *dal* (a thin lentil broth), stewed vegetables and pickles are served at these places, with unlimited top-ups available for the hungry. Locals usually eat with their right hand, mashing the different dishes together between their fingers, but if you ask a *chamchah* (spoon) can usually be conjured up from somewhere.

Even smaller than *bhojanalayas*, open-air street stalls sell various simple meals including momos (steamed dumplings filled with buffalo mince or vegetables), grilled corn, or skewered meat. Food from these places is often served up in disposable plates made of dried leaves, a logical and sustainable practice.

It's a far more refined affair at the grand restaurants serving traditional cuisine in Kathmandu. Most of these places offer a mix of Nepalese and more local Newari dishes. The latter cuisine is based around flaky beaten rice, known as *chiura*.

Many restaurants have set tasting menus which allow you to sample several dishes and so discover things that you might not otherwise have tasted.

At the best of the Nepalese and Newari restaurants dinner comes with a side order of traditional dance and music.

DRINKING NOTES

Nepal's national drink is undoubtedly the sweet, milky Indian-style masala tea, known here as *chiya*. The spice blend that gives *chiya* its distinctive flavour includes cardamom, cinnamon, cloves, ginger, nutmeg, star anise and pepper. If you want your tea served English-style, be sure to ask for "milk separate" or you may find leaves, milk, water and sweetening all boiled together in the same pot.

Up in the high mountains you may encounter the distinctive Tibetan-style yak butter tea, where black tea is mixed with salt and the pungent butter of the domestic yak. It's certainly an acquired taste, but locals maintain that it helps fight off the high-altitude chill.

There are plenty of harder drinks on offer too, and alcohol consumption is far less of a social taboo in Nepal than in some neighbouring countries. The commonest local beverage, which you'll find on offer in every grimy roadside café, is *chhang*, a milky white beer made of fermented millet or barley. It's surprisingly drinkable, and incredibly cheap (as little as Rs10 per glass), but it packs a deceptively powerful punch.

Still more potent are the local moonshines, *arak* (potato alcohol) and *rakshi* (wheat or rice liquor), which are also consumed in large quantities.

Those with a little more money to spare favour locally bottled lagers including Tuborg, San Miguel and Nepal Ice. Locally distilled rum, gin and brandy are cheap at hole-in-the-wall liquor stores, while upmarket supermarkets sell all manner of imported alcohol. There are a few locally produced red and white wines, though none of exceptional quality.

KATHMANDU

Baithak
Babar Mahal Revisited
Tel: 01- 426 7346
www.baithak.com.np
Inside the cool maze of Babar Mahal Revisited, this exceptionally grand Newari restaurant captures something of Rana-era decadence in its lavish decor and flawless service. The set "Royal menu" features such authentic palace dishes as *kukhura ko masu* (chicken cooked with spices) and *bandel tareko* (fried wild boar). There is a nightly cultural performance to accompany dinner service. **$$$**

Bhanchha Ghar
Kamaladi
Tel: 01-422 5172
www.bhanchhaghar.com
In a fine old house with paved floors and a warren of whitewashed rooms, this is an excellent place to sample authentic Newari cuisine. Food comes served on heavy brass platters, with lime-tinged chilli sauce and *chiura* (crispy beaten rice). The lunch menu is exceptionally good value, while more expensive evening meals are accompanied by a cultural show with traditional Newari music and dancing. **$$$**

Brezel Bakery and Restaurant
Thamel
Tel: 01-426 5601
Set in a breezy courtyard garden, this European-style café has a good range of pasta dishes, as well as Chinese and Indian staples. The pasta carbonara is suitably creamy, and there are generous hunks of chocolate cake available from the attached bakery for desert. **$$**

La Dolce Vita
Thamel
Tel: 01-470 0612
This upstairs restaurant offers some of the best Italian cuisine in the Thamel area. The menu doesn't stray far beyond the usual standards, but they are well executed and authentic, with good gnocchi, ravioli and tiramisu. There is inside seating or alfresco dining on the terrace, and excellent coffee. **$$$**

Fire and Ice Pizzeria
Tridevi Marg
Tel: 01-425 0210
www.fireandicepizzeria.com
Ever-busy and attracting as many middle-class locals as tourists, Fire and Ice is named for its offerings of crisp-crusted stone-baked pizza followed by home-made gelati. It's worth booking to be sure of a table, especially at the weekend. **$$$**

Panak paneer curry (cheese curd and peas).

Ghar-e-Kabab
Hotel de l'Annapurna, Durbar Marg
Tel: 01-422 1711
www.annapurna-hotel.com
Decked out like a Mughal durbar hall, this is one of the best Indian restaurants in Kathmandu. The focus is on north Indian regal cuisine, with plenty of tender tandoori-cooked kebabs, fluffy pilaffs, and rich, creamy curries. There are performances of classic *ghazal* music most nights. **$$$–$$$$**

Himalayan Java
Thamel
Tel: 01-442 2519
www.himalayanjava.com
The smell of roasting coffee beans hits you the moment you enter this first-floor American-style coffee shop perched above the busy Tridevi Marg. All the usual lattes, espressos and cappuccinos are on offer here – brewed from locally grown beans – as well as good continental breakfasts and light meals. There are upright seats on the small terrace area, and comfy sofas inside, and it's a very popular spot with local fashionistas. **$$**

Kaiser Café
Garden of Dreams
Tel: 01-447 9488
www.kaisercafe.com
Set inside one of the neoclassical pavilions in the Garden of Dreams, this elegant eatery offers a sophistication that the garden's Europhile Rana founder would surely have appreciated. Run by the same management as Dwarika's, and with a similarly high standard, the decor is understated Italianate and the food is precisely executed European fare, from Wiener Schnitzel to savoury crêpes. Tables are laid with sparkling silverware and stiff napkins, and the formally attired waiting staff move between the Doric columns with effortless efficiency. **$$$–$$$$**

Kizuna
Thamel
Tel: 997-9818 970583
Tucked away in a quiet courtyard off a busy Thamel street, this hole-in-the-wall place does excellent and authentic Japanese food. The *katsudon* (rice with fried pork, egg and sauce) makes for a filling meal in itself, but there are plenty of tasty side dishes too, and the miso soup is thoroughly flavoursome. Takeaway is available; diners who eat at the open-air tables get complimentary green tea with their meal. **$**

Mike's Breakfast
Naxal
Tel: 01-442 4303
www.mikesbreakfast.com
A long-standing Kathmandu institution, Mike's Breakfast

PRICE CATEGORIES

The following prices are based on a meal for one, without drinks:
$$$$ = more than US$10
$$$ = US$7–10
$$ = US$4–7
$ = less than US$4

occupies a charming Rana-era building with a beautiful garden. Originally set up by the eponymous Mike – an American Peace Corps worker – in 1988, the restaurant continues to offer huge American-style breakfasts, as well as excellent locally produced coffee, hearty lunches and filling Mexican dinners. **$$$**

Nanglo
Durbar Marg
Tel: 01-422 2636
www.nanglo.com.np
The original pub in Kathmandu, this café, bar and restaurant at the upmarket end of Durbar Marg has been in action since 1976. The pub is comfortable and cosy, and there is a more formal restaurant area in the back, serving decent steaks and other Western dishes. **$$$**

OR2K
Thamel
Tel: 01-442 2097
www.or2k.org
In the heart of the Thamel action, this popular vegetarian restaurant does a fine line in informal sophistication, with comfy floor-level seating, and alternative artwork. The handwritten menu straddles the globe, but the focus is on Middle Eastern dishes, with top-notch *shakshuka*, Israeli salads and flatbreads. The hummus may well be the best in Kathmandu, and the associated takeaway counter downstairs does a roaring trade in falafel wraps. **$$**

The Organic Café and Salad Bar
Thamel
Tel: 01-421 5726
www.loveorganic.com.np
In a place where proclaimed green credentials are often hard to verify, this is an authentically organic eatery using produce from its own farm. There is an excellent selection of vegetarian dishes, including generous portions of salad and some tasty tofu-based dinners. There are meat and fish dishes too, and some delicious fresh juices. The open kitchen is spick and span, and there is a small retail section selling various organic produce including local honey. **$$**

Roadhouse Café
Thamel
Tel: 01-476 2768
This comfortable, cosy restaurant in the heart of Thamel has decent pasta dishes, and a few Nepalese specialities, but it's the pizzas from the wood-fired oven that are the main attraction. There is also good coffee to round things off, and the warm chocolate brownie with ice cream is a real treat. **$$$**

Freshly baked puris for snacking.

Royal Penguin Restaurant
Thamel
Tel: 01-421 5013
www.royalpenguinhotel.com
The interior is bright and breezy with striking orange seat covers and some unusual art installations. The menu is just as fresh, with some crisp salads and generous juices, tender burgers, and a selection of fish dishes, which are much better executed than is normal in a country so far from the sea. **$$$**

Thamel House
Thamel
Tel: 01-441 0388
www.thamelhouse.com
In a beautifully restored Newari townhouse, this restaurant is still run by the same family who have lived in the building for more than a century. There are Newari and Nepali set menus, and an extensive choice of à la carte dishes. Highlights include the *kalo dhal* (slow-cooked black-eyed lentils) and *bara* (flatbread made from lentil flour). There are nightly cultural performances in the airy central courtyard and diners receive a complimentary Nepalese gift. **$$$$**

Third Eye
Thamel
Tel: 01-426 0160
Rather more formal than many Thamel eateries, this restaurant has neat little tables behind the large windows, and low-level cushioned seating further back. There are a few local and international dishes on the menu, but the Indian options are the best. The various tandoori-cooked kebabs are succulent and the naan bread is light and fluffy. **$$**

Yangling Tibetan Restaurant
Thamel
Tel: 01-470 1225
Up a flight of gloomy steps above a busy Thamel intersection, and with all the ambiance of a truck-stop, this bustling, no-frills restaurant is nonetheless an excellent place to sample authentic and tasty Tibetan cuisine at bargain prices. There are meat and vegetable momos, steaming bowls of *thukpa* (noodle soup), *thenthuk* (pasta broth), and other hearty dishes from the north. **$**

Yin Yang Restaurant
Thamel
Tel: 01-470 1510
This Thamel eatery is best known for its Thai cuisine, with excellent *massaman* and *penang* curries, but there is also an extensive Western menu, with satisfyingly succulent steaks and proficiently presented pasta dishes. The portions are generous and the staff are attentive. There's a choice of seating in the downstairs courtyard or in the more formal upstairs dining room, and a small attached bakery serves good deserts. **$$$**

PRICE CATEGORIES

The following prices are based on a meal for one, without drinks:
$$$$ = more than US$10
$$$ = US$7–10
$$ = US$4–7
$ = less than US$4

AROUND KATHMANDU

Patan

Dhokaima Café
Patan Dhoka
Tel: 01- 552 2113
www.dhokaimacafe.com
Set in the courtyard of a restored Rana outbuilding with open brickwork and shady trees, Dhokaima serves up a fine selection of sandwiches and salads, as well as more substantial meals. The marinated pork chops are excellent, and the fish and chips come with home-made tartar sauce. A small selection of cakes and pastries are offered for dessert. **$$**

Café Soma
Jhamsikhel
Tel: 01- 552 8732
www.cafesoma.wix.com/cafesoma
West of Durbar Square in the upper echelons of Jhamsikhel, this is a seriously sophisticated little café-cum-bookshop, attracting a mix of expats and middle-class locals. There are excellent breakfasts, including well-executed eggs Benedict and fresh croissants. The filled rolls make for a fine lunch, and there are good pasta and pizza dishes for dinner. **$$**

Café Swotha
Swotha
Tel: 01-555 1184
Attached to a boutique hotel in a restored Newari house, this friendly little café offers good European fare in an airy setting. Expect dishes such as home-made quiche, generous portions of Caesar salad with grilled chicken, and a "Not so English Breakfast" with bacon, eggs and yak cheese. There is also a small selection of wines and cocktails. **$$**

Bhaktapur

Café Beyond
Itachhe
Tel: 01-661 4815
On the way into town, this sweet little café is run by a small Korean-Nepalese NGO, Beyond Nepal (www.beyondnepal.org), which aims to encourage alternative means of social improvement, as well as organic agriculture. The handwritten menu has some good Korean dishes, including vegetarian *gimbap* (sushi-style rice rolls), as well as a selection of Nepalese and international dishes. The staff are exceptionally welcoming. **$$**

Café Nyatapola
Taumadhi Tol
Tel: 01-661 0346
In an authentic temple pagoda peering out over the action on Taumadhi Tol, this is Bhaktapur's original destination restaurant. The menu covers the usual touristic standards, from pasta carbonara to chicken chow mein, all reasonably well executed. The real draw here, however, is simply the opportunity for people-watching from the upper balcony with its epic temple views. **$$$**

Palace Restaurant
Durbar Square
Tel: 01-661 4815
www.palacerestaurantbkt.com
In a beautifully restored building directly opposite the Royal Palace, this is a great spot to take in the views of Durbar Square over a meal. Seating is on a long, wooden balcony, and the menu has the usual array of Indian, Chinese and European dishes, but the Nepali set meals are the best option for some local flavour. **$$**

KATHMANDU VALLEY

Boudhanath

Boudha Stupa Restaurant
Tel: 01-213 0681
www.boudhastupacafe.com.np
With a fine view over the stupa, this restaurant has some good Tibetan dishes on its mixed menu, including the usual *thukpa* and momos. There is also a wide range of vegetarian dishes, including vegetable curries and pizza. **$$**

Flavor's Café
Tel: 01-449 8748
www.flavorscafe.org
There is a fine view across the square from the roof terrace at Flavor's, and the food is decent too, with crispy salads and generously filled sandwiches. There's a good selection of cakes and breads from the attached patisserie, and some tasty Thai dishes. Some of the waiting staff are handicapped, making this one of the only restaurants in Nepal to have a deliberate policy of employing people with disabilities. **$$**

Pharping

Lakeside Garden Restaurant
Bansbari
Tel: 984-132 6730
A few kilometres outside of Pharping town, this simple little roadside café serves standard snacks, meals and drinks. What sets it apart is the epic panorama from the garden terrace. The Chobar Gorge lies below, while to the left the towns of the Kathmandu Valley are in view, with the high mountains rising beyond. The staff are very friendly, and the vegetable *pakodas* are satisfyingly crispy. **$**

KATHMANDU TO POKHARA

Bandipur

Gaun Ghar
Tel: 065-520129
In the charming boutique hotel of the same name, this excellent Newari restaurant has inside tables facing the town, and a terrace at the back perched above rolling green hillsides with a view of the high mountains beyond. The decor follows the same earthy, rustic style as the rest of the hotel, and there is good Newari cuisine served on heavy earthenware plates, as well as passable sandwiches and momos. **$$$**

Pokhara

Black & White Café
Lakeside
Tel: 061-460267
This open-fronted place towards the southern end of the Lakeside strip is a little gloomy, but the food makes up for the lack of atmosphere. The menu offers the usual eclectic mix of European and Asian fare, but the real strength here is the baked goods, with fluffy croissants, and wonderfully moist apple cake. There's also a small bar serving beer and spirits. **$$**

Byanjan
Lakeside
Tel: 061-466271

www.byanjan.com
Occupying a prime position looking out over Phewal Tal, Byanjan has excellent views from the garden and upper terrace along with attractive whitewashed stone walls and distressed wood tables and chairs. The menu focuses on European fare with excellent pizzas and decent pasta, though there are also all sorts of exotic interlopers from Moroccan wraps to Thai green curry. **$$**

Chilly Bar and Restaurant
Lakeside
Tel: 061-463614
A tempting scent of frying spices wafts out from the front of this cheery little restaurant towards the northern end of Lakeside. There is a wide range of Asian, European and Mexican dishes. The wild boar with chilli is particularly good, and there are excellent views across the lake from the garden area at the back. **$$**

Caffe Concerto
Lakeside
Tel: 061-463529
With rough walls painted in whites and earthy browns, vintage porcelain set into wall niches, and excellent pasta dishes, Caffe Concerto successfully conjures up Mediterranean ambiance and cuisine. The menu ranges beyond the usual Nepalese-Italian standards, with succulent chicken saltimbocca, gnocchi with home-made basil pesto, and excellent, paper-thin home-made lasagne and ravioli. There's a good cocktail menu too. **$$$**

The Lemon Tree
Lakeside
Tel: 061-463246
On the main road through Lakeside, this shady restaurant has comfy wicker chairs and vintage photos of Nepal as it once was on the walls. There are good European dishes, including fine spinach and mushroom cannelloni, and an expansive cocktail menu – everything from the familiar whisky sour to the offbeat Dylan's disco (tequila, beer, whisky and sugar). **$$**

Daal bhat tarkari.

Moondance Restaurant
Lakeside
Tel: 061-461835
A long-established Lakeside eatery that has successfully kept pace over the years, Moondance has an excellent and eclectic menu, with Chinese and Indian standards, as well as grilled wild boar, imported Australian beef and lamb, and a drinks menu featuring excellent mojitos. The best tables are on the internal wooden balcony that encircles the central dining area. **$$**

Newari Kitchen
Lakeside
Tel: 061-462633
www.newarikitchen.com
Amongst the plethora of international eateries in Pokhara, the Newari Kitchen offers a beacon of authentic Nepalese cuisine in a softly lit setting. There are set menus offering a good opportunity to sample a range of traditional Newari specialities, as well as à la carte choices including hearty *mustang dal* (black bean stew). There are also a few European choices for those who still want to forget that they are in Nepal. **$$**

Perky Beans
Lakeside
Tel: 061-53975
A tiny café on the main drag, Perky Beans has some of the best coffee in the Lakeside area. The beans are perfectly roasted; opt for a double shot if you want an extra kick. There is also a small selection of cakes – the chocolate caramel slice is thoroughly moreish – and simple meals. **$**

Tansen

Nanglo West
Tel: 075-520184
www.nanglo.com.np
In the centre of sleepy little Tansen, this offshoot of the Kathmandu-based Nanglo chain is unexpectedly sophisticated. Set in a restored building with pleasant outdoor seating, the menu stretches from traditional Newari beaten rice to American-style hamburgers. There is also an excellent bakery attached for breads and cakes, and good freshly roasted coffee. **$$**

THE TERAI

Chitwan National Park

K.C.'s Restaurant and Bar
Sauraha
056-580309
www.kcsrestaurant.com
With a long garden stretching down towards the river, this is the best place to eat outside the resorts in Sauraha. There are a few Mediterranean and Chinese dishes on the extensive menu, but the focus is on professionally executed Indian cuisine. The paneer butter masala is wonderfully rich and creamy, and there is crisp, refreshing Long Island ice tea to sip as the sun sets. **$$$**

Sunset View Restaurant and Bar
Sauraha
056-580249
www.saurahabeach.com
Beautifully located on the banks of the Rapti, this is the spot for an evening drink as the sun slips down over the forest and a cacophony of exotic insect noise rises from the undergrowth. The menu has a good range of Western, Indian and Chinese dishes, including the usual pasta dishes, and some decent Mexican snacks, but it's the view that's the real highlight. **$$**

PRICE CATEGORIES

The following prices are based on a meal for one, without drinks:
$$$$ = more than US$10
$$$ = US$7–10
$$ = US$4–7
$ = less than US$4

ACTIVITIES

THE ARTS, NIGHTLIFE, SHOPPING, OUTDOOR ACTIVITIES AND SPORT

While Nepal sometimes seems to have been designed as an adventure playground for adrenaline junkies, with everything from turbulent whitewater rivers to the highest mountains on earth, there's plenty to occupy those in search of more serene pastimes. The country has a rich artistic culture. For the most part this is still typified by traditional craft and performance, but modern interpretations are beginning to appear. The arts also coincide with Nepal's wealth of shopping opportunities – the seething bazaars are a happy hunting ground for those seeking an exotic souvenir, be it a cheap trinket or a lavish example of the finest Newari craftsmanship. Around Kathmandu there are plenty of other leisure activities too, from luxury spa treatments to a round of golf in the shadow of the Himalayas.

THE ARTS

Cinema

Nepal has a popular cinema scene, and in Kathmandu there are plenty of cinemas, generally featuring an array of Hollywood blockbusters and Bollywood tearjerkers, as well as low-budget local attempts to emulate both. Western visitors may enjoy the reactions of the audience more than the action on the screen. **QFX** (www.qfxcinemas.com) inside Civil Mall in Sundhara is a modern multiplex with plenty of English-language screenings.

For Western films, check the programmes of the European, American and Russian cultural centres. The **Alliance Française** (www.alliancefrancaise.org.np) also shows the occasional film. **Film South Asia** (www.filmsouthasia.org) holds a film festival in Kathmandu every two years, showcasing the best documentaries from around South Asia.

Museums

Kathmandu Valley

National Art Gallery
Durbar Square, Bhaktapur
Tel: 01-661 0004
In a section of the old Royal Palace, this museum houses a remarkable collection of Hindu paintings, as well as sacred manuscripts and some fine Buddhist thankas (Wed–Sun 10am–5pm, Mon 10am–3pm; charge, which also includes access to the nearby and worthwhile **National Woodcarving** and **National Brass and Bronze museums** on Dattatraya Square).

National Museum
Chhauni, near Swayambhunath
www.nationalmuseum.gov.np
Tel: 01-427 1478
Housing the country's oldest and largest collection of archaeological relics, folk objects and historic exhibits, the National Museum is reasonably well presented, and usually quiet (Wed–Mon 10.30am–4pm, winter to 3pm; charge).

Patan Museum
Durbar Square, Patan
Tel: 01-552 1492
www.patanmuseum.gov.np
Situated in the restored Mani Narayan Chowk, this is Nepal's best museum, and a "must-see" cultural experience, with displays of Nepalese art, handicrafts and religious items, as well as a garden restaurant (daily 10.30am–5.30pm; charge).

Pokhara

Annapurna Regional Museum
Prithvi Narayan Campus
Tel: 061-521102
Managed by the Annapurna Conservation Area Project (ACAP), this museum has an exceptional collection of butterflies, insects, birds and geology (Sun–Thu 9am–5pm, Fri 9am–noon; free).

International Mountain Museum
Southeast of Pokhara
Tel: 061-460742
www.internationalmountainmuseum.org
This huge museum is dedicated to everything mountain-related, from the ecology of the Taiwanese uplands to the myth of the yeti. There's also a climbing wall in the garden (daily 9am–5pm; charge).

Gurkha Museum
Tel 061-541966
On the edge of Pokhara, this museum presents the history of the famous Gurkha regiment, from the first encounters of the British Empire with Gurkha troops in the 18th century to the present day (Thu–Tue 8am–4.30pm; charge).

Around Nepal

Kapilavastu Museum
Tilaurakot, west of Lumbini
Tel: 076-560128
Ancient coins, pottery and toys are on display here, dating from the 7th century BC to the 4th century AD (Wed–Sun 10am–5pm, Mon 10am–3pm; charge).

Lumbini Museum
Tel: 071-580318
Located in the Cultural Zone, this museum contains coins, manuscripts and sculptures. Opposite is the **Lumbini International Research Institute** (tel: 071-580175) which provides research facilities and

has a collection of some 12,000 books (both Wed–Mon 10am–4pm; charge).

Jomsom Eco Museum
Jomsom
This museum contains artefacts from old burial caves of Mustang, ethnic objects from Mustang culture and herbal medicine (Tue–Sun 10am–4pm; charge).

Tharu Cultural Museum
Thakurdwara, near the entrance to Bardia National Park
Tel: 084-489719
This small museum exhibits costumes, accessories and household objects, which highlight the art and lifestyle of the Tharus (Sun–Fri 12pm–4pm; charge).

Theatre and dance

The **National Theatre** *(Rastriya Nachghar)* in Kathmandu puts on plays and music performances.

Many of Kathmandu's luxury hotels host nightly cultural performances, including traditional music and dance. Some of these are fairly tawdry tourist shows, but the best function as serious outlets for the arts. **Hotel Vajra** (tel: 01-4271545; www.hotelvajra.com) near Swayambhunath is one of the best places for cultural gourmets. The hotel is the home base for the **Kala-Mandapa Institute of Nepalese Performing Arts** (www.kalamandapa.com). There are performances of the Buddhist Charyia dance every Tuesday at 6.30pm, and concerts of Newari music and dance, as well as visiting classical and folk music groups. An institute of classical Nepalese music, a permanent art exhibition and a library complete the picture.

Cultural performances are also held nightly at many of Kathmandu's upmarket Newari restaurants, including **Thamel House** (tel: 01-441 0388; www.thamelhouse.com) where a programme combining elements of music and dance from around the country complements the Nepalese tasting menu.

The best show of all is the dancing amid ancient squares and courtyards lit by oil lamps in Patan or Bhaktapur. This must be arranged in advance and is available for groups only – ask your travel agent for details.

Live music in Pokhara.

NIGHTLIFE

Bars and clubs

Nepal goes to bed early, and even in the Thamel tourist quarter of Kathmandu most bars shut up shop at around 11pm. Good places for a beer in this area include **Tom & Jerry Pub**, up a flight of stairs on the main Thamel drag. The staff are cheery, the beer is cold, and there's a solid soundtrack of soft-rock classics. The long-running **Rum Doodle Bar** (www.rumdoodlebar.com) is a little more sedate – and a little more pricey – with an open fire and walls decorated with the autographs of every noteworthy mountaineer ever to pass through Kathmandu. Also in Thamel, the **Maya Cocktail Bar** (tel: 01-470 0371) is rather more sophisticated, and attracts some trendy locals as well as tourists. Classier still is **J-Bar** (tel: 01-441 1595), popular with some of the slickest local sophisticates, and has good DJs.

There are a number of exclusive nightclubs, many inside the luxury hotels, such as **Galaxy** inside the Hotel Everest (open until 1am), and **Rox Bar** in the Hyatt Regency Boudha (open until midnight). **Club Dynasty** on Durbar Marg is a top-end nightclub that stays open until late.

Art galleries

The **Nepal Association of Fine Arts (NAFA)** (tel:01-441 **1729;** www.nafa.org.np), Bal Mandir, Naxal, Kathmandu organises various art exhibitions (some also with exhibits for sale) featuring traditional and modern Nepalese paintings.

Kathmandu also has a range of active private art galleries, including the **Siddhartha Gallery** (tel: 01-421 8048; www.siddharthaartgallery.com) in Babar Mahal Revisited, the **Park Gallery** in Pulchowk, Patan and the **Indigo Gallery** in Naxal.

At the other end of the spectrum, local working-class men – and a surprising number of women – like to settle down over a glass or two of *chhang* (millet beer) of an evening. All over Nepal you'll see little cafés open at night – a scrap of dirty curtain across the door is a sure sign that the place is a drinking den. Not many tourists pop into these places, but you can generally be sure of a warm welcome if you do.

Casinos

Kathmandu has several casinos, all attached to luxury hotels, aimed squarely at wealthy Indian tourists and with bets placed in US dollars or Indian rupees.

Casino Nepal
Soaltee Crowne Plaza Hotel
Tahachal
Tel: 01-428 0588
Here you can fritter away small fortunes on baccarat, blackjack, roulette and other games around the clock. The casino has a free bus service to ferry you back to your hotel.

Casino Royale
Hotel Yak & Yeti, Durbar Marg
Tel: 01-422 5550
One of the most popular casinos with the Indian high rollers; free drinks flow here and the gaming tables are arranged over two floors in an elegant former Rana palace.

SHOPPING

Kathmandu is a treasure trove for shoppers. Traders appear wherever tourists stray and merchants wait on temple steps. Wares are spread on every pavement but watch out for the junk, fake antiques and souvenirs. Peer into shops, take your pick or take your leave; try the next boutique or the next stall. There are good buys among the bewildering and dazzling array.

Antiques

Unless they are bought from a reputable antiques gallery or certified by specialists, assume that most "antique" pieces have been made yesterday and pay accordingly. Tibetans and Nepalese will not willingly part with their jewels and adornments and, especially when you encounter people on the trail, it is impolite to try to persuade them to part with their personal heirlooms.

Remember when buying that antiques are forbidden for export if they are more than 100 years old. Certificates are required to prove their younger age if there is any doubt. These and export papers, if necessary, can be obtained from the **Department of Archaeology** (see page 337). Here you can also get expert advice on precious and semiprecious stones.

In addition to the old carpets many of the tempting antiques to buy are from Tibet. They include *thangkas*, carved and painted side tables, metalwork from east Tibet, and jewellery and trinkets made with turquoise, coral, amber, gold and silver. Painted wood chests and cupboards from Tibet blend well with Western interiors but beware of modern copies. Prices are on a par with the world market.

Bookshops

Kathmandu has some fabulous bookshops, many carrying spectacular collections of specialist literature on Nepal and Tibet and obscure vintage titles impossible to find overseas.

Pilgrims Book House
Thamel
Tel: 01-422 1546
www.pilgrimsonlineshop.com
The original Pilgrims Book House was a destination in its own right, a magnificent treasure trove of a place housing a mind-boggling array of specialist and out-of-print books. Tragically, the shop was destroyed by fire in 2013 and the entire stock, including thousands of rare and second-hand books, went up in flames. Nothing can replace the lost material, but happily Pilgrims endures in a second, slightly smaller branch a few hundred metres further down J.P. Road in central Thamel. While it isn't quite the glorious literary Aladdin's cave of the original, the management have successfully restocked from their warehouse and their own India-based publishing arm, and it is still the most sophisticated bookshop in town, with a list spanning the gamut of South Asia from the Mekong Delta to the Hindu Kush. The shop also has an impressive collection of fixed-price arts and handicrafts.

Gurkha knives, or khukris, for sale as souvenirs.

Tibet Book Store
Thamel
Tel: 01-441 5788
An upmarket bookstore on the busy Tridevi Marg, this place gives a particular focus to Buddhism and Tibetan history and culture. There is a particularly impressive collection of glossy photo books on offer, and a good range of spiritual titles.

Himalayan Maphouse
Basantapur
Tel: 01-423 1220
www.himalayan-maphouse.com
This excellent shop is the hub of a chain of stores which extends from Pokhara's Lakeside to Namche Bazar on the Everest Trail. The same company also publishes the Nepa brand of maps – all of which are on offer here. There are good-quality large-scale trekking maps for all the major mountain routes, and detailed street maps for major towns, along with a good collection of books.

Clothing

Clothes are good value and can be fun, from the lopsided *topis* (caps) to knitted sweaters, mittens and socks; from Tibetan dresses *(chubas)* to men's Nepalese cotton shirts buttoned diagonally across the chest. *Topis* come in two types: sombre black ones and multi-coloured variations. They are a must for all Nepalese visiting government offices, and their asymmetric shape is said to be a replica of Mount Kailas, the most sacred mountain for Buddhists and Hindus.

Nepalese cloth, in red, black and orange, hand-blocked and chequered with dots or geometric designs, is worn by women as blouses or shawls. It is also made into cotton quilts, covered on both sides with thin muslin, giving pastel overtones to the colours.

There is a wide variety of raw silk – from coarse linen-like textures to fine ones – available in all colours including undyed natural silk yarns.

Wool shawls in a wide variety of colours are established as a major international fashion item; made of the finest goat's wool called pashmina, they are extremely soft, warm and strong (see page 85). Note: Don't be tempted by under-the-counter offers for special *Shahtoosh* pashminas; they are illegal, and up to three endangered Tibetan antelope may be killed to produce one shawl.

Buying fabric for saris at Kathmandu's Durbar Square.

Several shops sell items made from *girardinia*, the Himalayan nettle. It is knitted, crocheted and woven into shawls, garments and bags, and makes a distinctive souvenir to take home.

Folk art

Among the various Nepalese folk objects available and produced in Kathmandu is the national knife, the curved *khukri*, worn in a wooden or leather sheath at the belt and sometimes highly adorned with silver and gold. Dozens of shops specialise in these blades, though most are cheaply made for the tourist market, and will not retain a good cutting edge when sharpened.

The *saarangi* is a small four-stringed fiddle cut from a single piece of wood and played with a horse-hair bow by the *gaine*, the traditional wandering minstrels. Bamboo flutes, sold by vendors who carry them as a huge "tree", make cheap and enchanting gifts. Try them out first though, to make sure they work.

There are all kinds of hand-beaten copper and brass pots, jugs and jars, sold by their weight but rather heavy to carry home. Tibetan tea bowls are carved from a special wood and lined with silver, and silver offering bowls, newly made, are available in Boudhanath.

Handmade paper is beautifully block-printed or tie-dyed in a variety of designs by the women of Janakpur and sold as wrapping paper, cards and booklets (see page 286).

Intricately painted *thangkas* (religious scrolls mounted on silk) are sold at a variety of prices. Look for the detail of the work and the amount of gold leaf used (see page 80). Papier-mâché dance masks are popular, as are the puppets made and sold by the people of both Bhaktapur and Thimi.

Statuettes of Hindu and Buddhist deities are produced semi-industrially with the ancient "lost wax" process, a speciality of the people of Patan (see page 180).

Costume jewellery abounds in Katmandu's Thamel at reasonable prices. Silver and gold is sold by weight. Inexpensive bead necklaces are to be found in Indra Chowk (see page 81).

Handmade carpets, for which there is a flourishing export market, are excellent value. They come in traditional Tibetan designs in either bright colours or more subtle "vegetable dyes", though all are in fact chemical colours. The density of knotting, straightness of lines and overall quality of workmanship influence the price of new carpets (see page 84).

Replicas of Newari woodcarvings seen on temples and 16th- to 17th-century homes can be purchased in handicraft emporiums or at woodcarvers' studios in Bhaktapur, Bungmati and other centres.

Shopping areas

The best selection and the best prices are available in the Kathmandu Valley, though you will find things to buy all over Nepal. As you sightsee in the valley you will encounter many good shopping areas and, as a general rule, if you see something you really like and the price is not too exorbitant, it is better to buy it than regret not being able to find anything similar. To get an idea of the variety on offer and of the relative qualities and prices, visit the following areas.

Thamel, the tourist area in old Kathmandu, has a good selection of most things, though the crowds may distract you.

The shopping and restaurant complex of **Babar Mahal Revisited**, located just south of Singha Durbar, is highly recommenwded (see page 159). A series of purpose-built Rana-style courtyards, it offers an excellent selection of quality shopping for those pressed for time. Look out for the paper shop with imaginative lamp fittings. Pasal, with branches in Babar Mahal Revisited and Durbar Marg, is good for gifts with imaginative local and regional decorative items.

For antiques there are two reliable galleries on **Durbar Marg** with beautiful showrooms: Tibet Ritual Art Gallery is above the Sun Koshi Restaurant and the Potala Gallery is on the first floor across from the Yak & Yeti Hotel.

The main shops in Kathmandu for imported articles are on **New Road**, with supermarkets located in Thapatali and Lazimpat. Jewellers and shops selling handicrafts to tourists are centred around Durbar Marg and the big hotels.

Jawalakhel, south of Patan, is an excellent place for carpet shopping, and for hunting out other authentic Tibetan handicrafts. You can buy carpets and watch the weaving process at the Tibetan Refugee Camp (see page 181).

Patan itself is famous for the manufacture of jewellery and metalwork, still made by traditional methods. Also check out the Patan Museum Shop for unusual gifts (see page 178). Sana Hastakala (tel: 01-552 2628; www.sanahastakala.com) is an NGO originally set up with the help of UNICEF to promote Fair Trade manufacture and export

Bargaining

Bargaining is an intrinsic part of the Nepalese trading culture, and prices are negotiable at most small boutiques and street stalls. Bear in mind that many trinket hawkers will attempt to charge whatever they think a tourist is willing to pay, and an initial asking price will often bear no relationship to the true value of the item. Don't be embarrassed to offer a tiny fraction of the vendor's initial demand as your own opening gambit. It's worth scouting out some of the fixed-price shops beforehand to get an idea of maximum sensible prices if you are planning on some serious street-side souvenir shopping: Pilgrims Book House in Thamel (see page 327) has a fine collection of most of the same curios you'll find on stalls nearby.

A microlight flying over the Pokhara Valley.

of Nepalese handicrafts. The organisation has an excellent store in the Kupundole area of Patan, and a comprehensive online shop as well.

OUTDOOR ACTIVITIES

Adventure sports

Last Resort Adventures
Thamel, Kathmandu
Tel: 01-470 0525
www.thelastresort.com.np
Nepal's original bungee jump, located 160 metres (525ft) over the Bhote Koshi gorge, just 5km (3 miles) from the Tibetan border, is operated by **Last Resort Adventures**.

The Borderland Adventure Centre
Thamel, Kathmandu
Tel: 01-470 0849
www.borderlandresorts.com
Rock climbing, canyoning and mountain biking is organised by **The Borderland Adventure Centre**, which is located 16km (10 miles) from the Tibetan border off the Arniko Highway on the banks of the Bhotse Koshi River.

Aerial activities

Avia Club Nepal
Tel: 01- 426 7633 (Kathmandu), 061-463338 (Pokhara)
www.aviaclubnepal.com
Spectacular views above Pokhara come from the motorised glider flights operated by Avia Club Nepal. This is the longest-established aviation team in Pokhara. Highly professional.

Balloon Sunrise Nepal
Lazimpat, Kathmandu
Tel: 01-443 1078
An unparalleled view of the Kathmandu Valley and the mountains ringing it can be obtained from the hot-air balloon flights arranged by Balloon Sunrise Nepal.

Fishtail Nepal Paragliding
Lakeside, Pokhara
Tel: 01-977 614 66237
info@fishtailparagliding.com
Highly professional and qualified paragliding team.

Mountain biking

There are plenty of mountain biking agencies in Kathmandu and Pokhara with their own quality equipment for hire, but some bikers prefer to bring their own gear and travel independently. If you choose this option do not count on borrowing any specialised tools for on-the-road repairs. Self-sufficiency is essential within practical limits. Bring all the tools you will need for repairs and routine maintenance, including tyre irons, a tube patch kit, an extra tube, a chain tool, a spoke wrench, allen keys and screwdrivers. Less frequently required components are cone wrenches, a headset wrench, a bottom bracket tool, a spanner, extra spokes, extra brake cables and pads, and an extra rear derailleur. And do not forget the obvious, such as water bottles, a sturdy lock that can stretch around a fixed object, a helmet, gloves, a pump and definitely a bell.

Mountain bikes on the Annapurna Trail.

Panniers are the preferred mode for carrying your gear while cycling in Nepal. Racks and panniers must be durable as many roads are rough and full of potholes. Bring small padlocks to protect them. Riders taking to the trails may prefer to carry their equipment in a medium-sized, snug-fitting backpack, as panniers often hinder a bike's manoeuvrability on rugged terrain. Also, it is easier to carry a bike on your shoulders this way.

A "portager" is an essential piece of gear for carrying your bike, which you will probably be doing frequently if riding off-road. The "portager" is a strap which mounts beneath the central bar and allows the bike to rest fairly comfortably on your shoulder. But on long, uphill totes, you may want to attach the bike to your backpack with nylon webbing to better distribute the weight.

Before leaving home, test your equipment thoroughly and take an extended ride on bumpy terrain fully loaded to make sure that the panniers and rack sit solidly and that you can balance and ride easily wearing a loaded pack.

Be cautious at all times, on roads or trails, of other travellers: loaded porters and stock animals, women and children regularly ply the way and hardly expect to encounter a fast-moving cyclist. Ring your bell habitually. Move to the inside when animals are passing to avoid being nudged off the trail. Stay on the roads and trails at all times, as off-road riding only contributes to Nepal's already serious soil erosion problems.

Dress modestly as far as possible, and try to be tolerant of villagers' curiosity, which is generally good-natured. In some parks and reserves, bicycle use is strictly prohibited. Check the rules before leaving Kathmandu.

Participant sports

While most Nepalese people make a proud point of their essential difference from India, in one field they follow their gargantuan neighbour closely: Nepal subscribes fully to the general South Asian passion for cricket, and on every patch of dusty ground in towns and villages across the country you'll see impromptu matches in progress, often played with home-made bats and balls. Football (soccer) is also popular, with the English Premier League getting most attention.

Some sports can be enjoyed in and around Kathmandu, though facilities are limited and mainly belong to hotels and private clubs.

Fishing

Lowland rivers and valley lakes are often good fishing grounds. Besides the small fry, the two main catches are *asla*, a kind of trout, and the larger *mahseer* which can grow to huge proportions. February, March, October and November are the fishing months. Permits are required in national parks where the fish must be returned. Keen anglers should bring their own tackle. Contact **Tiger Tops** for information on fishing in the Karnali, Babai and Narayani rivers.

Tiger Tops
Lazimpat, Kathmandu
Tel: 01-441 1225
www.tigertops.com

Golf

Nepal has several beautiful golf courses, most around the Kathmandu Valley. Teeing off in view of the Himalayas is a fine experience.
Gokarna Forest Golf Resort
Kathmandu
Tel: 01- 445 1212
www.gokarna.com
Nepal Golf Club
Kathmandu
Tel: 01-449 4247
Himalayan Golf Course
Pokhara
Tel: 061-521882
www.himalayangolfcourse.com

Tennis and swimming

Hotel guests and members can use the tennis courts and pools at the Soaltee Crowne Plaza, Yak & Yeti, Radisson, Everest, Annapurna, and Shangri-La hotels and for small entrance fees some allow drop-in day use *for non residents*.

Prudence is needed when bathing in mountain torrents because of swift, treacherous currents. The larger rivers in the Terai are safe – but keep an eye out for the occasional crocodile.

River rafting and kayaking

River trips last from one to several days and your choice depends on the time available and where you are heading. White water varies with the time of year as the rivers rise and fall dramatically during the season, depending on rainfall and snowmelt. As a general rule they are at their highest (and the white water at its biggest) during and after the June to September monsoon and drop to their lowest in February and March. By April the snowmelt in the mountains raises the water level.

Most popular is the two-day Bhote Koshi trip east of Kathmandu and the three-day Trisuli or Seti river trips down to Chitwan National Park (see page 288). More remote and adventurous are the three-day Kali Gandaki trip, the four-day Bheri and the 10-day Karnali river trip from above Nepalganj to Bardia National Park. Most exciting of all are the huge rapids on the Sun Kosi River in east Nepal, which take 10 days to run.

In autumn (mid-Sept–mid-Nov) and spring (Mar–May) shorts and bathing suits, a sunhat, T-shirts, trainers and a torch are all that is needed for a short trip. For early autumn and late spring bring a long-sleeved shirt, light trousers, an umbrella (for shade and in case it rains) and plenty of sunblock to protect you from the glare off the water. During winter (mid-Nov–Feb), in addition to the above bring a thick sweater, warm trousers, down jacket and rain poncho. Ensure you have a complete change of dry clothes and shoes for use in camp.

A good river company will provide tents, sleeping bag and liner, foam mattress, towel and a waterproof bag to stow your clothing. You will be given a life jacket and your guide will instruct you in its use. Safety must be taken very seriously on the remote big rivers of Nepal and should be a consideration when you choose your operator. A waterproof "ammo can" is also provided to carry cameras, binoculars, sunglasses and personal items. This is clipped to the boat and is accessible during the day.

Standard kayaking trips operate on the same rivers as the rafts, and often use the same camps. Kayaking companies provide plastic boats suitable for beginners, while also keeping high-performance boats for more experienced paddlers.

Trekkers take a break from their backpacks in the Langtang Valley.

Trekking

Nepal is one of the world's premier trekking destinations, with a vast array of routes on offer – from gentle strolls through the foothills, to pioneering high-altitude routes in newly opened wilderness areas. The country is incredibly well endowed with professional trekking agencies, catering to all budgets and aspirations, and it is generally easy to organise even a thoroughly ambitious trek at relatively short notice in Kathmandu or Pokhara. However, even if you are heading out independently along one of the so-called "teahouse trails", there are certain preparations that need to be made.

Permits

Since 2008 all trekkers have been required to register through the government Trekking Information Management System (TIMS). Registration can be carried out at the **Tourist Service Centre** at Bhrikuti Mandap, where the TIMS counter is open every day except Saturday. Travel agents in Thamel or Pokhara can handle the process for a small fee. After registration trekkers are issued with a card. Individuals must pay US$20; members of groups are charged US$10. The cards are checked at registration posts on all the main trails. The rationale for the new system is that it allows the authorities both to raise revenues, and to monitor tourism numbers on the various trails, and to make provisions for environmental management. For more details see www.timsnepal.com.

Additional permits, charged at varying rates depending on the specific area, are required for those visiting restricted areas such as Dolpo and Mustang. Trekkers heading to these areas must go with a group and make their arrangements through a registered trekking agent who will usually secure the necessary permit as part of the service.

If you are attempting a trekking peak (see page 126) your trekking agent must obtain a Trekking Peak Permit from the **Nepal Mountaineering Association** (tel: 01-443 4525; www.nepalmountaineering.org). Permits for mountaineering are processed by the **Ministry of Tourism** (Mountaineering Section). Fees per person range from

US$350–500 for a trekking peak to a staggering US$25,000 for an individual climber tackling Everest by the Southeast Ridge in spring.

In addition to trekking and mountaineering permits, there are entry fees – generally Rs1,000 – for all the major national parks, which trekkers must pay. You can pay these in advance at the Tourist Service Centre in Kathmandu, or at the park entry points. For trekking in the Annapurna region it is also necessary to pay the Rs2,000 ACAP fee at the ACAP headquarters in Pokhara.

Physical fitness

Anyone who is reasonably fit can trek, but the fitter you are the more you will enjoy it. Do as much walking and exercise as possible in the weeks prior to your trek to prepare for the effort that will be required of you in Nepal. A thorough medical check-up is recommended before you go. Inoculations against typhoid, hepatitis, paratyphoid, tetanus and meningitis should be on your list too and they should start at least six weeks before your departure (see page 338).

What to bring

As you are going to walk four to eight hours a day, shoes are of paramount importance. They must be sturdy and comfortable with good tread on the soles. Many trekkers hike in trainers at low altitude (with ankle support when walking on rough surfaces), though in snow at higher elevations or on rough and rocky terrain good boots are essential. They must accommodate one or two layers of heavy wool or cotton (not nylon) socks, of which you should have a plentiful supply. Light tennis shoes or trainers will help you relax when the day's walking is over.

Many trekkers assume that it will be cold at all times, whereas when treks start low it can be quite hot for a few days. It is best to wear several thinner layers which can be removed. For women, cotton trousers or below-the-knee skirts are fine; in deference to local sensibilities, neither shorts nor tight or revealing tops should be worn. Men should wear either hiking shorts or loosely fitting long trousers, which also help prevent insect bites. Thermal underwear can be useful in particularly cold months and at high altitudes.

When trekking with an organised group, you will normally be asked to fit all your gear in one pack, to weigh no more than 15kg (35lbs). You will carry only a day pack with daytime essentials, such as water bottle, rain gear, sweater or pile jacket, camera and personal items. Your pack should be tough, compact, easily opened, lockable and packed in an organised fashion.

Even if you do not usually use walking sticks at home, collapsible trekking poles are an invaluable addition as they go a long way to reduce strain on the knees – particularly during long descents. For treks above 4,500 metres (14,750ft) it's worth bringing a pair of gaiters or light waterproof trousers for walking through snow. Good quality sunglasses are essential at all altitudes, replaced by proper glacier goggles if you will be walking extensively through snow. Much of this gear can be bought or rented from trekking shops in Thamel and Pokhara, but it is best to arrive fully prepared.

Altitude sickness

Anyone trekking above 2,500 metres (8,200ft) may suffer from altitude sickness. Known as AMS or acute mountain sickness it can ruin treks and should be treated seriously. Nearly half of the people who have trekked to Everest Base Camp, for instance, suffer mild AMS and in some cases lives are endangered.

The only reliable prevention is to give one's body time to adjust to high altitude. Those who go too high too fast are liable to be victims of AMS. To minimise the pitfalls of AMS during a trek, travellers should:

Drink adequate fluids. At 4,300 metres (14,100ft) for example, the body requires 3–4 litres (5–7 pints) of liquid a day – more if losing much sweat. At lower altitudes, especially in the heat, try to drink at least 2–3 litres (3–5 pints) a day.

Accept the fact you cannot go very high if your time is short.

Plan for "rest days" at about 3,700 metres (12,100ft) and 4,300 metres (14,100ft). This means sleeping at the same altitude for at least two nights. You can be as active as you wish during the day, and go as high as you like, but descend again to sleep. Above 3,700 metres (12,100ft), do not set up camp more than 450 metres (1,500ft) higher in any one day, even if you feel fit enough.

Learn the symptoms of AMS and be alert for them. If you begin to suffer, do not go any higher until the symptoms have disappeared. Often they will clear up within one or two days. Should any of the more serious symptoms appear, descend at once. Even a descent of 300 metres (1,000ft) can make a difference.

Do not go to a high altitude if you have heart or lung disease. Check with your doctor if you have any doubts.

Do not expect everyone in your party to acclimatise at the same rate. It is possible that you will need to divide the party so that people who acclimatise more slowly will camp lower than others. Be aware that general physical fitness at sea level is no reliable indicator of resistance to AMS: the fittest and healthiest of trekkers can be stricken at relatively low altitudes, while those who have done little training may be able to ascend higher before feeling the effects. Take extra precautions when flying into high-altitude airstrips. Take two "rest days" before proceeding further.

Symptoms and treatment

There are three main types of AMS. Early mountain sickness is the first and acts as a warning. If it goes unheeded, it can progress to pulmonary edema (waterlogged lungs) or cerebral edema (waterlogged brain).

Early mountain sickness manifests itself in headache, nausea, loss of appetite, sleeplessness, fluid retention and swelling of the body. The cure is to climb no higher until the symptoms have gone.

Pulmonary edema is characterised by breathlessness, even while resting, and by a persistent cough accompanied by congestion in the chest.

Cerebral edema is a very serious condition. The symptoms are extreme tiredness, vomiting, severe headache, difficulty in walking (as in drunken, uneven steps), disorientation, abnormal speech and behaviour, drowsiness and eventually unconsciousness. Should any of these symptoms appear, victims must be carried to a lower altitude immediately, either on a porter's back or on a yak or pony, and their trek abandoned. Do not delay descent for any reason and begin at night if necessary. Do not wait for helicopter evacuation. The patient must be accompanied and may well not be capable of making correct decisions. You may need to insist that they descend. Medicine is no real substitute for descent. If a doctor is available, he may give medication and oxygen but even with treatment the patient must go down.

Food and water

Water contamination is a problem. On the trail all water should be well boiled or treated with iodine or chlorine.

Bring your own high-energy goodies like chocolate, dried fruits and nuts, powdered drinks and herbal teas. On the major trekking routes Western chocolate bars can be bought, and a trekking mix of dried fruit and granola can be purchased in Thamel supermarkets.

Medication

Minor ailments are to be expected. Being at high altitudes and around exotic bacteria puts a strain on the body so that cuts take longer to heal and colds or coughs drag on. On organised group treks, a collective medical kit is provided and the *sirdar* (guide) will occasionally have some knowledge of first aid. Some items might be in high demand, however, and it is best to bring your own first-aid kit. This should include:

Gauze bandages
Crepe bandage/elastic knee support
Sterile compresses
Plasters
Laxatives
Pain-relief tablets with codeine
Strong pain-relief tablets
Vaseline
Mild sleeping pills
Decongestant or other cold remedy
Throat lozenges or cough drops
Ophthalmic ointment or drops
Cream against insect bites
Diarrhoea tablets
Medicine for other gastric problems
A broad-spectrum antibiotic
Blister pads or moleskin
Antiseptic and cotton
A good sunblock
Lip salve

Trekking trails and when to go

There is an overwhelming number of trekking trails to choose from. Your final choice depends upon the length of time you have available, the season, and your personal interests.

The following list will give you some guidelines. Consult the trekking sections of this book and your trek and travel agent for more information.

January to February

This is the best time of year for low-level walks at elevations up to 3,000 metres (10,000ft) offering pleasant sunny days with clear skies and good mountain views. It is also an excellent time to trek the old trade route between Kathmandu and Pokhara, visit the lower Lamjung Himal areas or trek in the valleys north of Gorkha.

Three good winter treks are recommended from Pokhara. The so-called **Royal Trek** follows the footsteps of the Prince of Wales for three or four days in the Gurung and Gurkha country northeast of the Pokhara Valley. Great views of Annapurna, Machhapuchhre and Dhaulagiri are highlights of the six- to ten-day **Ghandruk to Ghorapani Circuit Trek**. For those with more time, the 15–18-day **Kali Gandaki Trek** to Jomsom and Muktinath along the new trails pioneered by ACAP to replace the old lower Annapurna Circuit is in good condition in the winter, although snow is possible at Ghorapani.

North of Kathmandu, the **Helambu Trek** is an excellent winter option as it stays at relatively low altitude, as is the **Tamang Heritage Trail.** You may come across snow above the Sherpa villages of Tarkeghyang and Melamchigaun, but it should not hamper progress.

Khumbu in winter is only for the hardy as temperatures are low, but there is sensational scenery and few trekkers.

In late February, spring arrives in Nepal and flowers and rhododendrons begin to bloom at lower altitudes. Trek before mid-March if you want to beat the spring rush up to 4,000 metres (13,120ft).

March

Although spring has arrived in the Kathmandu Valley and at the lower levels, high-altitude conditions can still be harsh. Do not plan on being able to cross high passes (5,000 metres/16,400ft) before mid-April.

March is a good time to start a long trek into **Solu Khumbu** from **Shivalaya**, although it is still a little early for Rolwaling. Further east, start mid-month on an excursion to the rhododendron forests of the **Milke Danda** ridge or for a botanical trek up the **Arun River**, but not yet into Makalu Base Camp. **Jugal** is also rewarding for wilderness treks but expect spring flowers only late in the month.

All **Langtang**-, **Helambu**- and **Pokhara**-based treks are feasible, though some mountain haze may develop during the second half of the month. The **Dhorpatan** (from Tansen or Beni) and lower **Dhaulagiri** areas are a lovely alternative to the Annapurnas late in the month.

Short two- to five-day treks around the **Kathmandu Valley** are popular now as they are higher, therefore cooler, than short treks out of Pokhara.

Out west, the valleys below **Khaptad** are pleasantly temperate and the rhododendrons are brilliant.

April

In this high season, temperatures are warm in the lower altitudes but there is a likelihood of afternoon clouds and showers in most areas south of the main Himalayan chain. This is the best month for flowers in the mountains and the favoured season for alpine treks and climbing.

April is a superb month to spend high in the mountains around **Manang** and climbing is possible on **Chulu** and **Pisang**. After mid-April the **Thorung La Pass** is usually open, critical to completing the classic **Annapurna Circuit** trek. Beware of avalanche danger in the Annapurna Sanctuary, though the Machhapuchhre Base Camp area is good for wildlife after the middle of the month.

For the adventurous, the high altitudes of the **Dhaulagiri Glacier region** are at their best, as is the rugged remote terrain of **Manaslu** and **Dudh Pokhari**.

This is an excellent time for treks to the higher altitudes, such as in east Nepal, to the **Milke Danda** ridge and alpine treks to the Base Camps of **Kanchenjunga** and **Makalu**. It is also one of the best times to visit **Khumbu**, although the low-level walk in from Shivalaya can be disappointing due to increasing haze and heat. Now is the time for alpine and climbing treks to **Rolwaling** and the **Hinku** and **Hongu** and climbs of **Island Peak** and **Mera**.

Treks into the **Jugal Himal** are fairly tough but rewarding for the off-the-beaten-track adventurer. Spring flowers are beautiful. Between Helambu and Langtang, visits to the **Gosainkund Lakes** are attractive. En route to Langtang, **Trisuli Bazaar** and **Dhunche** are hot, but are worth enduring to reach the high-altitude forests and wild flowers. A return via the **Tirudanda** or on to **Gorkha** enters seldom-trekked highland areas.

In the far west of the country, treks to **Rara Lake** and **Dolpo** start in **Jumla**. The "Upper Dolpo" region is only open to organised groups with special permits. "Lower Dolpo" is open to individual trekkers but is logistically complex because of difficult access and food deficits in this remote region. Don't start a trek before late April or snow will bar the way.

May to June
In these pre-monsoon months, there is haze and heat at all lower elevations and occasional heavy showers. Treks that stick to higher altitudes are preferable at this time of year. Some of the better areas at this time are **Khumbu**, flying in and out of Lukla, **Rolwaling**, **Hongu**, the Ganja La or Tilman's Col areas of **Langtang** and the **Annapurna Circuit**. **Kathmandu Valley** walks are still pleasurable, though daytime temperatures rise sharply (see page 195).

July to Mid-September
Keen botanists and students of leeches will enjoy this monsoon time of year. Although not generally recommended for trekking, the terrain is lovely in the higher regions and rainshadow areas, such as **Muktinath**, **Manang** and **Langtang** to a certain extent, as well as **Dolpo** and the far west. Although rainfall is not continuous and sunny days and mountain views will be experienced, trekkers must realise that rain, leeches, slippery paths and swollen rivers will hamper their progress. Various alpine wild flowers and plants are at their zenith at this time, and particularly spectacular in **Upper Khumbu**. These months are also ideal for **Dolpo** and the **Mustang** region near the Tibetan border, which remain largely unaffected by the monsoon.

Mid-September to Mid-October
The monsoon tails off about this time and the countryside is fresh and green. When the mountains are free of clouds, the views are crystal clear though there are still a lot of showers at lower altitudes. Recommendations for trekking routes are much the same as for April and May, though high passes may be snowed over.

Mid-October to Mid-November
This is the "high season" for trekking and with good reason. It is the classic time for high-altitude alpine and climbing treks and in general has the most reliable clear weather, although rain is not unheard of. The more popular routes are congested at this time; these include the Khumbu where the sheer weight of numbers creates flight delays at Lukla. Even more crowded is the Pokhara region, especially the Kali Gandaki Valley, though weather-wise, the Annapurna Sanctuary is at its best.

This is the time to choose less popular areas and enjoy trips to east or west Nepal, **Jugal Himal**, **Ganesh Himal** and **Tirudanda** or routes between **Pokhara** and **Kathmandu**. Throughout this autumn period many colourful religious festivals take place to ensure a good harvest in the fields.

Mid-November to Mid-December
This period offers stable winter weather as the rain and snow do not start until mid-December. It also has the added advantage of avoiding the previous month's crowds. With crops harvested, the countryside lacks colour but the clarity of mountain views is superb, and there is plenty of variety and walking conditions are pleasant.

Low level and short treks up to about 3,700 metres (12,000ft) are at their best at this time of year. The **Pokhara** region is ideal as are **Helambu**, **Langtang** and **Gorkha**. The **Khumbu** is still good though getting colder and the Lukla flights more reliable than at the height of the season. Remember that most of the high passes cannot be safely crossed because of snow after the middle of December.

Trekking etiquette

Learning a bit of Nepali will open doors and help when asking directions – though bear in mind that local estimates of distance and walking time may bear little relation to your own capacities. Trail directions should be repeatedly sought as each villager may have his own version. Distance is generally measured in hours rather than kilometres, which are irrelevant in such up-and-down terrain.

Whereas no one is likely to openly criticise you if you make a cultural faux pas, out of respect for the Nepalese and to ensure a better rapport between you, your staff and the villagers, try to be sensitive to religious beliefs and local practices. For example, on your trek you will come across stupas and *chortens* of various sizes and conditions. They are revered, regardless of their size, with great devotion and were built to pacify local demons, deities or the spirit of some dead person. It is inappropriate to sit or climb on *chortens* and they should be passed with the right shoulder in a clockwise direction. Lamas' prayer wheels whirl prayers out in a clockwise direction only.

In Buddhist areas you will see *mani* stones placed around *chortens* or stacked to make a *mani* wall. These flat stones are carved with inscriptions, prayers and supplications, which have been artistically engraved with devotion. Though the temptation may be great, because of the beauty and small size of these stones, do not take them for souvenirs. The removal of these stones from their place of offering is sacrilege.

When looking for a toilet spot in the bush, be sure that you are not close to running water or to any holy places or relics such as prayer flags or *mani* walls. Burn and bury, or carry out, all toilet paper. Carry all litter to a rubbish pit or to camp where the staff can burn or bury it. Help to minimise the burning of firewood in lodges by being adequately clothed so as not to rely on the fire's heat for keeping warm, by limiting hot showers heated with wood and by combining orders for similar food items.

On the trails

A typical day, when trekking with an organised outfit, begins around 6am with a cup of tea or coffee. After packing, breakfast of porridge, eggs, toast or pancakes is served. Walking starts around 7–7.30am. Late into the morning, trekkers halt for a substantial hot brunch or lunch, the cook having gone ahead to select the site and prepare the meal. As early as 3 or 4pm the day's walking is over. Camp for the night is set up (usually with a toilet tent), dinner is served, and by 9pm everyone is thinking of sleep.

You are free to walk at whatever pace you prefer. Fast or slow, there will always be a staff guide in front or behind you. If you wish, you can take the time to make endless stops to enjoy the scenery or chat with passing locals, take photos or sip tea in a wayside shop.

If trekking independently, it is best not to trek alone. Team up with other trekkers or hire a guide, preferably from a trekking agency rather than at the trailhead. If you are completely unable to find anyone to trek with ahead of departure, stick to the well-trammelled trails like the Annapurna Circuit, where you will run into other hikers along the way.

A few hints may increase your enjoyment:

Do not try too much too soon. Walk at your own pace, no matter what others may say. Watch the way the porters walk, slowly and steadily. Go uphill in short steps, feet flat on the ground, weight forward.

Go downhill with your knees bent, using your thigh muscles. Rest as often as you feel like.

Drink as much liquid as you can to compensate for the sweaty hours under the sun; at high altitudes, this also helps your body to acclimatise.

Shielding your head from the sun with a hat or umbrella, as well as applying sunscreen to your skin, helps prevent sunstroke, which along with dehydration is one of the most common ailments on the trail.

Ensure that your feet are in good condition to walk. Treat potential blisters before they develop.

Be careful in the night as in certain areas thieves sometimes slit tents to steal cameras and other valuables. Keep your belongings close to you, well inside the tent, and keep your tent closed when you are not in it.

Finally, add to your luggage a strong dose of patience, understanding and congenial curiosity for the values and ways of a world that is different from, and at times better organised than, your own.

Mountain rescue

The **Himalayan Rescue Association (HRA)** (tel: 01-444 5505; www.himalayanrescue.org) is a non-profit organisation that strives to prevent casualties in the Nepal Himalaya. The HRA runs Trekkers' Aid Posts at Pheriche in Khumbu and at Manang in the Annapurnas. They are staffed by doctors and equipped to treat and advise on acute mountain sickness (AMS) and other medical problems.

As this is an entirely voluntary organisation, donations are welcomed directly to the HRA or channelled through your trekking agency. The HRA has no facilities to arrange helicopter evacuations, which must be done through your trekking agent or embassy.

The HRA does not routinely recommend any medicine for preventing AMS, though there are two medicines which under certain circumstances are considered useful. Diamox (acetazolomide) is the safest for helping to cope with symptoms of mild AMS. The standard dose is 250mg every 12 hours until symptoms are resolved. Dexamethasone is a powerful drug, which can be useful in the treatment of cerebral edema. It should only be used under experienced supervision.

Additional information for independent trekkers can be obtained from the **Kathmandu Environmental Education Programme (KEEP)**. This non-profit organisation is designed to minimise impacts of individual travellers and maximise benefits for local people. A visit to their information centre is highly recommended.

Thamel Kathmandu
Tel: 01-441 2944
www.keepnepal.org

Jungle safaris

Most camps and lodges around Chitwan and Bardia supply facilities you would expect of any hotel. Take casual, washable, safari-style clothes in jungle colours – beige and green are the most suitable. Wear baggy shorts in the summer months but take long trousers to protect legs from swishing tall grass while riding elephants. Trainers are the most suitable footwear and jungle hats, mosquito repellent and suncream are useful. The winter months are cold and morning mist makes it chilly – sweaters and jackets are essential from December to February. As a guideline, the Terai is about 1,200 metres (4,000ft) lower in altitude than Kathmandu and so the weather is always several degrees warmer.

Taking a jungle boat trip in Chitwan National Park.

A – Z

A HANDY SUMMARY OF PRACTICAL INFORMATION

A

Admission charges

There are admission charges for most of the high-profile sights around the Kathmandu Valley, and there is usually a three-tiered price system, with visitors from countries belonging to the South Asian Association for Regional Cooperation (SAARC) grouping paying less than those from further afield, and locals paying still less. For major attractions tickets for non-SAARC residents generally range between US$5–10. As the various historic attractions are generally run by separate managements there are few combined tickets. However, general entry to Kathmandu's Durbar Square and the Hanuman Dhoka Durbar have been combined, and there are plans to bring some other sights in Kathmandu under a single ticket.

There are entrance fees for all national parks, including those traversed by trekking routes. These fees are typically around US$10, payable in dollars or rupees.

B

Begging

Beggars are a common sight in Kathmandu, often stationed around bus stations or on busy pedestrian walkways. Major pilgrimage centres such as Pashupatinath and Swayambhunath were attracting large groups of beggars long before the first tourists arrived in Nepal, and they continue to do so today.

As well as these "genuine" beggars, you may be targeted by children around tourist sights, often speaking excellent English, and offering a slick tale to elicit sympathy. A typical approach is to ask tourists to pay for school books, and even to lead them to a shop where they can make the purchase directly. This is generally a scam and the beggar later returns the book and splits the cash with the shopkeeper. While a few street children have used their savvy and their language skills to make their way in the legitimate tourist trade, many others slip into a life of drugs and crime, and local NGOs strongly caution against giving handouts, arguing that doing so encourages children to stay on the streets. If you want to help, make a donation to a local charity.

Budgeting for your trip

Bottled beer: Rs350
Glass of house wine: Rs500
Main course meal: Rs:250 budget; Rs:600 moderate; Rs:1,200 expensive
Hotel cost: from Rs500 budget; from Rs:2,500 moderate; from Rs5,000 expensive
Taxi ride within Kathmandu: Rs200–500
Bus journey: Kathmandu to Pokhara on a "tourist bus" Rs500–1,000

C

Children

Travelling with children in Nepal is a wonderful way to break the ice and meet local people as the Nepalese love youngsters. Be aware of health and hygiene concerns, however, and before travelling take medical advice about vaccinations and other issues. Disposable nappies can be bought at upmarket supermarkets in Kathmandu and Pokhara, but they are hard to come by further afield. Cots are a rarity in hotels, so ask in advance when booking if you need one.

Climate

Nepal crams an extreme variety of climates into a remarkably small geographical area. In terms of temperature variation the seasons correspond roughly with those in Europe – with the added complication of a summer monsoon. But when the Terai is sweltering in a tropical fug, temperatures a day's drive to the north can still be below freezing. Generally speaking however, winters (Nov–Feb) are dry across the country with most of the annual rain falling during the monsoon months (June–Aug). Autumn, winter and late spring are generally the best times to visit Nepal.

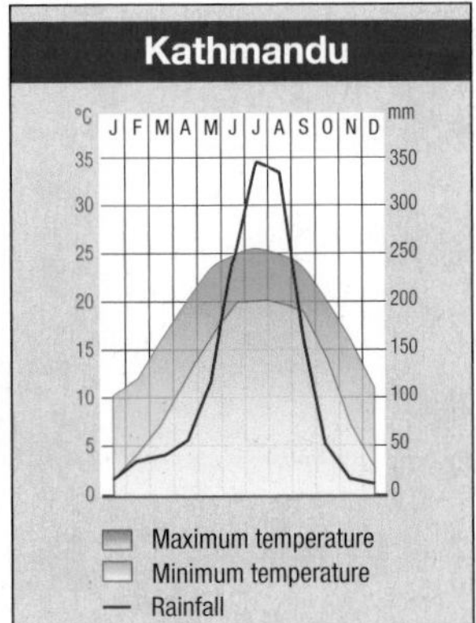

The Terai has a warm and humid climate. During winter, night-time temperatures can drop below 8°C (46°F) but the daytimes are mild and dry and this is generally the best time to visit. In the pre-monsoon months of April and May temperatures rise towards 37°C (99°F) and humidity spikes, making travel uncomfortable. The monsoon rains are particularly heavy in the Terai, and this is not generally a good time to visit.

With an elevation of about 1,350 metres (4,400ft), the Kathmandu Valley has a more temperate climate. Though nocturnal temperatures can drop to freezing point in January and February, daytimes remain mild, and the air is usually clearer in winter – after the frequent morning mists have dissipated. October and February are particularly pleasant months.

The weather is noticeably warmer in the Pokhara Valley, where spring temperatures rise to 30°C (86°F) at midday. In April, May and early June the weather becomes hot and stuffy, with occasional evening thunderstorms. The mountains are often shrouded in haze at this time of year.

Travel is by no means impossible during the rainy season, and it rarely rains all day. However between June and late August the Himalayas usually remain out of sight, and most trekking trails fall quiet as mud and leeches take over. Flooding does occur in both the Terai and the Middle Hills, and roads are sometimes washed away. Temperatures remain high at lower altitudes, but the stuffy humidity of the pre-monsoon generally clears. In trans-Himalayan regions such as Mustang and Dolpo there is no monsoon and the weather remains largely dry year-round.

The rains generally clear in September, bringing lush colours and blue skies. In the mountains temperatures plummet with the onset of winter. Many trekking routes remain accessible throughout the winter but those which traverse high passes – such as the Annapurna Circuit – are usually off-limits from around mid-December until March.

What to wear

From mid-September to March light clothing is fine in the Kathmandu Valley during the daytime but for evenings and early mornings bring a fleece, heavy sweater or a thick jacket. Comfortable shoes are a must, even if you do not intend to go trekking.

At high altitude, night-time temperatures are cold enough year-round to make fleeces, hats and gloves necessary – though on the trail in the heat of the day you'll likely strip down to a single layer. Special gear for trekking can be hired or bought in Pokhara or Kathmandu in Western sizes. Wearing plenty of clothing reduces your need for fuel to keep warm.

From April to September only light clothes, preferably cotton, are necessary in Kathmandu. Avoid synthetic fibres as they can irritate the skin.

The Terai, being lower in altitude, is generally warmer than Kathmandu throughout the year. Safari-type clothing is most appropriate for visits to the lowland national parks. But the cold winter nights in both December and January make a sweater and jacket essential. Jungle areas require light cotton clothing. Light colours are much less attractive to mosquitoes. Remember to bring a sunhat and suncream.

Crime and safety

Ordinarily, Nepal is regarded as a safe place, but in Kathmandu, as in any capital city, it pays to be careful, especially after dark. Theft and pickpocketing are the major problems – be especially alert during crowded festivals, at currency-exchange counters and bus stations, and on buses.

Since the end of the Maoist insurgency the overall security situation in Nepal has improved markedly, and there are no longer any parts of the country which are off-limits for security reasons. However, Nepalese politics is still a turbulent business, and large-scale demonstrations – prompted by domestic or international events – can flare up, so keep abreast of the current situation ahead of your visit. The governments of the **UK** (www.fco.gov.uk) and **US** (www.travel.state.gov) provide up-to-date information on travel and security.

There are a few specific hazards. Violent crime is very rare, but petty theft has been reported from some trekking villages on the fringes of the Kathmandu Valley. Much more of an issue are the scams perpetrated by hustlers in tourist areas. Be wary of any get-rich-quick scheme involving gemstones, and any child or mother with remarkably good English requesting money to ease some family misfortune.

While various locally grown marijuana products are widely available throughout Nepal, and are consumed by some locals, there are stiff penalties for possession and the authorities do sometimes clamp down on foreigners.

Country-wide strikes *(bandhs)* and demonstrations against the government may be called at short notice, which cause transport delays and may erupt into violence. Avoid large public gatherings.

The English-speaking Tourist Police are trained to assist visitors and have offices in Thamel (tel: 01-442 9750) and in Bhrikuti Mandap at the Tourist Service Centre (tel: 01-424 7041).

Customs regulations

Travellers may bring in 250 cigarettes, one bottle of liquor and up to 12 cans of beer. Electronic items for personal use can be brought into the country on condition that they are subsequently re-exported when you leave. In practice there is little enforcement of this rule for laptops, cameras and other everyday items, but if you are bringing particularly large

Police officers.

photographic equipment you may be required to make a formal declaration on arrival.

Passengers arriving at Tribhuvan International Airport without any dutiable articles can proceed through the Green Channel for quick clearance without a baggage check. Those carrying dutiable items are required to pass through the Red Channel for detailed customs clearance. Prohibited items include firearms and ammunition (unless an import licence has been obtained in advance), beef products and radio transmitters. It is forbidden to import or export Nepalese or Indian currency, and in theory it is necessary to declare cash totalling more than US$2,000, though in practice this is seldom enforced.

Souvenirs can be carried or posted out of the country freely but antiques and art objects (such as metal statues and sacred paintings) require a special certificate from the **Department of Archaeology** (Ramshah Path; tel: 01-425 0683) in Kathmandu. It takes at least two days to secure. It is forbidden to export any object more than 100 years old that is valued for cultural and religious reasons. For more information, contact the **Chief Customs Administrator** (www.customs.gov.np). Keep receipts for any handicrafts and purchases you have made.

D

Disabled travellers

Nepal is not well set up for disabled travellers; streets and pavements are narrow and uneven; lavatories designed for people with disabilities are virtually unknown; there is a surfeit of stairs and a deficit of lifts, and very few hotels or public spaces have ramps for wheelchair users (although wheelchairs are available at Tribhuvan International Airport). However, people with disabilities have successfully climbed Everest in recent years, so with the aid of a well-informed agency a tour around Nepal ought still to be possible.

Electricity

Major towns in Nepal are electrified with 220-volt alternating current, though some fluctuation is usual, so when using a computer or other sensitive electrical equipment, it is essential to use a voltage stabiliser. Electric razors, hairdryers, etc. can be used with adaptors. Outages – known here as "load shedding" – are a fact of life in Nepal, with scheduled and unscheduled cuts most days. Hotels generally have a backup system, though it may not provide full power.

Always take your shoes off before entering a temple.

E

Embassies and consulates

Foreign embassies in Kathmandu

Australia: Bansbari. Tel: 01-437 1678; www.nepalembassy.gov.au
Bangladesh: Maharajganj. Tel: 01-437 2843
Canada: Lazimpat. Tel: 01-441 5389
China: Hattisar. Tel: 01-441 1740; www.np.china-embassy
India: Lainchhaur. Tel: 01-441 0900; www.indianembassy.org.np
New Zealand: Rani Pokhari. Tel: 01-442 6427
Pakistan: Maharajganj. Tel: 01-437 4024
Sri Lanka: Maharajganj. Tel: 01-441 9289; www.slembktm.com
Thailand: Bansbari. Tel: 01-437 1410
UK: Lainchhaur. Tel: 01-441 0583
US: Maharajganj. Tel: 01-400 7200; www.nepal.usembassy.gov

Emergency Numbers

Ambulance: 102 or 01-422 8094
Fire: 101
Police: 100
Tourist Police: 01-424 7041

Etiquette

Nepalese cultures are very different to those in the West, and many visitors are uncertain how to deal with people directly because they do not speak their language and do not know their customs and values. Misunderstandings and prejudice can make everyday encounters difficult. The more you know about the history, the economic and political developments and particularly the cultural background, the more you will be able to understand what you see and hear. Nepalese people are generally friendly, helpful, polite and tolerant towards visitors and will make you feel at home. The first greeting is not marked by shaking hands but by folding the hand in front of the chest and saying "*Namaste*". It is normal to use first-name terms.

A sideways shake of the head usually means "yes", though a "yes" may only signify an attempt to avoid a negative answer which is deemed to be impolite. Effusive thanks for assistance or a gift are not the norm here as the pleasure is normally evident from other gestures. Self-control is highly valued in Nepal, and anyone showing lack of self-control or aggression in public loses respect. Displays of physical affection between couples are not acceptable. Immodest or revealing clothing should also be avoided.

Although the various local cultures across Nepal differ greatly, they all have a deep-rooted religious underpinning. Always respect religious sites and rites. Walk clockwise around a stupa, *chorten* or *mani* wall. Take your shoes off before entering a temple or a shrine; leather is prohibited inside temple precincts. Seek permission before entering a Hindu temple and comply with good grace if you are asked not to enter a certain precinct or not to photograph a shrine or cultural event.

Long exposure to tourism has left locals in places like Kathmandu and Pokhara, and along well-known trekking routes, used to what they may actually regard as uncouth

English-language newspapers and maps for sale.

behaviour by foreigners. This familiarity, coupled with a general hospitality and tolerance of guests, is mistaken by some travellers for a liberal acceptance of Western values. In fact, such behaviour may still be viewed as offensive and bizarre, even if there are no expressions of disapproval. You should always make a concerted effort to respect local norms, even in the most touristic areas.

Men and women dressed in white are in mourning and should not be touched under any circumstances. Stepping over the feet or the body of a person rather than walking around him should be avoided. Never point at a person with your foot as it is believed to be "polluted".

If you are invited into a Nepalese home, follow these rules: take off your shoes before entering a house or a room; treat the kitchen or the cooking and eating area with the utmost respect; on no account should you go without an explicit invitation. Remember that the hearth in a home is sacred – never throw rubbish into the fire. Little presents for the children are welcome but will not be opened before your eyes.

Locals use water and the left hand to clean themselves after going to the toilet, therefore nothing should be accepted, and especially not offered, with the left hand only. Never offer to share your "polluted" food – that is food you've already tasted, bitten into or even touched with your used cutlery. Nepalese people often eat squatting on the ground. Do not stand in front of a person who is eating as your feet will be in front of his plate of food. The sociable part of the evening takes place before the meal so that the visit draws to a close with the end of the meal. Do not forget to praise the food before you leave.

G

Gay and lesbian travellers

Unlike in most neighbouring countries, gay people are not criminalised in Nepal. In 2007 a long-standing ban on homosexual activity was overturned by the Supreme Court, and there are even moves afoot to make legal provisions for same-sex marriage. The local human rights organisation **Blue Diamond Society** (www.bds.org.np) continues to advocate gay rights, and works in the field of HIV awareness. Despite the admirable legal situation, however, Nepal does not have a notable local LBGT scene readily accessible to travellers, and discrimination does continue, so discretion is still advisable.

H

Health and medical care

While life-threatening infectious diseases are rare in travellers to Nepal, it is essential to get some good pre-travel advice regarding vaccinations. Arrange an appointment with your GP, ideally three months before you set off to discuss your vaccine requirements and any medicines you should bring.

Make sure all the vaccines you receive are recorded in your International Vaccine booklet and carry this in your hand luggage. As well as ensuring you are covered for tetanus, MMR, polio and diphtheria, you should consider receiving vaccines against typhoid fever, hepatitis A and B, Japanese encephalitis (for visitors to the Terai or travellers engaging in extensive outdoor activities in rural areas) and rabies. Meningitis A/C should also be considered, especially if you are planning to visit Nepal in the winter months, as well as cholera for high-risk individuals such as relief workers.

Much of Nepal lies high enough to be free from the threat of malaria. The disease does still occur in the Terai, however, especially during monsoon months. Around Chitwan the risk is minimal, but in more remote areas it pays to take precautions. Use repellents and cover up, especially at dawn and dusk. Sleep under a net, if possible, and get specific advice about anti-malarial medicine from your GP. Get good travel insurance and make sure you are covered for helicopter evacuation to Kathmandu and for air-ambulance evacuation to a regional hospital.

Never drink unboiled or untreated water or ice cubes. Avoid eating raw vegetables, and peel fruit before consuming. Never walk barefoot and wash your hands often.

Should you be taken ill, drink plenty of fluids and take enough sugar and salt. Glucose/electrolyte packs, available from your chemist at home, are essential and can be difficult to obtain in Nepal. Minor problems can occur soon after arrival. "Traveller's tummy" should clear up after a couple of days but if you find it is severe and persistent get medical assistance. Many visitors find that Kathmandu's chronic air pollution sets off low-level respiratory problems – it may be worth following the local example and wearing a facemask when out walking the busy streets. Use disinfectant and cover even the smallest wounds. Cover your head in the sun and avoid contact with stray cats and dogs or wild animals. HIV/Aids is a major problem in Nepal so take the usual precautions of avoiding unprotected sexual intercourse. For information on altitude sickness, see page 331.

Medical services

Top-end hotels usually have a doctor on call, and embassies can provide a list of recommended hospitals and practitioners. A new combined ambulance service has recently been launched in Kathmandu (tel: 102). Otherwise call the Red Cross (tel: 01-422 8094). Avoid the chaotic government-run Bir Hospital near the Tundhikhel.

There are a number of private hospitals and clinics in the Kathmandu area which have experience in treating foreigners – though fees are usually steep.

The **CIWEC Clinic** in Lainchaur (tel: 01-442 4111; www.ciwec-clinic.com) has foreign staff and a good reputation, and experience in arranging emergency medical evacuation. **Nepal International Clinic** in Hitti Durbar close to Thamel (tel: 01-443 5357; www.nepalinternationalclinic.com) offers similar services. **Patan Hospital** in Lagankhel (tel: 01-452 2278; www.patanhospital.org.np) has a full range of services and is the best place to tackle serious problems.

Pokhara lacks similarly sophisticated services, but the **Manipal Teaching Hospital** (tel: 061-440387) in Fulbari can handle most cases.

Pharmacies

An alarming array of powerful medicines, supposedly only available on prescription, are readily and cheaply sold over the counter in Nepal. Despite the temptation to self-medicate or to stock up on powerful antibiotics in case of illness on the trekking routes, get a proper diagnosis and advice from a doctor before heading for an *aushadhi pasal* (literally "medicine shop"). Look out for the well-known brand names manufactured under licence in India but check the label carefully as contents may be different from those you are familiar with back home. Check the dosage and expiry dates carefully.

Pharmacies can be found in all the major towns of Nepal, although even simple medicines can be hard to find in remote rural areas. In Kathmandu, **Gust Medicine Concern** (daily 10am–7pm inside Center Mart, Thamel, tel: 01-470 0326) are particularly helpful. They have a nurse/chemist on staff who can give advice on vaccinations and various ailments.

I

Internet

Wi-fi has become ubiquitous in Kathmandu and Pokhara, and even the lowliest budget guesthouses generally provide free wireless internet access. As a consequence the demand for internet cafés has dwindled, though a few remain in areas such as Thamel. Expect to pay around Rs100 per hour in an internet café. Most tourist restaurants also provide free Wi-fi. Internet access has even started appearing on the better known trekking routes, though connection speeds are generally slow.

Kathmandu's Thamel district is packed with tourist-friendly services.

M

Media

Newspapers and magazines

Nepal has a vibrant newspaper industry, *The Himalayan Times* (www.thehimalayantimes.com) and *The Kathmandu Post* (www.ekantipur.com/tkp/) are the most widely available English-language dailies, and can be bought from news-stands across the Kathmandu Valley. They are usually also available in Pokhara. Both have good coverage of local news and politics, as well as agency stories from the region and the world. *The Nepali Times* is an English-language weekly.

Amongst the various magazines published in Kathmandu, the glossy *Nepal Traveller* has good travel and lifestyle content and lots of useful travel information. *Vibes* is a similar glossy magazine, with interesting articles on travel, culture and food. The excellent, environmentally orientated *Himal* magazine (www.himalmag.com) covers all of South Asia monthly and is highly recommended for a regional overview.

Various international publications, including Indian editions of the main news weeklies, are available in bookshops across the capital.

Radio, television and online

Radio Nepal (www.radionepal.gov) broadcasts a mainly Nepali programme of folk songs, news and stories on 576, 648 and 792Khz, and FM 98–100Mhz, though there are a number of English bulletins throughout the day. Private radio stations have music programmes in English as well as Nepali. These include FM Kathmandu on 100Mhz, Kantipur FM on 96.1Mhz and Radio Sagarmatha on 102.4. Reception of BBC World Service, on 103 FM, is good within Kathmandu Valley.

Most of the main hotels offer a wide variety of international channels including BBC, CNN, sports and movie channels. Nepal Television presents Nepali programmes as well as nightly news in English. The private news website Nepal News (www.nepalnews.com) has excellent English-language coverage.

Money

Currency

Nepal's national currency is the Nepalese rupee. Notes come in denominations of 1,000, 500, 100, 50, 20, 10, and 5. Coins are issued in denominations of 10, 5, 2 and 1. Many hotels and travel agents accept payment in US dollars, and foreigners booking flights within Nepal must pay in foreign currency. Entry fees at major attractions can also be paid in dollars.

Credit cards and ATMs

Credit cards such as American Express, Diner's Club, Mastercard and Visa are widely accepted in the Kathmandu Valley, particularly in upmarket hotels, restaurants and gift shops. However, Visa or American Express stickers on the windows of smaller gift shops may turn out to be a false promise. Many shops will add the card company's 5 percent commission onto bills. For lost or replacement credit cards contact the local representatives for Visa and Mastercard, **Alpine Travel Service** (tel: 01-422 5362; www.alpinetravelnepal.com) on Durbar Marg or the American Express agent, **Yeti Travel & Tours** (tel: 01-422 1234; www.yetitravels.com), also on Durbar Marg.

Nepalese currency.

Traveller's cheques are still accepted in some places but are becoming less common due to the use of ATMs, which are found throughout Kathmandu and most other mid-sized towns. There is often a relatively low withdrawal limit on stand-alone ATMs, so try to find a machine attached to a bank to take out a larger amount.

You can receive money quite conveniently through MoneyGram (tel: 01-441 7775) or Western Union Money Transfer.

Exchanging money

Money can be changed at Tribhuvan International Airport (though rates are much worse than in town) and at any number of banks and foreign exchange counters in Kathmandu. Hotel exchange rates are generally slightly below the bank rates, which fluctuate against a basket of currencies and are published daily in the local press. Be sure to save encashment receipts as you will need these if you want to change any surplus rupees back to hard currency before departure. It is impossible to exchange Nepalese rupees overseas. There is no black market for foreign exchange in Nepal.

Most banks are open Mon–Fri 9.30am–3.30pm, and some on Saturday morning. The counters of licensed moneychangers are usually open 12 hours a day. Most hotel, airline and travel agency payments must be made in foreign currency.

O

Opening hours

Government offices are open Mon–Fri 9am–5pm for most of the year. Banks open Mon–Fri 9.15am–2.30pm. The best time to do business with embassies and international organisations is between 10am and 3pm. Check if they close for lunch.

Many private businesses work a six-day week (Sun–Fri), though a seven-day week with half-day opening on Saturday is increasingly common in the Kathmandu Valley. Shops seldom open before 10am but do not usually close until 8pm or 9pm (although some open early and close at noon on Saturday). In Thamel and Pokhara's Lakeside many shops stay open until 10pm or even midnight.

Some museums and other tourist attractions close on Tuesdays or Mondays.

P

Photography

When it comes to taking photos of the Nepalese and their surroundings, tread carefully. Bear in mind that religion and superstition play an integral part in Nepalese life. Do not simply click away at people, statues, shrines, buildings, trees and boulders; what may appear to be innocuous may have deep spiritual significance for the locals. Seek permission when in doubt. It's always better to forgo a shot rather than risk offending your hosts.

Film processing is still available in a few labs in Kathmandu, though the quality is often questionable. Fresh transparency and black and white film is very hard to find in Nepal, so bring stock from home. There are many well-stocked photographic shops, however, which can supply batteries and repair cameras. Try **Photo Concern** on New Road, Kathmandu (tel: 01-422 3275).

Postal services

The General Post Office (tel: 01-422 7499; www.gpo.gov.np) in Kathmandu is located on Kantipath, near the Bhimsen Tower. It is open Sun–Thu 7am–6pm, Fri 7am–3pm, and sells stamps, postcards and aerogrammes. Airmail of parcels up to 10kg (22lbs) and surface mail of up to 20kg (44lbs) can be sent at the foreign post office next door. Officials may ask to see the item before it is wrapped. Express Mail Service (EMS) is available at the General Post Office, as well as at Thamel, Basantapur and airport postal counters, at Bhotahiti and Dillibazar area post offices; and in Lalitpur and Pokhara district post offices.

The postal service is surprisingly reliable, and relatively fast. Letters posted in Kathmandu or Pokhara usually reach Europe within a few days. Ensure that stamps on both letters and postcards are franked in front of you. Main hotels, handicraft shops and private communications centres will also handle mail for a small commission, and this is certainly the easiest way to send things back home.

Federal Express has an office in Kamaladi, tel: 01-426 9248; email: fedex@edc.com.np.

Public holidays

Festival dates vary from year to year because of the difference between the lunar and solar calendars and, as many are determined only after complex astrological calculations, your best bet is to contact the **Nepal Tourism Board**. The Nepalese are usually more than happy to allow you to share in their festivities, but do remain respectful and keep some distance. Remember they are predominantly religious in character, even though they can often get a little rowdy.

Amongst the major fixed public holidays are the birthday of Prithvi Narayan Shah on 10 January, Bisket Jatra (Nepalese New Year) on 14 April, and Constitution Day on 9 November (see page 87).

R

Religious services

While the overwhelming majority of Nepalese are Hindu or Buddhist, there are local Christian communities scattered throughout the country, as well as expat congregations in the major cities. The Kathmandu International Christian Congregation (www.

kiccnepal.org) conducts interdenominational services at 10am at the Church of the Assumption, Dobighat, Patan (tel: 01-543 6910). Catholic services are held at 5.30pm, also at the Church of the Assumption in Dobighat. For details of Jewish services contact the Israeli Embassy (tel: 01-441 1811). Kathmandu's main mosque is on Durbar Marg.

T

Tax

A 13 percent government tax is usually added to bills in all but the cheapest hotels, and in most mid-range restaurants. In more upmarket places a 10 percent service charge is sometimes added to the bill too. When this is the case there is no need to leave a further tip.

Telephones

International telephone connections are now excellent, and direct overseas dialling is available in most hotels as well as from many small communications shops in Thamel. The latter are open daily 8am–11pm. Most internet cafés offer internet telephone calls, which are much cheaper.

The country code for Nepal is 977. The area code for Kathmandu is 01. Telephone numbers are six digits except in Kathmandu, Lalitpur/Patan and Bhaktapur, which have prefixes of 4, 5 and 6 respectively. Do not use the area code if dialling from a landline within the same area.

Mobile phones

Mobile phone use has really taken off in Nepal, and anyone with an unlocked triband phone can get a SIM card for mobile phone access throughout the country. However, bear in mind that mobile phone coverage is non-existent in many rural and high-altitude regions.

You can obtain a SIM card from local providers including **Ncell** (www.ncell.com.np) and **Nepal Telecom** (www.ntc.com.np). These companies and others have outlets all over Kathmandu. To obtain a SIM card you need to present your passport and a passport photo at one of these offices. There are kiosks providing SIM cards outside the arrivals hall at Tribhuvan International Airport. Top-up cards can be bought in various denominations. The main mobile phone providers also offer 3G internet packages.

Operator services

Enquiry from a mobile: 1414 (pre-pay only) or 1498
Fault reports: 198
Internal long-distance calls: 180
International operator: 186
Operator for India: 187
Telephone enquiry: 197

Time zone

Nepal is five hours and 45 minutes ahead of GMT. This makes the country 15 minutes ahead of India, which is in fact the intention of this strange zoning: it is Nepal's way of making it very clear that it does not automatically follow India in all things. There is no daylight saving time in Nepal.

Tipping

Tipping is not a traditional practice in Nepal, though it has become common in tourist areas. Many restaurants add a service charge to the bill, and there is no need to tip when this is the case. As it is usually necessary to bargain for a taxi ride, tipping is not expected – though it is reasonable to round up the fare for a long journey. For porters and guides a tip of around 15 percent of the total fee/wage in recognition of good service is the norm.

Tour operators and travel agents

Nepal is home to a huge number of travel agencies and tour operators – from hole-in-the-wall set-ups issuing bus tickets and putting together shoestring tours, to major organisations with multiple branches. Other operators specialise in biking, river trips or mountaineering. The following is a small selection of the well-established operators.

Adrenaline Rush Nepal
Thamel, Kathmandu
Tel: 01-470 1056
www.adrenalinenepal.com
A well-run company specialising in watersports, offering kayaking, rafting and canyoning. The company has its own camp on the Trisuli River, and excellent, internationally trained river guides. There is a branch office in Pokhara.

Annapurna Travel & Tours
Durbar Marg, Kathmandu
Tel: 01-422 2339
www.annapurnatravel.com
A slick, professionally run agency offering tours throughout Nepal, and in neighbouring India, Bhutan and Tibet.

Asian Trekking
Tridevi Marg, Kathmandu
Tel: 01-442 4249
www.asian-trekking.com
A long-standing outfit running treks and mountaineering trips in the Himalayas.

Equator Expeditions
Thamel, Kathmandu
Tel: 01-470 0854
www.equatorexpeditionsnepal.com
A rafting and kayaking company, specialising in tailor-made river tours, but also running trekking and mountaineering trips.

Himalayan Spirit Adventure
Thamel, Kathmandu
Tel: 01-425 8792/7997
www.himalayanspiritadventure.com
Specialists in ecotourism, expertise covers all areas of Nepal and includes everything from peak climbing to rafting to jungle safari. Knowledgeable and friendly English-speaking team.

Mission Eco Trek
Thamel, Kathmandu
Tel: 01-444 2922
www.tibetnomad.com
A Kathmandu-based operator specialising in tours across the border to Tibet.

President Travels & Tours
Durbar Marg, Kathmandu
Tel: 01-422 0245
www.pttnepal.com
A long-established travel agent at the upmarket end of Durbar Marg, this is a good option for booking both international and domestic flights.

Sherpa Trekking Service
Kamaladi, Kathmandu
Tel: 01-442 1551
www.sts.com.np
A specialist trekking agency, with a good reputation.

Three Sisters Adventure Trekking
Pokhara
Tel: 061-462066
www.3sistersadventuretrek.com
Based in Pokhara, this award-winning agency is owned by a team of local women, and uses female guides to lead its tailor-made treks and tours.

Ultimate Descents Nepal
Khusibu, Kathmandu
Tel: 01-438 1214
www.udnepal.com
A rafting and kayaking company with a good reputation for running trips on the Trisuli and Seti rivers.

Yeti Travel & Tours
Durbar Marg, Kathmandu
Tel: 01-422 1234

www.yetitravels.com
A long-established operator, offering treks, safaris and cultural tours.

Tourist information

Nepal Tourism Board

Bhrikuti Mandap, Kathmandu.
Tel: 01-425 6909/6229
www.welcomenepal.com
The Nepal Tourism Board is located alongside the Tourist Police and the trekking registration (TIMS) office in the Tourist Service Centre, just off Durbar Marg near the Tundikhel. It has a few brochures and simple maps, and staff are friendly and do their best to be helpful, but the centre is not particularly useful. Its website has some general information. There are smaller branches at the airport and in Pokhara, but services are limited.

Useful addresses in Kathmandu

Alliance Française
Tripureshwor
Tel: 01-424 1163
www.alliancefrancaise.org.np
Amnesty International
Basantanagar, Balaju
Tel: 01-436 4706
www.amnestynepal.org
British Council
Lainchaur.
Tel: 01-441 0798
www.britishcouncil.org/nepal
CARE Nepal
Krishna Galli
Tel: 01-552 2800
www. carenepal.org
VSO Voluntary Service Overseas
Lazimpat.
Tel: 01-441 0606
www.vso.org.uk

Visas and passports

Except for Indian citizens, all passport holders require a visa for entry into Nepal. Visas may be obtained from any Nepali Embassy abroad or upon arrival at Kathmandu's Tribhuvan International Airport, Indian border entry points into Nepal (see page 308) or the Kodari border with China/Tibet. You will need a passport valid for at least six months and one passport-size photo, and it is useful to bring exact money with you.

The visas issued on arrival are valid for 15, 30 or 90 days, and cost US$25, 40 or 100 respectively. At the airport the fee can be paid in most major currencies, but you'll need dollars at the land borders. Children under 10 are exempt from the visa fee.

Multiple-entry visas are available in advance from Nepalese consulates overseas, and a single-entry visa issued on arrival can be converted to a multiple-entry visa at the Kathmandu Central Immigration Office.

Visa extensions

Tourist visas can be extended up to 120 days on request in Pokhara or Kathmandu but the application must be made before the visa expires. A 30-day extension costs US$60 and is usually available within an hour from the main immigration office after submission of a completed application form with the fee and a passport photo. Given that a one-month extension is more expensive than the visa itself, it is worth paying for a 90-day visa in the first instance if you may be staying for more than a month.
Kathmandu Central Immigration Office
Dilli Bazaar
Tel: 01-442 9659
www.immi.gov.np
Open Mon–Fri 10am–5pm (mid-Nov–mid-Feb until 4pm).
Pokhara Immigration Office
Ratna Chowk
Tel: 061-565167
Open Mon–Fri 10am–5pm.

Visas for China and India

Travellers wishing to visit Tibet and China must apply for a Tibet Tourism Permit at the Chinese Embassy, for which you need confirmation from your travel agent that you are booked onto a tour. Travellers coming from China may get their visa at the Kodari border point. Agencies organising tours to Tibet from Kathmandu will arrange the necessary paperwork.

Travellers wishing to visit India can get their visas before they leave home, or from the Indian Embassy at Lainchaur in Kathmandu (tel: 01-441 0900; www.indianembassy.org.np), but allow two weeks for the application and clearance process.

W

Weights and measures

The Nepalese use the metric system, but in some circumstances they also stick to traditional measures. As elsewhere in South Asia, they count in *lakh* (unit of 100,000) and *crore* (unit of 10 million). Heights are usually measured in metres, but sometimes in feet. (One foot equals 0.305 metres; one metre equals 3.28ft.) Distances are counted in kilometres. The term *muthi* means "handful", whether it be of vegetables or firewood.

Weights are measured in kilograms with the following exceptions:
Rice and other cereals, milk and sugar: 1 *muthi* is a handful; 10 *muthi* = 1 *mana* (just under half a litre, 0.8 pints, 16.5 fl oz); 8 *manas* = 1 *paathi* (3.75 litres, 6.5 pints, 1 US gallon); 20 *paathis* (160 *manas*) = 1 *muri* (75 litres, 16.5 UK gallons; 19.8 US gallons).
Vegetables and fruit: 1 *pau* equals 200g (7oz); 1 *ser* equals 4 *paus*, or 1kg; 1 *dharni* equals 3 *sers*, or 2.4 kg (5lbs).
Metals: one *tola* is equal to 11.66g (0.5oz).
Precious stones: 1 carat equals 0.2g.

Women travellers

There are no particular safety concerns for women travellers in Nepal, but this is a conservative country so women should dress modestly in trousers, long shorts or skirts below the knee; wearing revealing clothing will gain unnecessary attention and lose respect. In some areas showing bare shoulders is also frowned upon.

Women travelling alone can expect a certain amount of attention, and even low-level harassment from local men. For the most part this is harmless, but be cautious about accepting invitations. There have been a number of attacks on foreign women in remote parts of the Kathmandu Valley, so it is best to avoid wandering these areas alone. Some women have reported harassment when travelling alone with a local guide, so take guides based on personal recommendation whenever possible. A handful of Nepalese women work as guides in the mountains and the national parks – ask locally.

LANGUAGE

UNDERSTANDING THE LANGUAGE

There are as many languages spoken in Nepal as there are races and almost as many dialects as there are village communities. Just as centuries of intermarriage have left the nation without a single distinct ethnicity, throughout history, the main languages have intermingled and influenced one another. As with everything from its architecture to its food, Nepal's linguistic geography forms a collision zone between Indian and Chinese influences. Most of the individual indigenous languages in the hills and mountains, including Newari – the language of the Newar people, predominant in the Kathmandu Valley – belong to the Sino-Tibetan family, related the languages used everywhere from Burma to Beijing. In the south, meanwhile, the Terai dialects belong to the Indo-Aryan group, closely linked to languages spoken across north India and in turn part of the larger Indo-European language family which includes English.

The official language, Nepali, is part of the Pahari or "Hill country" branch of the Indo-Aryan family, closely related to Hindi. Nepali and Hindi use the same writing system called Devanagari. Nepali has also borrowed heavily from some local dialects as well as from Sanskrit, an ancient scholarly language that has survived, like Latin, as a religious medium. Nepali, Sanskrit and Newari each have their own distinctive traditions.

In northern Nepal the Tibetan language – another traditional vehicle for religious teaching – remains widespread both in its classical form and as derived dialects (including Sherpa and Thakali). Of the southern Indo-Aryan dialects, three times more people speak Maithili, an eastern Terai dialect, than Newari, reflecting the uneven population distribution in Nepal.

A few words of Nepali are helpful when shopping in less touristed places.

English is spoken and understood in both official and tourism-related circles, and is widely used by the urban middle class. Most taxi drivers and merchants in the Kathmandu Valley region have a working knowledge of English, as do most Sherpas. English does not have the same reach as in neighbouring India, however, and outside of urban zones and tourist areas you may find it difficult to make yourself understood.

It is strongly recommended that you learn a few basic words and expressions. You will get big returns on this small investment in terms of hospitality and respect.

If you are interested in learning more about Nepali, there are many phrasebooks and home-learning book and audio packages available. In Kathmandu both introductory and longer courses can be arranged.

Pronunciation

Nepali is an atonal language. Whatever the length of the word, the accent is always placed on the first or second syllable. Words are pronounced as they are spelled. Consonants are pronounced as in English, with a few peculiarities:

ch = tch as in bench
chh = tch-h as in pitch here
th = t-h as in hot head
kh = k-h as in dark hole
ph = p-h as in top hat
j = dj as in Jesus
dh = d-h as in adhere

The t, d, th and dh with a dot beneath them are pronounced by rolling the tip of the tongue back to the centre of the roof of the mouth, instead of against the teeth. Vowels are pronounced either long or short:

e = e (ay) as in café
u = oo as in moon (never yu as in mute)
y = yi as in yield (never ai as in my)
i = i as in bin (never ai as in bind)
o = oh as in toe

Nepalese do not usually use the different greetings "good morning", "good afternoon" or "good evening". Instead, when greeting someone, it is polite to clasp your hands together in front of you, bow your head slightly and say *Namaste* (pronounced na-ma-stay). This simple phrase will evoke a smile and warm greeting in return.

Intercultural Training & Research Centre (ITC)
Thamel
Tel: 01-441 2793
www.itcnepal.com

Kathmandu Institute of Nepali Language
Bhagawan Bahal
Tel: 01-443 7454
www.ktmnepalilanguage.com

USEFUL VOCABULARY

Hello *namaste*
How are you? *sanchai chha?*
Yes *ho*
No *hoina*
Thank you *dhanyabadh*
Please *kripaya*
Good morning (formal) *subha prabhat*
Goodnight (formal) *subha ratri*
Goodbye (literally: we'll meet again) *pheri bhataunla*
Sorry/Excuse me *maph gaurnus*
How much is it? *kati parchha?*
Where is (place)...? *kahaa parchha?*
Where is (object)...? *kahaa chha?*
Where is (person)...? *kahaa hunnuhunchha?*
How far? *kati tada chha?*
How long (length)? *kati lamo chha?*
Good/OK *thikchha*
Cheap *sasto*
Expensive *mahango*
Hot (temperature) *tato*
Hot (spicy food) *piro*
Cold (temperature) *chiso*
Cold (feeling) *jaro*
Free *furshad*
Open *khula*
Closed *bhandha*
I don't understand *bughina*

NUMBERS

1 *ek*
2 *dui*

Catching up on events in a local paper.

3 *tin*
4 *chaar*
5 *paach*
6 *chha*
7 *saat*
8 *aath*
9 *nau*
10 *das*
11 *eghaara*
12 *baarha*
13 *terha*
14 *chaudha*
15 *pandhra*
16 *sorha*
17 *satra*
18 *athaara*
19 *unnais*
20 *bis*
21 *ekkaais*
22 *baais*
23 *teis*
24 *chaubis*
25 *pachchis*
26 *chhabbis*
27 *sattaais*
28 *aththaais*
29 *unantis*
30 *tis*
40 *chaalis*
50 *pachaas*
60 *saathi*
70 *sattari*
80 *asi*

Indigenous languages are spoken in Nepal's hills and mountains.

90 *nabbe*
100 *sae, saya*
1,000 *hajaar*
100,000 *lakh*
1 million *das lakh*

DAYS OF THE WEEK

Sunday *Aityabar*
Monday *Somabar*
Tuesday *Mangalbar*
Wednesday *Budhabar*
Thursday *Bihibar*
Friday *Sukrabar*
Saturday *Shanibar*

MONTHS OF THE YEAR

Nepalese months vary from 29 to 32 days in length, and any one month may have a different number of days from year to year. Therefore, no exact correspondence with the Western calendar is possible.

April/May *Baisakh*
May/June *Jesth*
June/July *Asadh*
July/August *Srawan*
August/September *Bhadra*
September/October *Ashwin*
October/November *Kartik*
November/December *Marga*
December/January *Poush*
January/February *Magha*
February/March *Falgun*
March/April *Chaitra*

PLACES

Tourist Office *paryatak office*
Bank *bank*
Museum *shangra laya*
Chemist *aushadhi pasal*
Bus stop *bus bishoni*
Post Office *hulak*
Hospital *ashpatal*
Church *girgha ghar*
Hotel *hotel*

FURTHER READING

FICTION

Arresting God in Kathmandu Samrat Upadhyay. Nepal's pre-eminent writer of fiction in English won acclaim for his first collection of short stories, with its clipped, crisp accounts of modern Nepalese life. He has since published two novels – *The Guru of Love* and *Buddha's Orphans* – and another short story collection, *The Royal Ghosts*.

Himalayan Voices: An Introduction to Modern Nepali Literature edited by Michael Dutt. This anthology provides rare access to a wide array of translated work by the cream of Nepal's 20th-century poets and prose authors.

The Mountain Is Young Han Suyin. Published in 1958, between the conquest of Everest and the opening of the Hippie Trail, this bestseller of love and reawakening in the Himalayan foothills did more than its fair share to bring the exotic allure of Nepal to Western attention.

Mountains Painted with Turmeric Lil Bahadur Chettri. Originally published in Nepali more than half a century ago, this translated novel is a beautiful but bleak depiction of the hardships of village life, which in many corners of the country have changed little since it was written.

Nothing to Declare Rabi Thapa. A collection of sharp short stories exploring the modern underbelly of Kathmandu and the tensions of immigrant lives lived between Nepal and the West.

Palpasa Cafe Narayan Wagle. Originally a Nepali-language bestseller, this translated novel by a respected journalist is part love story, part vivid indictment of the violence that wracked rural Nepal in recent decades.

The Tutor of History Manjushree Thapa. Best known for her non-fiction, Thapa has written two novels: this story about four Nepalis set in the late 1990s at the time of political uncertainty; and *Seasons of Flight* and a short story collection, *Tilled Earth*. In each she turns her characteristically wry eye on Nepalese life.

HISTORY, CULTURE AND POLITICS

An Account of the Kingdom of Nepaul William Kirkpatrick. This book was written in 1793 by a British army officer deputed by the East India Company in a clumsy attempt to mediate in a clash between Kathmandu and China. Kirkpatrick's political mission was a disaster, but he brought back the first English account of the kingdom.

Blood Against the Snows: The Tragic Story of Nepal's Royal Dynasty Jonathan Gregson. This book begins and ends with Crown Prince Dipendra's gun-toting rampage through the royal palace in 2001, but in between it provides a snappy and highly readable account of the blood-soaked history of the Shah Dynasty. The book was published in the USA as *Massacre at the Palace*. Gregson is also the author of *Kingdoms Beyond the Clouds*, a travelogue examining the royal dynasties of the Himalayas, including those of Kathmandu and Mustang.

Forget Kathmandu Manjushree Thapa. Part memoir, part reportage, part polemic, Thapa's book about modern Nepal's convoluted history and the turbulence that followed the 2001 royal massacre crackles with unrestrained indignation at the sorry state of her country.

The Great Arc John Keay. A highly readable account of the efforts to map the Indian subcontinent and the Himalayas in the days of the British Empire, including the story of the naming of Mount Everest.

A History of Nepal John Whelpton. The standard overview, this short history is decidedly dry, but it provides plenty of insight and an admirable synthesis of a vast array of sources and perspectives.

Nepal in Transition: From People's War to Fragile Peace edited by S. von Einsiedel, D.M. Malone and S. Pradhan. The most up-to-date scholarly assessment of Nepal's current state of affairs and recent troubled past.

Trespassers on the Roof of the World Peter Hopkirk. A fascinating account of the clandestine manoeuvres of the pundit surveyor-spies who mapped out the Himalayas in the era of the Great Game, and of the unsavoury British invasion of Tibet in 1904.

Send Us Your Thoughts

We do our best to ensure the information in our books is as accurate and up-to-date as possible. The books are updated on a regular basis using local contacts, who painstakingly add, amend and correct as required. However, some details (such as telephone numbers and opening times) are liable to change, and we are ultimately reliant on our readers to put us in the picture.

We welcome your feedback, especially your experience of using the book "on the road". Maybe we recommended a hotel that you liked (or another that you didn't), or you came across a great bar or new attraction we missed.

We will acknowledge all contributions, and we'll offer an Insight Guide to the best letters received.

Please write to us at:
Insight Guides
PO Box 7910
London SE1 1WE
Or email us at:
insight@apaguide.co.uk

TRAVEL AND MEMOIR

A Balcony in Nepal: Glimpses of a Himalayan Village Sally Wendkos Olds. A light and readable travelogue by an American writer about a remote village in eastern Nepal where she helped to set up a library for local children.

Among Flowers: A Walk in the Himalaya Jamaica Kincaid. A short and somewhat whimsical, but elegantly written, account of a trek in the Annapurna region in search of mountain plants.
East of Lo Monthang Peter Matthiessen and Thomas Laird. In the 1990s Matthiessen and Laird travelled through Mustang, shortly after it was first opened to the outside world, and produced this beautiful, evocative book.
Himalaya Michael Palin. The former Python had moved beyond the genuine intrepidness of his earlier journeys for the BBC by the time he visited Nepal and the other Himalayan nations in 2003, but he delivers his account with the usual engaging breeziness. The hardback edition features beautiful photographs by Basil Pao.
Little Princes: One Man's Promise to Bring Home the Lost Children of Nepal Conor Grennan. Although it reads like an obvious attempt to climb aboard the *Three Cups of Tea* bandwagon, the bright and positive tone of this account of work with Nepal's orphans is thoroughly engaging.
The Snow Leopard Peter Matthiessen. A true classic of travel literature, Mattiessen's account of a winter journey into Inner Dolpo, long before the trekking parties turned up, alternately soars to metaphysical heights and plunges to crystalline details of life on the trail. The snow leopard of the title is both a real, if unseen, presence in the mountains, and a cipher for unattainable enlightenment.
Stones of Silence George B. Schaller. A description of a journey to study the blue sheep of Dolpo in 1973, and an intriguing counterpoint to the account of Schaller's companion, Peter Matthiessen, in *The Snow Leopard*.
Tiger for Breakfast Michel Peissel. The rollicking tale of exiled Russian ballet dancer Boris Lissanevitch, the man who introduced chicken Kiev to Calcutta, founded the Yak & Yeti Hotel and kick-started Nepal's tourist industry.
Video Night in Kathmandu Pico Iyer. The book ranges widely beyond the city of the title – as far as Burma and Bali – but it remains a classic account of the intersection of tradition and globalisation in Asia by one of the most unusual, sensitive and insightful of all modern travel writers.
The Waiting Land: A Spell in Nepal Dervla Murphy. A classic account by the indomitable Irish travel writer of her experiences in a Tibetan refugee camp in Pokhara, and in the remote Langtang region, in the 1960s.

MOUNTAINEERING

Annapurna: First Conquest of an 8,000-Metre Peak Maurice Herzog. An unembellished but nonetheless gripping account of the audacious ascent that kicked off the "Golden Decade" of Himalayan mountaineering, with extreme frostbite and field amputations to boot.
The Ascent of Rum Doodle W.E. Bowman. First published in 1956, at the height of the mountain madness of the "Golden Decade" this hilarious spoof account of the ascent of a "40,000-and-a-half-foot peak" successfully skewers all the more absurd conventions of mountaineering literature.
Chomolungma Sings the Blues Ed Douglas. In a counterpoint to all the celebratory stories of summit triumphs, this travelogue by a respected British mountaineering writer examines the manifold problems besetting the Everest region, from litter and deforestation to social tensions amongst the Sherpas. While there has been improvement in some areas since the book was first published in 1997, it remains apposite.
The Crystal Mountain Reinhold Messner. The mighty Tyrolean mountaineer is also a very fine writer, with a number of impressive books to his name, including,this account of his epic solo ascent of Everest and a reflection on those who had gone before him, and *My Quest for the Yeti*, an intriguing reflection of the intersection of myth and reality in the high Himalayas.
Everest 1953: The Epic Story of the First Ascent Mick Conefrey. Published to mark the sixtieth anniversary of the first ascent, this sharply written account of the efforts to reach the summit draws on a formidable range of sources and is one of the best overviews of the conquest of the world's highest mountain.
High Adventure Edmund Hillary. The first man successfully to reach the summit of Everest published an impressive array of books during his long lifetime, including this original account of the first ascent, and *View from the Summit*, an autobiography covering his entire array of adventures.
Into the Silence Wade Davis. A magisterial account of the early attempts on Everest and the disappearance of Mallory and Irvine, which manages seamlessly to incorporate the histories of World War I, Tibet, the Bloomsbury Set and more into a compelling narrative of high altitude derring-do.
Into Thin Air: A Personal Account of the Mount Everest Disaster Jon Krakauer. A factual, first-hand account of the 1996 Everest disaster that reads like a fast-paced thriller. A number of other participants have challenged some of Krakauer's interpretations, but what is most striking is that despite the lessons of 1996, Everest is now more crowded with commercial groups than ever.
Nepal Himalaya W.H. Tilman. An account of the early journeys in Langtang and the Everest region by Bill Tilman delivered in classic light-footed, self-deprecating English travel-writing style.
Sacred Summits Peter Boardman. A beautifully written account of climbs on Kanchenjunga and Gauri Sankar by one of the finest mountaineers and mountaineering writers of his generation. Boardman died with his climbing partner Joe Tasker on the Northeast Ridge of Everest in 1982; the Boardman Tasker Prize for Mountain Literature was established in their memory.

OTHER INSIGHT GUIDES

Among nearly 200 companion books to this one are several *Insight Guides* highlighting destinations in the region. Titles include *Insight Guide India*, *Insight Guide China* and *Insight Guide Myanmar (Burma)*.

CREDITS

Photo Credits

Alamy 209
AWL Images 207
Bigstock 248, 249, 259, 265B, 268/269T, 271, 303, 305
Chandra Shamsher 24/25
Corbis 27T, 39, 90, 91, 93, 132, 158, 206B, 215
Dreamstime 99, 133, 134, 206T, 208, 258B, 261, 264, 275, 301
FLPA 94/95, 106, 136, 252
Fotolia 266T, 289T, 291, 304
Getty Images 27B, 31, 32, 34, 35, 36, 37, 38, 40, 41, 92, 103R, 107, 128, 130, 131, 135, 138, 268R, 269ML, 272, 276B
IHG Hotels 313, 314
iStockphoto 2/3, 5B, 101, 102, 120, 124, 125, 129, 236, 263, 266B, 269BL, 273, 276T, 288T, 318, 345L
James Tye/Apa Publications 1, 4BR, 4ML, 4MR, 4BL, 5TR, 5ML, 5ML, 5MR, 5TL, 6BR, 6M, 6BL, 7TR, 7TL, 8/9, 10/11, 12/13, 14, 15T, 15B, 16, 17, 18, 19, 20, 21, 22, 23, 42/43, 44, 45, 46, 47, 48, 49, 50, 51, 52, 53, 54/55, 56, 57, 59, 60, 61, 62, 63, 64, 65, 66, 67, 68, 69, 70/71, 72, 73, 74, 75, 76, 77, 78, 79, 80L, 80R, 81, 82, 83, 84BL, 84/85T, 84BR, 85ML, 85BR, 85BL, 85TR, 86, 87, 88, 89, 96, 97, 98, 100, 103L, 104, 105, 108, 109, 110, 111, 112, 113, 114, 115, 116, 117, 118/119, 121, 122, 123, 126, 127, 141, 142BL, 142/143T, 143ML, 143BL, 143TR, 144/145, 146/147, 148/149, 150, 151T, 151B, 156, 157, 159, 160T, 160B, 161, 162T, 162B, 163T, 163B, 164, 165, 166T, 166B, 167, 168, 169, 170, 171, 172, 173B, 173T, 174, 175B, 175T, 176, 177, 179T, 179B, 180T, 180B, 181, 182, 183, 185T, 185B, 186B, 186T, 187, 188, 189B, 189T, 190BL, 190/191T, 190BR, 191ML, 191BR, 191BL, 191TR, 192/193, 194, 195, 196, 197, 200, 201T, 201B, 202, 203T, 203B, 204T, 204B, 205, 210, 211, 213B, 213T, 214, 216, 217, 218, 219, 220, 221B, 221T, 222, 223T, 223B, 224/225, 226, 227, 229, 230T, 230B, 231, 232T, 232B, 234T, 234B, 235, 237T, 237B, 238T, 238B, 239, 240, 241, 242, 244, 245B, 245T, 246, 247B, 247T, 250/251, 253, 254T, 254B, 256, 257T, 257B, 258T, 262B, 262T, 265T, 268L, 269BR, 269TR, 277, 278/279, 280, 281, 282, 284, 285T, 285B, 286T, 286B, 287, 288B, 289B, 292B, 292T, 293, 294T, 294B, 295, 296T, 296B, 297B, 297T, 298, 299, 306, 308T, 308B, 309, 310, 311, 312, 316, 317, 319, 320, 321, 322, 324, 325, 326, 327T, 327B, 328, 329, 330, 334, 335, 336, 337, 338, 339, 340, 343T, 343M, 344T, 344B
Photoshot 137, 300
Public Domain 26
Robert Harding 142BR
Scala Archives 28, 30
SuperStock 270
The Art Archive 29
TopFoto 33, 58, 260, 267
Ultimate Decents Nepal 7BL, 139, 140, 143BR

Cover Credits

Front cover: Phewa Lake against Annapurna Mountain Range with Annapurna, *4Corners*
Back cover: (top) Kathmandu; (middle): Sadhu, all *James Tye/Apa Publications*
Front flap: (from top) Pokhara; Holi Festival; Buddhist Prayer Wheels; Trekking in Langtang-Gosainkund, all *James Tye/Apa Publications*
Spine: Flag of Nepal, *iStockphoto*

Insight Guide Credits

Distribution
UK
Dorling Kindersley Ltd
A Penguin Group company
80 Strand, London, WC2R 0RL
sales@uk.dk.com

United States
Ingram Publisher Services
1 Ingram Boulevard, PO Box 3006,
La Vergne, TN 37086-1986
ips@ingramcontent.com

Australia and New Zealand
Woodslane
10 Apollo St, Warriewood,
NSW 2102, Australia
info@woodslane.com.au

Worldwide
Apa Publications GmbH & Co. Verlag
KG (Singapore branch)
7030 Ang Mo Kio Avenue 5
08-65 Northstar @ AMK
Singapore 569880
apasin@singnet.com.sg

Printing
CTPS-China

First Edition 1991
Sixth Edition 2014

www.insightguides.com

Project Editor
Sarah Clark
Series Manager
Carine Tracanelli
Author
Tim Hannigan
Picture Editor/Art Editor
Tom Smyth/Shahid Mahmood
Map Production
Original cartography Colourmap Scanning Ltd, updated by Apa Cartography Department
Production
Tynan Dean and Rebeka Davies

Contributors

This comprehensively revised new edition of *Insight Guide: Nepal* was commissioned by Senior Commissioning Editor **Sarah Clark**, Insight's Indian subcontinent specialist, and copyedited by **Naomi Peck**.

The book was thoroughly updated by Nepal expert **Tim Hannigan**, an award-winning author, who travelled through the country researching this book. He has written extensively about the subcontinent and the Himalayas, with a special interest in mountaineering.

The stunning new pictures in this book are the work of travel photographer, **James Tye**.

Thanks also go to **Deepak Joshi** of the Nepal Tourist Board.

The book was proofread by **Leonie Wilding** and the index was compiled by **Penny Phenix**.

About Insight Guides

Insight Guides have more than 40 years' experience of publishing high-quality, visual travel guides. We produce 400 full-colour titles, in both print and digital form, covering more than 200 destinations across the globe, in a variety of formats to meet your different needs.

Insight Guides are written by local authors who use their on-the-ground experience to provide the very latest information; their local expertise is evident in the extensive historical and cultural background features. All the reviews in **Insight Guides** are independent; we strive to maintain an impartial view. Our reviews are carefully selected to guide to you the best places to stay and eat, so you can be confident that when we say a restaurant or hotel is special, we really mean it.

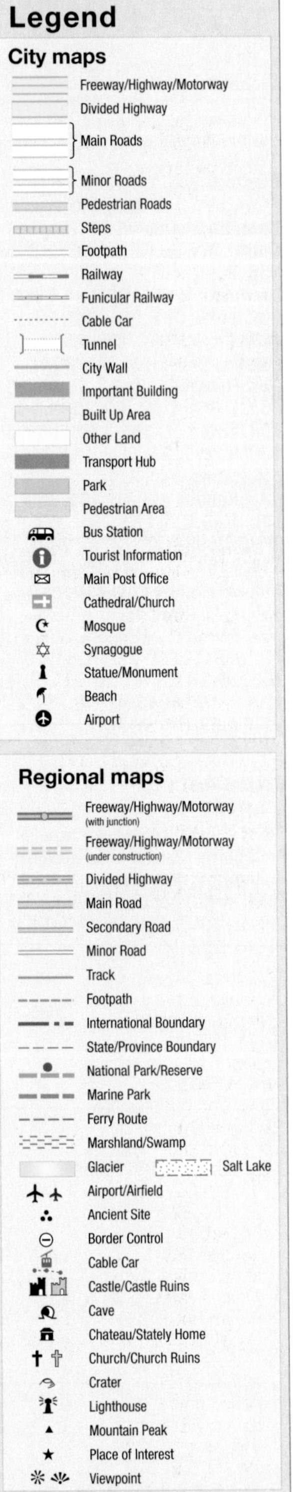

INDEX

Main references are in bold type

Travel guides, ebooks, apps and online
www.insightguides.com

INSIGHT GUIDES
AQUA LUNA
99P.

Kathmandu
0
200 m
0
200 yds
N
NAYA BAZAR
PAKNAJOL
KALDHARA
THAMEL
LAINCHAUR
LAZIMPAT
GAHIRIDHARA
NAXAL
HATTISAAR
KAMALADI
KWABAHAL
JYATHA
KAMALACHI
THAHITI
NAGHAL
CHHETRAPATI
TENGAL
NARDEVI
DHALKO
DHOBICHAUR
Balaju
Balaju Sourkhutte Sadak
Ropeway Sadak
Layata Marg
Vintuna Marg
Suman Marg
Yekikaran Sadak
Swoyanbhu Marg
Kaldhara Marg
Luti Ajima Mandir
Bjeshowri Bridge
Swayambhunath Natural History Museum
Lekhnath Marg
Pipalbote Marg
Z Marg
Paknajol
Samakhusi Marg
Lainchaur Marg
Library
British Council & British Embassy
Lazimpat
Budhanilkantha
Uttar Dhoka Road
Kanti Path
Bahadur Bhawan
Keshar Mahal
Garden of Dreams
Tridevi Marg
Narayanhiti Palace Museum
Narayan Mandir
Narayanhiti Path
Naxal
Narayan Hiti
Seto Durbar
Everest Cultural Society
Casino Royale
Nepal International Clinic
Jai Nepal Chitra Ghar
Nag Pokhari
Siwa Mandir
Kamal Pokhari
Pashupatinath, Boudhanath
British Council
Durbar Marg
Lal Durbar
Royal Nepal Academy
Kamaladi
Jana Masjid
Clock
Jamal Sadak
Rani Pokhari
National Theatre
Makhan Tole
Annapurna
Bhagwan Bahal
Kwa Bahal
Musya Bahal
Chusya Bahal
Jyatha
Thahity
Thahiti Stupa
Chhetrapati
Chhetrapati Bandstand
Swachapu Ganesh
Dhobichaur
Purano Dhalakwo Mg
Gangalal Marg
Nyata Ganesh
Kathe Simbhu
Uma-Mahesvara
Dhoka Bahal
Ikha Narayan
Haku Bahal
Vaisha Dev
Hum Bahal
Bangemudha
Nara Devi
Raktakali
Chittadhar Marg
Tamsipakha Bridge
Vishnumati